# RAMBLES ABOUT PORTSMOUTH.

FIRST SERIES.

---

## SKETCHES

OF

PERSONS, LOCALITIES,

AND

INCIDENTS OF TWO CENTURIES:

PRINCIPALLY FROM TRADITION AND UNPUBLISHED DOCUMENTS.

---

By Charles W. Brewster.

---

[SECOND EDITION.]

PORTSMOUTH, N. H.
PUBLISHED BY LEWIS W. BREWSTER,
Portsmouth Journal Office.
1873.

# PREFACE.

To the Sons and Daughters of Portsmouth scattered throughout the Union, and to those who are resident at home, is respectfully inscribed this effort to put in permanent form some of the varied incidents which have given interest to the local history of our ancient town.

These Rambles, gathered from the recollections and traditions of our old citizens, from our town records and from documentary sources, are not only wanderings from street to street, from the river to the forest, from the ball room to the cemetery—but are necessarily ramblings from the regular chronological order of history. The main object being to collect the incidents of unwritten history, there have been but few extracts taken from Adams's "Annals of Portsmouth," which is a valuable chronicle of events in our early town history. The Rambles were not originally written for the purpose of making a book, but to interest the readers of the Portsmouth Journal from week to week, and were usually published on the week on which they were written, generally without any serial connection.

In complying with the request to give these sketches in book form, a revision has been made, and new incidents and several new Rambles have been added. While historical accuracy has been aimed at, it would not be surprising if we have made some errors, or been misled by some wrong traditions.

One object of these Rambles has been so to connect *incidents* and *localities*, that as we pass the streets we may at the turn of almost every corner be reminded of some early historical event. If some of these incidents appear trivial, we have only to say that it is not the prominent figures only in a picture that give it intersst—the background touches and the little details of the dress are as essential for effect as the profile of the countenance.

PORTSMOUTH, N. H., May 1, 1859.

## PREFACE TO SECOND EDITION.

---

The author of the "Rambles" passed away Aug. 4, 1868. In preparing this second edition for the press, the corrections suggested by him have been carefully made, and with a view to changing as little as possible the original cast of the stories. This edition is therefore presented to the public very nearly as it originally came from the pen of the "Rambler," as doubtless most of its readers will prefer to receive it.

LEWIS W. BREWSTER.

PORTSMOUTH, July 1, 1873.

# CONTENTS.

---

RAMBLE. PAGE.

1. Pring's Visit to the Piscataqua—Smith's Discoveries on the Coast—Vision of the Future—Early Scenery.......... 9
2. Visit of M. Champlain at Odiorne's Point—The Manor House erected—Gorges and Mason—Emigrants—The Great House—Stock of the Plantation—Relics—Garrison Houses—Early Water Courses.......... 16
3. Adoption of the name of Portsmouth and Town Lines—Hubbard's Sketch of the Early Settlements.......... 22
4. Fines for Cutting Timber—The Distribution of Town Lands—Names of Inhabitants in 1657—Portion assigned to each.......... 25
5. The Cutt family—John the first President of New-Hampshire—The Estates of John and Richard—Their Wills—Murder of Ursula—Providential Escape of the Waldron Family.......... 29
6. The Glebe Land—Its Location and Occupancy.......... 41
7. John Pickering—His sons, John and Thomas—Great Bay Farm—Descendants—The Old South Church—Point-of-Graves Cemetery—The Foot Path.......... 49
8. The Pickering Family—Incidents of John's Life—Captain, Lawyer, Moderator, Carpenter—Prowess of Thomas—The first South-end Meeting House.......... 54
9. Tythingmen of Portsmouth—Names of Inhabitants in 1678—Designation of Neighborhoods.......... 61
10. The First Meeting House—Seating of the Occupants—Old Inhabitants—Moody and Cranfield—Rogers—Emerson—Scenes at the Old Meeting House.......... 64
11. Settlement at Plains—Old Roads—Military Scenes—Indian Massacre of 1696—The Surprise—Scalping of Mary Brewster—List of Killed and Wounded—The Retreat—Pursuit—Breakfast Hill.......... 70
12. Bridget Graffort—Gift of Daniel Street—Lot for the First Town School House—Ichabod Plaisted—Early School History—Samuel Keais—Style of the Early Town Records.......... 78
13. Newcastle—The Jaffrey Residence—Atkinson—Church Yard—The Old Cemetery—John and Abigail Frost—Rev. John Blunt—Funeral Items—Captain John Blunt and Family—Cromwell Anecdote—Newcastle Pastors.......... 86
14. Rev. John Emerson—Rev. William Shurtleff—Trials of a Pastor—Rev. Job Strong and his Successors at the South Church.......... 93
15. Old House on the Corner—High School House Site—Daniel House—Mark Hunking and Hunking Wentworth.......... 96
16. The Creeks—First Wentworth House—Samuel and John Wentworth.......... 98
17. Gov. Benning Wentworth—His Seat at Little Harbor—Its Present State—Molly Pitman—Romantic Marriage of the Governor with Martha Hilton—Col. Michael Wentworth—Washington's Visit there—Cushing Family—Residence of Gov. John Wentworth, 2d.......... 101
18. Atkinson House—Theodore Atkinson—His Style of Life—Descendants—Legacy to the Church.......... 107
19. Theodore Atkinson, Jr.—His Marriage—Death—Funeral—Gov. Wentworth's Attentions—Mrs. Atkinson a Widow but Ten Days—Style of the Times—The Town and Country Residences—Lake Story—His Character—Illustrative Anecdote—Departure for England.......... 110

20. Col. Joshua Wentworth—His Offices—Incidents of his History—His Descendants—George Jaffrey ... 116

21. Factory Site—Nathaniel Adams' Seat—Discovery of Lady Stanley's grave—Her husband William Parker—Sketch of the Parker family: William, John, Samuel, Matthew Stanley, Noah, John 2d ... 119

22 The earliest Pauper Work-House, 1716—Almshouse on Court Street—Clement March and his family—Superintendents ... 127

23. King Street—John Tufton Mason—His Premises and Family—John Gains—Charles Treadwell ... 131

24. Charles Treadwell—His Marriage—Successful Store-keeping—Building of three Large Houses—Death of Mrs. Treadwell—Her Character ... 135

25. The Warner House—Capt. Macpheadris—Jonathan Warner—Paintings Developed—First Lightning Rod ... 140

26. Pleasant street—Livermore—The Church—Vestry—Parsonage—Matthew Livermore—Samuel—Edward St. Loe—The Mansion ... 143

27. John Sullivan—The House Boy—His First Law Case—His Advancement—His Sail on the Piscataqua ... 147

28. Fire of 1802—N. H. Bank House—Jotham Odiorne—His Family—William Whipple—The Marriage put aside—His First Declaration of Independence—His Slaves—Prince's Freedom—Dinah—Cuffee—The Garrison House ... 151

29. Description of the Whipple Garrison House—Construction and Use ... 156

30. Portsmouth in 1727—Inhabitants—Property—Location of Neighborhoods ... 159

31. Residences on Market and Bow streets—Judge Pickering—John Penhallow—Boyd—J. McDonough—Disappearance on Wedding Night—Boyd's Riches ... 162

32. G. Boyd's Seat near the North Mill—Grenadiers' Heads—Boyd's Early History ... 165

33. Ropewalks in Former Times on Islington Road, Elm and Middle Streets—Present Ropewalk on South street—Improvements in Machinery—Longfellow's Hempen Lines ... 169

34. The Old Cellar—Rock Pasture—Myrick's Ropewalk—His Departure—The Buried Gold ... 174

35. Vaughan street—The Old Assembly House—Michael Whidden—Nathaniel Meserve—The Stamp Act—George Meserve—Revolutionary Scenes—Liberty Bridge—Occupants of the Meserve House—Old Trees ... 176

36. Doctor Moses—Single Tens—Small Glass—Congress at Albany—"Dr. Moses's Bottle"—Conjuration—His Widow ... 182

37. Samuel Moses—Samuel, Jr.—Fish Story—Shaving—Theodore Moses ... 186

38. Stavers's Hotel—John and Bartholomew Stavers—First Stage to Boston—Progress of Travel ... 189

39. Earl of Halifax Hotel—Meetings of Royalists—Mob Assault—Mark Noble Injured—Stavers's Escape—John Langdon—French Fleet—Distinguished Visitors—Lafayette—Louis Philippe—Washington ... 192

40. Scenes on Market Square—William Pottle the Tory—Whipping of a Woman at the Town Pump ... 197

41. Residences on Middle street—Sketch of the eccentric Shepherd Ham—Middle street Church Site ... 200

42. Sagamore Creek—Origin of Name—Residences—The Bridge—Lear the Hermit ... 205

43. Slaves in Portsmouth—Their Standing—Cyrus—Prime Fowle—Cuffee Chase—Sambo Stevens—Peter Warner—Negro Elections—King Nero—Black Court—Continuance of Slavery ... 210

44. The Association Test of 1776 ... 214

45. Capt. Thomas Pickering—Capture of Fort William and Mary—Langdon—Sullivan—Scarborough's Boat Conflict—The Hampden—Death of Pickering ... 218

46. Major Samuel Hale—Latin Grammar School in State street—Patriotism—First Province School ... 226

47. New Custom House and Post Office—Former Custom Houses—Eleazer Russell—His Peculiarities—Collector and State Postmaster—His Death ... 229

48. The Buckminster House—Occupants—Nathaniel Warner's Disappointment—Lettice Mitchel—Wyseman Clagett—The Marriage—Domestic Troubles—Sketch of his Life—Official Acts—Character........ 233

49. Eliphalet Ladd—Early Life—Family—The Hercules—The Archelaus—Buildings—Portsmouth Aqueduct—The Challenge—His Death and Character........ 239

50. Frenchman's Lane—The French Fleet Three Months at Portsmouth—The Murder—Their Laundry at the Creek........ 245

51. Richard Fitzgerald—His Residence—Interview with Com. Hull—His Garden—Old Rose Bush—Love of Flowers—Death of Husband and Wife same day........ 250

52. Washington's tour to New Hampshire in 1789—His own Account........ 254

53. Washington's Visit to Portsmouth—Committees—Reception—Reply to Town Address—Attendance at Church—Dr. Buckminster's Address—Fishing—Little Harbor........ 258

54. Gardner and Hunking streets—The Old Linden—The Lear House—Tobias Lear, Washington's Private Secretary—Washington's Family—Washington's Visit to Mrs. Lear—Memorials of the President and his Lady—Tobias Lear's Political Life........ 267

55. Andrew and James Clarkson—The Pretender's Ensign—The Tan Yard—Rev. John Murray........ 272

56. Pierse Long—Early History—Revolutionary Sketch—Family........ 275

57. Charles Chauncy—Family History—His Interest in the Revolution—Anecdotes—Character—Descendants—Charles W. Chauncy—Finale of the Old House........ 280

58. Market Square in 1789—First Store of Three Stories—Knight's House—The Robber Discovered—Inspection of Travellers and Goods........ 286

59. Auburn street Cemetery—First Training Field—Cotton's Burying Ground—Execution of Ruth Blay—Duel by Frenchmen—Laighton's Poem........ 289

60. William H. Rindge—Noble Act of an Unknown Sailor—Mrs. Sigourney's Sketch—Disclosure at Death........ 294

61. William Brewster—Display of Dauntless Bravery at New York—The Fatal Disaster on Ship-board—A Model of Self-devotion........ 295

62. Paved street in 1780, by an Old Lady—Location of Buildings on the East and West Sides—Dearborn's School—Dedication of his Academy........ 298

63. Market street—Dearborn's Residence—Its Builder—Romantic Incident........ 300

64. Jefferson Hall—Its School Scenes—First Public Female School, Montague's—Only Town Grammar School, Taft's—The first Sunday School........ 303

65. Gardner's Arch—Gardner Family—William Gardner's History—Sacrifices in the Revolution—His Appointment and Removal—Thomas Manning—Gardner's Character........ 307

66. Daniel Webster—His Residence in Portsmouth—His last Visit to Portsmouth—Public Reception at Jefferson Hall—Meeting at the Cameneum........ 311

67. Stoodley's Hotel—Masonic Hall and Ball Room—Etiquette of last Century........ 315

68. Decorations of Market Square—The Packer House—Deacon Penhallow—The Langdon and Thompson Houses—Great Elm—The Old Man's Sketch—Sandemanian Church—Brimstone Hill........ 317

69. Rev. Dr. Haven—Settlement and Residence—Manufactures—Revolutionary Anecdotes........ 322

70. Old North Church—Rev. Dr. Buckminster—Last Service—Pew Occupants in 1812—The Vane's Appeal........ 326

71. Revolutionary Meeting at North Church—Resistance against Tea Importation... 332

72. Town Security against Foreign Paupers—Orders for Strangers to Leave—Promptness of Town Officers—Who Built the Forts........ 334

73. Newmarch and Billings House—Bell Tavern—Melcher House—Waldron's—Jenny Stewart's—Mary Martin's—John Francis—The Privateer Adventure........ 336

74. Market street—Bow street—Penhallow's garden—Penhallow's family—Theatre......342

75. Deer street—Why so named—Houses of Newmarch, Collings and Fitch—Christian Shore—Tradition of the Beehive........ 344

76. Three Generations of Trees—Lombardy Poplar—Sycamore—Elm and Maple........ 346

77. The Three Episcopal Churches, of 1638, 1732 and 1808—Richard Gibson, Arthur Brown, John C. Ogden, Joseph Willard, Charles Burroughs, William A. Hitchcock, Rectors........ 349

78. Opening of Middle street—The Naming of Congress street—Thomas Manning—Houses on Congress street—Jail History—The Keeper's Story........ 353

79. Gov. Vaughan's Residence—North Burying Ground—Buildings on Market Square........ 357

80. Peirce Family—Sketches of Joshua, Daniel and John........ 359

81. Langdon Family—Tobias—Family Genealogy—Samuel—Woodbury—John—The Revolutionary Services of John Langdon........ 362

82. Badger's Island—The Seventy-Four America—John Paul Jones—Progress of Building—Description—Difficulties—The Final History........ 367

83. River Scenery—Navy Yard Island—Trefethren's—Peirce's—Shapley's—Salter's—John Salter—The Cautious Ferryman—The Close........ 373

Alphabetical Index of Names........ 378

# Portsmouth Sketches.

## RAMBLE I.

Pring's visit to the Piscataqua—Smith's discoveries on the coast—Vision of the future—Early scenery.

FOR more than a century after COLUMBUS had discovered America, the noble Piscataqua was unvisited and unknown. The first rambler on its shores, of whom we can find any record, was MARTIN PRING, who, in 1603, came here with a ship of fifty tons and thirty men, and a bark of twenty-six tons and thirteen men. This small fleet was fitted out under the patronage of the mayor, aldermen and merchants of the opulent English city of Bristol, to prosecute the discovery of the northern parts of Virginia. The flag-ship was called the Speedwell, and the bark the Discoverer. They first touched at some of the islands near the entrance of Penobscot Bay, then visited the mouths of the Saco, Kennebunk, and York rivers, which Pring says they found "to pierce not far into the land." They next proceeded to the Piscataqua, which Pring calls the westernmost and best river, and he explored it ten or twelve miles into the interior.

This visit to our harbor was made in the pleasant month of June, when the landscape wore its freshest aspect. We may easily imagine the Speedwell anchored in the lower harbor, while the Discoverer, not much larger than one of our pleasure sloop-boats, receives on board the adventurous Pring, who, aided by sturdy oarsmen, carefully and slowly ascends the river,—now and then sounding its unusual depth and calculating upon the safety of the navigation. They look with some fear as they approach the Narrows—but that point safely passed, and a broader basin opening, they begin to admire the "goodly groves and woods," as Pring terms them. The bold shores on either side invite them to land, now on this point, then on that,—sometimes making a short excursion on an island, and then a more extended one on the main land,—wending their course now in a grove where hundreds of ships instead of trees are in future time to spring up—and then pursuing their way through a forest where wild beasts are prowling, which in after years is to give place to graded streets, lined by well-designed places of business, dwellings and public edifices. Timber which was then standing in that forest may even now be found in some of our old structures—while, solitary and alone, yet stands one venerable oak, under the shadow of which perhaps Pring passed in this first ramble about Portsmouth,—that old oak which afterwards became an ornament in the large garden of John Tufton Mason, the heir of the grantee of the State, and in its green old age is still the cherished heritage of his descendants.

The party have not yet discovered the main object of their pursuit, nor do they find a red man in the present site of Portsmouth, although the embers of extinguished fires were frequently visible, showing the spots where they had encamped earlier in the Spring. June was the season when fish were plenty at the falls, higher up the rivers, and thither they had then probably gone. We may imagine Pring and his company again entering the Discoverer at the Spring, and proceeding further up the river. They pass the Pulpit, and, encouraged by the great depth of water, proceed on, until spread before them, in all its quiet beauty, lay the placid waters of Great Bay. Again they land and rove through the forest, scrutinizing every tree; but among them all not a Sassafras can be found—that valued tree whose medical virtues in that age were regarded as the elixir of life. Thus again disappointed, they seek the mouth of the harbor, and the Speedwell and Discoverer depart for a more southern excursion. This was the close of the first ramble by foreigners on the Piscataqua. The Speedwell, or a vessel of about the same size bearing the same name, seventeen years after, received on board the Plymouth Pilgrims, but proved unseaworthy, and her passengers were transferred to the ever-blooming May-flower.

Eleven years roll on before we find mention of another excursion on the Piscataqua. The next visitor was one whose adventures form an important chapter in English as well as American history. The name of JOHN SMITH was no myth in the seventeenth century. He was a man of great daring, energy and perseverance. His own account of his romantic adventures among the Turks, shows him well fitted for the severe trials he was destined to pass through as a pioneer in America, and evinced in him that firmness so coolly displayed before Powhatan in Virginia, when he was providentially rescued from death by the noble conduct of the Indian girl, not yet in her teens, whose generous devotion, in view of its great results, radiates, as a star, in the firmament of history, the name of POCAHONTAS.

It was in 1614, that Captain John Smith, with two vessels, arrived at Monhegan, on the coast of Maine, and while his men were engaged in fishing, he with eight of his company in one of his boats, ranged the coast from Penobscot Bay to Cape Cod. He was the discoverer of the Isles of Shoals, which so pleased him that he gave them the name of *Smith's Isles*—a name which they *should* still retain, to hold in remembrance one for whose valuable services in the early settlement of the country no pecuniary reward was bestowed. Smith drew the first map of our coast, and, on presenting it to Prince Charles, with a request that he would give the country a name, it was for the first time by him called New-England. On this map, Smith gave to the locality of Portsmouth the name of *Hull;* to Kittery and York he gave the name of *Boston.*

The exalted opinion Smith had of the wild country he was exploring, and his conceptions of its high destiny, as exhibited in the poetic address, reflecting his own ideas, made to him on his return to England,* warrant us in

* TO HIS FRIEND CAPTAINE SMITH, UPON HIS DESCRIPTION OF NEW-ENGLAND.

SIR: your Relations I haue read: which shew,
Ther's reason I should honour *them* and *you:*
And if their meaning I haue vnderstood,
I dare to censure thus: Your *Project's* good;
And may (if followed) doubtlesse quit the paine,
With honour, pleasure and a trebble gaine;
Beside the benefit that shall arise
To make more happy our Posterities.
  For would we daigne to spare, though 'twere no more
Than what ore-fils and surfets vs in store,
To order *Nature's* fruitfulness a while
In that rude *Garden* you *New-England* stile;
With present good, ther's hope in after daies
Thence to repaire what *Time* and *Pride* decaies
In this rich Kingdome. And the spacious *West*
Being still more with *English* blood possest,
The proud *Iberians* shall not rule those Seas,
To check our ships from sailing where they please;
Nor future times may any forraine power
Become so great to force a bound to *Our.*
  Much good my minde foretels would follow hence
With little labour and with lesse expence.
Thrive therefore thy *Designe,* who ere envy;
*England* may joy in *England's* Colony,
*Virginia* seeke her Virgin sisters good:
Be blessed in such happy neighbourhood.
  Or, whatsoere Fate pleaseth to permit,
  Be thou still honour'd for first moving it.
*George Wither,* e societate Lincol.

the supposition that his visit to the Piscataqua aided in the formation of his favorable opinions. We may easily imagine him, after visiting the group of islands to which he gave his own name, tracing his way towards our coast, marking the outlines of Agameticus, nearing the outer harbor, and proceeding up the deep-channeled river to what he called "a safe harbor with a rocky shore." To his keen perception might then have arisen visions of the future—for his was the pioneer's life, and his joy was in opening those fields which others were to cultivate and develop, and to contemplate the results the hidden future might produce. Had some vision then passed before him, unrolling as in a moving panorama the history of succeeding centuries, how impatiently would he have looked upon the slow growth of this locality! For nine years the green forest which extended back from Strawberry Bank would continue to grow, and the river to flow, undisturbed, before the erection of the first frame house near the entrance of the harbor. And after the completion of Mason Hall, eight more years transpire before another like structure, the "Great House," is seen rising near the river at the Bank. As the scene progresses, he discerns matters of interest more rapidly increasing, and there is an evident awakening to future prosperity. The year 1631 now opens, and Smith sees a numerous company begin to locate in this new land of promise. Log cabins are now constructed, salt works put in operation, and the saw-mill, then a new invention, cuts the forests into forms for civilized use. The panorama moves on—the White Mountains, or "Crystal Hills," are now, in 1632, first visited by the white man, and the internal resources of the State are beginning to be developed. He sees, too, rebellion among the tenantry. A banner is unfurled on the picture, and its inscription is "freedom and independence." The stewards at the plantation, in 1639, enter on the business of dividing the goods and cattle of the Mason estate among themselves, and take possession of the buildings and land, claiming the soil as the right of those who cultivate it. And he might now, in 1644, see another evidence in favor of the inscription on that banner, in the decision of the local court that African slavery could not here be tolerated. There is a darker shadow now passing before his mental vision—the fanaticism of witchcraft swaying the better judgments of the colonists. Now on the borders of the Piscataqua he sees rise the residence of the first royal governor sent into New-England—he sees the young nation eventually maturing, and the first evidence of rebellious prowess manifested in the capture by the colonists of the royal castle "William & Mary" at the harbor's mouth—he sees building on the banks of the Piscataqua, and floating in its waters, the first line-of-battle ship New-England produces.—But the scenes are too numerous and the panorama passes too fast for us to trace them. Smith might have looked upon them with deep interest, until there came a display of ships without sails, plying in the river, stemming its rapid current—carriages on land running without horses—invisible letters passing from place to place on wires. Surprised that such vagaries should enter his brain, Smith looks upon the whole as a fancy sketch, and awakes from his reverie. He now turns from our harbor, passes again his adopted isles,—and we have no record that he ever returned.

Smith being the intimate friend of Fernando Gorges, it was probably on Smith's representation that the Laconia Company made selection of the banks of Piscataqua for their plantation. John Smith died in London, in 1631, at the age of 52. Although he had given many years' labor, and had spent five hundred pounds in the service of Virginia and New England, he complained in his latter days that in America he had not a foot of land

—what he had discovered had been shared among those who only knew the lands by his description. His memory should be held in esteem by a nation for whom he had a fatherly care, when it was in its earliest infancy.

The early scenery of the Piscataqua was happily adverted to in the centennial oration of Mr. Haven, in 1823. "Two hundred years ago, the place on which we stand was an uncultivated forest. The rough and vigorous soil was still covered with the stately trees, which had been, for ages, intermingling their branches and deepening the shade. The river, which now bears on its bright and pure waters the treasures of distant climates, and whose rapid current is stemmed and vexed by the arts and enterprise of man, then only rippled against the rocks, and reflected back the wild and grotesque thickets which overhung its banks. The mountain, which now swells on our left and rises its verdant side 'shade above shade,' was then almost concealed by the lofty growth which covered the intervening plains. Behind us, a deep morass, extending across to the northern creek, almost enclosed the little 'Bank,' which is now the seat of so much life and industry. It was then a wild and tangled thicket, interspersed with venerable trees and moss-grown rocks, and presenting, here and there, a sunny space covered with the blossoms and early fruit of the little plant, that gave it its name."

In the following apostrophe to the Piscataqua, another writer presents some idea of the scenes of early days. The reference to Ohio arises from some discoveries there made which tend to show a higher state of civilization in the early days of the aborigines.

Through how many rolling ages
  Have thy waters, broad and free,
In their grandeur and still beauty
  Swept their current to the sea!
Thou hast seen the tangled wild wood,
  Where the lonely wigwam rose,
Thou hast echoed the wild war-whoop
  When the red men met as foes.

When the pine and oak and maple
  Over them their shadows threw,
Then was heard the rippling eddies
  Of the glancing birch canoe;
When the wild beasts, unmolested,
  With the birds of air, roamed free,
And the beaver built his dwelling
  Where the mason's art we see.

Thou didst mirror the new dwelling
  Rudely reared in this wild land.
When the deep and lonely forest
  Swayed before the white man's hand;
Thou didst echo the last struggle
  When the hatchet fell no more,
And with the forests of the red man
  Passed the Sachem's lordly power.

Say, what didst thou see, O river,
  In the centuries gone by?
Saw you the same tangled forest
  All along your borders lie?
Did no fair and spreading city
  Rise up in that distant day,
With a race whose wealth and honors
  From the earth have passed away!

From the lands of broad Ohio
  Did no restless wanderers come,
Here, amidst our sunny landscapes,
  To construct a busy home?
Did the fate which strangely scattered
  In the dust their homes and race,
Sweep along thy banks, O river,
  And their memory efface?

Away in the distant future
  Thou still on thy course wilt flow,
When we to our rest are gathered,
  And these busy homes laid low:—
Through the wrecks of time and changes
  Thou unfettered still wilt flow,
Through the ages of the future,
  As the centuries come and go.

## RAMBLE II.

Visit of M. Champlain at Odiorne's Point—the Manor House Erected—Gorges and Mason—Emigrants—the Great House—Stock of the Plantation—Relics—Garrison Houses—Early water courses.

An hour's walk from Market Square, over Sagamore bridge, will find us on the seacoast at Odiorne's point—a peninsula on which there is a slight eminence, a few rods from the sea, which affords a good view of the ocean and of the neighboring country. It is said that in 1605, a French vessel touched at this point, where Champlain met with a small company of Indians, to whom he made presents of knives, &c., and from them obtained information of the coast. The Indians, with charcoal, marked out the coast as far as they knew it—delineating the entrance of the Merrimac impeded by sand bars, and making the first disclosure of the existence of that river.

Odiorne's point was the spot selected by the Laconia Company for the site of the first building erected on the grant. The first settlers were sent from England by the Company in 1623, "to found a plantation on Piscataqua river, to cultivate the vine, discover mines, carry on the fisheries, and trade with the natives." The month in which they arrived is supposed to be May, and under the direction of David Thompson, the Manor house, or Mason's Hall as afterwards called, was erected for the Company. There is no record of the vessel by which they came, or any sketch left to give us an idea of what sort of house was built. As the materials of many of the early houses were brought from England, it is probable that in the liberal provision made for the plantation, those of this house were also. The Manor house was a little north of the hillock, which was between it and the ocean,—and on that elevation there was a small fort built, to protect from savage incursions. Fishing being one of the objects of the settlement, salt works were early erected in connection with the establishment.

A few rods south-west of the fort at Odiorne's Point they erected their fish flakes, which gave the name of Flake Hill to the knoll, which is still retained. During the first few years of the existence of the colony, remarks Potter, the people suffered every hardship, and not being acclimated, many of them were carried off by disease. The graves of such are still to be seen a few rods north of the site of the fort, and it is worthy of remark, that the moss-covered cobble stones at the head and foot of the graves, still remain as placed by mourners of two hundred and thirty years since, while a walnut and a pear tree, each of immense size, and possibly of equal age with our State, stand like sturdy sentinels, extending their ancient arms over the sleepers below. Evidence is now apparent that a smith's shop was erected near the house. There were between three and four thousand acres regarded as attached to this branch of the plantation. The provisions of the grant were ample for carrying out the idea of the proprietors, which was to establish a Manor here agreeably to the English custom—the occupants of the land to be held as tenants by the proprietors of the soil.

The most interested and active men of the Laconia Company were Fernando Gorges and John Mason. In 1634, these gentlemen became owners of the grant, and Gorges disposed of his right in New-Hampshire to Mason, also his right to the saw-mills at Newichewannock (the Berwick lower falls). Gorges held his possession in Maine, and founded there the first city in New-England, called Gorgiana. The city form of government was observed for only two years, when the Mayor, Thomas Gorges, returned to England. A laxity of morals being manifest, and the citizens being few, there being no clergymen nor schools, the city form of government was abandoned, and its place the quiet town of York has ever since supplied.

Although Mason never visited his possessions, he took a deep interest in his Manor, and in 1631 sent about eighty emigrants to locate here and act as stewards, agents, workmen and servants. Among the men were many whose surnames are yet familiar with us. Neal, Gibbons, Camocks, Raymond, Williams, Vaughan, Warnerton, Jocelyn, Norton and Lane were his stewards; Renald Fernald was the surgeon; there were forty-eight others of various occupations, and twenty-two women. Among the forty-eight men were the following names; Goe, Cooper, Chadborn, Matthews, Rand, Johnson, Ellins, Baldwin, Spencer, Furrel, Herd, Chatherton, Crowther, Williams, Knight, Sherborn, Goddard, Withers, Canney, Symonds, Peverly, Seavey, Langstaff, Berry, Wall, Walford, Brakin, Moore, Beal, James, Jones, Ault, Newt, and Bracket.

In 1631, the "Great House" was built by Humphrey Chadborn, about three miles up the Piscataqua from Mason's Hall. Its location was on our present Water street, on the south-east corner of Court street. It was from this point, over Church hill and further north, that there was a large growth of strawberries near the bank of the river, which circumstance, for thirty years from the first settlement up to 1653, gave what is now the compact part of Portsmouth, the name of *Strawberry Bank.*

The Great House, which was also a part of Mason's property, was the second house reported to have been built here, although the circumstance that a fort was early erected on the eastern part of Great Island goes to show that probably there were some fishermen's cots on that island at the time.

To the Great House there were attached about a thousand acres of land, consisting of marsh, meadow, planting and pasture grounds, and much of it under improvement. The bounds of this farm cannot now be accurately defined; it probably extended over a large portion of the present compact part of the city, taking in the whole peninsula between the ponds, and extending west and north of them. An old document shows that Strawberry Bank was the planting ground and pasture of the Great House.

In 1632, Mason imported a large breed of yellow cattle from Denmark. We find that in 1635, there were twenty-four cows and thirty-four other neat cattle, ninety-two sheep, twenty-seven goats, sixty-four hogs, and twenty-one horses and colts on the plantation. The imported cattle increased so well that, thirteen years after, one of Mason's unfaithful stewards drove a hundred of them to Boston and the vicinity, where he sold them on his own account for about twenty pounds a head. Some of this stock is yet to be found in this vicinity.

While we are rambling about the Manor, the Great House, and the Saw-mill establishment, which compose the three divisions of the Mason plantation, we will look in upon their stores, a schedule of which, made in July, 1635, at the time of Mason's death, is before us. We find them not only provided with food in abundance, but also with ample means of defence. For use in their little forts were furnished some articles of armament such as their descendants now rarely see. Here are twenty-two *arquebusses*, capable of carrying a three-ounce ball, and cocked with a wheel; three *sakers*, two *chambers*, and four other pieces of ordnance called *murtherers;* here, too, are four muskets, forty-six fowling pieces, twelve pistols, sixty-one swords and belts; and to make the guns effective, thirteen barrels of gunpowder, and about a thousand pounds of bullets and shot. For music, here are two drums for the training days,—while no less than fifteen hautboys and "soft recorders" are provided to cheer the emigrants in their solitude. Looking into their store-house, we find 220 bushels of corn and meal, 20 bushels of oatmeal, 15 barrels of malt, 29 barrels of peas, 610 pounds of sugar, 512 pounds of tobacco, 6 pipes of wine and 2 of brandy. Tea and coffee were then unknown, and chocolate had not come into use. So if we stop at the Great House, or at the Hall, for refreshments, we must put up with an Indian cake, pea porridge, a flagon of ale, and after whiffing a Dutch pipe, a cup of wine. It is very doubtful whether we can be accommodated with any crockery or glass ware from which to partake our treat, for the twelve hundred and seventy-six utensils made of wrought pewter, which they possessed, would seem enough to supply every use to which crockery might be appropriated. We must be careful to keep good hours—for in the whole establishment can be found but about fifteen pounds of candles.

The Great House was occupied up to 1644 by Thomas Warnerton, who was an assistant to Gov. Williams, (officers appointed by Mason.) In 1644, Warnerton seized upon some of the arms and ammunition of which we have just given an account, as well as on some other goods belonging to the estate of Mason, shipped them to Port Royal and accompanied them. Soon after he had disposed of his cargo, he fell in a rencontre with some of the inhabitants. Sampson Lane then became the occupant of the Great House, and continued there until 1646, when it passed into the possession and occupancy of Richard Cutt, who occupied it till his death, in 1676. The Great House then went into the possession of his brother President John Cutt, (if not before owned by him,) for we find in 1680 the President, by his will, gives the house to his son Samuel. The house was then probably in a dilapidated condition,—for in 1685 it is recorded that the house had fallen down, and the ruins were then visible.

Col. John Tufton Mason, of the fifth generation from the original grantee, John Mason, to whom his estate descended, lived in Portsmouth, on Vaughn street, more than a century ago. That house will be visited in a future ramble.

The only relics of the articles brought over by the company of 1631 in our knowledge, are two of the chairs brought over by Dr. Renald Fernald, which have probably been inmates of Mason Hall. One is now in the possession of A. R. H. Fernald, Esq., a descendant of the sixth generation. It is a handsome chair of the Elizabethan age, and has been carefully handed down from generation to generation. The other chair is at the residence of John L. Hayes, Esq., in the city of Washington.

We have no knowledge of the exact time when the old garrison houses in Portsmouth were built; but within a century there was a garrison house at the head of Jacob Sheafe's wharf on Water street, another near the mansion of the late Alexander Ladd, on Market street, probably the residence of President John Cutt, and a third was the Russell house near the Ferryways. These were probably some of the first houses built on the Bank, after the erection of the Great House.

In former times it is not unlikely that at high tides the Bank was nearly, if not quite, an island. Before any bridges were erected at the entrances of the North and South ponds, the tide rose much higher in those ponds than it has since. That the water from the North pond has flowed through Hanover, Vaughn and Congress streets to where the stone stable now stands in Fleet street, is very evident; for recently there has been dug in Fleet street, at the depth of four feet, the sward of a salt marsh, in good preservation,—showing that in former times the salt water had flowed there. It is also said that the marshes of the South Mill pond have extended into Court street. If so, the water has doubtless, in former ages, flowed between the North and South ponds; as it has also from Puddle dock to the South pond, over Pleasant street; thus making one island of what was formerly called "Pickering's Neck," and another of "the Bank."

## RAMBLE III.

Adoption of the name of Portsmouth and town lines—Hubbard's Sketch of the early settlements.

For thirty years from the first settlement, we might roam through forests without leaving the present limits of the thickly settled part of Portsmouth. The growth of the colony was slow, the Great Island portion being more rapid than at the Bank. In 1653 there were but fifty or sixty families in the limits of what now comprises Portsmouth, Newcastle, Rye, Greenland and Newington.

In May of that year the inhabitants petitioned the General Court of Massachusetts for a definite township, and the privilege of taking the name of Portsmouth. As this petition, obtained by Rev. Dr. Burroughs from the file in the early documents in Massachusetts, has not been placed in our town records or annals, we give it here, verbatim, for preservation.

"To the hon'd Gen'l Court at Boston, this present month of May 1653. The humble petition of the Inhab'ts of the Towne at present called Strabery Banke, showeth. That whereas your petitioners petitioned to the last Gen'l Court to grant to the P. Inhab'ts, a competent portion of land to make us a township, whereby we may be enabled to subsist and be useful to the church and Common'th. Our desire is, that this honor'd Court will be pleased to show their favor and good will towards us, and willingness to accommodate us to the uttermost. And for that purpose have desired the honor'd Capt. Wiggins to bringe his pattent to this present Court. Now it may please this hon'd Court to take our case into consideration; and to consider of our extreme necessities, first in respect of the number of families, which are between 50 and 60, of w'ch some are constrained to remove from want of land to accommodate them with their stocks—secondly the qualities of the land wee live upon is soe badd, its incredible to beleeve except those who have seen it—thirdly the place being settled a plantation, the first of any in these parts, and our willingnesse in submitting to yr government—fourthly, that all the neighbouring plantations about us, w'ch were settled since wee, have their townshipps settled and bounded; onely we as yet have none—fifthly, that whereas there is much benefit by saw mills in other townes in this river and adjacent townes there is none in this town but onely one, w'ch was never perfected nor like to bee. We humbly intreat his honor'd Court to take into theire view this necke of land w'ch we live upon; w'ch nature itselfe hath bounded with the maine sea and river, as may be seene by the draft of the river, w'ch was presented to the last Gen'l Court, and now presented againe by our deputie, w'ch necke of land is farre less than any neighboringe towne about us. The desire of yr humble petit'rs is, that this hon'd Court would grant us the necke of land, beginning in the great bay at a place called Cotterill's delight, soe runninge to the sea according to the former petition. And whereas the name of this plantation att present being Strabery Banke, accidentally soe called, by reason of a banke where straberries *was* found in this place, now we humbly desire to have it called Portsmouth, being a name most suitable for this place, it being the river's mouth, and good as any in this land, and your petit'rs shall humbly pray.

"BRIAN PENDLETON, RICH. CUTT and
"RENALD FERNALD, SAMUEL HAINES,
"JOHN SHEREBOURN, In behalf of the rest."

On this petition it was first proposed to postpone "because of Mr. Mason's claim on the land," afterwards granted 28 May, 1653, allowed to be called Portsmouth, "and the line of the township of Portsmouth to reach from the sea by Hampton lyne to Wynnacot river, leaving the propriet'rs to their just right."

In 1652 the records of the Bank were copied, suppressing all the selectmen regarded not worth preserving, thus depriving us of many of the early incidents of local history.

Hubbard, the early New-England historian, quaintly says of the slow settlement of *North America*, "this posthumous birth of time, is as to its nativity of the same standing with her two elder sisters Peru and Mexico, yet was suffered to lie in its swadling-clothes one whole century of years, nature having promised no such dowry of rich mines of silver and gold to them that would espouse her for their own, as she did unto the other two, which possibly was the reason why she was not so hastily possessed by her first discoverers, nor yet so early courted by any of the Princes of Europe." In 1676, Hubbard remarks, "All or most of the towns and plantations are seated upon and near some river greater or lesser, whose streams are principally improved for driving of saw-mills, those late inventions, so useful for destruction of wood and timber, specially of fir trees, which do so abound in those coasts; that there is scarce a river or creek in those parts that hath not some of those engines erected upon them. The upper branches of the famous river Piscataqua, being also imployed all of them that way, namely, Sturgeon Creeke, Salmon Falls, Newechewannick, Queechecho, Oyster River, Swamscot, Greenland, Lamprey-Eele river, together with the towns of Exeter and Dover, seated upon or near some of the main branches thereof, whose principal trade is in deale boards, cut by those saw-mills, since their rift timber is near all consumed. On each side of that brave navigable river of Piscataqua down towards the mouth of it, are seated, on the north side the town of Kittery, (a long scattering plantation made up of several hamlets,) on the south side the town of Portsmouth, to which belongs the great island, lying in the mouth of the said river, a place of considerable trade these late years, the which together with Strawberry Bank, the upper part of the said town of Portsmouth, are the magazine, and chief, or only place of commerce and trade at the plantations, betwixt it and Casco bay."

## RAMBLE IV.

Fines for cutting Timber—the Distribution of Town Lands—Names of Inhabitants in 1657—Portion assigned to each.

ALTHOUGH in 1631 eighty emigrants came into the colony, yet twenty-six years after, the citizens of Portsmouth over twenty-one years of age, and females unmarried over eighteen, numbered scarcely a hundred.

At a town meeting held by the Selectmen January 13, 1660, a penalty of five shillings for every tree was imposed upon any inhabitant, for cutting timber or any other wood from off the town common, except for their own building, fencing or firewood.

Robert Elliot, John Lewis, Mr. Fryer and Goodman Mussell were fined £10 each for building on or appropriating portions of the town commons to their own use, without orders, license, or town grant, in general, or Selectmen in particular. Subsequently the fine of Goodman Mussell was remitted, and the lands illegally taken conveyed to him by the Selectmen.

"At a general town meeting, held February 3, 1660, those gentlemen the town had chosen to consider of the plans and proportions unto whom land ought to be given, presenting the town with what they had done therein, the which when the town had considered and debated, there were some of the old planters made a motion to have 600 acres of land distributed among them, and others of a shorter standing to have a lesser proportion of land added over and above to them, gave occasion to the following votes:

*Voted,* That the old planters should have six hundred acres of land distributed among them, three hundred acres whereof is rendered up by Capt. Pendleton, Mr. John and Richard Cutt, out of their proportion of three hundred acres, to make the sum aforesaid to be out of the town's land. And furthermore it was voted that the above six hundred acres should be to relieve those that stand in need, together with the old planters.

*Voted,* That they are to distribute the six hundred acres mentioned in the former vote, shall not exceed above fifty acres to any man. William Seavey and John Pickering were added to the committee to distribute the land among the inhabitants."

The Selectmen were prohibited from granting any more of the town's lands, until the lands are distributed and a vote of the town again renews their power of making grants, and it was voted that all owners of lands be at equal charge for defending the same, according to their proportions.

The following is the report of the committee appointed to proportion the land among the inhabitants.

"Whereas, at a general towne meeting held by the inhabitants of Portsmouth the 22d of January, 1660, it was agreed upon for the distribution of their lands undisposed and not yet granted, that there should be a distribution thereof, be made up to such of the inhabitants as hitherto have had little or none given them in some proportion to those that have already lands granted to them. And for an equal proceeding therein did then and there choose us whose names are underwritten, for to consider the persons and proportions unto whom the said lands should be divided and distributed, which said persons then chosen have considered accordingly with reference unto both, and for a more just and equal way of proceeding, according to the premises, have drawn up and concluded upon these propositions following:

1*st.* That all such as were reputed inhabitants and free comyuers unto the year 1657, (when at a town meeting held the 24th of February, the town looked at and respected after-comers under another consideration,) are the persons unto whom right of land belongs in this distribution.

2*d.* That all sons as are of the age of 21 years and upwards have right to land in this distribution, and further that all sons that are married, although under the age of 21 years, as like right as those aforesaid.

3*d.* That all daughters of those mentioned in the first proposition, whether married or unmarried at the age of 18 years and upwards, are capable of and ought to have a proportion in this distribution.

THE PERSONS TO HAVE LAND AND PROPORTIONS.

| | | | | | | | | |
|---|---|---|---|---|---|---|---|---|
| Thomas Ornyon | 20 | | Agnus Turpin | 13 | | William Earle | 37 | |
| Robert Puddington | 19 | 6 | Antho. Brackett, jr. | 13 | | Wm. Ham | 35 | 35 |
| Jno. Jackson | 86 | | Ellinor Brackett | 13 | | Rich. Jackson | 50 | |
| Jno. Lock | 16 | | Jno. Berry | 13 | | Rich. Seaward, sr. | 13 | |
| Jno. Jones | 19 | 31 | Jos. Berry | 13 | | Rich. Seaward jr. | 13 | |
| James Cate | 13 | | Jno. Foss | 19 | | Rich. Martin | 62 | |
| Rich. Comings | 91 | | Fran. Rann | 50 | 30 | Robt. Mattoone | 15 | 10 |
| Walter Abbott | 100 | | Antho. Brackett, sr. | 100 | | Math. Ham | 25 | |
| Jno. Webster | 26 | 14 | Edward Clark | 25 | | John Pickering | 101 | 50 |
| Jno. Hunkins | 56 | | Jno. Partridge | 13 | | Tho. Walford | 68 | 42 |
| Wm. Cotten | 38 | 35 | Jos. Atkeson | 13 | | Jno. Sherburne | 101 | |
| Geo. Walton | 120 | | Rich. Sloper | 78 | | Tho. Peverly | 40 | 35 |
| Robert Mussell | 15 | 10 | Christ'r Jose | 13 | | Tho. Hincson | 28 | |

| | | | | | | | | |
|---|---|---|---|---|---|---|---|---|
| Alex. Jones | 19 | | Elias Stileman | 31 | | Jos. Walker | 18 | |
| Capt. Pendleton | 350 | | Hen. Sherburne | 151 | | John Moses | 42 | 43 |
| James Pendleton | 31 | | Tho. Jackson | 37 | | Hen. Beck | 17 | 43 |
| Caleb Pendleton, | 19 | | Otho Tuckerman | 13 | | Jno. Heart | 13 | |
| Wm. Lux | 13 | | James Drew | 13 | | Anthony Ellens | 50 | |
| Robt. Taprill | 13 | | Sarah Fernald | 13 | | Wm. Brookin | 33 | 7 |
| James Leach | 25 | 10 | Sam'l Haines | 101 | | Hen. Seavey | 28 | |
| William Seavey | 161 | | Walter Neale | 39 | 31 | Robert Davis | 13 | |
| Tobey Langdon | 38 | | Leon Weeks | 34 | 10 | Tho. Furzin | 13 | 12 |
| Tho. Seavey | 38 | | Charles Allen | 25 | 10 | Roger Knight | 13 | 37 |
| James Johnson & | 112 | | Tho. Avery | 13 | 10 | Martha Walton | 13 | |
| Mr. Wallis | | | Phil. Lewis | 105 | | George Row | 13 | |
| John Odihorne | 43 | | John Cutt | 350 | | John Pottle | 13 | |
| Mr. Mason | 35 | | Rich. Cutt | 410 | | Caleb Becke | 13 | |
| Nath. Drake | 50 | 20 | Mr. Moody | 100 | | Mary Pickering | 13 | |
| Tho. Fernald | 13 | | Wid. Mary Walford | 13 | | John Jackson, jr. | 13 | |
| Peter Abbut | 13 | | Margaret Washington | 13 | | Edw. Melcher | 13 | |
| Francis Drake | 37 | 13 | Fran. Jones | 13 | | | | |

The proportions abovesaid are made to every inhabitant as if noe land had been given them at all, and all such as have received above the proportions aforesaid by former town grant, such are to possess the same still, and must not expect further enlargement, as none is to be taken from them, and all those that have not yet had the abovesaid proportions such are to have the proportions aforesaid.

The 2d column contains the addition of acres given to every one against whose names they be sett, according to the discretion of those appointed for the distribution of the 600 acres of land as per the town's order.

Capt. Pendleton, Mr. John Cutt and Mr. Richard Cutt's full proportions are entered above as they were before they rendered back 100 acres apiece to be distributed, which are to be taken when the land is laid out to them."

Signed by Brian Pendleton, Richard Cutt, Nath'l Drake, Philip Lewis, Elias Stillman, Wm. Seavey, John Pickering.

The above distribution covers not quite five thousand acres. The land was in the limits of what now makes up Portsmouth, Great Island, Rye, Newington and Greenland.

## RAMBLE V.

The Cutt Family—John the First President of New-Hampshire—the Estates of John and Richard—their Wills—Murder of Ursula—Providential Escape of the Waldron Family.

AMONG the settlers in this vicinity previous to 1646, were three brothers from Wales, John, Robert and Richard Cutt. (Their descendants bear the name of Cutts.) John settled at the Bank, and acquired much wealth from mercantile pursuits. Richard at first carried on the fisheries at the Shoals, and then removed to this place. Robert, after a short residence at Barbadoes, located on Great Island. He afterwards went to Kittery, where he carried on ship building.

In 1679, when New-Hampshire was separated from Massachusetts, the king appointed John Cutt as President. The royal charter then given was the only one ever granted to New-Hampshire. The first general assembly held in the State was convened by President Cutt in Portsmouth, on the 16th of March the next year. Portsmouth, Dover and Hampton sent each three representatives, and Exeter two. These were all the towns in the State. The whole number of voters in the four towns was 209.

On Green street, a few rods south of the railroad track, is an enclosure of fifty feet square, walled with brick, where repose the remains of John Cutt, the first President of New Hampshire, and his family. It will be seen by the last ramble that he and his brother Richard were the largest landholders in Portsmouth in 1660. They owned the principal portion of what is now the compact part of Portsmouth. At that time, the inhabitants principally resided in the vicinity of the "Great House," on Water street. In all other parts between the ponds were only about a dozen dwellings, and as many warehouses, half of which belonged to these two brothers. Richard

Cutt's residence was at the "Great House." President John Cutts's mansion was situated on the spot near the C. & P. Railroad wharf, now occupied by the stone store of Joshua Brooks & Co. That of Capt. Samuel Cutts (whose son Edward had his mansion in the large house on Christian Shore, now James W. Emery's) was next south of the family seat of the late Alexander Ladd, on Market street. A well discovered beneath the street in that vicinity in 1858, probably belonged to his house before the street was made public.

The following last Will of Richard Cutt, made 1675, the year before his death, and the accompanying Will of President John Cutt, made in 1680, exhibit the way in which a large portion of the compact part of Portsmouth was parcelled out a century before the Revolution:

WILL OF RICHARD CUTT.

"I, Richard Cutt, of Portsmouth, in Piscataqua, being in perfect memory and good health, yet considering that man's life is short and his end oftentimes sudden, and not knowing how the Lord may deal with me, I thought meet, as becomes a Christian man, to set my house in order before my death, and do therefore make and appoint this my last will and testament, thereby revoking all wills by [me] formally made.

Imp.—I commit my soul into the hands of God that gave it through Christ Jesus, who I hope hath redeemed it, and believe that he is able to keep what I have committed to him untill that day. I allso committ my body to a decent buriall in the earth, in hope of a joyful resurrection. My worldly estate I dispose of as followeth:

First.—I give and bequeath unto my beloved wife, Elenor Cutt, my now dwelling house, with the bake house, brew house, barn, and all houseing thereunto belonging; with the log ware house and wharfing, my stone ware house only excepted; together with my garden, orchard, and all the land in fence in the home field, adjoining to my house; as allso my corn mill, with my house and barn up at the creek, with all the upland and meadow thereunto belonging, so far as home, unto the land which I bought of Hughbertus Mattone, excepting the tanyard and building thereunto belonging and the land on that side of the floom. All which premises before mentioned, except what is excepted, I will shall be in the hands and to the use and behoof of my dearly beloved wife, aforesaid, during her natural life. And, after her death, I give and bequeath my whole estate, aforesaid, unto my grandson, Cutt Vaughan, with all the privileges and appurtanances thereunto belonging, to be to him and his heirs forever; and it shall come into his hands att the age of twenty-one years. But if he die before that age, then I give it to the next heir, male; and if there be no heirs, male, then to the next heir that shall survive. Furthermore, I give unto my said wife, all my plate, brass, pewter, iron, beding utensils belonging to the house, together with all my stock of cattle, to be absolutely at her disposal, when and to whome and where she pleases—and the five Negro servants.

2d. I give to my daughter Margaret Vaughan, my stone ware house, and that part of the woodfield joining unto that which was John Pickrins, and reaching home to Wm. Hart's on the west, with my brother, Jno. Cutt, on the west, the way that goes to the Creek on the north, and Christopher Jose on the east, together with the tanyard, houseing and the stock therein, and the little field on the south of the floom; always excepting and reserving the highway as it is now to the farm and to the other mill, which is to be kept free for the use of the mill and the house by it. All which I give to my daughter Margaret and her children. If they fail, then to my daughter Bridget and heirs after the decease of my said daughter Margaret.

3d. Unto my beloved daughter Bridget and her heirs for ever, I give the remainder of the field commonly called the grate field, to say all besides what is already given to her and her husband, and already sould to several persons, to be to her and her heirs for ever, with all the privileges and appurtenances thereunto belonging. I give allso unto my daughter Bridget, that part of the wood field on the south of the highway up to the Creek, as it is now fenced. The other part, between the highway and the Creek, her mother shall have the liberty to use during her natural life, and that part allso shall be Bridget's after her mother's decease. Likewise I give Bridget, my land in the long reach, next to that which was Capt. Pendleton's, being thirty-three pole broad front on the river, and so back the whole depth; which land afore said shall be Bridget's and her-heirs for ever. If she die without heirs, then it shall fall to the heirs of her sister Margaret, after the decease of my said daughter Bridget.

4th. I give my son, William Vaughan, my land on the Grate Island, bought of Mr. Mason, and that acre given me by the town, which was laid out with an acre of Mr. Fryers. I allso give him two hundred pounds out of my estate, and all my houseing at the Isle of Shoals, on Star Island; together with that estate both in stock and debts that is in partnership with him there, provided he rest satisfied therewith upon the account of partnership in trading, betwixt us there. If he be not satisfied so, then, that the Island to be sould and the estate there valued and the balance to be given him out of my other estate, when our accounts are made up. And I do by these presents oblige my son, William Vaughan, not to expect any more out of my estate, for salary or anything done for me, at home or abroad, besides what he hath already received and is above expressed.

5th. I give my well beloved son, Thomas Daniel, two hundred pounds out of my estate.

6th. Furthermore, I give to my grandson Cutt Vaughan, one hundred pound.

7th. I give to my grandchild, Elenor Vaughan, that house and land I bought of Mr. Mattoon, with that part of my land that comes from the Pulpit, the whole breadth of Mattoon's land, till it comes to my brother, John Cutt's land on the north, together with two hundred pounds, the legacies to be paid in money or equivalent.

8th. I give to my grandchild, Mary Vaughan, two hundred pounds in money, and the hundred and fifty acres of land and the meadow belonging to it, as I bought of Edward Hilton, as appears by bill of sale of Jno. Wegewood.

9th. Further, I will that what remains of my twenty pounds per annum subscribed to the college for myself and sons, be carefully discharged by my executors.

10th. I give to my brother Jno. Cutt ten pound to bie him

mourning and ten pound to his wife and five pound to each of his children.

11th. I give to my sister Ann Shipway ten pound to bie mourning and five pound to my brother Shipway and five pound to his son Jno. Shipway.

12th. I give tø my brother Robert Cutt's wid'r five pounds, and to each of his children five pound, as allso do I forgive the debt due on the book.

13th. I give Mr. Joshua Moody thirty pound and to his five children to say forty shillings to each of them.

14th. I give to my coz, Jno. Hale and his wife, five pound each of them.

15th. I give to the church of Portsmouth ten pound, to bie a piece of plate for the use of the church.

16th. I make my wife Elenor and my two daughters Margaret and Bridget my executors to whom I give the rest of my estate as well shipping or what else due to me in any part of the world, my debts and legacies paid and what remains to be divided in equal thirds between my wife and daughters. I make my brother Jno. Cutt, Mr. Joshua Moody, my son William Vaughan, and my son Thomas Daniel, my overseers, to see this my will performed. To the truth or this I have hereunto set my hand seal this tenth of May, 1675, Portsmo' in Piscataqua.

Per mee, RICH'D CUTT. [L. S.]

We whose names are under written do attest that Richa d Cutt did own this to be his volentary act and deed.

JNO. WINCALL, JNO. FLETCHER."

## WILL OF PRESIDENT JOHN CUTT.

" I, John Cutt, being in perfect memory, but crazy and infirm in body thro' many weaknesses by reason of age and otherwise, do ordain and declare this to be my last will and testament, hereby revoking all other wills by me formerly made.

1st. I commit my soul into ye hands of God in Christ Jesus, trusting yt it shall be kept by him until that day; and my body unto a decent buryall in my orchard where I buried my wife and children that are deceased. And I will that there be a wall of lime and stone made about my grave and the rest there already buried, with room convenient for a burying place for the residue of my family relations.

2d. I give unto my beloved son, John Cutt, my house and land where I now live, with the orchard, gardens, wharfing, ware-houses and other housing (except what is hereafter excepted, which I give unto my daughter Hannah,) with all the privileges and appurtenances thereunto belonging, together with my wood field lying upon the creek behind my house, and adjoining to ye land of John Hunking; and all my fresh marsh at ye head of the creek next to Richard Commins's marsh, with my share of ye land bought of Major Waldron and Capt'n Lake near Greenland; as also all the land I bought of Mr. Andrew Wiggin, being 160 pole, by ye water side, (more or less, according to bill of sale) and three miles back into ye woods, toogather with ye marsh or meadow abreast of it, and my ten acres of land on ye Grt. island, (excepting out of it what is hereafter excepted for my daughter Mary,) and my warehouse on Star Island.

3d. I give unto my beloved son, Samuel Cutt, my house commonly called the grt. house, with the orchard and field adjoining, (excepting what is hereafter given to his sister Mary,) with all ye privileges thereunto belonging, together with my land near ye Pulpit, being 70 pole in breadth, by ye water side, and running up ye whole length into ye woods, according to the agreement between me and Bro. Richard Cutt, together with yt half of William Williams' plantation in Oyster river, which I bought of him; and ye farm lying near it, which I bought of Thos. Doughty, with ye fresh and salt marsh belonging to it; and my land at Spruce Creek, bought of Mr. Morgan and his wife and Eph'n Lynn, being 160 acres more or less, and yt part which is mine of ye house and land yt was Mr. Corbett, lying at Kittery Point; and my one acre of land lying on ye Great island, with ye warehouse on Smutty Nose island; as also a parcel of land purchased of Rich'd Abbott, lying near Mr. Wilson's at Newichawonit.

4th. I give unto my beloved daughter, Hannah Cutt, my new ware-house, with ye wharfing belonging to it, ye land and wharfe so far as ye smith's shop, with the smith's shop and so far as ye high way, with half an acre of land out of ye windmill field, at ye corner next Bro Richard's barn, fronting upon ye high way between yt and ye river, to run up ye lane between Bro. Richd's land and mine for ye depth of it; ye front to be so wide as yt ye double of ye front shall be in ye length to make ye half acre; and ye little field by William Hart's; and all my land in ye long reach, to say 50 pole breadth which I had at first, with ye addition afterwards laid to it, and ye land I had of Ralph Twamlin per execution; and ye land I had in Dover of Phillip Cromwell per execution, which was sometime belonging to Joseph Austin, to say eleven acres, with the free hold or commonage belonging to it; as also my farm at Wells, both upland and meadow, with ye housing and priviledges belonging thereunto; and that hundred acres of land which I had of Joseph Beard of Dover, lying in or near Cocheco.

5th. I give to my beloved daughter, Mary Cutt, the little field being part of that commonly called ye great field, lying next to ye highway going to ye meeting-house, with half an acre of land butting upon ye river on ye one side and ye creek yt goes up by ye great house on ye other, to take in ye point over and above, and so up toward the great house and the river; and a parcel of land out of that ten acres I gave to my son John upon ye Great island, to say that where my frame now lies or formerly did lye, from ye house that was Capt'n Pendleton's to that which was Otho Tuckerman's, and all below ye rock and so down to ye river; and ye land I bought of John Alt, and the land I bought of Will'm Williams, lying in ye woods at the head of Oyster river; and the 13 acres at Boyling Rock, bought of Jaffray Currier; and further, I will that her brother John shall summer two cows for her in his pasture at home freely during her natural life, and because her proportion of land is smaller than what the rest of my children have, I will that she shall pay nothing towards what I hereafter give to her mother out of her proportion of moveables.

6th. As to the remainder of my estate lying in moneys, plate, household goods, wares of any sort, stock, shipping, debts, or any estate whatsoever, anywise of right appertaining to me, and not already disposed of, I doe dispose of it as followeth, viz: one third part of the whole to my eldest son, John Cutt, the other two-thirds shall be divided into four parts, of which my son Samuel Cutt shall have the one half, the other half to be equally divided between my two daughters, Hannah and Mary Cutt, unto each of which daughters I give besides their portion a silver plate marked T. S.

7th. Provided always yt I give and bequeath unto my beloved wife, Ursula Cutt, the full sum of five hundred pounds, to be taken out of that portion which I have given to my sons, John and Samuel, and to my daughter Hannah, each of them to pay their proportions of the said five hundred pounds, according to ye quantity of goods yt falls to their shares when the whole is summed up and divided to them, and they shall pay it in each species yt they receive their portion in, whether money, goods, shipping or otherwise, according to ye value of what they receive—the moveables to be apprized at price current.

Moreover I will that my beloved wife shall have liberty to dwell in my house till my son John come to age or marry if she continue a widow, whom I request to have respect to my children and be a mother to them. If my son John marry while my wife continues a widow, she shall have ye use of a couple of rooms in ye house, such as shall be judged most convenient by my executors and overseers together; and may be comfortable for her accommodation, or shee shall have liberty to build an house upon that piece of land which she hath lately taken in as an addition to ye orchard, and may therein dwell during her widowhood; and when she leaves it my son John shall have it with what is built upon it—or she shall have liberty to dwell in ye new warehouse, which shall be fitted up for her till my daughter Hannah comes to make use of it; moreover she shall have ye use of that land at ye Pulpit which I have given to my son Samuel, till he come to age, and may improve so much of it as shee sees meet, and build upon it if she pleases, and shall have ye benefit of it dureing her natural life, and then both ye land and all ye improvement and building shall return unto my son Samuel Cutt.

8th. Furthermore, I will that if any of my children die before they come to age or marry, the portion I have given them shall be equally divided between those of them yt survive; and if any of my children die without issue after marriage, I will yt the housing and land I have given them shall goe to the next kin; and with these provisos it is to be understood that I give the above mentioned houses and lands to my children and their heirs forever—provided also that it is to be judged meet for the peopleing of the place to sell any part of the grt. house field into house lots, and my overseers and execu'rs approve of it, may be done, and ye money for ye land so sold to redound to the behoofe of the person to whom I have given the lands; and if it may be done for the good of the whole, I advise that by the consent of my exec'rs and overseers, the shipping or part of them may be sold as soon as may be.

9th. For the good of the town where I dwell, I give and bequeath one hundred pounds towards the erecting of a free school—provided the town shall set it up within seven years after my decease. Unto the church in Portsmouth to which I belong I give fifteen pounds, and thirty pounds to the poor of the town, which said thirty pounds shall be disposed of at the direction of my overseers. Unto ye children of my bro. Robert Cutt, I give wt. was owing to me from their father, to be equally divided among them. Unto my cousin John Shipway I give ten pounds, and to my servant Bathiah Furber fivety shillings.

10th. Finally, I make my beloved son John and my daughter Hannah, execu'rs to this my last will and testament; and I request and appoint my good friends, Mr. Joshua Moody, Mr. Richard Martin and Mr. Reuben Hull of Portsm. and Capt. Thos. Brattle of Boston, to be my overseers; and unto ye sd. Moody I give as a legacy fivety pounds, and to the other three overseers thirty pounds a piece, whom I do earnestly desire to be careful for the concerns of my children, and to order matters so for them as may be to their best behoofe and for the maintaining and promoting love between them; and if there happen any difference among my wife and children about the interpretation of the will, or about any matter referring to these concernments therein, my will is that the partie or parties concerned shall chuse each of them a man to join with the overseers for the decision of any such controversy; and wt. they or the major part of them shall determine I will shall be the final issue of any such matter.

The management of my buriall I leave for the prudence of my beloved wife and my overseers; and do oblige my exec'rs with the advice of my overseers to see to the paying of the legacies above mentioned, and discharging of all my just debts and funeral charges out of my estate.

In testimony to all and singular ye premises, I set to my hand and seal this 6th day of May, in the year 1680—by the premises I mean wt. is written on ye side above and on ye other side. JOHN CUTT. [L. S.]

We whose names are und'rwritten, saw Mr. John Cutt, Sen'r, set his hand and seal to this instrument, and heard him declare it to be his last will and testam't, this 6th May, 1680.

JOHN FLETCHER, SAM'L KEAIS."

The will contains a codicil, made Jan. 3, 1681, in which he says, "upon the consideration of ye grt. wasting of my estate by reason of long sickness and other bad Providences attending me," he gives his beloved wife £400 instead of £500.

The corn-mill at the Creek, to which reference is made in the will of Richard, was near the spot where the stocking factory was afterwards built. The wind-mill field was in front of the present locality of the jail. The windmill was on the site now occupied by Mr. Goodall's house. The foundation stones remained undisturbed until the erection of that house, in 1851.

Richard Cutt died in 1676, within one year after making his will. President John Cutt died in 1681. The place in his orchard where he was buried is the spot above referred to on Green street. This family burying ground is substantially enclosed by a wall of masonry, as directed.

This ground has a tombstone inscribed to the President's first wife, Hannah Cutt, who died Nov. 19th, 1674.

There is no stone however to tell the resting spot of President Cutt, or any other of the family, although it is probable that many of the relatives rest there. Among them his second wife, the beloved Ursula, with whom he could not have lived more than five or six years. He provides for her in his will, either rooms in his house, a residence in the warehouse, or a farm on the river, as her preference might dictate. Like a wise woman, after his death she preferred an independent residence, and therefore took the farm at "the Pulpit," about two or three miles up the river on the west side. The spot selected for her residence was the farm since owned by Ichabod Bartlett and now by Mark H. Wentworth. It is between the Freeman farm and that of John N. Sherburne. Here the lady of the first President of New Hampshire presided over the acres of her domain, and by her industry and good taste the beauty of her situation was developed. Thirteen years was she thus happily situated. But there came at length a day of sad calamity. It was in the summer of 1694—the year when the Indians from the East, instigated by the French, had committed many outrages on the settlements o the whites. There had been intelligence of their visit at Dover, but little apprehensions were had of a nearer approach to the Bank. Although friends had warned her of being in a dangerous position at her retired residence, she decided, as it was haying time, to do up that important business before leaving home; and while her three haymakers were improving a good day to the best advantage, Madam Ursula, with her maid at a wash tub or kettle, might be seen between the house and the shore, attending to some culinary process. "The Indians!" exclaims the lynx-eyed maiden —and with a rapidity which could only be produced by the terror of their deeds, she flew to a retreat, and soon on the shore a mile distant, she takes a skiff and passes to the Bank from Freeman's point, for there was no bridge then at the mouth of the North mill pond.

Here turn a moment from the dreadful scene she left, to another feature of Providential preservation.

Col. Richard Waldron (the successor of Cutt as President of New Hampshire) married President Cutt's daughter Hannah, who, it will be seen, was well provided for in his will. In about two years, in 1682, she with her only son, fourteen months old, were buried in that "Orchard" enclosure. Col. Waldron took a second wife; and on this day, with his wife and infant child, he had arranged to visit the Pulpit farm, and enjoy the company and hospitality of Madame Ursula. The boat and everything was in readiness, when—how they regretted the disappointment!—some friends arrived, and the visit was reluctantly abandoned. There were some sighs for the scent of new-mown hay—for a taste of the strawberries and cream, and for a sight of the flower-garden—but all had to be foregone, and at home they must stay. They sit down to dinner, the meal is partaken, and the disappointment is becoming less thought of.

"The Indians!—the Indians!"—exclaims a terrified girl, as she hastily enters in her working dress, almost exhausted by effort—"They are all killed!"

A visit to the farm proved the intelligence too true. The three men in the mowing field had all been shot down, Madam Ursula had shared the same fate, and their scalps had all been taken as Indian trophies! The savages finding some difficulty in removing the rings from her fingers, severed and bore away her hands!

Such is a picture, which we have gathered in part from history and in part from tradition, of a scene in our early local history. The providence which frustrated the intended visit to the Pulpit, saved three lives at least—that infant then preserved was afterwards Secretary Waldron, so distinguished in our State history.

# RAMBLE VI.

## The Glebe Land—Its location and occupancy.

In former times there was a stronger alliance between church and state than the spirit of republicanism now countenances. Every man felt as much obligated to pay his town tax for the support of a minister, as he now is to pay his school tax. It made no difference whether he attended church or whether the minister held sentiments utterly at variance with his own, the tax for the minister's support was to be paid. It thus became a subject of municipal policy to make such provision for the ministers as would relieve the public taxes.

In 1640, only seventeen years after the first settling of Portsmouth, Francis Williams, (the governor,) Ambrose Gibbins, William Jones, Renald Fernald, John Crowther, Anthony Bracket, Michael Chatterton, Jno. Wall, Robert Puddington, Matthew Coe, Henry Sherburn, John Lander, Henry Taler, Jno. Jones, William Berry, Jno. Pickering, Jno. Billing, Jno. Wolten, Nicholas Row and William Palmer, the principal inhabitants of Portsmouth, made a deed of fifty acres of land in Portsmouth for a Glebe, or Parsonage. Three fourths of it was the "full tenth part of the fresh marsh lying at the head of Strawberry bank creek," and land adjoining. The other fourth part, or twelve acres, was given in a square lot in that part of Portsmouth between and including the North Church, to the garden of J. K. Pickering on the east, thence by the southern bounds of the Court House lot to the west garden line of John E. Salter, thence north to the garden line east of late Wm. Sheafe's estate, on Congress street, and east on that street to the North church.

On this minister's field, of which three acres were then enclosed in a pale for a corn field, there was at that time erected "a parsonage house, with a chapel thereto united." This house and chapel were on the spot where John K. Pickering's house now stands.

It does not appear that the minister's field was turned to any public account, except the erection of a house therein by Thomas Phipps, probably on the spot where the Rogers mansion now stands, and the erection of a prison in that vicinity, for some sixty years after 1640.

In 1705 the inhabitants of Portsmouth residing principally at the south and eastern part of the town, looked upon the glebe land as our national government does upon the western territory—and took precisely the same means for inducing settlers. What is now doing in the way of *pre-emption* in the west, was, more than one hundred and fifty years ago, introduced here, as the following copy of a lease given in 1709, to Charles Story, Judge of the Admiralty,—fully explains:

"This Indenture, made the fifth day of September, in the year of the reign of our sovereign lady Ann, Queen of Great Brittaine, between William Vaughan, Sam'll Penhallow, John Plaisted, William Cotton, Thomas Phipps, Edward Ayers and Samuell Weeks of the town of Portsmo. in the province of New Hampshire in New England of the one part, and Charles Story of the same place, gentleman, of the other part.

Whereas, that tract of land or pasture in Portsmo. afore s'd, comonly called or known by the name of the town field, or minister's field, lying att the entrance of the Bank, in which field the said Thomas Phipps hath built a house and now dwelleth: was at a public town-meeting the twentieth day of April, Anno Dom. 1705, ordered to be laide out into house lotts for peopling the town as by the following vote appears, viz.:

Voted that the minister's field formerly given for the use of the ministry, be by consent of Mr. Rogers, our present minister, divided off for house lots for peopling the town, and that the advantage which arises thereby be to the benefit of the ministry. Preserving a conveniency for a Meeting house, Court house, Alms house, and Burying place, as the Selectmen for the time being, with a comitte chosen for that end may judge most meet for the town interest, and that each lot consist of fifty foot front and eighty foot deep. Soe as to make a square of eighty and fifty, and that evry p'son that may incline to buy, to agree with the said Selectmen and comitte, who are hereby impower'd to give leases for the same, that noe man have more than one lott, and the same built upon within three years, and every byer to enclose the same att his own proper cost, and maintaine the same on his and theire proper accomp't and charge forever; voted that Maj'r William Vaughan, Mr. George Jeffrey, John Plaisted, Wm. Cotton and Samuell Penhallow be of the comitte to joine with the Selectmen for the time beinge in disposing of house lotts out of the said minister's field.

And wheras the field above s'd being laid out, and divided into house lotts which are number'd 1, 2, 3, 4, &c. as by a plat recorded in the town books of Portsmo. upon file. Reference being thereto had will plainly appear.

Now this Indenture will [*here the manuscript is obliterated*] consideration of the annual or yearly rent therein expressed, and pursuiant to the aforesaid vote have demised, granted, sell and to farm, let and by these presents doe fully, freely and absolutely demise, grant, and to farm, let oute the said Charles Story for himself,—his heirs, exect'r, administrators or assignes one house lott in said field, entered in the said number (10) and is fronting upon the northerly side of the said minister's field on the—[*obliterated*] of the prison adjoining to the lott of Thomas Phipps, Esq. and is fifty-three foot front and seventy-five foot deep, holding the same breadth in the back as in the front.

To have and to hold the said house lott or lotts of land with all priveleidges, benefitts and appurtenances whatsoever to the same belonging or in any wise appertaining unto him the said Charles Story—his heirs, exec'trs, administrators or assignes, for and during the full space and term of nine hundred ninetie and nine years fully to be compleated and ended, to commence from the five and twentyeth day of March last past—yielding and paying therefor yearly and every year during the whole term and space of nine hundred ninety and nine yeares, eight shillings in money, according to the custom and manner of money in [*obliterated*] between man and man to be paid upon the five and twentyeth day of March—in every yeare during the said term, unto Mr. Nathaniel Rodgers, our present minister, during his continuence in the ministry of this town, or to the Selectmen of the said town for the time being or theire order for the support of the ministry of this town. And att the end and expiration of the said term of nine hundred and ninety nine years he the said Charles Story, his heirs, execu'rs, adm'rs or assignes shall yield and deliver up peaceable and quiet possession of the premises unto the Selectmen of the said town of Portsmo. for the time being, or to other p'sons that may then be appointed and delegated in their room to manage that concerne. And further the said Charles Story doth hereby for himselfe, his heirs, executors and assignes, covenant and agree that he, they, or some of them shall from time to time during the term afores'd, at his and theire owne proper cost and charges, stone in the said house lott or lotts of land; and shall also within those years build a house upon the same. In witness whereof the parties aforesaid to these presents interchangeably have sett their hands and seals the day and yeare before written. Anno Dom. 1709." [Duly signed by the committee and selectmen.]

This Charles Story was an Englishman, who in 1697 received, while in England, the appointment of Judge of the Admiralty for New Hampshire, and took up his residence in Portsmouth. He was also appointed Secretary of the Province, but refusing to produce the books of the Province when in his possession, he was discharged from the latter office for contempt of the Council.

The following is a diagram of the division of lots in the glebe land, agreeably to the plan referred to in the above lease as being recorded on the town books:

CONGRESS STREET.
PLEASANT STREET.
M. H. 1 2 3 4 5 6 7
8 9 10 11 12 13 14 15
22 21 20 19 18 17 16
Prison Lane.
Fetter Lane. (now Warren st.) Pond Lane.
29 28 27 26 25 24 23
36 35 34 33 32 31 30
Church street.
Fleet street.
(now Chestnut st.)
51
Broad st. (now State st.)
43 42 41 40 39 38 37
50 49 48 47 46 45 44
Negro Burying Ground.
Jaffrey st. (now Court st.)
Parsonage.

The Jail, formerly on the corner south of the Temple, was built in 1759. Previous to that time, from a boundary given in the above lease, it appears that it was in the vicinity of lot No. 10, but exactly where does not appear.

Charles Story did not comply with the requisition to build a house in three years,—and so the lot was still in the market for any other occupant. We have before us a lease of the same lot No. 10, together with lot No. 20 in the rear of it, given to Charles Treadwell in 1729, for nine hundred and ninety-nine years, he paying a rent of fifteen shillings annually, on the 25th of March, to the Parish wardens for the use of the Parish. This deed is given by the wardens and parish committee, the selectmen of the town taking no part in the transaction. All leases after that time were given in the same manner.

The following are the conditions of Mr. Treadwell's lease:

"To have and to hold the premises with the privileges and appurtenances thereto appertaining, or in any wise belonging unto him the said Charles Treadwell, his exe'ts, administrators or assigns, for and during the full space and term of nine hundred ninety-nine years, from the day of the date of these presents, and from thence to be fully compleated and ended, he, the said Charles Treadwell, or his exe'ts, administrators, on yielding and paying therefore yearly, and every year during the aforesaid term, to the Church wardens of the said Parish and committee for the time being, upon the twenty-fifth day of March, the sum of fifteen shillings in cur't money of New England or good bills of credit on the province of New Hampshire, which shall be applied to the use of the aforesaid first parish of Portsmouth from time to time, and at the end and expiration of the said term, shall quietly and peaceably surrender up the premises—without strip or wast to the Church wardens of said Parish for the time being, and to the committee for the ruling, ordering and governing the premises."

We find on the back of this lease an endorsement dated March 1, 1792, which acknowledges the receipt by the Parish Wardens of £3 16s. 8d. for the rent of lots numbered ten and twenty for the remaining term of the nine hundred and ninety-nine years for which the lease was given.

Lot No. 4, was leased to John Plaisted, in 1730, for eleven shillings per year. And in the course of a few years after there were many more of the lots taken up and leases given, at various annual rents, which were regularly collected annually up to the time of the Revolution. The pre-emption principle had the effect of settling that portion of the town which was less attractive at the time than the immediate vicinity of the river, and brought in some persons from other towns who otherwise might not have been attracted this way.

It appears that during the time of the Revolution there was no attention paid to the collection of the rents. In 1789 the North Parish appointed a committee of investigation, which reported the sums then due for back rents, and what sums would be received from the lessees in full for the unexpired terms of the leases. Many of the tenants in 1792 settled in full. Nothing more was done until 1821, when the parish wardens made claims against those who had not settled previously, and some further settlements were made for rent, but no quitclaim deeds of land, to our knowledge, were given. A few years since James Smith, Esq., by the payment of forty dollars, received a deed from the Parish, which will entitle his heirs, if the estate should remain in his family, to the inheritance of the property after the nine hundred and ninety-nine years expire.

The sum paid, if put on interest to the time when the right thus purchased shall be enjoyed, is rather large—several times the value of all the wealth of earth! For *one cent* at compound interest, for one century, produces $3 40; in two centuries, $1,156; in three centuries, $393,040; in four centuries, $133,633,600; in five centuries, $45,435,424,000. This is only for half of a thousand years; but it is useless to go further to show how much was paid for the security of the right of some heir thirty generations off, who will probably never know the true worth of him who bestowed the benefit, or even his name, unless he finds it in some musty old book entitled "Rambles about Portsmouth."

Happy for us, perhaps, that there are no speculators among us who can feel assured of a Methusalian age: otherwise we might begin to hear of the price of prospective Glebe stock, division to be made in the year 2730! Though all must sleep before that day, yet it will arrive, the nine hundred and ninety-nine years leases all expire, and the twelve acres with all the improvements may come again into the possession of the old North Church! We might speculate on their ownership of the Stone Church, one of the three only buildings in the minister's field likely to continue to that day; but as time will make great ravages in nine hundred years, even among the stones, we will not venture now to predict how valuable the old North will then estimate their claim. Nor will we venture to say that some Solon of the year 2730 may not prove that the whole property belongs to the Episcopal or South Church, and that the old North may not be placed under an annual rent. There is much doubt in law—and the more distant the day the greater the doubt.

Had our fathers taken but the first year's rent of their fifty lots, at nine shillings each, and placed it at interest, it would at the present time, after expending $30,000 for building the new church, have left a fund large enough to pay from the interest an annual salary to a minister of $1500, besides having $2500 annually for other purposes. But had they done so, is it certain that preaching which costs nothing is so highly valued?

That portion of the glebe land called the minister's field, of twelve acres, was located in the centre of the city. The other thirty-eight acres of the glebe were laid out in one lot, the entrance to which was through a lane which formerly opened opposite a little north of the residence of Daniel H. Spinney, on White's road. In 1790 or '91, Islington road was opened from the Creek to the Plains, passing directly through the glebe lot. Until that time it had been let by the Parish for pasturing. After the road was opened, one object of which was to give value to the land, the North Parish leased it for nine hundred and ninety-nine years, in separate lots, to Joseph Akerman, Dr. A. R. Cutter, Elijah Hall, Edward Parry, and to some others, for about twenty dollars an acre. The land extends about equal distances each way from the powder house, taking in those fields on the west side of the lane that extend to D. R. Rogers' farm. Its northern bound is not far from the Eastern railroad; and the western extent is the western side of Peter Emery's field. It also takes in all the fields on the opposite side of

Islington road, to the same extent. The object of the sale of leases was to obtain the means for building the parsonage house, (where Charles Robinson now lives,) which was erected in 1792, and was owned by the Parish, and occupied by its ministers, for about forty years before it was sold to its present occupant.

---

## RAMBLE VII.

John Pickering—His sons John and Thomas—Great Bay farm—Descendants—The Old South Church—Point-of-Graves Cemetery—The foot-path.

As early as 1636, John Pickering, the father of the several Pickering families in this county, came to Portsmouth from Massachusetts, coming originally from England. He appears to have been a man of good reputation and business capacity, although he could not write his name. He was confided with some of the most important business of the early settlers, and such matters as settling the lines between Portsmouth and Hampton were left to his decision—the settlers giving him full power to decide for them. He was one of the company who in 1640 gave the fifty acres of glebe land for the ministry. He selected his location on the shore north of the south mill, then well covered with wood which was not speedily removed,—for, nearly a quarter of a century after, a portion of the frame of the South church was cut on the spot where it was erected. The original Pickering house was built a few rods west of Marcy & Petigrew's ship-yard, and some fifty feet further from the shore than the present front of the houses on Mill street. Here were born two sons and four daughters—John born about 1640, Thomas, Rebecca, Abigail, Mary and Sarah. After living here thirty-three years in 1669, John Pickering, senior, died—the estate was entailed, and came into possession of his oldest son John.

In February, 1655, the town granted John Pickering, senior, "the land lying between Swaden's creek and Pincomb's creek in the Great Bay, so that it be no man's right of property. The said land is to extend into the swamp, and no further." In 1660, fifty acres in addition, in that vicinity, were granted by the town.

Thomas, the second son, took the farm of more than five hundred acres on Great Bay, (then in Portsmouth but now in Newington,) which, after a lapse of nearly two centuries, still remains in the family. About one hundred and seventy acres of it are now occupied by James C. Pickering, Esq., who was born thereon in 1770.

It has descended in a regular line to him—there never having been a deed made of the land since the original grant to the first John Pickering by the town, in 1655. Portions of it are also owned by Winthrop Pickering, Esq., who occupies the house built by his grandfather's grandfather, the first Thomas; seventy acres of it by the children of the late Judge James Pickering, lineal descendants; and valuable farms by Messrs. Reuben L. Lane, Samuel H. Tarlton and S. Fabyan, who are allied by marriage. It is from this Thomas that all who now bear the name of Pickering in this and the neighboring towns have descended.

In 1658, the town granted the south mill privilege to John Pickering, on condition of his keeping in repair a way for foot passengers over the dam in going to meeting. He then built the mill.

John Pickering (2d), who inherited the mill-dam, married a daughter of Anthony Stanyan of Hampton, by whom he had eight children, three of whom died young and unmarried. John (3d) married Elizabeth Munden in 1688, and died in 1713, six years before his father. He left three sons and three daughters: John, Thomas,

Daniel, Mary (who married Ambrose Sloper,) Deborah and Sarah. Of the history of John (4th) and Daniel we have no account. Thomas, the second son, was slain by the Indians in 1746, in the vicinity of Casco bay in Maine. The population about Casco bay was at that time very sparse, and the incursions of the Indians for depredatory purpóses frequent and sometimes especially cruel,—so that the aid of the settlement at Portsmouth and vicinity was needed for their protection. Thomas Pickering was captain of a military company, and was sent with them to Casco. While there he was violently seized with inflammatory rheumatism. The Indians knowing this, surprised and routed the company while in camp, and when they entered his tent none were with him but his orderly sergeant, who, faithful to his promise, did not leave his captain. The sergeant crept under an empty sugar hogshead, which had been used in the transportation of the camp equipage, and while therein his ears were shocked with the cruelty of the savages, who, with their knives, sliced Capt. P. from head to foot, until they had completely dissected him. Not having been discovered by them, the sergeant escaped a like fearful end.

The children of Capt. Thomas Pickering and Dorothy his wife, were three sons, John (5), Daniel and Thomas, and six daughters.

John Pickering 5th, had three sons and three daughters. Abigail, (the mother of John P. Ross) Sarah, Jemima—John 6th, (died in Bristol, England,) Thomas and Daniel. None of the sons left children, and the name of Pickering in the line of Capt. John, here became extinct. John 5th was the last inheritor of the south mill estate, the entail being docked about seventy years ago, when the Pickering's mills came into possession of James Sheafe.

Daniel was lost by shipwreck on Block Island, leaving no descendants.

Thomas, the third son, had command of the Hampden, a privateer of twenty guns, and was killed in an engagement in which a valuable prize was captured. His age was about thirty-two;—he was unmarried.

The six daughters of Capt. Thomas Pickering were all married and had children, and five of them lived to the average age of ninety-two years!

The name of Elizabeth's first husband was Lambert, that of her second, Prowse. Capt. Daniel Prowse was her son. She died at the age of ninety-one.

Abigail married Thomas Patterson, who was the father of the late Mrs. Timothy Gerrish and Mrs. Richard Lowe. She afterwards married Mr. Janvrin, had one son, and in 1832 died at the age of one hundred years and eight months.

Dorothy married Capt. Nelson, father of the late Capt. Isaac Nelson, and died at eighty-six years.

Olive married George Jerry Osborne, the father of the printer of that name, and died at the age of about twenty-five.

Lydia married John Underwood, the father of the rope-maker of that name, and died at eighty-four years.

Mary married Samuel Drown, the son of Rev. Samuel Drown. Messrs. Daniel P. Drown and Thomas P. Drown were her sons. She died in 1841, at the age of ninety-seven years and six months.

The most venerable relic of antiquity left as the representative of places of worship of former times, is the old South Church, which now bears the age of 128 years. In the days of its erection, "Let there be light" must have been a favorite text, judging from the number of its windows. There was a reason for those windows which does not regulate the lighting of churches generally. As has been the custom in later days, subscriptions were solicited for the erection of the church. One of the richest men of the day, Henry Sherburne, we think, when the paper was presented, said he would pay for the windows. This *carte blanche* to operate with, a much larger surface of the building was left for glass than otherwise probably would have been.

In connection with the old church we will, for the purpose of our ramble, although apart in their locality, look into the Cemetery of the Point-of-Graves. Like the church, it readily shows evidence of its antiquity. Its rudely cut and moss-covered slabs of two centuries are surely the monuments of age as well as of mortality.

In this sacred enclosure, in 1669, was deposited the remains of John Pickering, whose estate covered the Point-of-Graves Cemetery and extended over the site of the South church to the mill bridge, taking in the whole shore, from the cemetery probably around to near the site of the Universalist church—for in 1754, when the Pleasant street burying-ground, near Livermore street, was deeded to the town, it was said to be "situated on *Pickering's Neck*"— the name of the small and pleasantly situated farm of the first John Pickering.

As an evidence of the extent of the possessions which his oldest son inherited, we give the following extract from the town records:

"1651.—At a town meeting it was agreed, that whereas there has been a *foot path* usually made over John Pickering's grounds from over his dam, and from thence along by the mill path into his next path, and so direct as conveniently may towards the present meeting house—[then near the site of the Universalist church] to be continued for the more ease of the inhabitants and others that shall have occasion to travel that way, at all times hereafter without leave of said John Pickering, or any one else, to be continued forever."

The tenacity with which families hold to an old inheritance, as shown by the Pickering farm on Great Bay, may be seen in other localities in our neighborhood. As we look over Portsmouth bridge from Church Hill, a handsome house in Kittery, erected as a summer residence by Samuel Adams, of the firm of Barker, Adams & Co. of this city, on the land of his fathers, at once arrests the attention of every observer.

The land upon which it is erected has been in the family one hundred and ninety years, having been purchased by Christopher Adams of Nathaniel Fryer, a merchant of Portsmouth, in 1668, for eighty pounds for one hundred acres. It descended to John Adams, and to his son John, who was the father of Mark Adams. The latter gentleman for more than twenty years was the regular representative of Kittery in the Massachusetts legislature. He died about forty years ago. Many will recollect the old gentleman, who could be seen in his three-cornered hat, sculling his yawl boat across the river every Sunday, and occupying his seat in the old North as regularly as Dr. Buckminster did the pulpit. Mark left three sons, Mark, John and Christopher. The latter lived in the old mansion house until his death, in 1858, at the age of eighty-two. The situation of the new house is one of the most prominent on the river. The original farm was divided by Mark between his two sons, John and Christopher. Samuel and Franklin Adams, the present owners of the whole farm, are the sons of John.

## RAMBLE VIII.

The Pickering Family—Incidents of John's Life—Captain, lawyer, moderator, carpenter—Prowess of Thomas—The first South-end Meeting-house.

In our last Ramble it was stated that the two sons of John Pickering Senior, were John (2d) and Thomas. John was the inheritor of "Pickering's Neck" and the mill dam—Thomas, of the farm at Great Bay.

John Pickering (2d), the inheritor of "Pickering's

Neck," is first noticed as a military man, for which his talents and character seem eminently to have qualified him. He had command of a company in Portsmouth for a number of years. In 1680, the colony of New Hampshire, which for almost forty years had been united with Massachusetts, was erected by the king, into a separate government, whereof John Cutt was appointed the first president. In the first assembly called by the president, Capt. John Pickering was a representative for the town of Portsmouth. He was also a member of the assembly called by Lieutenant Governor Cranfield, in 1684, which he (Cranfield) dissolved in great wrath, for vetoing a bill to raise money, previously passed by the council. It is mentioned by Dr. Belknap, and some others, that during the suspension of government consequent on the imprisonment of Sir Edmund Andros in 1689, Capt. John Pickering, a man of "a rough and adventurous spirit, and a lawyer," went with a company of armed men to the house of Richard Chamberlain who had been secretary of the province under Andros, and clerk of the superior court, and demanded the records and files, which were in his possession. Chamberlain refused to deliver them without legal warrant or security. Pickering took them by force and carried them to the house of Major Joseph Hammond, in Kittery, where they were concealed.

Afterwards, in 1692, Pickering was summoned before Lieutenant Governor Usher, threatened and imprisoned, but for some time would neither deliver the books nor discover the place of their concealment, unless by order of the Assembly, and to some person appointed by them to receive them. At length, however, he was constrained to deliver them up, and they were handed over to the secretary by Usher's orders.

Capt. Pickering was a member of the Assembly most of the time from 1697 to 1709. In 1697, 1698 and 1699, he was elected speaker, and had the good fortune to be a favorite of Governor Allen in one of those years. He was again chosen speaker under the administration of Dudley in 1704, and continued to be annually elected to that office until 1709. In 1707, the great cause, Allen *vs.* Waldron, involving Allen's title to the Province of New-Hampshire, was tried on appeal, at the August term of the Superior Court. As this was the last trial, all the strength of the parties was brought into action on this occasion. It affords unequivocal evidence of the legal and popular talents of Capt. Pickering, and of the confidence reposed in him by the defendants of this cause, which embraced some of the first men in the Province, that he was selected as one of the counsel to defend the homes, the houses and lands of the inhabitants, from the rapacity of the plaintiff and those who were especially interested in his behalf. Charles Story was associated with him as counsel. The verdict of the jury was a confirmation of the former judgment for the defendant.

In March, 1671, soon after his father's death, an agreement was made between Capt. John Pickering and the town, "That the town shall have full liberty, without any molestation, to inclose about half an acre on the neck of land on which he now liveth, where the people have been wont to be buried, which land shall be impropriated forever unto the use of a burying place—only the said Pickering and his heirs forever shall have liberty of feeding the said with neat cattle." "Provided also that the town or any of them, as there is occasion, shall have liberty to pass over the land of said Pickering to bury their dead." This was at the Point-of-Graves.

In 1673, John Pickering gave to the town a highway two rods wide through his land to the dam. This was the opening of Pleasant street.

The remembrance of John Pickering (2d), who gave the Point-of-Graves Cemetery for a public burying place; and who bequeathed to the South Parish the lot on which, ten years after his death, the old South Church was erected, should be kept fresh in our local history.

Capt. Pickering was the leading man in all matters, both of Church and State. If any doubtful question came up, the voice of the populace was—"What does the captain of the Port say?" He was a standing moderator, and could sway the people as well as any political leaders of the town meetings held in after days.

It could be well said of the early settlers of Portsmouth, that "there were giants in those days." Not long after Thomas Pickering had built his log hut on the Bay, and had commenced clearing the land, an English man-of-war came into the harbor of the Piscataqua. A press gang was sent on shore to obtain recruits for the service. Two of these minions went into the outskirts, as the best place to secure persons who might be found alone, and met Thomas Pickering, on his premises, felling trees. They stopped and conversed with him awhile, complimenting his muscular appearance, and after saying he was just such a man as his majesty needed, with official importance commanded him to leave his work and follow them. Thomas declined, saying he had a young family, and was needed at home. "*No excuse, sir—march!*" were words which the lord of the forest could not brook,—so, seizing one of the officials by the back of his neck with his left hand, he placed his face in the ground, and with the right raised his axe in the attitude of chopping off the fellow's head. His terrified companion seized his arm and begged for mercy. Thomas permitted the arrogant fellow to arise, and the way they hasted from the scene was evidence that they felt they had escaped as from a lion's power.

Capt. John was a man of might, and was not willing that Thomas should excel him. One day a test of strength was made on a wager. It was made by carrying bags of corn up the steps into the mill. Capt. John had the bags piled up, until ten bushels were upon his back. This he thought sufficient, and with them walked into the mill. Thomas bore eleven and a half bushels, and with a firm step went over the same track. Such is the tradition.

As early as the year 1662, it was in general town meeting "*Ordered*, that a cage be made, or some other means invented by the Selectmen, to punish such as sleepe or take tobacco on the Lord's day out of the meeting in the time of the publique exercise."

The press of other matters delayed the carrying out of this order for nine years. In 1671, the Selectmen made a contract with Capt. John Pickering (who appears to be a carpenter as well as miller, lawyer and commander of a company), to build a cage twelve feet square and seven feet high. The studs to be six inches broad, four inches thick, and the openings between them to be three inches. "The studs are to be round the said cage, and at the bottom and overhead. The said Pickering to make a good strong dore, and make a substantial payre of stocks and place the same in said cage—and also build on the rough of said cage a firm pillory. All which cage, stock and pillory to be built and raised some convenient space from the westward end of the meeting-house by the last day of October next ensuing." The bargain also included a ladder.

In 1672, we find Capt. John Pickering and Edward West were authorized by a vote of the Selectmen to "keep houses of publique entertainment."

The 4th of July, 1676, a general town meeting was held for the choice of a constable. We will return from the meeting house with Capt. Pickering, and converse with him at his mill door. He first directs our attention to the two-story meeting house of Rev. Mr. Moody, a few rods south of the mill, directly on the spot where the residence of E. Fitzgerald now stands. His father had aided in its erection eighteen years before. The road then branched off as it now does, leaving the meeting house near the corner. It is of two stories and has a low belfry. The bell, which has been hanging here for a dozen years, has been merrily ringing this 4th of July, but being just a century before the declaration of Independence, it told not of any such event. There was a cheering sound in that lone bell, perhaps at that time the only one in New-Hampshire. It had brought together men to exercise the freeman's right of suffrage, and therefore had an ennobling sound. The Captain had met many of the members of his company in the meeting, and the salutations of "Captain" had a far from depressing influence. The small diamond glass windows and the front door, on which were marks where the wolves' heads had been nailed to secure the captor's bounty, are all distinct objects in our eyes.

The house was without pews, nor had it any until fifteen years after. A little to the west of the meeting-house the Captain points to the open cage he made for the town, and tells of this one who had been put in for smoking tobacco on Sunday—and of that, whom the Tythingmen had set there in the stocks for drinking—and of Goodman Such-a-one, who was placed in the pillory on top for disturbing the meeting. And a little further west, he points to the school house (the remains of which were in use a century and a half afterwards), where the boys were enjoying the advantages of learning to read and write—if their parents saw fit to pay for their instruction—a privilege which his father had told him was not everywhere enjoyed in his day. He points to his snug farm house north from the mill, the only house in sight in that direction—and speaks of the grave-yard beyond where his father rests. He tells of the settlement on the other side of the dock—of the great house of Cutt, and of the lesser houses in the neighborhood—and of the

Glebe land, to which he had given a road through his land from the mill, but as it was not much needed, he had delayed fencing, and he yet kept up a gate near the rocks at the north end of the Neck. He thinks the time may come when the town will be larger, and at some distant day even allow of a meeting-house on his land—and he points to a good location, on a rise of land in his forest a few rods north as the place, should the growth of the town extend on the north side of the dam. He now looks down upon his bridge, on which we stand, six feet wide, capable of bearing a foot passenger or a horse, but not a wheel-carriage. It was a work of art as important then, in his estimation, as an Atlantic cable would now be to the world.

And for what use, Captain, is that small shed building near the meeting-house? Oh, that was built by Nat Fryer, a Boston merchant, who some years ago lived further up the river. He built this house for his family to stop in to warm themselves and take a dinner when they came down to meeting. That Boston is becoming a great place—it will soon have several thousand inhabitants, if Philip's pesky Indians don't destroy it with the other towns. Hope they won't burn the college, which our town is paying £60 every year to sustain. With a hearty shake of the hand, the Captain leaves us for the mill and we—go on in our ramble.

Capt. John Pickering was truly democratic in one sense of the word, and it was by looking upon an equality of rights among his fellow-men that he attained his popularity; more particularly on an occasion which was manifest to the whole town. It was in 1671, after Mr. Moody had been preaching here twenty-three years without being settled or collecting a church around him, that movements were made for his ordination. It was a great occasion for so small a meeting-house—and as Cabot and Wheelwright and others from abroad were expected to be present, it was necessary that some powerful man should be marshal for the day, to keep the people in such positions that the dignitaries of the occasion might enjoy the best locations. Capt. Pickering was therefore chosen as the best man to provide seats for the people. Regarding one man as good as another, he let every one who entered take whatever position he chose—making no reservation for the pastor's guests. For so doing he was summoned before the ecclesiastical body, and censured for neglect of duty. His only apology was, that regarding one man as good as another, he could make no such invidious distinctions as preferred seats would give. Though censured for his course, he became popular by the incident, and a standing moderator at public meetings for many years after.

He was a man for the times in which he lived. For fifty years he appears to have been a very active public man—sometimes controlling town matters in a spirit of obstinacy, and at others seeking to serve the public for the promotion of their good. Like many other men, Capt. John Pickering liked to have his own way—unlike many others, he generally enjoyed the power.

---

## RAMBLE IX.

**Tythingmen of Portsmouth—Names of Inhabitants in 1678—Designation of Neighborhoods.**

A VIEW of the municipal police, of the names of the inhabitants, and the neighborhoods in which they were located in 1678, cannot be better presented than in the appointment of Tythingmen, in that year, whose duty it was to look after the good morals of their neighbors. It appears that special Tythingmen had the charge of every individual or family, excepting that of the minister—who probably was a sort of supervisor of the Tythingmen.

At a town meeting held on the 22d of March, 1678, it was voted "that the selectmen at the next meeting appoint some honest men to inspect their neighbors, as the law directs, for preventing drunkenness and disorder."

On the third of June, 1678, it was voted by the selectmen—"In pursuance of an additional law of the General Court, made on the 23d of May, 1677, touching the prevention of the profanation of the Lord's day, enjoyning the selectmen to appoint Tythingmen to inspect ten or twelve of their neighbors' families, the selectmen do nominate and appoynt the persons here undernamed to perform that service:

*Mr. Wallis, for*
famylies of
Mr. Hen. Sherburne
James Rendle
Jno. Odiorne
Tho. Seavey
Mr. Tucker
Wm. Seavey
Robert Purrington
Sergt. Moses
Fardi Hoof
Tho. Creler
Joseph Walker
Hugh Leare
Robt. Lange
Goodm. Lucomb
Edw. Bickford
And. Sampson
John Bowman
Sa. Harris
Ric. Shortridge
Mark Hunking
Goodm. Goss

*Sergt. Brewster, for*
Tob. Leare
Sergt. Sloper
Xtoph'r Noble
Jno. Peverly
Jno. Westbrooke
Jno. Hoomes
Jno. Sherburne
Hen. Savage
Wm. Brooking

*Tho. Jackson, for*
John Jackson
Peter Ball
Rich. Dore
Nath'l White
Rich. Manson,
Dan Duggin
Wm. Walker
Jam. Jones
Jno. Whidden
Jno. Banfield
Tho. Stevens
Jno. Picker
Ant. Row
Wid. Cate.

*Jno. Light, for*
Wm. Cotten
Leo. Drowne
Wm. Richards
Mr. Comins
Ano. Ellens
Sam'l Whidden
Neh. Partridge
Jno. Preston
Sam. Rawlins
Hen. Herke
Peter Glanfield

*Jno. Dennett, for*
Wm. Earle
Jno. Cotten
Wm. Rackley
Sam. Clarke
Math. Nelson
Geo. Hunt
Jno. Place
Jno. Dennett, Sen'r
Rich Jackson
Wm. Ham.

*Docter Fletcher, for*
Mr. Jno. Cutt, Sen'r
Mrs. El. Cutt
Lt. Vaughan
Mrs. Cowell
Mr. Tho. Harvey
Jno. Cutt, Jun'r
Jno. Tucker
Mr. Martin
Mr. Shipway
Clem't Merserve.

*Obadiah Morss, for*
Geo. Lavers
Edw. Melcher
Joseph Clarke
Tho. Dew
Adri Fry
Goodm. Bond
Rob't Williams
Ephra, Lyn
Hen. Crowne
Tho. Wacomb.

*James Leech, for*
Wido. Johnson
Jno. Lock
Geo. Walton, Sen'r
Jno. Menseene
Sam. Robey
Wid. Joanes
Jno. Clarke
Math. Estes
Geo. Harris
Arth. Head
Mr. Jordan
Wm. Haskins.

*John Lewis, for*
James Paine
Jos. Messeet
Aron Ferris
Steven Webster
Tho. Joanes
Tho. Westcote
Mrs. Taprell
Wid. West
Mr. Harvey
Geo. Walton, Jun'r
Jno. Abbott
Rich'd Palmer
Wm. Row
Ed. Rendle.

*Robert Eliot, for*
Rich. Rogers
John Kettle
James Robeason
Henry Russell
Edw. Beale
Sam. Wintworth
Fran. Tucker
Wm. Lux
Edw. Cranch
Silo. Herbert
Hump Spencer
Mr. Nath. Fryer.

*Phineas Ryder, for*
Waymon Bickfon
Tho. Parker
Dorm. Oshaw
Jno Turbet

*George Bramhall, for*
Mr. Ladbrooke
John Pickerin
Rich. Webber
John Partridge,
Rich. Waterhouse and rest of famylies on the island.

*Sam'l Kaise, for*
Mr. Monday
Capt. Daniel
Jno. Seaward
Mr. Mercer and rest yr.
Ben. Hull
Caleb Beck
Jno. Hunking
Mrs. Joce.

*Phineas Ryder, for*
Geo. Jaffrey
Mr. Rich. Stileman
Rich. Abbett
Steven of Graffum
Tho. Paine
Wm. Lucas
Capt. Elias Stileman.

*Lt. Neale*, for all the famylies at Greenland.
*Ens. Drake*, for all the famylies at Sandy Beach.

In the Constables' rates made in Dec. 1688, we find the following names given as the residents of Sandy-Beach and Greenland. Some of these are known to have been residents at and in the vicinity of Portsmouth Plains; it is therefore evident that Greenland, in that document, includes the western part of Portsmouth, Greenland and Newington. Sandy Beach was then the name of Rye.

Phillip Lewes
Edward Fox
Christopher Kempstone
William Davis
Abraham Lewes
Charles Alling
Richard Andrews
Thomas Avery
Robert Bryan
John Johnson, Jun'r
Robert Hinkson
Joseph Berry
Jothan Lewes
Samuel Nele
Leonard Weeks
Walter Nele
John Johnson, Sen'r
Samuel Haines
Mathias Haines
Samuel Whiden
Sadwick Fowler
Clem Misharvie
Justinion Richards

Mr. Packer
Nathaniel Drack
William Berry
John Berry
John Mardin
John Foss, Sen'r
John Foss, Jun'r
Thomas Pickrin
William Keat
John Hill, Jun'r
John Odihorne
Anthony Bracket
John Bracket
Frances Ran
Thomas Ran
Thomas Bearnce
William Wallis
James Allard
James Randel
William Seavie
Thomas Seavie
John Sherburn, seaman
Peter Harvie

James Gerrish
Thomas Beck
Georg Walker
Tobias Langdon
Richard Sloper
John Peverly
Thomas Edmonds
John Brewster, Sen'r
John Brewster, Jun'r
John Sherburn, Sen'r
John Sherburn, Jun'r
John Westbrook, Sen'r
John Westbrook, Jun'r
John Vrine
Robert Pudington
Thomas Pudington
James Berry
Samuel Ran
John Seavie
Anthony Libbe
Henry Sherburne
John Sloper, Jun'r
Nicholas Hodg.

Any one acquainted with the family owners of the farms on the road from Rye Beach to Great Bay, may see for a considerable distance, almost in the order of their names, the places where the sons are now occupying the lands held by their fathers more than one hundred and seventy years ago.

## RAMBLE X.

The first Meeting-House—Seating of the occupants—Old Inhabitants—Moody and Cranfield—Rogers—Emerson—Scenes at the old Meeting-House.

THAT old town Meeting House, built in 1658, two centuries ago, on the rise of ground a few rods south of the south mill bridge, where Mr. Fitzgerald's house now stands, would be an object of much interest, could we again see it rise on its old site, and the parishioners of Rev. Joshua Moody again seeking seats in the sacred place, to them the nearest approach to heaven the earth afforded. But as the old house has departed, and its shadows on the memory are every year becoming less distinct, it will be the effort of this ramble to bring back and daguerreotype some impressions which may not only give it perpetuity, but also be a chronicle of the families of 1693 in this vicinity, and of the positions assigned to each individual in their only place of worship.

The Meeting House probably faced the bridge, and being between fifty and sixty feet in length, and not far from thirty feet in width,—its first story about eleven feet, and the second story about ten feet in hight,—the roof on an angle of about forty-five degrees, being somewhat elevated, gave the structure, in comparison with everything around it, a rather imposing appearance.

Those who have seen the Billings house, which was removed in 1846 to give place to Congress Block, can form some idea of the old Meeting House—for that dwelling house was a part (probably half) of the old edifice. In 1738 a building occupied by Robert Macklin, the old baker who lived to the age of one hundred and fifteen years, was burnt on the site of the Billings house. Soon after a portion of the meeting house was removed to the spot, and was owned and occupied by John Newmarch, merchant, son of Rev. John Newmarch, of Kittery. In

1743, Paul March, who married a daughter of Mr. Newmarch, built the Bell Tavern, next west, which is still standing. [1859.]—Some of the original diamond glass windows remained in the Billings house until it was taken down, thirteen years ago. The panes were about four inches long and three wide, set in lead, and strengthened by small oak bars on the inside.

We have therefore a basis on which we can, in imagination, again erect the old edifice. Very fortunately we have been able to place our hand on a record which will at once give us a true idea of its occupants, and the mode of seating, nearly two centuries ago. Here is the curious and valuable document, verbatim, which having been written before any newspapers were published in America, has never before appeared in print:

"Whereas at a Generall Towne meeting held in Portsmouth the 3d of April, 1693, there was a vote passed impowering the Selectmen, together with Mr. Richard Martine, Capt. Walter Nele and Mr. Marke Hunking to be a comitte to regulate and order the seating of the people in the meeting house; also to order seats and Pews according to their discression, provided no charge acrue to the Towne thereby, wee whose names are hereto anexsed being the parties above-mentioned, and met togeather the day aboves'd, having well veied and considered of the order and power aforesaid, and finding it shuteable and convenient to have Pews round the said meeting house below, and the severall persons herein named desiring Pewes and ingaging to build them at their own charge and also to remove and compleat all the mens and womens seates below and build all the pews of one hith, and uniforme. Also to make a door by the womens stairs, to be done with all convenient speed. The persons names that are to have the Pews and do the work as afores'd, viz: Mr. Rich'd Waldron, Mr. George Jeffry, Mr. Wm. Partridge, Mr. Marke Hunking, Mr. John Knight, Mr. John Plaisted, Mr. Richard Jose, Mr. Langdon, Mr. George Snell, and John Pickerin, Sen'r, who are the persons that have ingaged to doe the worke. It is also promised to them that the towne, nor none by their order, shall have liberty to build any Pew or Pews before them or either of their Pewes, but that all the seats shall be according to the draft on file; and if it should happen that any person that hath pews as afores'd, shall leave the Towne, the Towne shall reimburse such person what said Pew cost him and have the disposing of it to whome they shall see fitt. And whereas the allies round the meeting house before the pews and round the seats cannot be so compleat and uniform without cutting the corners of Major Vaughan's, and that seat where Mr. John Cutt sat, and the sd Vaughan as far as he is concerned, being free thereto, so it be done of the same sort of worke as now it is; which the persons aforenamed are also to doe at their own charge. Wee have also seated the inhabitants according to their places as per their names, at the ends of the severall seats, both in the galleries and below, the list whereof is next following our names and hands.

WM. VAUGHAN, GEO. SNELL, JOHN PICKERIN, Sen'r, TOBIAS LANGDON, } Townsmen.

WALTER NELE, MARKE HUNKING, } of the Committee.

Here followeth the names of the persons seated below in those severall seats, viz:

*With the Minister in the Pulpit.*

| | | |
|---|---|---|
| Mr. John Fletcher, | Mr. Samuel Keise, | |

*In the seat under the Pulpit.*

| | | |
|---|---|---|
| Serg't Moses, | Henry Becke, | Allexsander Whidden. |

*The front seat before the Minister.*

| | | | |
|---|---|---|---|
| 1. | Mr. Rich'd Martine. | | |
| 2. | Phillip Lewis, | Lieut. Sloper, | Capt. Nele. |
| | Mr. Morse, | | |
| 3. | John Partridge, S'r, | Tho. Jackson, Sen'r, | John Dennet. |
| | John Jackson, Sen'r, | John Tucker, | |
| 4. | Thomas Waycome, | John Fabens, | Leonard Weeks. |
| | John Sherborne, Plaines, | | |
| 5. | John Johnson, Sen'r, | Francis Jones, | John Westbrooke, S'r, |
| | John Banfield | Rich'd Monson, | Joseph Berry, |
| | Peter Ball, | Daniel Westcoat, | |
| 6. | Charles Allen, Sen'r, | John Holmes, | Hubertus Mattone, |
| | Richard Webber, | Wm. Rackleife, | Will. Walker. |
| | John Bowman, | Nathan White, | |
| 7. | Robert Lange, | Thos. Lowrie, | Henry Kirke, |
| | Lewis Williams, | Robert Rowsely, | John Bartlett. |
| | Will. Davis, | Abr. Bartlett, | |

*In the Men's Gallery fronting the Pulpit, viz:*

| | | | |
|---|---|---|---|
| 1. | Capt. Thos. Packer, | Sam'l Rymes, | Capt. Job Alcocke, |
| | Mr. Nicholas Follet, | Mr. John Hunking, | Mr. Rich'd Gerish, |
| | Mr. John Hatch, | Mr. Phillip White, | Mr. John Cutt. |
| | Mr. Edward Kenard, | | |
| 2. | Richard Waterhouse, | James Lovett, | Aron Moses, |
| | Marke Ayeres, | Henry Sherborne, | Thos. Deverson, |
| | Rober Almory, | Thos. Becke, | Mr. Pitman, |
| | Geo. Walker, | John Ballard, | John Sloper. |
| | Splan Lovewell, | John Partridge, Jun'r, | |
| 3. | Rober Hinxson, | William Williams, | John Savage, |
| | John Cate, | Nathan Knight, | Rich'd Dow, |
| | John Foss, | Nath. Berry, | John Walker, |
| | Robert Gosse, | Samuel Jackson, | John Dockum. |

*In the Men's Side Gallery.*

| | | | |
|---|---|---|---|
| 1. | Mr. Basain, | William Partridge, Jun'r, | Thos. Pickerin, |
| | Capt. Ick. Plaistead, | Mr. Henry Crowne, | John Snell, |
| | Wm. Hunkins, | John Cotton, | Mathew Nelson, |
| | Wm. Cotton, | Mr. Aug's Bullard, | Nich Bennet, |
| | Nathaniel Ayeres, | Edw'd Ayeres, | Jacob Lavers. |
| | Mr. Togood, | | |
| 2. | Abraham Lewis, | Wm. Richards, | John Brewster, |
| | Wm. Philbrooke, | John Johnson, Jun'r, | Benj'n Cotton, |
| | John Abbot, | John Downing, | Edward Cate, |
| | John Peverly, | Sam'l Nele, | Thomas Edmons, |
| | John Vrin, | John Philbrooke, | Allen Loyd. |
| | John Clarke, | | |
| 3. | Clem't Meserve, | Jos. Alexsander, | Elisha Bryer, |
| | John Hill, Jun'r, | Richard Shortridge, | Rob. Bryant, |
| | Edw'd Wells, | Thos. Perkins, | Michael Hickes, |
| | Peter Wells, | Geo Kenistone, | Wm. Willowbey, |
| | Edw'd Pavey, | Daniel Allen, | Thomas Lewis, |
| | Charles Allen, Jun'r, | Thos. Avery, | James Drew. |
| | Peter Babb, | Sampson Babb, | |

Women seated below stairs as followeth, viz.:

*Seat fronting the Pulpit.*

1. Mrs. Moody, Mrs. Martine.

2. Mrs. John Partridge, Mrs. Dennet, Mrs. Keise.
Mrs Hannah Jackson, Mrs. Morse,

3. Mrs. Tucker, Mrs. Waycome, John Johnson's, wife,
John Westbroke's wife, Goody Monson, Mrs. Togood.
John Faben's wife,

4. Goody Ham, Goody Banfield, Goody Baker,
Widow Fabens, Goody Seward, Goody Webber.
Goody Rackleife,

5. Goody Goss, Goody Savage, Peter Ball's wife,
Lewis Williams' wife, Goody Bowman, Nath. White's wife.
Goody Brooking,

6. Goody Allen, Wm. Davis's wife, John Hill's wife,
Thos. Jones' wife, Rob. Lange's wife, John Homes' wife.

7. Hen. Kirke's wife, John Bartlet's wife, Goody Rousely,
Goody Ackerman, Joseph Berry's wife, Goody Dore.
Wm. Walker's wife,

*In the first seat between the Pulpit and Maj. Vaughan's pew.*

The widdow Hunking, Widdow Brewster, Mrs. Fletcher.
Mr. Phil. Lewis his wife,

*The next.*

Goody Waterhouse, Mr. John Jackson's wife, Widdow Jackson.
Mr. Sloper's wife,

*In the Women's seat in the Gallery.*

1. Mrs. Parker, Mrs. Clarke, widdow, Mrs. Hall,
The widdow Light, Mrs. Mary Hunking, Mrs. Kennard,
Mrs. Ursula Cutt, Capt. Plaistead's wife, Mrs. Jane Gerish,
Mrs. Hatch, Mrs. Rymes, Thos. Pickerin's wife,
Mrs. White, Mrs. Mary Hoddy, Mrs. Elizabeth Hoddy.
Mrs. Pitman, Mrs. Allcock,

2. Mrs. Hopley, Nath. Ayeres' wife, Mrs. Levett,
Wm. Cotton's wife, Mathew Nelson's wife, John Sherborne's wife,
Hen. Sherborn's wife, John Cotton's wife, Widdow Allkins,
Jacob Savers' wife, John Brewster's wife, Thos. Deverson's wife,
Widdow Jane Haines, The widdow Mary Haynes, Mr. Bennet's wife.

3. The widdow Widden, John Partridge's wife, Jr. Samuel Widden's wife,
Samuel Niles' wife, Abr. Lewis' wife, Wm. Richard's wife,
Aron Moses' wife, John Peverly's wife, Geo. Walker's wife,
John Clarke's wife, Thos. Becke's wife, Allen Loyd's wife,
Wm. Philbrooke's wife, Geo. Huntris' wife, Widdow Barnwell,
John Philbrooke's wife, Mrs. Crowne, The widdow Mary Lewis.

4. Widdow Beck, Edw'd Cateife, John Vrin's wife,
Thos. Edmond's wife, Elisha Bryer's wife, Benj'n Cotton's wife,
Splan Lovewell's wife, Clem't Meserve's wife, Michal Hicke's wife,
John Savage's wife, Peter Wells' wife, Abr. Bartlett's wife,
Edw'd Wells' wife, John Downing's wife, Nathan Knight's wife.
John Jackson, Junr.'s wife

The 5th seat being the back seat is left for young persons about 14 years of age, unmarried

The room over the women's staires is for the persons under named to sit in, viz.:

Robert Hinxson's wife, Rich'd Shortridge's wife, Rob. Bryant's wife,
Nath. Berry's wife, Jas. Howard's wife, Edw'd Fox's wife,
John Foss, Junr.'s wife, John Dockum's wife, Christop'r Keniston's wife,
James Kenist's wife, Wm. Willowbes' wife, Alias Gerish.
Goody Pomry,

*In the seat where Major Stileman's daughter satt.*

Mrs. Follet, Sarah Famsy till further order.
Elizabeth Plaisted's widow, Wm. Partridge's wife.

As for that seat where Capt. Fryer sat, Lieut. Redford and his wife are there placed till further order.

The back seats in the men's galleries is left for younge persons about 14 years old.

As for boys under that age they are to sit in the men's allyes, and the girls in the women's allyes. And also that no boys be suffered to sit on the staires or above staires, and that noe younge men or younge women offer to crowde into any seat where either the men or women are seated.

And whereas there is parte of the back seate in the women's gallery built uniforme, if there be any young women that will advance for building sd. back seat in the same forme the whole length hence to the stares, they may have liberty. And also young men that will advance for macking the two back seats in the men's galleries as uniforme, they may have the same liberty."

The term *goody* is probably applied to *maiden* ladies in the above.

The meeting-house was thirteen years without shutters. In 1671, it was agreed with John Pickering, for thirty shillings to make shutters for the windows, "to draw backwards and forwards; and in case it be too little, then the said Pickering shall have something more."

In 1672 it was "voted that Nehemiah Partridge and five or six more people have free liberty to build a payre of stayres up to the westward beame within the meeting-house, and a pew upon the beam, at theyr own charge; and the pew shall be to theyr owne use, and the stayres are not to be discommodious to the meeting-house."

1680—Town agreed with Nich. Bond "for to look after the demeanor of the boyes at meeting" at twenty shillings per annum.

In 1692, "it was proposed to the town whither William Wacker (Walker) should pay for the bell, whom he carlessly crackt. It was voted in the negative, because he was poor. It was voted that the selectmen take care to provide a bell, and as for the hanging of him as they may judge most convenient." Whether the latter "him" refers to the *bell* or the *man* who "crackt" it, the record does not plainly show.

It should be understood that the committee of ten had pews for themselves and their families, in which the man and his wife and children were permitted to sit together. There appears to have been one or two other pews previously erected, for the official dignitaries. We do not learn that Gov. Cranfield often occupied either of these pews.

It was in 1684, when George Jaffrey (not Janvrin, as reported in Adams's Annals,) had been subjected to ecclesiastical investigation for false swearing, after Cranfield had stopped legal proceedings, that the irritated Governor gave notice to Moody that he should appear at this place of worship on the next Lord's day, and dictated to him the mode in which the sacrament should be administered to him and his associates. Moody would not be dictated, and was imprisoned for three months at Newcastle. Being forbidden to preach here he went to Boston, and was absent for eight years. He had just been re-established in his labors here when in 1693 the above seating was made. His ministry closed by death on the 4th of July, 1697, at the age of sixty-four years. It is recorded that he probably wrote more sermons in the same number of years than any other man—in thirty years he wrote four thousand and seventy sermons, or two and a half each week. In those days sermons generally occupied an hour. He was succeeded by Rev. N. Rogers, in 1699, who removed from the old house to the North church in 1713. Rev. Mr. Emerson continued the services at the old church as soon as vacated, and from that day the *North* and *South* parishes took the names which they still hold, although their churches for more than thirty years have been but a few rods apart.

There is subject enough in the history for a lively indulgence of the imagination, but we will leave the reader to trace out the worshippers as they travel afoot, or the goodman and his wife as they dismount from the old horse at the door—he with his buckled shoes and knee bands—she dressed in all the simplicity and modesty of the times; the one followed by his boys seeking their seats in the aisle on one side,—and the goodwife with her girls filing off in an opposite direction. Imagine the niche where those just entered their teens were seated; and the terror Nich. Bond excited in the bare legged boys in their small clothes, when he pointed to the cage just by the door—an array of all the wolves' heads that had been taken off during the last week being visible between them and the cage. We might speak of the guns sometimes left in the porch,—but the length of this ramble warns us to close.

## RAMBLE XI.

Settlement at Plains—Old Roads—Military Scenes—Indian Massacre of 1696—The Surprise—Scalping of Mary Brewster—List of killed and wounded—The retreat—Pursuit—Breakfast Hill.

There was in former times quite a village in the vicinity of the Plains and on the road leading by the cattle pound down through Frenchman's lane. It was of such importance that a meeting-house was erected on the spot where Mr. Branscomb's house now stands, a few rods east of the Plains. The meeting-house was then on the east side of the road, although Mr. B.'s house is now, by a change in its direction, on the north. The direct road from the Creek to the Plains by the powder-house, was opened in 1792. Before that time the only way of reaching the Plains was by passing through Frenchman's lane and the road on which D. H. Spinney lives to the pound, then by the present road to a few rods west of Mr. Sheafe's farm house, from whence it inclined a little north of the present line, and opened on the Plains at the place where the Dennett house stood. The road from the pound towards Newcastle was early opened, but the one which extends from the pound to Middle street was not opened a century ago.

The Plains meeting-house did not appear to have been firmly "founded upon a rock," for in 1748 in a gale of wind it was blown down. Twelve years since, on the spot where the one-story house near the school-house now stands, was a large two-story dwelling, called the Dennett house, which was erected in 1722 by Samuel Brewster, a son of the lady who stands prominent in the dreadful tragedy which twenty-six years before took place near that spot.

The Plains has witnessed in the present century some scenes of a warlike aspect, not only in the so long continued annual musters, but also in the war of 1812 in the long-extended barracks, and a field in daily use for the drafted militia of New Hampshire. There were some scenes of sickness and of death there at that exciting time; and the beat of the muffled drum, and the long military processions which paid the last tribute at the grave, are not soon to be forgotten by those who witnessed them marching through our streets. A more dreadful scene, however, had the Plains previously witnessed.

We will now turn more than a century yet further back. It was on the 26th of June, 1696, that the Indians made their way to this very spot, after their fearful predatory incursions on Dover. Cotton Mather and Belknap refer to the event in short paragraphs. Adams in his Annals also records the incident in a single page. The following account has been furnished us, collected from history, old manuscripts and traditions, and is the fullest that has ever been published.

In the afternoon previous to the Indians' commencing their attack on the people and property of that vicinity, the clouds and chilled air portended rain. That night a thunder storm occurred; the cattle came frightened from the woods, and at an unusually early hour sought refuge around their owners' homes. Dover having suffered from the murdering hands of the treacherous Indians, the thinly settled neighborhood of the Plains had constant forebodings that they might soon be subject to like incursions. Their suspicions were awake, and whatever appeared to be ominous of the approach of the Indians was dreadful in the imagination.

Their cattle had been previously very frequently abused and lacerated by parts of wandering tribes which had been skulking through the woods for theft and cruelty. When the cattle and sheep on the day before the attack hurried to the yards, their frightened appearance caused much talk and alarm among the villagers; and although they suspected and even believed that their herds had fled from Indians they had seen, yet, not conceiving danger to be so nearly awaiting them, they sought repose in their habitations for one night longer. The people awoke at early dawn from their slumber and were greeted with the light of their burning barns. The Indians then sounded their warhoop, turned their havoc to the houses, rushed upon the inmates, and seized such valuable property as could be made portable with them. Such of the women and children as could flee, made their way toward the garrison-house; while the sick and infirm could at farthest only absent themselves from their homes to some near retired spot. The men fought the Indians with such implements as came nearest at hand, till contest became useless. The enemy overpowered them in numbers, then burned their houses and inflicted personal cruelties on all within their reach.

The men, when fully repelled from their desperate struggle, fled for the garrison to take fire-arms and swords; expecting there to find secure their wives and little ones. The Indians knowing the direction to be taken by those who would seek garrison protection, intercepted their course, and early lay in ambush to meet those who were passing by. By this means, solitary individuals were taken prisoners. Some were mained, some killed and others secured and carried off. But those who sought for the garrison in company passed on without interruption.

The garrison-house is said to have been located about north of the present site of the school-house, in the field between the barn of Mrs. Joseph Sherburne and the elevation on the east. A cellar and well are yet visible in the field not far east from the orchard.

When they had armed themselves for meeting the Indians on return, none were to be seen. The dead and the wounded they found in the pathway and around the houses.

The person named by Belknap as being scalped, was Mary Brewster, born Feb. 11, 1663, (daughter of Richard Sloper,) wife of John Brewster, Jr., who was the grandson of Wrestling Brewster* and great-grandson of Elder Wm. Brewster of Mayflower memory. The cellar of that house from which Mr. and Mrs. Brewster and their family were driven by the Indians, in this memorable scene, is to this time plainly discernible. It is a short distance south-easterly of the brick school-house on the Plains, situated on the northerly side of the discontinued old road which formerly led from the cattle pound to the Plains. The stones of the cellar remain principally in their first set position. Westerly of the house was a garden which extended to the stone wall. Amid the growth of wild shrubbery now occupying the spot, the cinnamon rose-bushes have retained their position, generation after generation, and afforded their annual bloom with the same blush and beauty as when planted and cared for by those who have ceased from their labors for upward of two centuries.

* Since the first edition was printed it appears by Gov. Bradford's Journal that Wrestling Brewster died young and unmarried. The name of John Brewster first appears in the town records about 1670. Where he came from, or what his connection was with Elder Brewster cannot be ascertained. He was probably a grandson.

When Mrs. Brewster was met by her friends, she was about mid distance between her house and the garrison, being but a few rods east of the present school-house. She was taken up for dead. Her scalp was entirely removed from her head, and she was deeply wounded by a tomahawk. She became a mother shortly after, and fully recovered her health. The fracture made in the cranium by the tomahawk, was closed by a silver plate, and her loss of hair was supplied by an artificial substitute. She was afterwards the mother of four sons, and lived till Sept. 22, 1744, then departed this life, aged 81y., 7m., 11d. The Brewster family in New Hampshire descended from this lady. This date is taken from a relief inscription of a beautifully enameled gold finger ring, which was made for and given at the obsequies of her interment. It was owned by Gov. John Langdon, to whose mother the ring was originally given. Gov. L. presented the ring to a member of the Brewster family.

Of dwelling-houses burned there were five, and nine barns. Capt. John Sherburne's loss by the fires exceeded that of any other individual. Two barns, well built, stocked with cattle, hogs and one horse, together with grain and hay, were entirely destroyed.

When news was sent from the plains to the Bank, the name by which the commercial part of Portsmouth was then known, Capt. Shackford rallied his military company, and the orders to the soldiers were that they proceed to a large rock which was then and has been till within the last six years, standing within a quarter of a mile east of the Plains; and was ever afterwards called "VALOUR ROCK." The company was there organized, and proceeded in pursuit of the enemy.

The Indians, about fifty in number, were observed in their canoes passing up the Piscataqua a day or two previous to their assault at the Plains. When the news of the attack reached the commercial part of the town, it was generally supposed by those who saw them when they were going up the river, that escape from the inhabitants would be effected by the Indians passing down the river in their canoes to avoid justice for their barbarity. The stratagem on the part of the Indians was too successful; it served to lead the attention of the people in a wrong direction and prevented any effectual action. The savages had moved their canoes in the night time, (unperceived in the town,) carried them down the river to Sandy Beach and secreted them in bushes.

Capt. Shackford pursued in the course supposed to have been taken by the Indians. Their direction was through Great Swamp, in a course for Rye. About four miles distant from the Plains the military company discovered the incendiaries with their plunder and captives; the four prisoners whom they had captured being placed in a position to receive the first effect of a discharge of guns should a military force appear for attack. The company rushed upon the ground, rescued the prisoners and retook the plunder; but the enemy escaped and concealed themselves in the swamp till night, then in their canoes took their departure. One party was sent out in boats, which were arranged in a line to intercept the enemy in their passage to the eastward. This enterprise would have been successful had not the commander indiscreetly given too early orders to *fire*. This caused the Indians to change their course, and thus make their escape by going outside of the Isles of Shoals.

When Capt. Shackford routed them at Breakfast-Hill and the boats in the river were waylaying them in their preparations to return to the eastward, it was discovered that those who were seen going up the river toward Dover were but a small party and the whole number which were then making their escape was much larger. It was from the circumstance of the Indians and their captives being engaged in taking breakfast on the declivity of a hill near the bounds of Greenland and Rye, that the location was called BREAKFAST HILL; and has ever since been known by that name.

The tribe to which these Indians belonged was not known by the populace; nor was it ever known what course they took for their homes after they had arrived on the high seas. It was evident, however, that the intention of the party was to commit murder and plunder in the commercial part of the town after it had sated its savage brutality on the outskirts. The resistance that met their progress at the Plains so delayed them, that the morning became too far advanced to warrant attempts on a more thickly-settled community.

Those killed were Thomas Onion aged 74, Joseph Holmes 20, Hixon Foss 17, Peter Moe 40, James Jaffrey's child 4, John Jones 32, William Howard 30, Richard Parshley 25, Thomas Meloney 13, Samuel Foss, Jr. 14, Betsey Babb 14, Nancy White 8, William Cate, Jr. 16, and Dinah, the slave of John Brewster. The wounded were Peggy Jones aged 76, William Cate's three children, and Daniel Jackson aged 41.

In the pleasant mornings of May and June, rising with the sun, a most excellent walk is an excursion to the Plains, going up one road and returning by the other. The local scenes of the past,—how much interest do they give the excursion.

Turning from the Plains, towards town, by the South road—how do you think this elevation on the left hand, as we leave the training field, would now do for a *Meeting House?* The one of which we have spoken was here erected in 1725, and stood for twenty-three years, and was a portion of the time occupied. We have never been able to find the records of the society, and doubt the existence of any such record. The house being a frail structure, it was blown down in 1748, and the parish became again united with the North parish, under

Rev. S. Langdon. We find the following document relating to its history in the Province papers, in the office of the Secretary of State, at Concord, vol. 6, fol. 15. It not only gives some important statistics of the neighboring towns in 1732, but also disproves a statement in Adams' Annals, where it is said the petition was *not* concurred in by the General Court. This record shows that it was "concurred in and consented to."

"Petition of sundry of His Majesty's freeholders of the southwesterly part of Portsmouth (at the Plains) to Governor Belcher, and dated March, 1732 and 3, setting forth that about seven years ago several of the petitioners, at vast expense, erected a house of public worship at the Plains, and from the month of January, 1725, to March, 1727, defrayed the charge of constant preaching in the said house, paying their full proportion of the parish tax at the Bank; but that burthen bearing too heavy, at length requested the parish to which they belonged to exonerate them from a further levy toward the subsistence of Rev. Mr. Fitch.

The parish by a unanimous vote, dated the 4th of March, 1727, in a full parish, complied with the request, and now ask for an Act of Incorporation for a parish by the metes and bounds in the aforesaid parish vote,—and state first: that to the best of their knowledge *eighty families* besides the families of six widows—*one hundred and one ratable heads* and *four hundred and fifty* souls, or thereabouts, within the bounds. N. B.—There are half a dozen families or more, consisting of thirty souls at least (not included in the bounds aforesaid), to attend public worship at the Plains meeting house rather than any where else. Second, that in 1727 (as they are informed), there were at Greenland but ninety-two ratable polls, though there has been a church there twenty or thirty years; at Newington but ninety-two, which has been a parish near twenty years; at Newcastle but eighty-two; at Newmarket seventy-eight, and at Rye but seventy-two, &c.

March 10th, 1732. Concurred in and consented to.

(Signed) J. BELCHER."

Number of petitioners about sixty-two.

## RAMBLE XII.

Bridget Graffort—Gift of Daniel street—Lot for first town school house—Ichabod Plaisted—Early school history—Samuel Keais—Style of the early town records.

In digging up subjects in our Rambles, to introduce new acquaintances to our readers, sometimes one appears uncalled, with whom we have had no previous acquaintance. Such is the case with an apparition now before us, who has been quietly resting for a century and a half. She bears the name of Bridget Graffort.

In the year 1700, we find that Bridget Graffort, of Portsmouth, the widow of Thomas Graffort, made a present to the town, which is expressed in the following terms:

"For divers good causes and considerations me herewith moving, but more especially for the love and affection I have unto the town of Portsmouth, the place of my birth, I have given unto the said township of Portsmouth forever all the bye way or street from the Fort at Strawberry Bank in said town, taking its beginning from the corner of the house of Ichabod Playsted, and so running easterly nearest to the river of Piscataqua, as it is now being laid out and fenced, being in the broadest part about thirty feet, more or less—together also with that highway or lane from my new dwelling-house to the house of John Hoddey mariner, being about twenty feet wide, as now laid out and fenced. As also one lot of land in my great field for erecting a school house and conveniences thereunto for the use of the same, which lot of land is to be forty-six feet front towards the south, and eighty-eight feet north in said field abutting upon the lot sold by my late husband, Thomas Graffort, merchant, to the east to John Dennett and others, my land in said field."

Ichabod Plaisted, whose house is referred to by Mrs. Graffort, was a man of some note. He was High Sheriff of Salem, Mass., and owned this house in Portsmouth. He was connected with the Rindge family, and a handsome portrait of his portly form, arrayed in the apparel of a royal Sheriff, was preserved in the family of Jacob Sheafe, Esq., until destroyed in the fire of 1813. Daniel Rindge occupied a house on the corner of Daniel and Market streets a hundred and twenty years ago, and it is probable that Ichabod Plaisted was the owner of that location before him; and that the gate which opened from the "great field" was at the place where Daniel street now connects with Market square.

In 1735, the above-described school house lot was purchased of the town by Ebenezer Wentworth, who gave in exchange the lot of land with a small school house upon it, the spot where the present brick school house in State street now stands. By the above description of the lot first given to the town, it appears that it was situated on the north side of State street, not far from Chapel street, and probably within a few rods south of the present site of that noble structure, our new high school house. It also appears that what is now Daniel street, extending from the Fort, (which was probably the ledge of rocks on which the old State House was sixty years afterwards built, on Market square, near the North church,) was then being fenced, and was the gift of Mrs. Graffort to the town. For half a century after Daniel street was opened it bore the name of Graffort's lane. One thing is certain, that the real founder of the State street school house was Mrs. Graffort, and as a tardy act of justice should it not even now bear her name?

In December, 1684, Thomas Graffort was married to widow Bridget Daniel, who was the daughter of Richard Cutt. To her reference is made in his will. Thomas Daniel, the first husband of Bridget Cutt, was the builder of the old Wentworth house in Daniel street, which was removed in 1855, to give a location for our high school house.

There is a singularity in the course of events that led our city authorities unwittingly to select, as the site of our high school house, the very spot which more than a hundred and fifty years before had been the residence of one who donated a lot in front of her house for a like purpose, but which the town did not improve as directed.

In turning over the musty volumes of our town records, which for many years have been in quiet repose, we find some interesting matters relating to the introduction of public schools into Portsmouth. At the time widow Bridget Graffort presented a lot of land for a public school house in the year 1700, there does not appear to have been any school house owned by the town. Schools for boys had been patronized by the town, but the teachers received some further compensation from the parents. The town clerk was doubtless a man of average education, or he would not from year to year have been elected to his office. The following literal extracts from his records are curiosities in more respects than one.

There may be earlier records of public school movements, but we have not found any made prior to 1696.

On the 16th of March in that year, among the votes passed was the following:

"That care be taken that an abell scollmaster be provided for the towen as the law directes, not visious in conversation: and yt Mr. Joshua Moody and Mr. Sam'l Penhalow be desired in behalf of the towen to treat with some mett persons for yt servis, that thirtey pounds mony pr anum be allowed sd scollmaster as a sallery to be raised as ye law directs. The persons hereafter named desent against the vote for sd scollmasters sallery:

| | | |
|---|---|---|
| "John Pickrin, senior, | Nathaniel Berry, | Lazarus Noble, |
| Henry Sherburn, | Robert Briames, | Hugh Banfield, |
| John Pattridg, | Francis Graves, | Tho. Avery, |
| Tho. Beck, | John Benson, sen'r, | John Philbrook, |
| Georg Walker, | Richard Sloper, | Lenord Weeks, |
| James Lovet, | Joseph Berry, | Aron Moses, |
| Benjamin Cotton, | John Jonson, jn'r, | Andrew Samson," |

It does not appear that any public school was established in that year. The next year the following proceedings were had :

"May ye 7th, 1697. At a meeting of ye sellecttmen agreed with Mr. Tho. Phippes to be scollmaster for the towen this yr insewing for teaching the inhabitants children in such maner as other schollmasters yuosly doe through out the countrie: for his soe doinge we the sellectt men in behalfe of ower towen doe ingage to pay him by way of rate twenty pounds and yt he shall and may reseave from everey father or master that sends theyer children to school this yeare after ye rate of 16s for readers, writers and cypherers 20s, Latterners 24s."

By the following proceedings it appears that the town at that time owned no school house, and disputed a bill of fifty shillings incurred by the teacher for a school room.

"May 5th, 1698. At a meeting of the sellect men this day Mr. Phipps ower scollmaster informing yt he has disburst 50 shil. for a house to keep scoll in at ye bank which he saith the towen ought to reimburst him again; agread that the case be refered to the commissioners yt assisted last years acco't and that the bargain made be declared to them with wt is a leaged by Mr. Phipps as to the payment of fiftey shillinges, and if the commissioners shall judg it rationall then to be paid by the towen, otherwise not."

"At meeting of the sellectmen May 5th, 1699. The day above sd the sellectmen and Mr. Phipps have agread and said Phipps doth promise to prosed in keeping scooll this yeare insuing from the date forward unto the years end according to the agreement last yeare made with them: and to have ye same sallerey in all respecs as last yeare: and if it soe happen that the commishoners should not allow any thing for wt sd Phipps has desbursted on ye hows for the scool in at the banck last yeare, that then wee sd sellect men in behalf of our town doe promise to pay unto sd Phipps forty shillings more yn his twenty pounds sallerey for this yeare insuing, but if any thing be alowed by the commissioners then the same to be alowed the yeare and noe forty shillings to be pd."

"At a meeting of the sellectmen the 19th of June, 1699, agread with Mr. Tho. Phips schoolmaster of our town that he prosed in keeping scholl in the town on ye termes as formerly viz 24s for a Latting scholler, 20s for a writer and cypher and 16 for a reader qualified as formerly; and the sd Phipps for his sattisfaction shall be paid by ye sellectmen 20s in mony by way of publick rate besides the pertickuler sumes aforementioned and shall allsoe be alowed 50s by ye towen for his house rent; the time to begine the 5th day of May."

"May 5th, 1700. Agreement with Mr. Phipps for keeping a school renewed, the town allowing him £6 of the public money."

"March ye 26: 1701. At a meeting of ye sellectmen and comite apoynted by ye towen to tack care for ye providing of an abell scoolmaster soe qualified in learning and good maners as to teach ower youth in reading writing and syphering, the tonges and other learning as may fit ym for ye colledg, then agread yt we will alow and will pay in behalfe of ye town such scoolmaster for his settellment amonst us fortie pounds pr annum: then also agread that we request ye honorable ye Leutt governor Pattridg and Mr. Georg Jeffrey to youse thayer atmost indeavors in enquiring out and procquring such fit person and send him forth with amonst us in order to his further settellment."

"At a meeting of ye sellectmen and commite: May ye 12th: 1701, for settling of a scollmaster—Voted that whear as Mr. Daniel Grenlefe of Newbery has been with us in order to a settlement as a scoolmaster and is at present at Newbery, yt we doe forthwith send to him to have his answare in comings amonst us in order to a settelment, yt we alow him forty pounds per anum while he abides amonst us in case he comes and dully performs his offise to ye satisfaction of the towne: Voted that Mr. William Cotten and Capt. John Pickering doe forth with hire a howse at ye bank as neare ye towen fort as may be for ye keeping of a scool in for this yeare or until ye townes school howse be fitted up: Mr. Grenleaf being com and present with us we have agread with him to alow him forty pounds per anum while he continews with us and faithfully performs ye offis of a schoolmaster and hoe lickwise doth promise and engage to continue with us this yeare for ye above consideration and so teach all towen children and servants as are able compettently to read from thayer Psalters."

In 1702, no record of school proceedings is made.

In 1703, it appears that Daniel Greenleaf had left the school and town. Mr. Joshua Pierce was sent to Ipswich, to make enquiry into the qualifications of Josiah Cotton. It does not appear that he came; for

In 1704, the town empowered the selectmen "to call and settell a gramer scoll according to ye best of ower judgments and for ye advantag of ye youth of ower town to learn them to read from ye primer, to wright and sypher and to learne ym the tongues and goodmanners," &c. Mr. Cotton was again sent for, but not accepting the invitation, the messenger returned with Mr. William Allen of Salisbury, who engaged "dilligently to attend ye school for ye present yeare, and to tech all children yt can read in thaire psallters and upward." He asked a dismission in six months.

The town this year also voted six pounds by way of "incoridgment" to Nathaniel Freeman, to assist Greenland, the Plains and Sagamore Creek, "provided he use his dilligenc and care to scholl thos parts."

We find no further record respecting the schools until 1708, when the following votes were passed, directing the building of the first public school house in Portsmouth:

"At a generall towen meetinge held this fifth of Apriell, 1708: Voted that the sellectmen tack care to build a scool howse apon the land Mrs. Bridget Grafort lately deceased gave for the youse of ye towen for a scool howse.

Voted that the sellectmen take care to build a scool howse in some convenent plase one ye south side of ye milldam.

December ye 23: 1708. The selectmen ordred that Capt. John Pickring tack care and agre with Left. Pears or any other person for erectting and building a scool howse one ye south sd of ye milldam, sd howse to be of ye same dimentions ye former sellectmen agread with ye sd Pears for and to be fernished as in theire sd agrement spesifyed in all respects and to be paid soe much as sd former agrement spesieth: thirty pounds whear of to be paid out of ye present towen rate, besides ye money in sd Pearses hands and ye remainder out of ye next years towen rate, and ye sd howse be finished at or before ye 15th of Apriell next insuing the dat above sd."

It thus appears that the old south school house, in front of the site of the Haven school house, was the first public school house ordered to be built.

By one of the above votes it appears that the Widow Bridget Graffort died about the year 1707 or 8. The value of her gift of a school house lot, in its tendency to draw the attention of the town to the ownership of a school house, a matter which had been neglected for over seventy years, is of more value than the land itself. It does not appear, however, that the vote to build a house on the lot given to the town was complied with.

A small school house, owned by the Wentworth family, had been for some time previous to 1735 standing on the site of the present brick school on State street. In 1735, the town exchanged the lot given by Mrs. G. for the Wentworth school house. It is probable that in that very house Mr. Phipps kept his school, as it is not known that any other school house was erected in the vicinity of Market Square for many years after 1735. Mr. Phipps' residence was the firet erected on the glebe land, a few rods west of the North Church.

The town clerk who kept the above records from 1695 to 1714, was Samuel Keais, who was also in that time a selectman and a representative to the General Assembly at Newcastle. The improvement in spelling in the succeeding records shows that the advantages of schooling were duly realized.

In 1713, a vote was passed requesting the selectmen to build a school house at the south side of the mill-dam.

In 1732, it was voted that an enlargement be made at the west end of the grammar school house. [The house at mill-dam.]

In 1737, it was voted that the school master south of mill-dam shall keep his school in December and January near Randle's farm. It was voted that the selectmen provide wood for the school at the Bank, at the town's expense. It was also voted, that a school be kept two months in the year on the north side of Islington creek.

The third town school house was that erected in School street, in 1751. It was removed several years since to give place to the Bartlett school house. The original structure, modified into a dwelling-house, is still to be seen on the east side of Auburn street, No. 15, the most southerly house now standing there.

In days before newspapers were printed, there were but few opportunities for learning to spell. The following we take from our town records, as specimens of the entries two centuries ago. The town clerk had heard of such a place as Boston, but had probably never seen it in print.

In 1663—It was "voted that the Selectmen have power to lay out thé hiwasė for the town."

1663, Sept. 3.—"At a generell town meten this day, the towen in generell have referede the case of Goodwife Evens to the selectmen in case she bee sent from Borstorne Jale, consarnen hir keepen in the towne or senden hir to hir husband."

We find by another record that Mrs. Evans had been charged with witchcraft.

When we look at the limited means of education enjoyed by our ancestors a century ago, and compare their opportunities with those now enjoyed, it should excite a more determined zeal in our young men to be useful according to the better circumstances in which they are placed.

## RAMBLE XIII.

Newcastle—the Jaffrey residence—Atkinson—Church yard—The old Cemetery—John and Abigail Frost—Rev. John Blunt—Funeral items—Capt. John Blunt and family—Cromwell anecdote—Newcastle pastors.

UNTIL 1693, Newcastle was a part of Portsmouth—and if we can estimate the proportion which that part held to the whole from the standing of the early residents of the island, we must call it a valuable portion. As we pass the bridges which now unite the two places, the eye is feasted with the continual change of rich and refreshing land and water scenery, and we enter upon the spot where were once the homes of the ignoble Gov. Cranfield and his associate, Judge Barefoot—of the no less celebrated Judge Charles Story—of Councillor Stileman—of those Honorables, Sampson and Jacob Sheafe, Theodore Atkinson, George Jaffrey, and some other individuals whose names were conspicuous in their day.

On the south part of the island, about a mile from Fort Constitution, may now be seen the early Jaffrey residence. This original mansion was erected about one hundred and eighty years ago. The place near which it stands is now called *Jerry's* Point. This name is no doubt a corruption of that of the original proprietor, and should be *Jaffrey's* Point. The house is kept in good repair, and, if no accident occurs, in a score of years will enter upon its third century. It must have been regarded a noble structure in its day. On the land of Mrs. Card some ruins still remain of the old Atkinson house, where it is said the General Court has been convened. There are many old moss covered hovels, which might have been places of renown in early days, but their history is now hidden, and even the old cellar where Cranfield stored his wine cannot now be pointed out.

Here is the neat little Church edifice, around which is

a white open fence, enclosing a refreshing green spot, handsomely laid out with gravel walks, mounds, flower beds, and ornamented with trees, shrubs, vines and flowers. And in its midst, bearing the date of 1856, is a handsome marble obelisk to perpetuate the memory of those who have been buried beneath that ocean which here lies open to the eye. Let us read the inscriptions. First on the north side:

"To the Memory of Citizens of Newcastle lost at sea. 'I saw the dead, small and great, stand before God—and the sea gave up the dead which were in it.' *Rev.* 20: 12, 13."

On the east and west sides are records which show how large a number of the inhabitants in the last eleven years have met with the sad experience of the perils of an ocean life. Here are their names:

"Ebenezer Yeaton, aged 52: Edward Martin, 51; William Amazeen, 49; John H. Gerrish, 33; James P. Baker, 30; Samuel Hall, 15; lost with the Inez, near the Isle of Sable, April 1847.

Benjamin Trefethen, aged 34; Benjamin Hunt, 33; Wm. Amazeen, 24; Nath'l B. Davis, 20; perished on the Balerma, near Prince Edward's Island, in the storm of Oct. 3d, 1851.

Charles Smith, aged 20, lost from the Mexico from Boston for West Port, N. S., Oct. 1851.

Calvin D. White, aged 21; lost from the Eliza, from Boston for Baltimore, Nov. 17th, 1854."

The side towards the ocean is yet blank—and many an ocean rover has been led to think of the chances of his own name's being recorded on it.

On the opposite side of the street is a more ancient enclosure, the resting place of some who were once the life and pride of the village. Here, among the numerous old monuments, is one which might receive some notice even in such a place as Mount Auburn. It is inscribed to ABIGAIL, the lovely daughter of Hon. JOHN FROST, who died in 1742, aged twenty four. Her monument presents a specimen of sculpture rarely excelled, probably the work of a foreign artist. Near the top is a group of figures in bold relief. In the centre a beautiful female—on the right a lofty pillar, a flame waving from the capital—below, an anchor and cable—and near it, a female half-reclining, in her hand a branch of olive—on the left among blooming roses, an angelic visitant, bearing in her hand a splendid coronet. Beneath is the following inscription:

> "Released from cares, at rest she lies,
> Where peaceful slumbers close her eyes.
> Her *Faith* all trials did endure,
> Like a strong *pillar*, firm and sure.
> Did adverse winds tempestuous roll?
> *Hope* was the *Anchor* of the soul.
> We, by the *Olive* in her hand,
> Her peaceful end may understand.
> And by the *Coronet* is shown,
> *Virtue*, at last, shall wear the *Crown*."

This is rare lore for a tomb stone—far, far above what can be found among many acres of grave stones in more extensive cemeteries. How appropriate to the scenery are the fifth and sixth lines. Who could thus have written more than a century ago, when epitaphs were matters of literary curiosity rather than of sterling worth? This question is readily answered by the respected pastor, by whose care not only the spiritual wants but the present outward adornings of the sanctuary are so well attended to. The writer was probably Mrs. Jane Turell, the daughter of Rev. Dr. Colman of Brattle street church in Boston. She was the first wife of Rev. E. Turell of Medford, of whom some account will be found in Prof. Brooks' excellent work on Medford. Mr. Turell's second wife was Jane, the youngest sister of Sir Wm. Pepperell.

Among the men of eminence in this ancient town, early in the last century, Hon. John Frost held a high rank. He was a native of Kittery, Me., born in 1681, and was the son of Major Charles Frost (who was slain by the Indians, on the Sabbath, July 4th, 1697, as he was returning from meeting), and grandson of Nicholas Frost, an emigrant from England, born in Tiverton, about the year 1595, and settled at Sturgeon Creek, in Eliot, in

1636, where he died in 1663. This grandson, Hon. John Frost, in 1702 married Mary Pepperell, sister of Sir William, the Baronet.

Hon. John Frost and his lady were early established at Newcastle, where he soon rose to eminence. He was a member of His Majesty's Council; at one time commanded a British ship-of-war, afterwards pursued the profession of a merchant, and was much distinguished and highly useful in civil life. His place of residence was on an eminence, westerly of the Prescott mansion (now the alms-house), commanding a view of the spacious harbor, the river and its table lands, with the lofty Agamenticus in the distance. Some remains of his extensive wharf may yet be traced.

His family was numerous and highly respectable—one of whom was Madam Sarah Blunt, born in 1713, consort of Rev. John Blunt, third pastor of the church in Newcastle; and after his decease, the wife of Hon. Judge Hill of South Berwick, Me. Hon. John Frost died February 25, 1732, in the fifty-first year of his age. It is for their daughter that the above well-designed memorial was erected more than a century ago.

Near by it is another moss covered monument, which bears unmistakable evidence that the same poet who sketched the above chaste epitaph, has also, in as smooth and as strong lines, drawn another marked portraiture. Let us read it.

"To the memory of Rev'd JOHN BLUNT, Pastor of the Church of Christ of this Town who died Aug. 7, 1748, in the 42d year of his age, whose body lies here interred, this stone is erected.

Soft is the sleep of saints, in peace they lie,
They rest in silence, but they never die;
From these dark graves, their flesh refined shall rise
And in immortal bloom ascend the skies.
Then shall thine eyes, dear BLUNT! thine hands, thy tongue—
In nicer harmony each member strung—
Resume their warm devotion, and adore
Him, in whose service, they were joined before."

Can any one tell us more of this servant of God, whom no mortal at present living has seen, but whose remembrance is beautifully chiseled in the stone? Here comes the patriarch of the isle, whose four score years have scarcely yet marked him beyond middle life. Capt. Oliver is as well acquainted with our subject as any one we could meet with, for he tells us that seventy years ago he terminated a three years residence in the family of Capt. John Blunt, one of the two sons left by the village pastor, and the father of the five ship-masters of that name who for many years sailed from Portsmouth.

William Blunt, the ancestor of the family, came from England in 1634, and settled in Andover, Mass. His son William (2), lived in Andover, had three sons, William Samuel and Hanborough, and died in 1709, aged sixty-seven. His grandson, William (3), born 1671, died in 1737. He had two sons, David, born 1699, and John, born 1706. John graduated at Harvard in 1727, and was ordained in Newcastle in 1732. As above stated, he married Sarah Frost, daughter of Hon. John Frost, and died in 1748, at the age of forty-two. He appears to have been a highly approved preacher and useful man. On his death, the town voted to continue his salary to his widow for nine months, and to pay £200 old tenor (thirty or forty dollars) on account of funeral expenses. Some of the items were—for coffin £66, for rings £30, for gloves £28, for grave £2, for rum £2 10s, for tobacco pipes £1. The use of rum as a cordial to the afflicted, and of tobacco as an assuager of grief, was in those days deemed indispensable.

Rev. John Blunt had three sons, William, Charles and John; and three daughters, Sarah F., Abigail F., and Dorothy. William married a Slade, and afterwards a March, and had twelve children. Among them was Edmund M. Blunt. Charles died unmarried. John married Hannah Sherburne, and had nine children.

Sarah F. married Thomas Furber of Portsmouth, and had three sons. Abigail F. married William Parsons of Alfred, and had nine children, among them Dr. Usher Parsons. Dorothy married a Mr. Campbell of Deer Island, and was the mother of a distinguished gentleman of that name of large estate who died at Newburyport not long since.

John, (the third son of the clergyman) was a shipmaster and farmer. He owned and occupied the peninsula at Little Harbor, which was afterwards owned by Jacob Sheafe and made up about one-half of the Sheafe farm. It was here that Capt. Thomas Oliver resided with the family, and in common with the sons had his seat in the unfinished room to receive instruction from the master of the family. It was here that those five distinguished shipmasters, the sons of John, received their primary instruction—recited their advanced lessons, and from this house they all graduated and entered upon the world. The oldest son, bearing the family name, John, born in 1757, was lost at sea during the revolutionary war. The other sons were Capt. George F. Blunt, born in 1761, who resided at the corner of Vaughan and Hanover streets; Capt. Robert W. Blunt, born in 1763, resided in No. 24 Washington street; Capt. Charles Blunt, born in 1768, resided in 57 Pleasant street; Capt. Mark S. Blunt, born in 1770, died at sea; and Capt. Oliver C. Blunt, born in 1774, resided in the house now occupied by John N. Handy, 88 State street. The several houses in which they lived were built by them. Of the daughters, Sarah married Mark Simes, Esq., postmaster. Frances and Mary Ann were unmarried.

The family attended meeting regularly at Newcastle. It was in revolutionary times when these boys were born, and the resolution and spirit which characterized their after life was rightly inherited from their father, who is described as a short man, with a bald head, covered with a wig, of full body, and carrying a cane which came down with firmness as he stepped. On the birth of the sixth boy, after a counsel between the parents, *William* was the name decided upon, and as usual the child was taken to the church at Newcastle for christening. The Rev. Joseph Stevens of Kittery, who that day officiated, leaned on the side of royalty, and gave a sermon expressive of his sentiments, in which Cromwell, as a revolutionist, was denounced in no measured terms. This was grating to the feelings of the patriotic Blunt, and he was determined to resent it. The child is handed up and with it the name, *Oliver Cromwell.* "What did you say?" said the wonder-struck preacher, hoping that he had misunderstood. In the tones of a boatswain, the reply filled the church "OLIVER CROMWELL!" There was no misunderstanding now, the babe was christened, and hence the name of Oliver Cromwell Blunt.

Edmund M. Blunt of New York, the author of the American Coast Pilot, and John Blunt, a merchant of Brooklyn, formerly of this city, son of Charles, are among the descendants of the old pastor.

Looking into the church, the desk of which for many years has been filled by Rev. Lucius Alden, we find among its neat fixtures a black walnut pulpit, the gift of two of the descendants of the old pastors. Its front panel presents a record of its pastors, on a plain, highly polished and beautiful marble slab. The inscription, in deep cut letters, is as follows:

Rev. JOHN EMERSON died Jan. 21, 1732, aged 62.
Rev. WILLIAM SHURTLEFF died May 9, 1747, aged 58.
Rev. JOHN BLUNT died Aug. 7, 1748, aged 42.
Rev. DAVID ROBINSON died Nov. 18, 1749, aged 33.
Rev. STEPHEN CHASE died Jan. 1778, aged 72.
Rev. OLIVER NOBLE died Dec. 15, 1792, aged 56.
PASTORS OF THIS CHURCH.
"The memory of the just is blessed."

## RAMBLE XIV.

Rev. John Emerson—Rev. William Shurtleff—Trials of a Pastor—Rev. Job Strong and his successors at the South church.

At the residence of Capt. Charles E. Blunt, in Gardner street, is a finely executed portrait of Rev. John Emerson, who was the first minister settled at Newcastle, in 1703, after it was separated from Portsmouth. He was a man of fine countenance, and, in the full wig of the day, of very commanding appearance. It is no wonder that such a man, when in the city of London in 1708 (when this portrait was painted), should have received the marked attentions of Queen Anne. He returned to Newcastle and preached there till 1712, when he was dismissed. In the course of a year, when the old meeting house below the south bridge, in Portsmouth, was vacated by Mr. Rodgers' society for the occupancy of the new North Church, Rev. Mr. Emerson became the pastor of those who did not wish to remove, and in 1715 was installed over the society. He continued to preach there very acceptably and with good results during his life. His last public service was a prayer on the frame of the new South Church, when it was erecting in 1731. He died June 21, 1732, aged sixty-two. His wife, Mary Barter of Salem, whose portrait stands near her husband's, was not possessed of much personal beauty, but her rare virtues are treasured in the memory of her descendants. She was the mother of five daughters: Mary was the wife of Francis Winkley, of Kittery; Ann, of Stephen Greenleaf of Portsmouth; Sarah, of Mr. Davis of Portsmouth; Dorothy, of Elihu Gunnison of Kittery; and Martha, of Mr. Flint of Plaistow.

The Rev. William Shurtleff was ordained at Newcastle the same year in which Mr. Emerson was dismissed, 1712. He was a son of William Shurtleff, of Plymouth, in Massachusetts. His grandfather, William Shurtleff, of Marshfield, was killed by lightning in 1666; while two children in his lap and one between his knees, and his wife by his side remained uninjured. The Rev. Mr. Shurtleff married Mary Atkinson, sister of Theodore Atkinson, but had no children. As he succeeded Mr. Emerson at Newcastle, so upon Mr. Emerson's death he became his successor at Portsmouth, and was installed over the South Church, Feb. 21, 1733; his connection with Newcastle having been dissolved the year before. He spent the remainder of his days at Portsmouth, and died May 9, 1747.

He was eminent for piety and pastoral fidelity. During his ministry in Portsmouth, he baptized more than seven hundred, and admitted one hundred and thirty communicants to the church.

Mr. Alden remarks, that "his name will long be mentioned with respect, for his uncommon meekness and patience under *great trials*, and for his distinguished piety, talents and pastoral fidelity." His troubles were of the domestic kind. Mrs. Shurtleff might have been beautiful in person, but was far from possessing that amiable disposition which is the better ornament. Neglectful in attendence on his wants, see the devoted pastor patiently bending over the coals of his kitchen fire, broiling a fish for dinner, which she has told him should not be cooked.

"Has this been salted, Mr. Shurtleff?" she enquires.

He replies, "It has." "Well, it needs peppering, then, said his prim wife, and taking up a shovel of ashes, the fish and his hopes of dinner disappear beneath the liberal peppering. One Sabbath, he in a retired room is in close study to the last minute before the church service, in preparation for the duties of his holy office. He is ready to depart—but lo! the door is fastened, and no one is in hearing. The bell tolls and tolls to thrice the usual time; the lady of the pastor is sitting primly and quietly in her seat, and the audience are all wondering what delays the pastor's attendance. The deacon enquires of the lady; she says he was at home when she left. A committee is despatched; the barricade at the study door is removed, and the whole matter at once explained. The indulgent pastor asked that the matter might be kept quiet, and it is left for the rambler, about one hundred and twenty years after the event, to give to-day the matter to the public—even at the risk of incurring censure for having and expressing no very exalted opinion of one of the departed. It is said that Richard Baxter married that he might receive discipline and have his virtues brought into exercise. Mrs. S. would have been an excellent wife for such a man. We are informed by one who knows, that, when her husband died, she appeared at his funeral in deep mourning, whereupon her brother, Hon. Theodore Atkinson, seized hold of her dress with some violence, and tore it, telling her that she who had been such a thorn in his side, should not now add to the offense the hypocrisy of pretending to mourn for him.

In the Historical Rooms in Boston is a well executed portrait of Mr. Shurtleff, in surplice and bands. The characteristics of the expression of his countenance are gravity, devotion and apostolic meekness.

Rev. Job Strong, a native of Northampton, Mass., was the successor of Mr. Shurtleff as pastor of the South Church, over which he was settled June 28, 1749. Was married December, 1750, to Abigail, daughter of Peter Gilman of Exeter. Their infant son died Sept. 28, 1751. The next forenoon he preached from these words: "Though I walk through the valley of the shadow of death I will fear no evil." At noon he was seized with bilious colic, and on Monday died, at the age of twenty-seven. His widow, in 1755, married Rev. Woodbridge Odlin of Exeter, and was the mother of Dudley, Woodbridge, Peter, John, Elizabeth, Abigail, (first wife of Hon. Nathaniel Gilman,) Mary Ann and Charlotte.

The successor of Mr. Strong was Rev. Samuel Haven, D. D., in 1752. From 1799 to 1805, Rev. Timothy Alden was his colleague, Rev. Nathan Parker, D. D., was pastor from 1808 to 1833, in which year Rev. A. P. Peabody, D. D., was ordained.* The three last pastorates have thus extended over a full century, after deducting those years in which a colleague was employed. A striking illustration of the affection of a people, and the correspondingly strong attachment of their spiritual teachers.

---

## RAMBLE XV.

Old House on the Corner—High School House site—Daniel House—Mark Hunking and Hunking Wentworth.

THE mansion removed from the corner of Daniel and Chapel streets, to give place for the high school house, bore marks of antiquity, although kept in a good state of preservation. It was a large, gambrel roofed house, of two high stories, with four square rooms on the floor, and an ell on Chapel street. Many fruitless inquiries have been made for the age and history of the erection of the old mansion. Not a solitary memorandum could be found chalked on any part of the frame, or any mark to show that the builders were ambitious of remembrance beyond their day. It is said that the house was built about one hundred and forty years ago, by Capt. Thomas Daniel, a merchant, for whom, in after time, the street was named. It was more than a century ago occupied by Hon. Mark H. Wentworth. The spacious arrangements for the wine-cellar, show that in old times ample provision was made to lay in a year's supply to meet any emergency. We cannot find any definite date about the premises, except "1752" on the brick wall on Chapel

* Rev. Dr. Peabody was succeeded by Rev. James De Normandie in 1862, who is still the pastor, in 1873.

street, which was probably put up by Mr. Wentworth long after the house was erected.

But if the builder is now unknown, not so the family which afterwards occupied the mansion. Mark Hunking Wentworth, who resided there until his death in 1785, was the son of John Wentworth, the Lieut. Governor of New Hampshire, who died in 1730,—and the father of John Wentworth, who received his commission as Governor of this province in 1767. Benning Wentworth, who was Governor from 1741 to 1767, was a brother to Mark Hunking Wentworth.

That "old house on the corner" was a mansion of the highest class—and even then those noble elms, which within a few years have gladdened the eyes of all who have looked upon their green foliage in passing from Market square to the Navy Yard landing,—even in revolutionary times, afforded shade to many who passed under them.

On the second day of August, 1855, the remains of the "old house on the corner" were sold at public auction. The big elm tree, which had lost its vitality and stood like a gigantic skeleton of olden time, was put under the hammer—but alas for its departed glory, the highest bid was only fifteen cents!

And so the "old house on the corner" has passed away, and we shall look in vain for its sombre front and projecting portico. Never again will its old tenants be permitted to tread its pleasant halls. No more will the wind whistle down its massive chimneys and whirl the sand in fantastic wreaths across the hard floor. No more will the rising sun throw his beams upon it, and no more will its setting cast pleasant glances through its antique cupola.*

* Although it has been a common opinion that the Daniel house was located on the spot now occupied by the high school house, yet there are some antiquarians who locate it two lots further east, on the present site of the Danielson boarding house, and say the "old house on the corner" was built by Wentworth, about 1720. As we cannot decide in this matter, it is right in the absence of proof that we should not speak of the location with certainty, although we think it was as we have given it.

The Committee of Safety, of which Hunking Wentworth (uncle of Mark H.) was chairman in 1774, met at the house next west of the North church, to discuss the best mode of procedure to throw off foreign tyranny. While his uncle was thus engaged, the Governor of the province was secretly employing agents to hire carpenters to construct barracks for the royal soldiers in Boston. Patriotism led the uncle to lay aside his personal feelings, kind and liberal though they ever were, and pronounce the person guilty of such conduct "an enemy to the community." The Governor then held the mansion on Pleasant street, now occupied by Eben. Wentworth. In 1775, while the manifestations of devotion to the cause of independence were growing warmer and warmer under the uncle's influence, a field-piece was placed by the people before the door of the Governor, who fled through his back yard to the fort. The mob entered the mansion, disturbed the whole premises,—even the ladies' toilets were robbed of the *rouge*, etc.,—and to this day the broken marble chimney piece is preserved in its place for the inspection of the curious visitor.

## RAMBLE XVI.

### The Creeks—First Wentworth House—Samuel and John Wentworth.

VERY different must have been the appearance of the scenery on our river in the early days of the settlement from what is now presented. Our creeks, north and south, (now mill-ponds,) as well as the Sagamore creek, were then open and deep enough for the vessels of the day to sail in; and as these creeks were successively visitited, (each doubtless abounding in fish,) their location must indeed have been a most inviting feature to induce a settlement. There was also then another smaller, but scarcely less beautiful creek, extending up into the south part of the town, with green banks, and a good depth of water. We wish we could give it a name better fitted to its earlier days, but can only designate it as the Puddle Dock of modern times. In the last century the water not only flowed up beyond its present bounds, but at high tides small boats passed from it over Pleasant street, near the Universalist church, to the South creek.

It was on the south side of this dock that the first *Wentworth house*, of which we have any record, was built, and that house still stands. It is known as the house of the first Gov. John Wentworth, who was married in the year 1693 or 1694, and then occupied the premises. It is on the south side of the dock, at the north end of Manning street.

Samuel Wentworth (the father of the first Governor John and son of Elder William Wentworth of Dover) was the first of the name in Portsmouth. He died of the small pox in 1690. In the year 1670, our town records show him licensed with "libertie to entertain strangers and sell and brew beare." At that time the vicinity of the "Point of Graves" was the principal business part of the Bank, and directly opposite, on the northern shore of the dock, near the present eastern terminus of Jefferson street, was the original "Great House." Some old citizens who have died in our day, recollect the time when the mart of business was in the vicinity of Water street.

The size of the house would seem to indicate that it was built by Samuel for a public house; but of this we are not certain, for in 1678 he appears to have been a resident of Newcastle. There is little doubt of its occupancy by his son John, afterwards Lieut. Governor, at his marriage, in 1693. The avenue extending south from the house, now called Manning street, until within the last twenty years was called Wentworth street. Gov. John, it is said, owned all the land on the west side of the street to where the South church was afterwards erected, and then on the north side of Whidden street to the mill-pond. It is very probable that the Wentworth premises extended so far north as to take in the land on which the last Gov. John Wentworth built the mansion in which Eben. Wentworth now resides.

The old Wentworth house at the dock yet presents a good exterior, and an examination of it shows that it was built in a most substantial manner. The beams on which the floor rests are twelve by eighteen inches, and timber to correspond may be seen in various parts of the house, all now in good preservation. The chambers and stairway are wainscoted, some of the panels of clear boards being thirty-eight inches in width. The size of the base of the chimney is ten feet by thirteen; the bricks are set in clay. Spikes of a foot in length and bearded are as freely used as if the house had been built to "stem tornadoes and the storms defy."

This house was not only the residence of a Governor of truly exemplary life, but was also the birth-place, among his sixteen children, of another Governor, Benning Wentworth, in the year 1695. Lieut. Gov. John Wentworth's commission, given in 1717, was signed by Joseph Addison, the writer of the "Spectator," as Secretary of State. He held his commission until his death in 1730, at the age of fifty-nine. One of his sons, Daniel, was the father of George, who was the father of our present fellow citizen, Eben. Wentworth.

This house, probably as ancient as any in Portsmouth, has been owned and occupied by William A. Vaughan for over twenty years, and for about twenty years previously by the Misses Purcell. As Gov. George Vaughan, son of Major William Vaughan, was a predecessor of the first Gov. Wentworth in the chief magistracy of New Hampshire, it is but right that one bearing the same name, and of the same lineage, should now hold possession of the once royal mansion.

---

## RAMBLE XVII.

Gov. Benning Wentworth—His seat at Little Harbor —Its present state—Molly Pitman—Romantic Marriage of the Governor with Martha Hilton—Col. Michael Wentworth—Washington's Visit there—Cushing family—Residence of Gov. John Wentworth, 2d.

We will now turn our steps to the residence of the next Governor, at Little Harbor. Benning Wentworth, in 1741, received the commission of Governor of New Hampshire, and entered upon the duties of his office with much *eclat.* It is probable that he resided at the homestead for several years, as it was not until 1750 that he built the retired and romantic residence at Little Harbor —about two miles from the centre of business—which became his residence ever after, to the termination of the twenty-five years during which he held his commission. His merits or demerits as a Governor we shall not discuss, but only draw attention to some of the incidents which belong to the locality, and give interest to the old walls when visitors look upon them.

The house is generally of two stories in height, with wings forming three sides of a square. Its style of architecture is non-descript. It appears a group of buildings, such as from time to time may have been attached to one another, of no particular height or size. It contained formerly fifty-two rooms—a part of the house was a few years since removed, leaving now forty-five apartments.

The house is so hid behind an eminence that it is not visible from the road, and cannot be seen until you enter the gate. On the north and east the prospect is open to the water. The cellar is extensive, and for safety the Governor kept his horses there in time of danger. A troop of thirty horses could here be accommodated.

The mansion has yet the Council Chamber, an imposing, high studded room, where meetings important to the State and nation were held by the Council for many years. By its side opens the Billiard room—where the ancient spinet of the family is still located—and in its corner the *buffet* which has held many a full and empty punch bowl. The little side-rooms where cards and other games were long ago played by the illustrious visitants of this hospitable home, still remain.

At the entrance of the Council Chamber the racks for twelve guns still remain, which were for guards when occasion required. The Council Chamber is finished in the best style of the last century—the carved work around the mantle being more than a year's labor with the knife and chisel of a carpenter.

Around the room are a variety of pictures of the family of the present residents, among them a choice painting by Copley of the beautiful Dorothy Quincy, who became the wife of John Hancock, and afterwards Madam Scott. She was connected with the family of Mr. Jacob Sheafe, and made frequent visits to Portsmouth. There were also in the room the elegant portraits of Secretary Waldron, grandson of the renowned Richard Waldron killed by the Indians at Dover, and his son Westbrook, and others of nearer kin to the present residents of this mansion. The closely jointed smooth white floor, "none the worse" for a century's wear,—these all give to this ancient hall a choice venerableness which the antiquarian can fully appreciate. The many curiosities of the room fill with interest an hour's visit.

Ascending a short flight of steps, we enter the spacious parlor—still as rich in its original finish as it was a hundred years ago. As we sat upon the sofa, it required no great stretch of imagination to bring back some scenes herewith connected, which occurred while the house was yet new.

Gov. Benning Wentworth by his first wife had three sons, all of whom died while he was in office, the last in 1759—leaving him a widower and childless.

The Governor in his loneliness saw a young lady to whom he took a fancy. He proposed marriage—but Molly Pitman had given her heart to another, who, although of humble life, she esteemed more essential to her happiness than the honor and riches of the Governor,—and so she married Richard Shortridge, a mechanic, in preference. The Governor, however, did not forget the indignity of her refusal, and yet hoped by adopting David's unwise example, to conquer. An English frigate was in the harbor, and not long after the marriage a press gang was sent to the house of Shortridge, which forcibly took him on board, and from the endearments of home. For seven long years did his faithful wife mourn his absence. He was removed from ship to ship, until one day he related to the chief officer the circumstances under which he was impressed. "Run off, and we won't pursue you," was the reply; and he soon availed himself of the privilege. His return brought happiness to his faithful partner, whose virtue was not to be invaded by the most tempting allurements of wealth. Their descendants are yet among us.

Let us turn for a moment from this to another illustrative picture. The scene is in what is now Court street. Mrs. Stavers, the wife of the first mail carrier, standing in the door of her boarding-house, is looking upon a careless, laughing, bare-footed girl, lugging a pail of water in the street, with a dress scarcely sufficient to cover her decently, and exclaiming: "You Pat! you Pat! why do you go looking so? You should be ashamed to be seen in the street." "No matter how I look, I shall ride in my chariot yet, marm," was her hopeful reply.

Martha Hilton afterwards left home and went to live in the Governor's mansion, at Little Harbor, doing the work of the kitchen and keeping the house in order, much to the Governor's satisfaction. The Governor has invited a dinner party, and with many other guests, in his cocked hat comes the beloved Rev. Arthur Brown, of the Episcopal church. The dinner is served up in a style becoming the Governor's table; the wine is of good quality, as all present are well qualified to say, and as tobacco clouds circle to the ceiling good humor enlivens the board. There is a whisper from the Governor to a messenger, and at his summons Martha Hilton comes in from that door on the west of the parlor, and, with blushing countenance, stands in front of the fireplace. She seems heedless of the fire—she does not appear to have brought anything in, nor does she seem to be looking for anything to carry out—there she stands! a blushing damsel of twenty summers,—for what, no visitor can tell.

The Governor, bleached by the frosts of sixty winters, rises: "Mr. Brown, I wish you to marry me." "To whom?" asked his pastor, in wondering surprise. "To this lady," was the reply. The Rector stood confounded. The Governor became imperative: "As the Governor of New Hampshire, I *command* you to marry me!" The ceremony was then duly performed, and from that time Martha Hilton became Lady Wentworth.

She could not, perhaps, boast of as noble descent as her husband, but her change of position had a speedy effect in exalting her dignity. But a few days after her marriage, she dropped her ring upon this very floor. She called her servant to pick it up. The servant, however, took occasion to be near sighted, and would not find it until her mistress put her finger down to touch it. After the wire-edge of elevation was worn off, she made a most excellent wife; and when the Governor died, in 1770, he gave her his entire estate. Her two sons had died in infancy before their father.

The widow did not long mourn in solitude here. Friends came to this parlor to impart consolation. And most acceptable was that consolation which was soon found in the offer of the hand and heart of Michael Wentworth, a retired Colonel of the British army, who came from England in 1767. They were married and had one daughter, Martha Wentworth.

In 1789, when Washington came to Portsmouth, he visited the Wentworth mansion by water, was received with characteristic hospitality by Col. Michael Wentworth and lady, and came to the town by land. The Colonel was a high liver, and spent nearly all his own and his wife's property. He prided himself on his horsemanship. One afternoon at six o'clock, he called at the house of Mr. Jacob Sheafe, in Portsmouth, bearing the compliments of Madam Hancock, whom he left well at Boston at eight that morning, having performed the whole journey on horse back. It was a great feat in those days. In 1795 he died suddenly in New York, it is supposed by suicide. His last words were—"I have had my cake and ate it"—referring to the bankrupt state of his affairs.

*Sir* John Wentworth, an Englishman, who was a lawyer in Portsmouth in 1800, married Martha Wentworth, and they occupied the house at Little Harbor until 1816, when they went to Europe. He died in France some years since, and his wife died in London in 1851.

In 1817, the Little Harbor estate was purchased by Charles Cushing, whose widow, a daughter of the late Jacob Sheafe, with her family, still resides there. By their kind courtesy visitors are permitted to view the romantic premises which are associated with matters of no little historic interest.

We will close this ramble with a short call at the mansion of Gov. John Wentworth, who went into office in 1767, and went out at the time of the Revolution. This house is on Pleasant street, at the head of Washington street. We shall have occasion in another ramble to say more of the original occupant. As we have already said, it was in front of this mansion, in 1775, that the populace, in pursuit of Fenton, a royalist, who sought refuge there, brought a field piece and threatened to bombard the house unless he was delivered up. There was, however, no dangerous powder or ball provided. He was given up, and the Governor, not feeling secure, immediately vacated the house and took refuge in the fort. In the parlor there are yet some marks of damage by the invaders. This room still presents the same aspect in which the Governor left it, seventy-five years ago. The elegant plush on the walls looks as fresh as though it had been on the room but a few years, and the various decorations of former times are preserved with remarkable care. In the extensive hall are displayed the full length portraits of the Governors, and some others who bear the family name. The garden, extending from Pleasant street to the river, is a very pleasant locality, with handsomely arranged walks and agreeable shade. At the bottom of the garden, beneath a summer-house, a refreshing bathing-room is provided, which opens to the river. The present occupant and owner is Eben. Wentworth, Esq.,* born in 1780, great-grandson of the first Governor John—a most excellent sample of the old school gentlemen, and a memento of those who have there been earlier residents.

It is a remarkable circumstance that the only specimens of the architectural taste of the three Governors bearing the name of Wentworth, should have continued through a century in these three old houses to the present time.

* Eben. Wentworth died in August, 1860.

## RAMBLE XVIII.

**Atkinson House—Theodore Atkinson—His style of life—Descendants—Legacy to the Church.**

As we pass down Court street there is to be seen on the north side, at No. 41, separated by only one lot from Atkinson street, the sad remains of a once handsome edifice. It was erected about a century and a quarter ago, by THEODORE ATKINSON, whose name stands conspicuous in our State history as a Councillor, Judge and Secretary of the Province. He was the son of Theodore Atkinson of Newcastle, where he was born in 1697. He graduated at Harvard in 1718. He returned to Newcastle, where he served as Lieutenant at the Fort for two years. He was then appointed Clerk of the Court and studied law. Up to 1733 he had been the Representative of Newcastle in the General Court, and in 1734 was admitted to a seat in the Council. Probably about this time he built the house on Court street above referred to, was then married, and made this his home to the close of his life in 1779. For many years Col. Atkinson had command of the first regiment; he was also Collector, Naval Officer and Sheriff of the Province. He was also delegate to the Congress at Albany in 1754, and held various other offices of trust. He was a man of great popularity, being of a lively disposition, social and fond of merriment.

In 1746, when John Tufton Mason sold his title to New Hampshire, Theodore Atkinson bought one-fifth of the whole State; that is, of such parts as had not previously been granted or settled.

Col. Atkinson's stable, which was on the north-east corner of Court and Atkinson streets, was furnished with the best horses, and his coach was *the coach* of the town. His house, though not quite so extensive, was finished on the model of Sir William Pepperell's. The hall and stairway are similar, and it was probably built about the same time. The original Corinthian caps to the columns of the front door were finely executed, and are still in tolerable preservation. We have a relic of the mantle carving, a head forming the cap of a pillar, presented to us by Leonard Cotton, the present owner of the premises.

Col. Atkinson was a man of much wealth, and in this house was probably to be found more silver ware than in any other house in New Hampshire. An old lady who died in 1858, said that in her youth she spent several years in the family, and that two whole days were required to make a general cleaning of the silver ware. An iron-grated closet in the chamber displayed the shining treasure beyond the reach of robbers.

In early times and until about the year 1770, the garden of the Atkinson house was on both sides of the street. The land now covered by the house of T. D. Bailey and the old Stavers house, to Jefferson street, was the front garden of Col. Atkinson.

He gave the name to the town of Atkinson in this State, as a large portion of it belonged to him. The town of *Francestown* and the adjoining town of *Deering*, in this State were named for his son's wife, *Frances Deering* Wentworth,—not named by him, however, but by Gov. John Wentworth, after his marriage.

Theodore Atkinson died in 1779, at the age of eighty-two years. His wife (Hannah Wentworth, a sister of Gov. Benning) died several years before him. After his death, most of his property by bequest came into possession of Mr. William King of Dover, who added Atkinson to his name and was afterwards known as Hon. William K. Atkinson. The country residence of the latter was on that eminence near the northern end of Piscataqua Bridge, called "Atkinson's hill"—commanding one of the most beautiful prospects in the State. Wm. K. Atkinson married Abigail Pickering, daughter of Judge John P. and sister of the late Jacob S. Pickering.

Hon. Theodore Atkinson left a legacy of about a thousand dollars to the Episcopal church in this city, to be expended in bread to be distributed on Sunday to the poor of the parish. This distribution of more than a dollar's value in bread every Sabbath has now been regularly made for about eighty years—in which time about five thousand dollars have thus been expended, and the well appropriated fund is unimpaired.

As the relation of some rather romantic incidents connected with this locality would occupy too much space for this ramble, we will close it with some extracts from a poem communicated to the Portsmouth Journal by T. B. Aldrich, in 1853. The poet spent many of his youthful days in the house opposite the Atkinson mansion.

That Old House stands alone,
A queer and crumbling pile;
And tho' its shattered gables tell—
Like the vibrations of a distant bell—
Of days and years, mayhap of centuries flown,
I cannot help but smile.

That Old House stands alone.
Over the windows and the oaken door,
There's something in the mouldings that's so quaint;
No knocker rings upon those pannels more;
Some urchin *rung* it off!
In these degenerate days an urchin is no saint,
But dares to laugh and scoff
At things that bear the holy taint
And impress of the past.

Its windows boast not one whole pane of glass;
And tho' it pains me, let it still be said,
That I have broken many a square, alas!
Nor 'squared accounts' with Cotton, I'm afraid.
I'm grieving now I ever threw a stone,
They used to echo thro' the dismal rooms
With such a mournful, melancholy moan.
Besides, the windows always blushed so red,
When sunset stooped to catch the winged gulls,
Or stripped him, shameless, for his ocean bed;
But now *they seem like eyeless skulls*
*Of some poor mortals dead!*

The Old House stands alone;
But years and years ago
Near the east corner an old elm stood;
With time 'twas bent as we 've seen some with woe,
Or famed Napoleon in his thoughtful mood—
It was cut down and used for fire-wood.
I saw them fell it—sorry sight to me,
For I had learned to love it tenderly.
I wept the while; my heart was tender then,
And things like those were sorrows deep for me.
They heard me not; it was mine eyes that spake,
My heart that cried, 'Oh, *Woodman*, spare that tree!'

In that half-rotted elm the Old House lost a friend;
It used to shield it from the snow-storms wild,
And over it with seeming fondness bend,
Just as a mother o'er her *sickly* child.
There was between that aged house and tree
A sure and palpable affinity.
The elm would bend to it with such an air
Of sweet anxiety and parental care,
That tho' its branches but appeared to creak,
I would not say those branches did not *speak*.
But it is passed, the loving tree is gone,
The pile remains, decaying all alone.

* * *

That structure seems ideal!
There's such an indistinctness in its form,
I sometimes doubt if really it be real.
So oft its roof hath felt the drenching storm,
So oft it has been danced upon by hail,
That *contour* seems washed out!
And when I view it 'tis with half a doubt,
As dimly through a veil.

Oh, ancient house, thou puttest me in mind
Of my dear grandmother, who on travel bent
Was always sure to leave something behind.
It seems to me that *Time* on flight intent
*Forgot thee* quite, and thus hath left thee
For the prey "of years,"
The food of storm fiends, and to feel the tears

Of cloudlets when they weep.
* * *
When first I oped these eyes, so soon to close,
That antique structure fed my childish gaze;
Its huge brick chimneys like leviathans' arose,
Or *tombstones* telling of departed days.
It was some six, or full eight years ago,
Those dear delapsed chimneys were removed.
Six or eight years? it hardly seemeth so,
(Not easily I forget the things once loved,)
So fresh comes back the memory of my woe.
When I beheld those chimneys dark and tall,
Tottering as if they knew not where to fall,
Bending like topmasts in a sudden squall,
Reeling like Samson when his eyes were out,
Through my half-blind and aching eyes
Each tear I shed was then about
A *three-cent piece* in size.
* * *
Ah, that Old House might tell a startling tale,
Could its cracked wainscots and dark closets speak;
One word might make the boldest lip turn pale,
Or send the heart's blood bubbling to the cheek.
Ere I was born, when my grandsire was young,
A legend curious, rather wild withal,
Around that lonely mansion hung;
And at some future time,
Should I possess a quantity of rhyme,
That legend shall be sung.

Those chambers drear, deserted save by storms,
Shall hear again the pleading lover's sigh;
I'll clutch the past! bring back its phantom forms,
And light with passion many a sightless eye.
* * *
Oh, let me tell thee one thing, trembling house,
That in thy days of former pomp gone by,
When light feet danced where crawls secure the mouse,
And thy bare walls were hung with drapery—
I tell thee truly—when thy haunted halls
Were scenes of bridal, birth and revelry,
And funeral wails resounded in thy walls,
None in those hours of pain and joy gone by
Could love thee then, more fondly now than I.

## RAMBLE XIX.

Theodore Atkinson, Jr.—Marriage—Death—Funeral—Gov. Wentworth's attentions—Mrs. Atkinson a widow but ten days—Style of the times—Their town and country residences—Lake story—His character—Illustrative anecdote—Departure for England.

Hon. Theodore Atkinson had but one child, Theodore Jr., who was born in 1736, and graduated at Harvard in 1757. He was a member of the Council of which his father was President, and was for several years Secretary of the Province. On the 13th of May, 1762, he married Frances Deering Wentworth, daughter of Samuel Wentworth, of Boston, a lady of rare beauty and accomplishments. She was his cousin. Her earlier affections had been placed on another cousin, John Wentworth, who graduated at Harvard College in 1755. John soon after going to England to be absent for an indefinite period, she was wooed and won by Mr. Atkinson; who is described as a mild, obliging and devout man. They lived with his father's family in this old mansion. He was of feeqle health, and in seven years after his marriage, at the early age of thirty-three, departed this life, leaving no children. Two years before his death her early lover, John Wentworth, returned clothed with the regalia of Governor of New Hampshire. Her early affection for him remained unabated, and the Governor frequently honored his uncle and cousin by a social call at this old mansion. At this time there was no building between Court and Pleasant streets to obstruct the sight between the houses of the Governor and Secretary Atkinson, and gossips used to say that signals from one to the other were passed. But as telegraphs have been used for good purposes since, why might they not have been then?

It was on Saturday, the 28th day of October, 1769, that Theodore Atkinson, Jr. departed this life. On Wednesday following the funeral took place. It was a day of public mourning. By order of the Governor, during the moving of the procession from this old house to the family tomb at the Episcopal church, minute guns were fired at the fort at Newcastle, and from on board the ship-of-war Beaver in the harbor. The widow was arrayed in the dark habiliments of mourning, which we presume elicited an intense shower of tears, as the fount was so soon exhausted. The next day the mourner appears in her pew at church as a widow, but that was the last Sabbath of the *widow*. On Monday morning there is a new call for the aid of the milliner—the unbecoming black, new as it was, must be laid aside, and the brighter colors which become a governor's bride, must take their place! There were no sewing machines then, but active fingers did wonders, and on Saturday morning, the 11th of November, just ten days after the funeral, every thing was ready, and there was another movement from this old house to the same church. The blooming widow and the gallant Governor were the leading personages—and the same venerable pastor, Rev. Arthur Brown, who so solemnly had just conveyed "ashes to ashes—dust to dust," sealed the union of the new couple "for better or for worse!" The following extract from the Boston News Letter of Nov. 17th, 1769, of a letter from Portsmouth, dated Nov. 11th, gives a full account of the occurrence:

"This morning His Excellency JOHN WENTWORTH, Esq., our worthy and beloved Governor, was married by the Rev. Mr. Brown to Mrs. FRANCES ATKINSON, widow of the Hon. Theodore Atkinson, Jr. Esq., deceased,—a lady adorned with every accomplishment requisite to make the marriage state agreeable. Long may this amiable and illustrious couple live happily; blessings to each other and all around them in this world, may they be the crown of each other's joys in the next, when the great Governor of all worlds shall make up his jewels—

May this thrice happy, happy pair,
Be heaven's peculiar charge, and care;
Unerring wisdom guide their way;
Their joys increase with each new day,
To the top of bliss beneath the skies!
At some far distant, distant time,
Quit every scene in this low clime,
Rise to heaven's empyrean ground,
And with eternal life be crowned!

The day is spending in innocent mirth. The colors of the shipping in the harbor are displayed, all the bells in the town are ringing, and the cannon roaring; in a word, joy sits smiling in every countenance on this happy occasion. Happy, thrice happy the ruler! thus riveted in the hearts and affections of his people."

Of the appearance of Lady Wentworth in her wedding dress we have no particular record, but the style of the times would lead us to imagine her locks strained over an immense cushion that sat on her head, touched with pomatum, and then sprinkled over with a shower of white powder; the height of this tower not far from a foot, perhaps bearing a white rosebud on its top; over her neck and bosom a lace handkerchief fastened in front by a large bosom pin; her form braced up in a satin dress, the sleeves as tight as the natural skin of the arm, with a waist formed by a bodice, worn outside, from whence the skirt flowed off and distended at the top by an ample hoop. The dress for church was not complete without a richly wrought apron and shoes of white kid, with peaked toes, and heels of two or three inches elevation, glittering with spangles.

We have no record of the Governor's apparel. We have before us, however, some bills of merchandise, which he paid about that time, in which we find these items:

| | |
|---|---|
| To pair of white silk stocking breeches, | £1 18 0 |
| To white cloth coat, unlined, | 2 14 0 |
| To blue corded silk waistcoat, | 5 0 |
| To a rich gold lace, | 12 0 |
| To gold button and loop, and hat recockt, etc. | 2 0 |
| To 3 yds. queue ribband, | 1 3 |

Such are the items; the reader can array him to suit his own fancy.

On the day of the wedding, soon after the ceremony, the Rev. Arthur Brown, whether excited by the rapid movement, or in a moment of aberration from wonder at what might come next, in going out of a door unfortunately fell over a number of stone steps and broke his arm.

For six years the Governor and his lady continued residents at the house now occupied by Eben. Wentworth, on Pleasant street, spending a portion of the summer at the Governor's farm at Wolfborough. The Governor was a large owner in that town, his farm extending over twenty-three hundred acres in that town and fifteen hundred acres in the adjoining towns of Brookfield and New Durham. The mansion house was one hundred feet by forty-five, and other buildings corresponded. A journey to Wolfborough before the revolution, was no small undertaking. When the Governor and his lady made a summer visit to his farm. Dr. Cutter was usually one of his company, to be in readiness to attend if any disaster occurred on the way. The Governor's mansion house was on the border of Smith's pond, (east of the Winnipiseogee,) about a hundred rods from its shore. A story has been told of an adventure of the Governor and lady which we give as we have heard it. It was said that his lady when at the farm would sometimes have her own way, and one evening attending a husking without him, was not a little irritated to find the door closed on her return. Hearing her threaten that she would jump into the lake, he rushed from his chamber in a fright to the rescue. She was out of his sight when the door opened, and he dashed on the path to the water, while she, standing close to the side of the door, quietly stepped in, turned the key, and left him rather thinly clad to get in as he might be able. There is an improbability about the story; but as it is not more strange than the hasty wedding proceedings, we let the tradition pass as apocryphal.

Gov. John Wentworth had many good traits of character, was liberal in his charities, and did much to benefit the town and state. He was active in the establishment of Dartmouth College, and did much in improving the roads of the state and for the advancement of agriculture. He was a man of sound understanding, refined taste, enlarged views and a dignified spirit, and with the people became as one of them. One anecdote will illustrate.

Recently in a walk down Pleasant street, we met an old gentleman bordering on a century, who well remembered the events of the revolution. Did you ever see Governor Wentworth! we inquired. O yes, that I have, he replied, as his countenance brightened with the remembrance. He has patted me upon my shoulder many a time when a boy, and bestowed on me his coppers and his ninepences liberally. The boys then used to pay respect to their ministers and their honorable men. We never passed one of them without removing our hats—

and if we were playing marbles, all play was left to do our manners. The people thought a great deal of the Governor, and strangers who came in from the country would strive to get a sight of him. The Governor was a great lover of horses. That old stable in front, on the corner of Washington and Pleasant streets, long called "Hall's stable," was the Governor's. He kept there sixteen horses for his own use, and gave them much personal attention. One morning, soon after five, a stranger from the country who had never before been in Portsmouth, wandered down near the Governor's seat, hoping to get a glance at his Excellency. After dodging around the premises for a time, he looked into the stable to see the horses. He asked a man who appeared to have charge, many questions about the Governor, and told him what they said about him in his neighborhood. "They say Johnny is short and thick, that he is fond of his wine, but on the whole a pretty clever sort of a fellow —how I should like to see him." "Well," said the one he was conversing with, "I'll try to give you a sight of him—walk into the house." They enter—the splendor of the furniture as they pass from room to room is opened to his wondering gaze. After being shown into this room and that, the stranger whispered—"I should like to get a sight of the Governor." "*Oh sir, here he is!*" said the Governor offering his hand.

Dumbfounded at the fearful disclosure, nothing but the good nature of his excellency prevented his hiding his shame in a speedy retreat.

In 1775, when the Revolutionary troubles compelled Governor John Wentworth to seek refuge in England, his lady accompanied him, and they never again returned to New Hampshire. They had one son born here in 1774, named Charles Mary. He acquired much wealth, was never married, and died at Kingsand, England, in 1844, aged seventy. To the time of his death he was by entailment owner of the property on which our high school house now stands.

Lady Wentworth was distinguished in England for her beauty, was conspicuous at court, and one of the maids of honor to the Queen. A portrait by Copely, now in the possession of Asa Freeman of Dover, (who married a daughter of Hon. William K. Atkinson,) is regarded as an excellent likeness and a rare picture.

Gov. John Wentworth was Governor of Nova Scotia from 1792 to 1800, and had a pension of £500 a year till his death, which occurred at Halifax in 1820. Lady Wentworth died at Berks, England, in 1813.

Thus have they all passed away, leaving as an apt memento of the stability of earthly grandeur, the half demolished mansion which is the text of our ramble.

## RAMBLE XX.

Col. Joshua Wentworth—His offices—incidents of his history—His descendants—George Jaffrey.

Among the home residents of Portsmouth during the Revolutionary war scarcely any one performed more business for the government, as Commissary, Navy Agent, etc., than Col. Joshua Wentworth. We have before us a large package of business letters addressed to him, as the Agent of the Board of War at Portsmouth, by Gen. Stark, Col. Joseph Gilman, Capt. Joseph Leigh, Maj. Bass, Gen. Sullivan, and many others—showing that through him came nearly all the supplies which were furnished to the New Hampshire soldiers. His letters show him to have been a business man; and no doubt his experience tended to promote the interest of the country, at a time when poverty held up its visage on every side. Col. Wentworth built and for many years resided in that house in Hanover street afterwards owned by Capt. Thomas Brown, and then by Joshua Johnson. The house was of excellent workmanship,—a beautiful garden was laid out in front, and the position of the occupant brought many distinguished visitors to his domicil. It was at a time when Gov. John Hancock with his lady and family were spending a week in Portsmouth, quartering at the boarding house standing on the spot where Richard Jenness now lives, that a grand entertainment was prepared at Col. Wentworth's to His Excellency. At this entertainment all the *elite* of the town were present, and a son of Gov. Hancock, of five or six years of age, richly attired, gave an attractive feature, by dancing a *minuet.* The impression left of that circumstance was made lasting, by the fact that this was the last display of his skill in this branch of education. Only a week or two after the child returned to Boston, he suddenly expired.

Among the sons of the first Lieut. Gov. John Wentworth, was Daniel, who had two sons, Col. Joshua and Capt. George,—the latter was the father of Ebenezer, [who died in 1860.] Col. Joshua Wentworth is the individual who is the subject of our present sketch. He was born in 1742, and married Sarah Peirce in 1774. They had fifteen children, of whom only four arrived to mature age; Ann Jaffrey, lately deceased, widow of Samuel Larkin; Joshua, whose daughter was the first wife of Capt. Wm. Parker; Elizabeth, first wife of William Bodge; and Adeline.

Col. Joshua Wentworth received his title from his commission in the first New Hampshire regiment in 1776. He was a Representative, Councillor in 1786, Senator four years, and appointed Delegate in Congress in 1779, but did not attend. In 1790, he received next to the highest vote for President of the State. In 1791, he was commissioned by Washington "Supervisor for the United States in the District of New Hampshire."

Col. Wentworth's place of business was on the northeast corner of Hanover (then Cross) and Vaughan streets —on the spot where Dr. Kittredge afterwards resided. Here some of our first merchants received their business education,—among them, the late William Gardner and John Haven. Business at that time was more diffused over the town than at present. The house owned and occupied by Benj. Carter, on School street, was the Portsmouth Sugar House, where sugar was for some years refined. And when Dr. John Goddard was burnt out in Market street in 1802, he removed his goods to the Sugar House, and there carried on his extensive business until Market street was rebuilt.

Col. Wentworth was the bosom friend and associate of Hon. George Jaffrey, and was the heir expectant to his great estate. Mr. J. however becoming his bondsman to Government, and Col. Wentworth being unable to meet the claims Government had upon him, Mr. J. met his liabilities, but became so embittered that he cut off Col. W. from his expectations,—at once willing his whole property to the late George Jaffrey, a youth of Boston, bearing the name of Jeffries, on condition of his assuming his name, becoming a permanent resident of Portsmouth, and following no other occupation than that of being a *gentleman*. These requisitions were strictly complied with.

Col. Wentworth spent the latter days of his life in the house which till 1813 occupied the site of the present residence of Mrs. Henry Ladd, on Middle street. He died in 1809, at the age of sixty-seven. His wife died two years previous, at the age of fifty.

## RAMBLE XXI.

Factory site—Nathaniel Adams's seat—Discovery of Lady Stanley's grave—Her husband William Parker—Sketch of the Parker family: William, John, Samuel, Matthew Stanley, Noah, John, 2d.

THE site of the Portsmouth Steam Factory has historical reminiscences of some interest. It is but a few years since that its premises, together with the whole land in front from Parker to Rock street and up to Islington street, was the seat of Nathaniel Adams, the Portsmouth annalist. His mansion was situated on the spot where the factory stands, and a red fence extending around the whole premises enclosed one of the most attractive gardens and prolific orchards to be found in Portsmouth. On the west side of the garden, nearly opposite the end of Marlborough street, (which then extended only from Brewster to Rock street,) might be seen some slate stones nearly buried in the earth, which indicated that graves had long ago been made there.

In opening that street in 1847, before the building of the factory, a drain was laid from the street to the water, which passed near the graves. In covering up the drain, some slabs were found which worked to advantage, and were used for a covering.

After the Steam Factory company had laid out the ground for a highway in front of the mill, a gentleman in Massachusetts made inquiry whether any graves had been discovered. One who had been employed to dig the drain, recollected handling a square stone, and placing it to cover a portion of the drain. He dug in the centre of the street and soon found it. On being cleansed, the following inscription was found:

"Here lies<br>Mrs. ZERVIAH, wife of Mr. WILLIAM PARKER,<br>Died August 18, 1718,<br>Aged 53 years."

Tradition says that Mrs. Parker was Lady Stanley, a

daughter of the Earl of Derby, who married William Parker in England, without the consent of the Earl; the current of her affections running more in the course of love than in pride of ancestry. She abandoned her claims to nobility, and with her husband fled to the new world. Portsmouth was the place of refuge—this lovely spot by the river side was selected for their residence—and here the fifteen remaining years of her life were spent. In a correspondence with the present Earl of Derby, he says that he finds no record of Zerviah in the family of his ancestors. Her name was either suppressed, changed, or she was not of regular descent. Her family nobility, if she ever had any, did not survive her; but the record shows that from her have descended some who need no ancestral fame. From the annals of the Parker family, and other sources, we have an opportunity of drawing some interesting details.

WILLIAM PARKER was married to Zerviah Stanley, daughter of the Earl of Derby, Feb. 26, 1703, and came to Portsmouth, N. H. soon after. The family tradition is, that this was a love match. He was a gentleman of education, but after arriving in this country it was necessary for him to support himself and her; and yet he feared her father's vengeance, who was an arbitrary and vindictive man. Both were very much frightened—our country then being subject to Great Britain he feared legal proceedings. He kept as obscure as possible, working in a tan yard on the east of his residence. It is said of his lady that she suffered sometimes great distress of mind, knowing that she would be disinherited and her children cut off from her father's house. They were buried in the garden which afterwards belonged to Nathaniel Adams, as above stated.

The Hon. WILLIAM PARKER, the oldest son of the above, was born in Portsmouth in 1703, received his education in one of the public schools, and then became apprentice to his father. He made himself thoroughly acquainted with that business, but relinquished it soon after he came of age, and was employed for several years as master of one of the public schools. In his leisure hours he pursued the study of law, and was admitted to the bar in 1732. He was clerk of the commissioners who settled the boundary line between New Hampshire and Massachusetts in 1737; was appointed Register of Probate by Gov. Belcher; afterwards became Judge of Admiralty, and was for many years the only Notary Public in the Province. From 1765 to 1774 he was a member of the general assembly. In August, 1771, he was appointed a Judge of the Superior Court, which office he held until all those who received their appointment from the King were in the Revolution removed.

After Judge Parker left the bench he was confined to the house with the gout. He took no part in the politics of the day; neither did his health permit him to attend to any other concerns than the education of his family. He died April 29, 1781, aged seventy-seven. Of his character, the annalist of Portsmouth says, "that he was esteemed a well-read and accurate lawyer; he had dilligently studied the law, not only as a profession but as a science. While at the bar he was consulted, and his advice relied on in the most important cases which came before the courts. But his studies were not confined entirely to the law. He gave much of his attention to classical literature and the belle lettres, in which he made great proficiency." In 1763 the corporation of Harvard college conferred on him the degree of Master of Arts, although his preliminary education was received in a tanyard. He was emphatically a *self-made man.*

His children were Zerviah Stanley, married to William Earl Treadwell, and died May, 1750, aged 22 years. William died June, 1813, aged 82 years. John died Oct. 4th, 1791, aged 59 years. Elizabeth married to Capt. Nathaniel Adams, (the father of the late Nathaniel Adams, many years clerk of the court, etc.) and died Nov. 20th, 1815, aged 81 years. Mary married to Hon. David Sewall of York, Me., for many years Judge of the U. S. District Court, etc. She died May, 1788. aged 50 years. Lydia married Samuel Hale, and died September, 1787, aged 47 years. She was the mother of the late John P. Hale of Rochester, who was the father of Hon. John P. Hale, U. S. Senator, of Dover. Catharine died unmarried September, 1817, aged 73 years. Samuel died December 6th, 1804, aged 60 years. Sarah married Hon. Christopher Toppan, and died July 26th, 1837, aged 91 years. Matthew Stanley died 1787, aged 40 years.

Of the sons above-mentioned, the first, William, was the Hon. William Parker of Exeter, and many years a Judge of the Court of Common Pleas and Register of Probate for the county of Rockingham. His children were: William, a distinguished physician, who died of yellow fever; Nathaniel, lawyer, Deputy Secretary and Secretary of State; Jeremiah, died at sea; John T., formerly Register of Probate; Samuel, teller in one of the Boston banks; Elizabeth, married Col. Samuel Adams; and Mary, who married Joseph Lamson.

The other son of the first William Parker, (the husband of Zerviah Stanley,) was John Parker, the father of Noah the Universalist minister, of whom we shall speak hereafter. He (John) died young, leaving Noah a dependent on his brother William.

JOHN PARKER (the second son of William), always known as Sheriff Parker, was an "old bachelor" of the very best sort; for he educated at his own expense nine of his nephews and nieces—among whom was the father of the present John P. Hale. The very first copy of the Declaration of Independence ever received in New Hampshire, was read by Sheriff Parker from the balcony of the Court House in Portsmouth. That scene has been fully described by an old revolutionary soldier, then present. The old cocked hat, the old fashioned coat, the sheriff's sword, the three times three cheers when Sheriff Parker mounted the balcony with the scroll in his hand, and the enthusiasm with which that document was received by those who were at that time present, has been pictured to the life; and yet this man for electioneering purposes has been called a tory! Gov. Wentworth appointed him Sheriff of the Province in 1771, and Sheriff of Rockingham after the Province was divided into counties. When the government was assumed by the people at the commencement of the revolution, he was re-appointed, by the authority of the State, Sheriff of Rockingham; and when the federal government went into operation, President Washington appointed him Marshal of the District of New Hampshire. He held these offices during life, and discharged the several duties of them with fidelity and care. He likewise had the direction of an insurance office, and conducted the business of it with accuracy and skill. He was never married, but his house was the asylum of the widow and orphan; and the children he took charge of were nourished and educated with paternal care. His benevolence was not confined to his relatives, but extended in many instances to strangers, who partook largely of his bounty. In the walks of private life, his virtues were conspicuous. He was a social companion, an accomplished gentleman, a disinterested friend.

Samuel Parker, the third son of Hon. William Parker of Portsmouth, was born August, 1744. He was elected assistant minister of the Trinity Church, in Boston, in October, 1773. On the 27th of June, 1779, Dr. Parker was unanimously elected rector of the church. His reputation extended throughout the Union, and was rewarded with a doctorate from a respectable university. He was looked up to as the head of the Episcopal church in New England, and inferior to no clergyman on the continent in the essential accomplishments for that sacred office. After the decease of Bishop Bass, he was unanimously elected Bishop of the eastern diocese, which office he accepted. He was consecrated in New York on the 15th of Sept. 1804. He died on the 6th of December, 1804. Bishop Parker was married in November, 1776, to Annie, daughter of Mr. John Cutler of Boston.

Their children were John Rowe, who kept the telegraph establishment in Boston; Samuel Dunn, District Attorney for the county of Suffolk; William has been one of the Aldermen in Boston; Thomas Ives, a physician, and James Floyd, twins, deceased; Benjamin Clark, an Episcopalian clergyman in the western part of Massachusetts, (Lennox, we believe); Richard Green, a distinguished teacher in Boston and author of several school books; Elizabeth died young; Mary Cutler single; Anna died young; Sarah Dunn married to Samuel H. Packer; Maria; Rebecca married Rev. Theodore Edson, Episcopal minister at Lowell, Mass.

MATTHEW STANLEY GIBSON, the youngest son of Hon. William Parker of Portsmouth, settled at Wolf borough, and had the charge of the celebrated Gov. Wentworth farm. He married Anna Rust, daughter of Col. Rust of Portsmouth, who moved in the time of the revolution to Wolfborough. They were married at the house of Col. Toppan, in Hampton, and he afterwards educated their only daughter, Anna Rust Parker, the first wife of Rev. Jaaziniah Crosby of Charlestown, N. H.

The children of Matthew Stanley Parker were, Henry Rust, a farmer in Wolfborough; William Sewell of Troy, N. Y., it is said, kept a bookstore; Matthew Stanley, for many years Cashier of Suffolk Bank; Samuel Hale, the publisher of the Waverly novels, etc.; Nathaniel Adams, who died young; John Toppan; Anna Rust married Rev. Jaaziniah Crosby. Hon. William Parker, 2d, of Portsmouth, had two wives. The first was Elizabeth Grafton. His second wife was Mrs. Abigail Forbes, daughter of Mr. Keais of Portsmouth. The children were by the first wife.

NOAH PARKER was the only son of John Parker, who

was the second son of the first William Parker, who married Zerviah Stanley. Noah's father, John, married a Miss Ward, and both died while Noah was an infant,—leaving him to the care of his brother William, who adopted Noah into his own family. He received a good education, after which he chose to learn a trade; but though working several hours a day at his trade, he was a profound student, and became well versed in all the literature of the day. Noah was born 17th March, 1734, and died August 17th, 1787, aged fifty-three years.

Noah had two wives. The first was Elizabeth Cate, who died, leaving three children, viz.: John, Nathaniel and Mary. The second wife was Rebecca Noble, by whom he also had three children, viz.: Edward Parry, Olive Rindge and Zerviah Stanley. His uncle William resided in the house which was afterwards occupied by Nathaniel Adams, where now stands the Portsmouth Steam Factory. There Noah passed his early days, and received his early education. He was a man of unbounded liberality of feeling, carrying his charity so far beyond his means, that he would sometimes borrow to aid one in want, trusting to Providence for the means of repaying.

At the time of the revolution it is said that the mansion setting out prominently on the south-west corner of Daniel and Penhallow streets, was occupied by Noah Parker. It was a great house in that day, and from that circumstance and the name of the occupant, it was called *Noah's Ark*. In naming the streets in 1778, the street which extended from this house south to Buck (now State) street, was called *Ark* street, which name it retained until a few years ago it was made a continuation of Penhallow street.

Noah Parker's last place of residence was the house sixty-six Market street, formerly owned by C. Cushing, and occupied in 1869 by Capt. John N. Frost. He was a black and white-smith. His work shop was on High street, on what is now the west end of Ladd street, before this street was laid out. He had two daughters, Zerviah, who died of yellow fever in 1798, and Mrs. Watts, who for many years kept a boarding-house in Portsmouth, and died here some eight or ten years since. He was the first Universalist preacher in Portsmouth, and for him the Church in Vaughan street was built in 1784. This church was latterly known as the Camenēum, but is now no longer the "Seat of the Muses and the Arts."

In the month of June, 1778, Nathaniel Adams and John Parker, Jr. completed a survey of the town and made a plan of it. At their request the town appointed a committee to name the streets, which was accordingly done, and the names entered upon the plan. The original map is still in the archives of the city. The draft is by JOHN PARKER, JR., and is a rare specimen of penmanship. We have also seen an elegant miniature from his pencil. He was the son of Rev. Noah Parker, and father of William B. Parker, of this city. John married Elizabeth B. Wingate, daughter of Moses and Elizabeth B. Wingate, who was the daughter of Elizabeth and George Bennett, who was daughter of George Vaughan, Lieut. Governor of New Hampshire. Madam Bennett was a very learned lady and well versed in the Latin language. She was quite near sighted when young, but as she advanced in life her eyesight became remarkably clear, so that she could see to read the finest print and sew the finest "Holland," as it was then called, without spectacles. After she passed the age of ninety she translated one of the books of Virgil, without the aid of spectacles. She was born about the year 1700, and lived to the age of ninety-three.

John Parker, Jr. was a surveyor, and entered into a contract, in company with several others. with the authorities of Georgia, for a survey of that State, and died at Savannah, in 1792, without prosecuting that survey. William B. Parker was at the time of his father's death five years old.

The tan yard of the first Parker was near his residence on the east, and was used for the same purpose for more than a century after his day. The street parallel with *Parker street* still bears the name of *Tanner's lane.* The one a lasting designation of the original residence of the proprietor, and the other of the honorable profession of the son-in-law of the Earl of Derby.

---

## RAMBLE XXII.

The earliest Pauper Work-House, 1716—Almshouse on Court street—Clement March and his family—Superintendents.

It may not be generally known, though the fact was stated in the valuable discourse of Rev. Dr. Burroughs at the opening of our new Almshouse in 1834, that in Portsmouth was built probably the first pauper work-house erected in this or any other country. It appears by our town records, that at a meeting held April 9, 1711, it was voted to build an alms-house; and the house was built on the spot where the Temple now stands, previous to 1716, when it was fit to be tenanted. Here paupers were put, and set at work by the selectmen. It was not until 1723 that an act was passed in England authorizing the establishment of parish work-houses, after which time they came into use in the old country, as well as in this.

Up to 1750, Rebecca Austin is the only name that appears as keeper of the Portsmouth Almshouse. In 1750, William Hooker was appointed keeper, who held the office to 1756, when the old Almshouse was abandoned, for the occupancy of the new one that year built on the glebe land, on the present site of our Court House. For the full history of the work-house system and a great variety of other interesting details, we refer the reader to the above discourse, which furnishes an important and very interesting chapter in Portsmouth history.

The opening of the second Almshouse in 1756, presents to our readers a man who in some respects was the most conspicuous in the last century, to whom the management of the House was entrusted for thirty-six years. Clement March was a man of giant size—his height six and a half feet, and his frame well proportioned. His presence was enough to command the obedience of all entrusted to his care. Nor was that presence always necessary—for his grandson, still living, has told us that when a boy he frequently visited him, and so much was the keeper feared by the inmates, that when any disturbance was heard in any room, he would say, "Nat, take my cane there." The boy shouldering the long, mysterious wand, and marching through the room, would restore quiet without saying a word. He was, however, a kind and affable man, and his company was sought for at all merry-makings. In 1758 we find him constituted the north parish constable, and his duty was to keep the unruly boys in and about the church in order, for which he was to receive four shillings old tenor each Sabbath. He was for many years the collector of the north parish, and as sexton for thirty years from 1760 his portly form might have been seen at the head of the funeral processions generally.

Soon after the death of Clement March in 1790, William Vaughan was by the north parish appointed sexton; and the town appointed Deacon John Noble, whose residence had been at the Plains, to be superintendent of the Almshouse. In 1801, Deacon Noble died, and William Vaughan, his successor, was appointed to the superintendency of the Almshouse, which trust was held by him until 1825, and then John Grant, his son-in-law, was appointed. In 1830, Capt. Robert Neal was appointed. In February, 1835, he resigned, and Capt Hanson M. Hart was appointed superintendent, and held his trust to March 25th following. It was under Capt. Neal's administration, Nov. 12th, 1834, that the inmates were removed from the old Almshouse to the new Almshouse on the town farm.

Col. John Crocker was next appointed superintendent, March 25, 1835, and held his trust till November 15, 1836, when Robert Morrison (our present Mayor), succeeded him. April 7, 1841, he resigned, and John Huntress from that date was superintendent for eleven years. April 23, 1852, Daniel P. Scott was appointed superintendent, and held his trust from that date till April 16, 1856, when William Moses was appointed superintendent.

The old Almshouse on Jaffrey (now Court) street, was a two-story building of large dimensions. It was built for £1275, old tenor, expenses of materials, etc., making the whole cost about £3838. It was not only a place of residence and labor for the poor, but it also afforded rooms for transacting town business. There was one room called the Chapel, and another called Union Hall. Here the overseers transacted their business—here the town library was deposited; and at the close of the business year Union Hall, with all its dismal surroundings, had its rich table spread and the fathers of the town, in one good supper, took up the pay for their year's services.

In this house Clememt March reared a large family of his own; three sons—John, Nathaniel and Jonas C.,—and four daughters, Margaret (who married Mr. Maloon,) Sarah (who married Barnet Akerman), Hannah (who married Mr. Clark, the father of Joseph and William Clark), and Elizabeth (who married Josiah Akerman).

Jonas C. March became a trader of some note at Rochester, and was the father of John, now a merchant in New York. Nathaniel March, who died in early manhood, was the father of the venerable Nathaniel B. March, now of this city. John March occupied a house on Congress street, fronting the opening of Middle street, on which spot the present house was built by his daughters. In a front projection of the old house was his saddler's shop, where he and his nephew, Nathaniel B. (who was brought up by him), might be seen in their leather aprons busily engaged, while the three side benches were not unfrequently filled with visitors of the highest rank in Portsmouth, and the poor as well as the rich discussing with him the topics of the day, gathering from his experience and apt aphorisms ideas which had no small influence on the administration of public affairs. He was a man of correct life, sound judgment, meek and affable—and of a disposition which placed him among that class of men whom every body called "uncle." He was regarded "a perfect man in his generation," and closed a happy Christian life in 1813, at the age of fifty-five years. He left two sons and three daughters—John, Nathaniel J., Sarah, Catherine and Elizabeth. John was married, and five of his children are now living: John S. March (cashier of the Hide and Leather Bank, of Boston); Martha, widow of John S. Cutts; Sarah, widow of James Nowell; Helen, wife of Moses P. Brown, of Brooklyn; and Catherine, wife of H. M. Whitney, postmaster of Honolulu.

The March family of Greenland is connected with the above, in a distant line.

There was yet another March family resident in Portsmouth, in a house in the rear of the present Academy yard, where Hon. John March, of Eaton, was born some seventy years ago. This latter John, who left town early in life, was a powerful man—he could raise with his hands the wheel of a hay cart, when loaded with a ton of hay. He acquired good estate and reputation. His death was caused by over exertion. The grass had been cut on a small field which was disputed property. His hay cart entered the field at the same time with that of the other claimant. Determined to load up as much as possible, he pitched it up with whirlwind speed, throwing up large stacks at a time, and thus he obtained the largest share—but the exertion on a hot day was at the cost of his life—he went to his house and soon expired.

## RAMBLE XXIII.

King street—John Tufton Mason—His premises and family—John Gaines—Charles Treadwell.

Previous to the Revolution, the avenue running west from Market square was called King street; and as almost everything relating to royalty underwent a change, so the more republican name of Congress street was at that time adopted.

Among the oldest houses now standing in the vicinity of Market square, on this street, is the Gaines house, next west and in the rear of the old Bell tavern,—a little further west, nearly on the same line, is the mansion of Col. John Tufton Mason, who held, by inheritance, the title to the State of New Hampshire. The house is now on Vaughan street, but originally it had a handsome front yard extending to King street. Its situation is directly opposite to the entrance to the Cameneum.

This house was built previous to 1746, at which time John Tufton Mason sold to twelve individuals for £1500, all his State title. Mason kept a spacious lot connected with this residence. It extended from what is now Congress street on Vaughan street to Hanover street, then east to High street, then south to and including the premises of the late Dr. Nathaniel A. Haven, taking up the entire square made by those four streets, except the front lots between Fleet and High streets. One of our aged citizens tells us that he has had good slides in that field commencing on the east side, and running into Vaughan street. Fleet street (for many years called Mason street), was not then opened across the premises. The mansion was elegantly fitted up for that day ; it was said to be the first house in Portsmouth that had tapestried walls. None of it now remains, but we have seen some fragments of that mark of its grandeur within the last thirty years. Repairs and alterations have done that damage to the house which the thoughtless servant did to the ancient shield, by scouring off the rust. The ancient oak, near the residence of C. H. Ladd, which was probably a hundred years old when the premises were first occupied by the grantee of New Hampshire,* is still a thriving sentinel of old landmarks.†

* The following is the genealogy of the MASON family:

1. JOHN MASON married Anne Wallaston, and died Nov. 26, 1635.

2. JOHN TUFTON Married Anne Mason, daughter of John.

3. ROBERT TUFTON, son of John, who took the surname of Mason, was born 1629. Came to this country, 1680, and brought his two sons, John and Robert. John was drowned in Virginia. Robert Tufton Mason died at Æsopus, New York, in 1688, aged 59.

4. ROBERT TUFTON MASON married Catherine Wiggin. In 1691 he sold his estate in New Hampshire to Samuel Allen of London. He died at sea, leaving two children, Elizabeth and John Tufton.

5. JOHN TUFTON MASON married in 1711 Susannah Peirce. He died in Havana in 1718. His widow married A. Martin, and their son was Capt. Thomas Martin of Portsmouth.

6. Col. JOHN TUFTON MASON married Maria Theresa Van Harts Bergen. Their children were Sarah Catherine and Anna Elizabeth. He was born in Boston, April 29, 1713, and died in Bugden, England, Aug. 8, 1787, aged 74. In 1746 he sold his title to the lands in New Hampshire. His daughter, Anna Elizabeth, married Peter Livius.

7. SAMUEL MOFFATT, only son of John Moffatt, married Sarah Catherine Mason. Their children were three sons and three daughters.

8. NATHANIEL A. HAVEN married Mary Tufton Moffatt. Their children were one son and two daughters.

9. NATHANIEL A. HAVEN, Jr. married Eliza A. Haven. Their children were one son and two daughters.

10. Horace A. who died at the age of 21. Eliza A. and Charlotte M.

9. AUGUSTUS LORD married Charlotte; her second husband is Rev. Charles Brooks.

9. ALEXANDER LADD married Maria Tufton Haven. Their children who lived to be married were two sons and two daughters.

10. Charles H. Ladd married Susan L. Fowle. Charlotte A. H. Ladd married Samuel E. Coues. Alexander H. Ladd married Elizabeth W. Jones. Caroline S. Ladd married John L. Hayes.

† The old tree, nearly if not quite lifeless, remains in 1873.

The present, which is the tenth generation dating from the original grantee of New Hampshire, still hold possession of a good estate on the original premises on High street, occupied by Charles H. Ladd, which has never been out of the family.

The names of Sarah Catherine and Anna Elizabeth Mason are inscribed on the elegant marble baptismal vase in St. John's church, presented by them in 1761.

In the year 1766 we find the Mason house was vacated by the family, as it was advertised to let, by Jonathan Warner. It is described as "the mansion house of Col. John Tufton Mason, with a large stable, a good garden, and small pasture adjoining—pleasantly situated on the main street near the State house."

John Moffatt built the spacious house on Market street, now occupied by the family of the late Alexander Ladd, more than ninety years ago. It was afterwards occupied by his son, Samuel Moffatt, who was the father of the wife of the late Dr. N. A. Haven.

Peter Livius built the North Mill bridge in 1761, and was proprietor of the Boyd estate, now Raynes's ship yard. He afterwards occupied the house in Deer street, near the depot, where George Annable now resides. At the time of the Revolution, he received a commission from the crown, and removed with his family to Quebec. The house which he last occupied here was known through the town as *the white house.* White paint was but little used on houses in those days.

The oldest house now standing on what was Col. Mason's premises, is the mansion of the late Col. William Brewster, near the corner of Hanover and High streets. It was built about the year 1768.

The nearest house to Col. Mason's was the Gaines house, to which we have above referred. This was built in 1728, by John Gaines. About the same time there was built on the opposite side of the street, by Charles Treadwell, the two-story building next west of the residence of Daniel R. Rogers. The ravages of fire have removed those marks of age which used to be a gratification to the antiquarian eye, but the foundation of the building is still the same, and as it yet retains about its original height, enough is preserved to make it the old house still.

Mr. Gaines, a cabinet maker, and Mr. Treadwell, a hair dresser, were natives of Ipswich, Mass. About the year 1724 the young men came to Portsmouth to commence business. They were successful, and in three or four years they built themselves houses. Mr. Gaines purchased a lot next west of the Bell tavern. His friend Treadwell took a lot on the glebe land. The houses were completed in 1728. Mr. Gaines married Ruth Waterhouse in 1727. That now dilapidated building, when entered by the young couple, was handsomely situated almost on the outskirts of the town. It was finished in good style. For architectural symmetry the remaining ornaments of the front door exhibit evidence of good taste which few of modern times exceed. The caps of the pillars retain their beauty to the eye of every architect, after more than a century's exposure. That Mr. Gaines made his own furniture not only handsomely, but faithfully, we have seen evidence in the now daily use of his first parlor chairs, which have passed down in the family for an hundred and thirty years, and are yet as good as new. They never had a price put upon them. The looking-glass, which the parents of Ruth presented her in 1727, in which her young and smiling face had often glanced, and which in its time has made many sad as well as pleasant reflections, hangs now in our office, a looking-glass in common, and a mirror to throw upon us reflections of the past.

John Gaines died in 1743. His only son, George, who was born in 1736, was a cabinet maker and house carpenter, and built a house in which he lived, on the east side of the lot where the Franklin house now stands. He took an active part in the Revolution, and was conspicuous among the most patriotic of the times in opposition to the stamp act. In 1773 he was elected selectman, and held the office upwards of thirty years. For thirty consecutive years (with but one intermission,) he was a representative to the general court. The office of State commissary he held for many years; and as Major he was present in the army at the capture of Burgoyne. He died in 1809. Of several children, the only one with issue was John Gaines, watchmaker, who died in 1853, at the age of seventy-eight, leaving two sons in New Orleans, who are distinguished in the mercantile line. We might add the remark that Ruth Waterhouse was an elder sister of the widow Dennett, whose adventure with Judge Plummer at the wool washing is recorded elsewhere.

The history of the friend and partner of Major Gaines in his journey from Ipswich, is of sufficient interest to occupy a separate ramble.

---

## RAMBLE XXIV.

**Charles Treadwell—His marriage—Successful Store-keeping—Building of three large houses—Death of Mrs. Treadwell—and her character.**

Our last visit was to the mansion built by Charles Treadwell in 1728, next west of the present residence of D. R. Rogers, which latter is a building of an older date, said to have been the first in Portsmouth in which the diamond shaped window glass was not made use of.

Charles Treadwell, who came from Ipswich in 1724, sought a helpmeet, and found a partner to his liking in Miss Mary Kelley, a daughter of English parents residing at Newcastle. Her family had enjoyed much affluence in England, but by a sudden reverse of fortune they were reduced to poverty. After coming to this country and taking up their residence at Newcastle, Mary's wardrobe was so limited, that a boy's jacket was worn by her for one winter for lack of suitable clothing. But nothing discouraged, she knit nets enough for the fishermen to buy her a new dress, and by industrious application she placed herself in the light of a better fortune. Her good reputation and pleasant manners commended her to her suitor, and in due time they were occupants of the new house. As their husbands were associates, so Mrs. Treadwell and Mrs. Gaines were ever happy in neighborly kindnesses; and so fond were they of an hour's converse, which their industry forbade them to pass in idleness, that Mrs. T. might frequently be seen with her work in hand crossing King street, to enjoy an industrious hour of conversation with her intimate friend. They were of nearly the same age, and their prolonged lives closed within a year of each other.

Mrs. Treadwell had known the worth of money, and was not content with the slow income of her husband's business. She induced him to open a shop in the house, in a small way, to which she would give personal attention. Her pleasant manners attracted customers; so they extended their shop and their stock by degrees, until they had on hand in the building in which they resided, groceries, dry goods, hardware, and in fact almost every kind of article the country trade needed. They purchased the country produce brought in, and paid out in goods. She was aided by her husband in the store, but was really the manager of the business. She well knew that the way to the heart is sometimes through the mouth. On a cold day, when a customer came in, she would anticipate his wants with the present of some warm drink to cheer him. Around the fire might be seen several tea pots—and a lady customer from the country would rarely refuse a cup of warm drink, tendered so kindly and opportunely. They made no pretensions to selling at lower prices than others, but her forte was, polite attentions to her customers. By her upright dealing she commended the place of business to the country around. On business days, horses might be seen hitched not only in front of the house, but also west to Fleet street. There were no market wagons in those days. All came on horseback: the better half frequently sitting behind with her arm around her husband—a model way of riding worth restoring. If any were bringing in provisions in their panniers or saddle-bags, their first call was at Mrs. Treadwell's; and here, more than to any other market, the townsfolks went to purchase their provisions.

The family in time increased. As two sons and a daughter were seen growing up around their table, their future occupied her thoughts. She induced her husband to purchase the corner lot adjoining their premises on the west, and on it erected the spacious Cutter mansion, the appearance of which is yet fresh in our recollection. A few years since it was remodeled into the City Hotel, and is now occupied as such. This was given to her only daughter Hannah, who was the wife of the eminent physician, Dr. Ammi R. Cutter.

From the income of the shop was next purchased that well situated lot, on the corner of Congress and Middle streets, and there was erected what has been called the Storer mansion. This she gave to her son Jacob Treadwell, which he occupied. Jacob had four sons and three daughters, William, Daniel, Charles, Jacob, Ann, Mehitable and Mary. Ann was married to Rev. Mr. Eliot of Boston. William and Daniel were the publishers of the Portsmouth Oracle, from 1801 to 1813. Charles and Jacob were merchants—the latter lost his property in the burning of Moscow, and died here a few years since.

She next purchased another lot, on the corner of what is now called State and Fleet streets, extending their premises from Congress to State streets. On this was erected that large square mansion for many years known as the Davenport boarding-house, now owned and occupied by J. M. Mathes. This she gave to her son Nathaniel, who occupied it.

Not finding another corner lot to suit, they built a vessel, and gave it to their two sons—and to equalize the favors, gave to their daughter Hannah the homestead house and store.

Mrs. Treadwell died in 1783, at the age of 73 years. She was a remarkable woman, of rare strength of mind, energy of character, and purity of life. Born in affluence, in early childhood, as she once said, she received a lesson which had a lasting influence on her eventful life. Her father gave to her mother a rich brocade dress. On finding soon after that a person for whom she had great antipathy had taken a dress from the same piece, she in a fit of passionate pride destroyed her own. The time soon arrived when by the visitation of providence the mother had to look upon a daughter on whom she had not even a comfortable dress to bestow. Mrs. T. never regarded any as her inferiors, was the model of politeness to all, and the attentive friend of those who were more immediately in her circle of familiar acquaintance. Notwithstanding her devoted business habits, she was ever seeking to do good. So prompt and soothing were her attentions to the sick and afflicted, that it was a common remark of her beloved pastor, Rev. Dr. Langdon, when called to the sick chamber, "You might as well send for Mrs. Treadwell as for me."

We have referred to her history not only to show the source to which Portsmouth is indebted for several of her conspicuous houses, which were reared in the last century —but also to bring out a hitherto unwritten history of a lady whose traits of character should leave an enduring impression. There is one trait which has not been mentioned, but should not be passed over. She had her particular hours for secret prayer, and when these hours arrived, no matter how pressing her business, she would retire from it all to seek communion with her Maker.

Jacob, a brother of Charles Treadwell, came from Ipswich about the same time with his brother, and built the house at the corner of Congress and Chestnut streets, now occupied by Dr. Perry. It was probably built as early as 1735. Jacob Treadwell was a tanner, and located his yard at the north end of Bridge street. The yard was afterwards owned by Toppin Maxwell. Daniel Treadwell, a son of Jacob Treadwell, graduated at Harvard in 1754, and was a professor at King's College in New York, until his death in 1760.

Another son, Nathaniel, occupied his father's house in 1781, when the first great fire in Portsmouth commenced in his barn. The barn was on the spot where the Temple now stands. Some boys had been making clay marbles, and built a fire in the barn to burn them. The barn was soon in flames, also two barns near by, the jail on the opposite corner south, and the mansion of Woodbury Langdon, where the Rockingham House now stands, were all consumed. The jail had been built but twenty-two years. From Nathaniel Treadwell descended William E., from him Robert O., and from him Daniel H. Treadwell.

The house on the corner of Chestnut street was afterwards owned by Capt. John Parrott, and was the birthplace of the late John F., Enoch G., and Wm. W. Parrott, gentlemen distinguished in the political and commercial world.

Thomas Treadwell, who is not directly connected with the Treadwell families above referred to, also came from Ipswich, in 1794, and learned the hatter's trade of Deacon Job Harris, in a small shop which was then on the spot where the centre front of the Franklin House now stands.

---

## RAMBLE XXV.

The Warner House—Capt. Macpheadris—Jonathan Warner—Paintings developed—First lightning rod.

Among the great variety of structures in and about our city which have been noted for connection with our past history, is one which is deserving of some prominence. It is the oldest brick house in the city, which at the time of its building was scarcely surpassed by any private residence in New England. The mansion to which we refer is called the Warner house. It is situated at the corner of Daniel and Chapel streets, is at present owned and occupied by Col. John N. Sherburne, and is apparently as sound, fresh and in as good repair as though it had been erected within twenty years.

Capt. Archibald Macpheadris, the projector and builder of this mansion, was a native of Scotland, a member of the King's Council, and an opulent merchant. The work was commenced in 1718 and finished in 1723, at an expense of £6000. The massive walls, eighteen inches thick, are of brick, which with some of the other building materials were brought from Holland. Hewn stone at that time was not in use. The brick work commences on the rough cellar walls. It is three stories in height—the third story has a gambrel roof and lutheran windows. The stories are very high for the style of the time in which it was built, the whole height of the building being about fifty feet.

Capt. M. was a leading projector of the first iron works in America. He was at the head of a small company which commenced the manufacture of iron from the ore at Lamprey river. In 1719 the General Court of Massachusetts granted to this company, by way of encouragement, a slip of land two miles wide, at the head of Dover line. This land was to furnish fuel for the iron works, and a location for settling the foreign operatives. How long the work continued or to what extent, we have no knowledge,—but some of the iron fixtures now in use in this mansion were from the Lamprey River Iron Works. The land of the company is now embraced in the town of Barrington.

Capt. Macpheadris married Miss Sarah Wentworth, one of the sixteen children of Governor John Wentworth. [After his death, in 1729, she married George Jaffrey.] Capt. M. occupied the mansion but six years, and died in 1729. They had but one daughter, Mary, who was married in 1754 to Hon. Jonathan Warner. The portraits of the mother and daughter, in Copeley's best style, still ornament one of the parlors of the house. Mr. Warner was one of the King's Council, until the Revolution closed his commission. He had but one child, who died young. We well recollect Mr. W. as one of the last of the cocked hats. As in a vision of early childhood, he is still before us, in all the dignity of the aristocratic crown officers. That broad back, long skirted brown coat, those small clothes and silk stockings—those silver buckles, and that cane, we see them still, although the life that filled and moved them ceased half a century ago. He was the great uncle of the present occupant of the mansion. But in speaking of the persons we have neglected the mansion, of which it was our principal purpose to speak.

At the head of the stairs on the broad space each side of the hall windows, there are pictures of two Indians, life size, highly decorated, and executed by a skillful artist. These pictures have always been in view there, and are supposed to represent some with whom the original owner traded in furs, in which business he was also engaged. In the lower hall of the house are still displayed the enormous antlers of an elk, presented to Capt. M. by the Indians.

Not long since the spacious front entry underwent repairs. There had accumulated four coatings of paper. In one place on removing the under coating, the picture of the hoof of a horse was discovered. This led to further investigation—the horse of life-size was developed, and a little further work exhumed Gov. Phipps on his charger. The progress of clearing the walls was now entered upon in earnest, with as much interest as if delving in the ruins of Pompeii.

The next discovery was that of a lady at a spinning wheel (ladies spun in those times) who seems interrupted in her work by a hawk lighting among the chickens. Then came a scripture scene, Abraham offering up Isaac —the angel, the ram, etc. There is a distant city scene and other sketches on the walls, covering perhaps four or five hundred square feet. The walls have been very carefully cleared, and the whole paintings, which are evidently the work of some clever artist, are now presented in their original beauty.

No person living had any knowledge of the hidden paintings—they were as novel to an old lady of eighty, who had been familiar with the house from her childhood, as to her grand-daughter who discovered the horse's foot.

The rooms in the house are finished with panelled wood walls, and the old Dutch tiles still decorate the fire-places. The pictures on some of them are rather unique. The antiquarian here will find in the treasured family relics more curiosities than our limits will allow us to detail, which are more pleasing to him than a feast.

This house is provided with a lightning rod, which was put up in 1762 under the personal inspection of Doctor Benjamin Franklin—and was probably the first put up in New Hampshire.

---

## RAMBLE XXVI.

Pleasant street—Livermore—The Church—Vestry—Parsonage—Matthew Livermore—Samuel—Edward St. Loe—The mansion.

ALTHOUGH not always the case, streets sometimes have significant names. In going south from Market square, we proceed for half a mile through what once was regarded the most attractive street in Portsmouth, on which governors, lawyers, clergymen and merchants had residences, and pass over a neck of land with water not very far distant on either side—hence *Pleasant* street was very appropriately named. Diverging from it there is now no street more spacious, level, and refreshing to the eye of the rambler, than Livermore. It was named for him who owned the site long before the latter street was opened.

At the entrance of Livermore street, on the south side, stands a brick block of three tenements, where thirty years ago the Pleasant street church was built. Its builders not heeding that prophecy which rather belongs to the profane than to the sacred,

> "Westward the star of empire takes its way"—

found out too late that the location was wrong, if nothing else,—and after trials by several societies, which were swept by the current to the more western localities,—the church at the age of twenty-five years passed under the hammer to an enterprising individual, and was laid aside from its sacred use. Its belfry was dismantled, the sanctum or western portion, with the pulpit, were cut off, and the building with its hundred and twenty pews was turned into three tenements, and its pastor, deacons, wardens and sexton, are now all represented by Thomas H. Odion, who finds the investment he has made more profitable, pecuniarily, than it ever was before.

The next building on Livermore street, though of no towering pretensions, has yet its history. In 1813, at the corner of Pleasant and State streets, where Mr. Thacher's store now stands, the N. H. Union Bank house was burnt. Many will recollect the brick safe standing prominent amid the ruins on the next morning. Over the safe a new banking-house was erected, and used until a new location was found. The house was then removed to Wentworth street, and arranged for a chapel and Sunday school room for the South Parish. In 1828 it was sold to the Pleasant street Society, and was removed to its present location. It was again used as a chapel and school room for several years by the new society, then sold to an individual who raised the roof and made it what it is, a comely dwelling. Next comes the brick residence of Capt. Thomas Tarlton, built by the South Parish for Rev. Dr. Parker, soon after the street was opened to the water. We now pass over to the only mansion on the north side of Livermore street, which sits alone and claims to be a primitive settler, being older than the street itself, having been built facing Pleasant street, much like the original position of the Jaffrey house on Daniel street, with a similar open yard and balustraded fence in front to the street. After remaining there for more than half a century, on the opening of the street to the water between forty and fifty years ago, its front was changed from Pleasant to Livermore street, and it was removed back a short distance to its present locality. It was early the place of residence of Hon. Matthew Livermore, if not built by him.

This gentleman, who was born at Watertown, Mass. in 1703, at the age of twenty-one came to Portsmouth as a school master, and kept the grammar school seven years. In 1731, he became an attorney-at-law, and was soon after appointed Attorney General of the Province, and Advocate for the King in the courts of admiralty. These offices were profitable to him. It was not unlikely that he built this house as early as one hundred and twenty years ago. Both this house and that of Rev. Dr. Haven, north of it, were gambrel-roofed; between them was a small building, used by Mr. Livermore for his office, and in later years was the office of Hon. John S. Sherburne, also of John Wendell.

Samuel Livermore lived in the house on Livermore street (probably with Matthew) during a part of the administration of Gov. John Wentworth. He was born in Waltham in May, 1732; was a relative, not a brother, of Matthew Livermore. He settled in Portsmouth about 1758; was appointed by John Wentworth King's Attorney for New Hampshire, and became his most necessary adviser in the troubles. From that moment till his death, in 1803, (except about two years required for deliberation before October, 1777,) he was in almost uninterrupted service of the King, or of his country—serving from the last named epoch as Delegate, Representative and Senator in Congress, and as Chief Justice of the State. The late James Sheafe, our Duke of Wellington in sagacity and in manners, spoke with unreserved admiration of his strong common sense. The late Judge Smith illustrated by amusing anecdotes the almost absolute influence with which he presided at the Convention which formed the present Constitution of New Hampshire. It is subscribed with his name. The author of the Life of William Plummer pronounces a eulogy upon his talents; and a far better judge, the late Charles H. Atherton, in his memoir of Claggett, declared that Samuel Livermore was *the* great man of New Hampshire in his time. Samuel had a farm in Londonderry, where he lived at two different periods. There Arthur Livermore was born. Edward St. Loe was born in Portsmouth in 1762. Here he received his education and practiced law; Arthur lived in Holderness and was about forty years ago a member of Congress. Edward married here, and occupied the Rindge house, on the present site of the Jacob Sheafe house, corner of Daniel street. He also occupied the Storer house near the Academy. He was the owner of the old mansion on Livermore street, but we do not know that he was ever an occupant. He sold it in 1809, to Dr. Nathaniel A. Haven.

It is said that Edward St. Loe Livermore and Jeremiah Smith of Exeter, were at one time attentive to two ladies in the same family in Concord. That was a pleasant day on which Edward invited his lady love to ride. One of the best vehicles and most sprightly horses were selected. The animal was restive, and Edward, on reaching the door, regarding it unsafe to take in company until the horse was subdued, drove by without stopping. Again he approaches from the opposite direction, and again drives by Jehu-like, and after again passing and re-passing in a manner very unaccountable to the lady and her indignant mother, who regarded the whole proceeding as a matter of trifling with their feelings, Edward at length stops and enters the house. Before he had time to make an explanation, the spirited mother boxed his ears with a little of other demonstration than that of favor. At least, Judge Smith so decided in his own mind, and who shall question such a Judge's decision? for the Judge, though a greater favorite, being a considerate man, shrugging up his shoulders, retired from his suit, not being willing to subject himself to similar treatment. Edward, however, persevered and the lady became his bride. He had three children: Samuel, Caroline and

Harriet. The last we heard of the latter she was in Jerusalem, having been twice thither, wishing to close her days in the Holy Land.

After the death of Matthew Livermore in 1776, the house was for some years occupied by his daughter, Mrs. Greenwood, who was, we think, his only child. Afterwards it was occupied by Nathaniel Sparhawk, Col. E. J. Long, Capt. John Porter of the Navy, John Wardrobe, Mr. Toscan, the French consul, Capt. Samuel Ham, and some others. In 1809, when Livermore street was opened, it came into the possession of the late Dr. Nathaniel A. Haven, and in 1813 was owned and occupied by Alexander Ladd. The spacious garden extended on one side of the house to Pleasant street, and on the other to the creek. It was afterwards owned and occupied by Samuel E. Coues, and in 1854 it was purchased by Albert R. Hatch, and is now his place of residence.

## RAMBLE XXVII.

John Sullivan—The house boy—His first law case—His advancement—His sail on the Piscataqua.

HAVING given a hasty sketch of the history of the Livermore mansion, we will go back a few years to take a more familiar view of the old occupants.

It was not far from the year 1758, that a lad of seventeen years, with a rough dress, might have been seen knocking at the door of this house, and asking for the Squire, who listens to his application, and inquires:

"And what can you do, my lad, if I take you?"

"Oh, I can split the wood, take care of the horse, attend to the gardening, and perhaps find some spare time to read a little, if you can give me the privilege."

John Sullivan, for that was the name he gave, appeared to be a promising lad, and so he was received into Mr. Livermore's kitchen, and was entrusted with various matters relating to the work of the house and the stable. Mr. L., finding him intelligent, encouraged his desire to read by furnishing from his library any books he wished; and with this privilege he improved every leisure moment. Libraries then were not so extensive as now, but the position of Mr. L. gave him a very good one for the times, and among them the most choice legal works of the day. John was permitted at times to take a seat in the library room, and he had the care of it in Mr. Livermore's absence.

One evening there had been some trouble in the town, which resulted in a fight. As has been the custom in later days, so then the party which fared the worse prosecuted the other for assault and battery. The case was to be brought before Deacon Penhallow (at his house on the south-east corner of Pleasant and Court streets). The best legal talents were needed for the defence, to save the culprit from the stinging disgrace of being placed in the stocks—in those formidable pieces of timber which were standing for years near the south-east corner of the old North church. The defendant at once resorted to the office of Mr. Livermore. He was absent, and John was reading in the library alone. The man, supposing that any one from an office so celebrated might answer his purpose, asked John if he would not undertake his case. John, on the whole, concluded to go, and, leaving word in the kitchen that he should be absent awhile, trudged off with his client. He soon learnt the merits of the case, and having given some attention to the law books, and acquired some knowledge of the forms of trial, he had confidence that he might gain the case. The charges were made; the blackened eyes and bruises were shown, and the case looked very doubtful for John's client.

While this trial was going on, Mr. Livermore returned from his journey; and on inquiring for John to take care of the horse, was told that he had gone off to Deacon Penhallow's to a court. Mr. L.'s curiosity was excited. He put the horse in the stable, and, without awaiting his supper, slipped into a room adjoining the court, and, without being seen by the parties, listened to the trial. John had just commenced his argument, which was managed with good tact, and exhibited native talent and as much knowledge of law as some regular practitioners. John was successful, his client was acquitted, and John received here his first court fee.

Mr. L. returned as obscurely as he entered. The next morning the young man was called into the library room, and thus addressed: "John, my kitchen is no place for you; follow on in your studies, give them your undivided attention, and you shall have what assistance you need from me until you are in condition to repay it."

The result is well-known. John Sullivan became eminent at the bar, became conspicuous as General in the war of the Revolution, and, after the peace, was for three years President of New Hampshire. He was afterwards District Judge. He died at Durham in 1795, at the age of fifty-four.

Gen. Sullivan was of Irish descent. His father was born in Limerick in 1692, came to Berwick, Me., as early as the year 1723, and died in 1796, aged one hundred and four years. His mother came over several years after, from Cork. She was born in 1714, and died in 1801, aged eighty-seven. Her mind was of a rough though noble cast. The father's education was good, and together they enjoyed honorable poverty in early life. When on her passage to this country, a fellow passenger jocosely said to her: What do you expect to do by going over to America? Do, said she, why raise Governors for them. Little did she then think that of two of her boys then unborn, John would become President of New Hampshire and James the Governor of Massachusetts.

James, in his minority, was engaged in gondolaing on our river, and it was when following this business that he broke both of his legs, the effects of which were ever after visible in his gait.

John Sullivan, in early life, was doubtless familiar with the navigation of the Piscataqua. Later in life, after the Revolution, when the General's commission had given place to that of President of New Hampshire, his Excellency, being a resident of Durham, one day saw a boat bound to Portsmouth. He asked for a passage, which was readily granted, one of the boatmen proposing the condition that the President should observe the usual custom of paying his respects to the "Pulpit,"—a name given to some stones projecting from the river, which the superstitious boatmen regarded as subjecting to bad luck if passed without raising the hat. The General said he never did nor never should pay respect to the devil's pulpit, and therefore they need not ask it of him. There was danger of *bad luck* to the boatmen. They however sailed and rowed on down the river. At length one of the boatmen raised his own hat, and casting his eyes up to the tri-colored hat with waving plume which decorated the head of his Excellency, in apparent wonder said, "sir, the birds seem to have flown over your hat?" His hand was speedily raised and the hat carefully brought down for inspection. "I see nothing," said he. "We've passed the Pulpit, sir," was the laconic reply. The superstitious boatmen were in good cheer; they had brought the President down and good luck rested on the voyage of that day.

The success of the Sullivans under great difficulties should give encouragement for perseverance to all young men. There is certainly a memento connected with Livermore street history which should never be forgotten.

## RAMBLE XXVIII.

Fire of 1802—N. H. Bank house—Jotham Odiorne—His family—William Whipple—The marriage put aside—His first declaration of independence—His slaves—Prince's freedom—Dinah—Cuffee—The garrison house.

LET us stir the ashes of the fire of 1802, on Market Square, and see what will come up. On the spot where now stands the Piscataqua Exchange Bank, began that great fire on Christmas night, in the building occupied in part as a boarding house by the widow of Daniel Hart, and in part by the New Hampshire Bank. The vault of the bank was in the basement, and over the banking room was the insurance office of John Peirce. The deposits in the vault were all found safe after the fire, but the papers in the insurance office were all lost. The building was gambrel-roofed, similar in structure but not quite so large as the Ladd house near the academy. It fronted on Market Square, and on a line with the new Market, as did also the Pearse house and store on the north of it. This fire extended from the Market (which was burnt,) north, burning Market street on both sides to the north end of the present Merchant's Row, and also all the buildings on the north side of the Parade, and in Ladd street, except one.

Now that the old banking and boarding house is reared in imagination from its ashes, and the reader can see its ancient form, we will look some years further back for an incident in its history.

Here, more than a century since, resided the Hon. Jotham Odiorne, who, about the year 1720, married Mehitable, one of the four daughters of Robert Cutt, of Kittery. The other three sisters were married as follows: Mary to William Whipple senior, "malster," seaman, and afterwards farmer; Catharine to John Moffat, merchant, and Elizabeth to Rev. Joseph Whipple of Hampton Falls.

Hon. Jotham Odiorne, who died in 1761, was a son of the member of his Majesty's council. In early life he was a resident of Newcastle, and the owner of a large number of fishing vessels. Sarah, one of his three daughters, married Mr. Henry Appleton, a brother of the first wife of Rev. Dr. Haven. On his decease she married Mr. William Appleton,—although of the same name yet in no way related to her first husband. The latter husband was the father of Capt. William Appleton, who formerly lived in Court street, and of Mehitable, the wife of Thomas P. Drown. After William, senior, died, his widow married Daniel Hart, and at the time of the fire in 1802 she was again a widow, and kept the boarding-house where the fire commenced. Before this time of her limited means of support, Mrs. Hart had been the owner of the Gov. Wentworth house, on Pleasant street, and of the McClintock house, on State street. Mary, another daughter of Jotham Odiorne, married Capt. Peter Pearse, and was the mother of Mr. Stephen Pearse, of this city, and of Mary, the wife of John Peirce.

For the better understanding of the drift of our ramble, it is necessary to refer to another family.

William Whipple, senior, had five children; William (the signer of the Declaration of Independence); Robert, who died young; Joseph, collector of Portsmouth; Mary, married to Robert Trail, comptroller of the port of Portsmouth; and Hannah, married to Dr. Joshua Brackett.

William Whipple, junior, was born in Kittery in 1730, and at an early age went to sea. Before reaching twenty-one, he had command of a vessel, and afterwards made not only succesful voyages to the West Indies and Europe, but also to the coast of Africa; and the blemish of that dark living freight, which his vessel brought away, has not been wholly obliterated by the fame which shines around his name on the immortal scroll of our country's glory. At the age of twenty-nine he retired from sea service, and turned his attention to mercantile business at home, and to the enjoyments of social life. We now come back to the old house on Market Square to which we referred at the commencement.

Among the daughters of Jotham Odiorne was Miss Mehitable, who bore her mother's name, and was the pride of the family. Among the suitors, in cocked hats, small clothes and ruffles, William Whipple received her especial favor. In due time the wedding was arranged, and one joyous evening there was a special illumination of these premises. The Rev. Samuel Langdon, in his flowing wig, might have been seen entering the house and two shiny faced negro boys, Prince and Cuffee, busy in attendance. The parlor fire-place was dressed with fresh spruce, bouquets ornamented the mantle, and the white scoured floor was freely sanded. The father, mother and children were gathered, the bride with her maids, and the groom with his attendants were all arranged, when the chief personage of the occasion suddenly leaves the circle for another room.

After waiting nearly half an hour, a message is received by the anxious bridegroom. He goes to another room and there finds his lady divested of her wedding suit, and in her common dress. She told him she had come to the conclusion not to be married that evening! He pleads, but in vain; he remonstrates, but with no effect—the wedding, she said, must be delayed to some other occasion. "We must be married now or never," was his decisive reply. It was unavailing—so, with a determination no less heartfelt than that of some years after placing his name to the immortal Declaration, he here declared his personal independence, retired from the scene, and never after made a call upon his cousin Mehitable. She was afterwards married to William E. Treadwell, who was the father of Capt. Robert O. Treadwell. Capt. T. was the commander of the first East

Indiaman which hailed from Portsmouth. It was a brig of ninety tons, owned by Matthew S. Marsh. The voyage was very successful, and laid the foundation of Capt. Treadwell's large fortune.

Capt. William Whipple afterwards bestowed his affections upon another cousin, Catherine Moffatt, daughter of John Moffatt. After their marriage they resided at the house of her father (now the residence of the family of the late Alexander Ladd) during his life, which closed in 1795. They had but one child, who died in infancy.

At the foot of his garden, facing on High street, has stood until within twenty-five years, the house in which the families of two of his slaves resided—Prince and Cuffee Whipple. They were brought to this town with a number of others of their color, in a ship, from the coast of Africa prior to 1766, then about ten years old. It was said that they were brothers, the sons of an African prince, sent over for an education, but retained in slavery.

Capt. Whipple was a member of the first Council after the organization of the government of the state—and being summoned to attend an extra session of the legislature at Exeter, on the advance of Gen. Burgoyne into Vermont, in 1777,—Capt. Whipple, according to the custom of the times, proceeded to Exeter on horseback, and took as his servant the black Prince, on another horse behind him. On the meeting of the Council, Mr. Whipple was appointed Brigadier General with the command of the first N. H. Brigade,—Gen. Stark to the command of the second Brigade—with orders to march forthwith, each with one-fourth of their command, to the North Western Frontier, "to stop the progress of the enemy." Prince was ordered by General Whipple the next morning to get the horses ready while he went to take leave of the Governor and Council. On returning he found that Prince had not exerted his usual diligence, and on setting out, probably without other attendants, Prince appeared sulky and in ill humor. His master upbraided him for his misconduct. "Master," said Prince, "*you* are going to fight for your *liberty*, but I have none to fight for." "Prince," replied his master, "behave like a man and do your duty, and from this hour you shall be free." Prince wanted no other incentive; he performed his duty like a man throughout the campaign, which ended in the surrender of Burgoyne, and from that day he was a freeman. Mrs. Mullineaux, his daughter, yet living, has always retained his free papers as a valuable keepsake.

Prince Whipple died in this town in 1797, twelve years after his former master. He was a large, well-proportioned and fine looking man, and of gentlemanly manners and deportment. He was the Caleb Quotem of the old fashioned semi-monthly assemblies, and at all large weddings and dinners, balls and evening parties. Nothing could go on right without Prince, and his death was much regretted by both the white and colored inhabitants of the town; by the latter of whom he was always regarded as a leader. Cuffee Whipple died about the year 1820. He also was prominent among the dark gentry of the day. For a quarter of a century Cuffee was a subscriber to the Portsmouth papers.

Dinah, the wife of Prince, was born of a slave in Newcastle, in the family of Rev. Mr. Chase, minister of that place. At the age of twenty-one she received her freedom and came to this town, where she was received into the North church, of which she continued an exemplary member during her life of eighty-six years.

Gen. Whipple, after the war, had intended to erect a house on the premises of the family estate, for Prince, Cuffee, and their families; but he died suddenly of the heart complaint, in the autumn of 1785, before he had accomplished it. His widow, Madame Whipple, gave them the use of a piece of land at the west end of her garden, on High street, during their lives and the lives of their wives. Into this lot, by their joint exertions, Prince and Cuffee hauled a small two-story house, above referred to, where they and their families lived during the lives of all but Dinah, who occupied the same until 1832, and for a number of years was the teacher, in that house, of the Ladies' Charitable African School for young children.

The house in which Gen. Whipple was born and spent his early life is at the head of a small cove in Kittery, on the east from the Navy Yard. Until within a few years it bore the external marks of being a garrison house. It has been modernized, and its antiquarian beauties are now shut from sight. The locality is, however, of some interest, and is worthy of note to those who take an hour's stroll from Portsmouth to Kittery.

## RAMBLE XXIX.

**Description of the Whipple Garrison House—Construction and use.**

Our last ramble closed at the Whipple garrison house. These places of protection from the Indians were formerly quite numerous in this neighborhood, and within fifty years many of them were standing; but they have, one by one, given place to more convenient dwellings, until scarcely any are left. Already a generation of men has arisen who do not know these objects even by sight; and the historian has scarcely given that description of the structure and the uses of garrison houses, which will enable their memory to be preserved, when the old houses shall be no longer seen. And as a description of one is substantially a description of all, we will describe the Whipple house, so called, being the last one, so far as we know, which was left in this neighborhood,

It was built on the east bank of the Piscataqua, about a mile from its mouth, in Kittery, opposite the Navy Yard. The house was only a few yards from the water, and stood on a spot of ground very well chosen for its purpose, having a cove (now called Whipple's cove) running half way round it, so that no savage could come that way unperceived. It also commanded a view of the harbor up and down, for a considerable distance.

The size of the house as it now stands is fifty-four by thirty-four feet, two stories high,—though when used as a garrison it was probably about thirty-four feet square; the remainder of the length being of a later date, is framed in the common way. The repairs made by the present owner, Mr. Jesse Philbrick, in the past fifteen years, have removed all the former external appearances.

The garrison part of this house was constructed of hemlock timber hewed square, dove-tailed together at the corners; when the present owner put the building in repair, this timber was found to be perfectly sound, and likely to last for centuries unless destroyed by fire. This house, like nearly all the garrison houses, was built with the upper story projecting beyond the lower about eight or ten inches on every side. Some of them projected twice as far. The design of this projection was not, as some supposed, chiefly to afford good loop-holes, through which to fire muskets at the assailants, though they might be used for that purpose, but the projection, with its loop holes or scuttles, was intended to give the women in the house a chance to pour down boiling water, at once to scald the Indians and put out the fires they almost always kindled in their attacks. The form of the building was doubtless copied by the colonists from European houses, in which projecting upper stories were common; and the preference for timber over stone probably arose from the destitution of lime in early days.

Many of the garrison houses were much larger than

this; and their great size, their awkward structure, and the difficulty of repairing them when the lower timber became rotten, has caused them to disappear. For very obvious reasons, they had but few windows, and those of small size, especially in the lower part of the house; and these furnished with strong shutters. The door was a ponderous thing, in some cases made of timber or joist, sometimes of oak, and not unfrequently hung on wooden hinges; generally, but not always, opening in two parts, well braced and barred.

Every neighborhood, of three or four farm houses, used to have one of them a garrison house, built in this way by the united efforts of the neighbors, but held as the private property of one man, and used as the residence of one family. In times of apprehended danger nearly or quite all the neighbors lodged at the garrison. This house seems to have been the capital of a little hamlet at Whipple's cove, and was probably built by all the neighbors, at an early period. The house may, not improbably, be nearly two hundred years old. It was, at a later date, the residence of Robert Cutt, who died in 1717, and whose daughter was the wife of William Whipple, senior, whose name is still retained for the house and cove.

There was a garrison house in another part of Kittery, near York, on a farm afterwards owned by the late Judge Sherburne, of this city. One at Portsmouth Plains; one at Newington; both demolished. There were also many others, but these all stood until within a few years.

## RAMBLE XXX.

**Portsmouth in 1727—Inhabitants—Property—Location of Neighborhoods.**

A VIEW of Portsmouth near the close of the first century from its settlement, is a matter of some interest. We have before us an Inventory of the Polls and Estates of the Town of Portsmouth in 1727, which was taken by Messrs. Stephen Greenleaf and John Pray, according to an order of government. It is the best record extant of the names of the citizens of this town at that time, and interesting to many of the present citizens of Portsmouth as a register of their ancestors residing here more than one hundred and thirty years ago; for a large number of the names are yet among us. The names of some widows who were reported as tax-payers—and a few names which were not legible, have been omitted.

The whole number of polls given is 475—oxen 121, cows 407, horses 154, hogs 108, slaves 52, houses 298, acres of tillage land 226, acres of meadow 520, acres of marsh 87.

Of the *slaves*, Capt. Walker had 4, William Vaughan 4, Col. Walden 2, Richard Wibird 3, R. Waterhouse 2, George Jeffries 2; the remaining 35 were owned singly in families. Richard Wibird owned 5 *houses*, William Vaughan 4, Moses Paul 3, John Downing 4, Nathaniel Mendum 3, and 19 individuals 2 houses each. The remaining 241 houses were owned by as many proprietors.

The thirteen persons who paid the *highest taxes* ranged in the following order: Richard Wibird £37, Joshua Peirce 36, John Rindge 32, Geo. Jeffries 31, Henry Sherburne 29, Joseph Sherburne 24, William Knight 22, John Bradford 22, Henry Keyes 22, Thomas Sibson 21, Jacob Lanes 20, William Vaughan 20, Thomas Westbrook 20.

## TAX PAYERS IN PORTSMOUTH IN 1727.

John Abbott
John Abbott, Jr.
Peter Abbott
Reuben Abbott
James Abbott
Samuel Adams
William Adams
Joseph Adams
Benjamin Akerman
John Almony
William Amos
Arcula's Arichson
Robert Armstrong
George Ayers
John Ayers
Joshua Babb
Sampson Babb
Sampson Babb Jr.
Phillip Babb
James Babb
John Babb
Thomas Barns
Abraham Barns
William Barns
Abraham Bartlett
Peter Ball
Hugh Banfield
Capt. Sam'l Banfield
George Banfield
Daniel Bailey
Mr. Bacon
Thomas Beasfelde
Thomas Beck, Sen.
Thomas Beck
Henry Beck
Samuel Beck
Henry Bennett
James Benson
Henry Benson
John Benson
Stephen Berry
Joseph Berry
William Bevens
Abraham Bevens
Thomas Bevens
William Bennett
Wm. Bickham
Thomas Bickford
Henry Bickford
Eliakim Bickford
Percy Bickford
Nicholas Bishop
James Boyd
Robert Bond
Michael Brooks
John Brooks
John Briar
Samuel Brewster
Joseph Brewster
Joshua Brewster
John Brewster
Frenchman Brackett
John Bradford
Samuel Brown
Charles Brown
Joseph Brown
William Broughton
John Broughton
Joseph Buss
Moses Caverly
Edward Cate
Edward Cate, Jr.
William Cate
Joshua Cate
Thomas Cass
Abraham Center
John Churchill
William Chandler
Ambrose Clearage
James Clarkson
Josiah Clark
John Clark
George Clark
Ichabod Clark
Wm. Cotton, Sen.
William Cotton, Jr.
Thomas Cotton
Thomas Cotton, Jr.
George Coolbroth
John Coolbroth
Joseph Crowell
Benjamin Crowell
William Crostwaite
Thomas Crocket
Capt. Benj. Cross
Capt. Wm. Cross
John Cutt
Capt. Richard Cutt
John Culverson
John Darling
Samuel Davis
John Davis
Timothy Davis, Jr.
Timothy Davis
William Davis
John Daniel
John Daverson
Wm. Dillaway
Francis Dittey
Ephraim Dennett
Alexander Dennett
Moses Dennett
Timothy Dennis
Timothy Dennis, Jr.
Samuel Dennis
John Dow
Benjamin Dockum
Richard Dolebear
John Downing
Joseph Downing
John Drew
Francis Drew
Nathaniel Dresser
James Dun
John Edmonds
Thomas Edmonds
Richard Elliot
Joshua Fanning
Wm. Fairweather
William Fellows
Wm. Fellows, Jr.
John Fellows
Nath'l Fellows
Amos Fernald
John Fitzgerald
Wm. Foss
Samuel Foss
James Fuller
John Frost
Capt. Furber
Alde Gammon
Francis Gammon
Phillip Gammon
William Gammon
John Gains
Benj. Gamblen, Esq.
Jeremiah Gordon
John Gowell
Stephen Greenleaf
Peter Greeley
James Gray
Joseph Grant
John Green
John Grindall
Robert Green
Caleb Grafton
John Griffis
John Guy
Thomas Harvey
Samuel Hart
Samuel Hart, Jr.
Robert Hart
Capt. Samuel Hart
John Hall
John Ham
Thomas Ham
William Ham
Samuel Ham
Samuel Ham, Jr.
Thomas Hammet
John Hardison
Thomas Harris
Mark Hattin
John Hill
Samuel Holmes
Lazuras Holmes
John Hooper
George How
Edward Hopkins
William Hook
William Howard
David Horney
Edward Hobrens
Nath'l Horne
Nathaniel Hodgdon
Mark Hunking, Esq.
Arcul's Hunking
William Hunking
William Hucker
Walter Hull
Capt. Huse
Clement Hughes
George Hunter
Capt. Ellis Husk
George Huntress
Moses Ingraham
Thomas James
Richard James
John Jackson
Ephraim Jackson
Nathaniel Jackson
Daniel Jackson
Daniel Jackson, Jr.
Ebenezer Jackson
Elisha Jackson
Joshua Jackson
Samuel Jackson
George Jeffries, Esq.
Daniel Jeffries
Simon Jeffries
James Jeffries
David Jeffry
Abraham Jones
Joseph Johnson
Richard Jose
Martyn Jose
William Jones
Henry Keais
Capt. Kennard
William Keniston
Capt. George King
Capt. Wm. King
Peter King
William Knight
John Knowles
Ezekiel Knowles
Jacob Lane
George Lane
Jacob Lane, Jr.
Robert Lane
Wm. Langdon
Tobias Langdon
Mark Langdon
Joseph Langdon
Benjamin Langley
Stephen Lang
William Lang
Robert Lang
John Lang
Nathaniel Lang
Nathaniel Lang, Jr.
John Lang
Stephen Lang, Jr.
Jacob Lavis, Jr.
Jacob Lavers
George Lavis
Jeremiah Lawry
James Leach
Zachariah Leach
William Lewis
Benjamin Lewis
John Lear
Capt. John Libbey
Jeremiah Libbey
Abraham Libbey
James Libbey
Benj. Libbey
Joseph Libbey
James Libbey, Jr.
Robert Lintle
John Low
William Lowd
John Locke, Jr.
Edward Lock
Joseph Lock
William Lock
James Lock
Jethro Lock
William Lock
Benjamin Lusey
Robert Macklin
James Mackeny
George Marshall
John Martyn
A. Macpheadris, Esq.
Samule Manson
Thomas Mane
John Marden
James Marden
Peter Mann
Peter Mann, Jr.
Michael Mann
John Marshal
George Marriner

Nath'l Meservey
Francis Merritt
Nathaniel Melcher
Thomas Mead
Joseph Mead
Nathaniel Mendum
Francis Merritt
Joseph Miller
Joseph Miller Jr.
Benjamin Miller
John Mills
Eben'r Morse
Peter Moe
Samuel Moore
John Moore
James Moses
Mark Moses
Josiah Moses
Joseph Moses
Joseph Moulton
Capt. Dan'l Moulton
Joseph Moulton
Daniel Moulton
Hugh Montgomery
William Nason
Jeremiah Neal
Joseph Nelson
William Nelson
John Newmarch
Mark Newmarch
Thomas Newmarch
Stephen Noble
Stephen Noble, Jr.
Thomas Noble
Matthew Nelson
Nicholas Norris
Christopher Noble
Moses Noble
Lazarus Noble
Nathaniel Odiorne
Wm. Parker, Sen.
William Parker, Jr.
Jonathan Partridge
William Partridge
Nehemiah Partridge
Capt. Wm. Pane
Henry Paine
Moses Paul
Thomas Packer
Thomas Palmer
Richard Parshley
Abraham Perkins
Stephen Pendergrass
John Peverly, Jr.
John Peverly, Sen.

Nath'l Peverly
William Pevey
John Peirce
Joseph Peirce
Joshua Peirce
Joshua Peirce, Jr.
George Peirce
Doctor Peirce
Capt. Thomas Peirce
Thomas Peirce
Edward Pendexter
Capt. Jno. Penhallow
John Peacock
Neal Phillips
Thos. Phipps
Doctor Pike
Solomon Pike
Joseph Pitman, Sen.
Joseph Pitman
Benj. Pitman
James Pitman
Jabez Pitman
Samuel Pitman
Ezekiel Pitman
Samuel Pickering
Robert Pickering
John Plaisted
John Pray
John Preston
Thomas Priest
Daniel Quick,
Frank Rand
Capt. John Rindge
Joseph Richards
Doctor Rogers
John Roberts
Doctor Ross
James Rowe
William Ross
Anthony Rowe, Jr.
Alexander Ross
Capt. Jno. Robertson
Auwell Roberts
Benj. Rust
Eleazer Russell
Agu. Russell
Samuel Rymes
John Savage
John Sargeant
Edward Saddler
John Sampson
John Saunders
Sylvanus Scott
Samuel Seaward
George Seaward

John Seaward
Wm. Seaward
Henry Seaward
William Sheaf
Richard Shortridge
John Shores
Samuel Sherburne
Sam'l Sherburne, Jr.
Capt. H. Sherburne
Capt. Jos. Sherburne
James Sherburne
John Sherburne
Henry Sherburne
Ephraim Sherburne
Capt. J. Sherburne, Jr.
Henry Sherburne, Sr.
John Shackford,
William Shackford
Samuel Shackford
John Simes
Joseph Sibson
John Sibson
Thomas Sibson
Thomas Simpson
Capt. Sloper
Ambrose Sloper
Richard Small
John Snell
Samuel Snell
James Springer
John Sparks
William Spriggs
Thomas Starboard
John Stevens
Joseph Stutely
James Stutely
Jonathan Stutely
Capt. Walter Stewart
John Stergen
John Steggins
Samuel Snalen
Richard Swain
Roger Swaine
Elias Tarlton
Jacob Tash
William Tarrett
Wm. Tapley
George Thompson
John Thompson
Capt. Geo. Tendell
James Titcomb
Edward Toogood
George Townsend
Richard Tobey
Samuel Tripe

Robert Triggs
Nath'l Tuckerman
Jacob Treadwell
S. Tripe
John Tucker
Francis Tucker
Oliver Tucker
William Vaughan
John Venson
George Vincent
William Warren
Samuel Waters
Matthew Watson
Sam'l Wales
Edward Wells
John Wales
Capt. R. Waterhouse
Capt. S. Waterhouse
Timothy Waterhouse
Walter Warren
Richard Ward
Gideon Walker
George Walker
Capt. Walker
John Walker
Joseph Walker
Col. Richard Waldron
Richard Waldron, Jr.
Moses Welch
Capt. Daniel Warner
Thomas Westbrook
Hunking Wentworth
Benning Wentworth
Capt. Eben Wentworth
Wm. Wentworth, 1st.
Wm. Wentworth, 2d.
Elisha Witham
Joseph Witham
Capt. Winkley
Nicholas Winkley
Mr. Willey
Samuel White
William White
William White, Jr.
John White, Jr.
Capt. Thos. White
John Whidden
Michæl Whidden, Jr.
Michæl Whidden
Thomas Wilkinson
Richard Wibird, Esq.
John Wibird
John Woodworth
John Woodin

Some errors may be made, as the spelling in old times was rather phonetic. For instance, the following from the town book of 1720:

Theodr ackinson
mickel Wheton
Jams Spiney
ben dunel
wedo Elet
ames fornel
Rich alett
hen Ries
Patr Gares
mos denet
dock Ros

Sam whit
Boid ye Shopkeer
Boid ye Barber
Gil mockfrders
Tim wartorhowes
Samuel Penholo Esqr
nemiah partrg
Ed ares
wedo marchel
hen Sowerd
moses pall

Capt. henry Slopr
danel quck
Rich warrhors
Jo burs
Gorg peairs
John Robrds
Zacrey Lech
Jo moyes
docker Pikk
walter warn [*Warren*]
Abram Kent

Rich Jos
Abr Sentr
humongromey
Phel Gamn
Willam Clarnbol
nat hach
Sam more
Enoch Grenlef
ben dockom
nat Roborson
ben gamlen

One striking feature in the preceding list of names is this: there is not a single case in which a man has more than one Christian name.

On the sixty-second and sixty-third pages of this book will be found a list of neighborhoods in 1678. We have no definite data from which to locate all those neighborhoods, but from the knowledge of the residences of some of the landholders of the same family names in later years, we think we are not far from right in placing the neighborhood under the care of Tythingman *Wallis*, near Sagamore creek. *Sargeant Brewster's* neighborhood, between Sagamore creek and the plains. *Thomas Jackson's*, on the South road. *George Branhall's*, in the vicinity of the South mill and on Peirce's island, where Waterhouse was known to reside at that time. *John Light's*, south of the South mill. *John Dennett's*, between D. H. Spinney's and Christian Shore. William Earle owned the land now Spinney's, to the creek, and Ham owned Freeman's Point. *Doctor Fletcher's*, *Morse's* and *Kaise's* neighborhoods probably extended from Water street to the north-end, near the river. The four neighborhoods last given, were probably on Newcastle, which at that time was a part of Portsmouth.

## RAMBLE XXXI.

Residences on Market and Bow streets—Judge Pickering—John Penhallow—Boyd—James McDonough—Disappearance on wedding night—Boyd's riches.

As has before been said, there is much of the romantic in the heretofore unwritten history of Portsmouth. A map of the position and a picture of the residences here at the close of the last century, before the desolating fires raged, would now be highly prized for the reminiscences they would awaken.

Taking that section on the east side of Market street, which extends from Commercial alley around to Bow street, we have the site of three houses of some note, which were swept away by the fire of 1802. First on the northern corner of Commercial alley and Market street, was the residence of Hon. John Pickering. It was a large two-story house, gable end toward Market street, with an entrance on the street, also a front entrance on the court. Judge P. was born in Newington in 1738, and graduated at Cambridge in 1761. A man of eminent ability, which was devoted to the service of his fellow-men. He was a member of the convention which framed the State Constitution, filled the office of Governor when Langdon resigned, and was chief justice of the supreme court for five years.

Next came the residence of John Penhallow, fronting the street, and occupying the spot where Jones & Mendum's store now stands.* The garden extended far back, and included nearly all the land afterwards called Penhallow street, from Daniel to Bow streets. Mr. P. was the brother of Deacon Samuel Penhallow and the father of Hunking and Benjamin Penhallow, who imbibed their father's conscientious nicety, and so long and so systematically and so honestly conducted business on the spot of their birth. If every body could be made to move with the same carefulness and affability, the world would have few accidents to record, and universal respect of man for his neighbor would cover the earth. The influence of such examples does not die in a single generation. John Penhallow, more than sixty years ago, owned and occupied the house on Islington street now owned by Capt. Wm. Parker, where he closed his days.

Now we approach the corner of Bow street. Here, with an open fence in front, seventy years since, was the resi-

* John A. Lamprey's, in 1873.

dence of William Boyd, a son of Col. George Boyd. In front of this very spacious mansion-house, which faced to the north, was an open fence enclosing a small garden plot.

Somewhere in the neighborhood, on what was then called Spring hill, was an English goods store, kept by James McDonough, an enterprising gentleman who came from England with some trading capital about the year 1757. He was successful in business, selling at what was regarded low prices, and his property accumulated so fast, that from a town and province tax of only £2 in 1758, it rose up to £27 in 1768. Mr. McDonough was an officer in St. John's Lodge, and acquired the highest standing in society. He gave his attentions to Miss Abigail Sheafe, the eldest daughter of Jacob Sheafe, and sister of the late Thomas, James, Jacob, William, etc.

Sometime in the year 1768, arrangements for the nuptials were made. The house selected was the one just described, afterwards William Boyd's, which was handsomely furnished, and rich plate provided. The long looked-for evening at length arrived which was to seal the matrimonial bond for better or for worse. At the mansion of the bride were collected the invited guests. But the bridegroom appeared not! No investigations could make any discovery of his mysterious disappearance; nor from that day to this, altho' ninety years have elapsed, has there been any discovery of what became of him! The suspense in which the bride was placed must have been appalling: in doubt whether to indulge in feelings of scorn at the treatment of him who had wickedly fled from her reach, or to give vent to feelings of grief for one who had been waylaid and murdered to prevent the marriage.

The mysterious disappearance was town talk at the time, but as there was a possibility that he might return, the papers of the day made no record of it. It was not until March, 1769, that the least public reference is made to Mr. McDonough, when a notice is published by Benjamin Parke, that having made several payments on a note held by James McDonough *when he left the country*, now in the hands of Col. George Boyd, he will not pay it.

It appears that all his property (with the exception of some silver ware which is still retained in the Sheafe family, bearing the initials J. McD.) passed into the hands of Col. Boyd, who at once became the richest man in Portsmouth. In 1770 his town and province tax was £67, (increasing £37 in one year,) while the highest tax paid by any other man in Portsmouth that year was £30.*

Miss Abigail Sheafe afterwards found a beloved partner in the Hon. John Pickering, whose former residence is pointed out above. She was the mother of the late Jacob S. Pickering, and also of Mrs. Lyman, still living, the mother of John P. Lyman.

---

## RAMBLE XXXII.

**George Boyd's seat near the north mill—Grenadiers' Heads—Boyd's early history.**

WE shall endeavor in this ramble to throw some light on an enquiry recently made respecting the "*Grenadiers' Heads.*" Col. George Boyd, (he was the father of Wil-

*As a matter of curiosity, we give a list of the principal tax payers in Portsmouth in 1770, with the proportion (dispensing with fractions) assessed on each. The list shows all those who paid over £10 for town and province expenses. The whole amount of tax was about £1659. The poll tax was 12 shillings. The whole number of tax payers in 1770 was 666.

| | | | | | |
|---|---|---|---|---|---|
| George Boyd | £67 | D. & S. Sherburne | £19 | Samuel Cutt | £13 |
| Mark H. Wentworth | 30 | Griffith & Bowles | 17 | Theodore Atkinson | 12 |
| Jonathan Warner | 27 | Thomas Atchinclass | 15 | George Jaffrey | 12 |
| James Mc Master | 27 | Samuel Griffith | 15 | Thomas Martin | 12 |
| Woodbury Langdon | 24 | Jacob Treadwell | 13 | A. R. Cutter | 10 |
| Daniel Warner | 20 | Richard Hart | 15 | William Pearne | 12 |
| John Penhallow | 20 | Daniel Rindge | 15 | George Cragie | 12 |
| Jacob Sheafe | 20 | Hugh Henderson | 13 | Wm. Appleton | 12 |
| Joshua Wentworth | 18 | Thomas Packer | 13 | Benj. Bigelow | 11 |
| John Moffatt | 16 | John Sherburne | 13 | James Stoodly | 10 |
| Charles Treadwell | 15 | James Stilson | 14 | | |

liam Boyd, and grandfather of Col. George W. Boyd now living in Portland, Me.) purchased the mill seat, now the Raynes' mansion and ship-yard, of Peter Livius, somewhere between 1767 and 1770. He enlarged the house, materially. His garden in front extended to the site of the present depot, (the land of ex-Mayor Walker and James Nowell being included in it), and water bounded his premises on the east. It was a magnificent seat, such as a nabob might envy, enclosed within a white open fence, and at regular intervals of some forty or fifty feet, those handsomely carved towering *Grenadier's heads* were placed on posts, and presented a very unique appearance

Col. George Boyd was in indigent circumstances in early life, and served as a house-boy to Henry Sherburne, a merchant who resided near Pier wharf. His master was very strict in his discipline. One Sunday finding some fresh fish on the table, he learned on inquiry that George had caught them in sacred time. The next morning George received a horsewhipping for Sabbath desecration. Not long after, George was one day sent into the storehouse to draw molasses. After taking out the tap, he stepped to the door to speak with an acquaintance. Forgetting his charge, he did not look back until the floor was pretty well covered with the sweet carpet! The terror of the whip forbade an effort for an explanation, so he took French leave of the town and soon after became an apprentice in Boston. He came to Portsmouth when of age, and was foreman of Myrick's ropewalk, which was built north of the line of the present jail premises, extending west from what is now the garden of Ira Haselton, on Rock street, to the site of the stable of Ichabod Goodwin. He was successful in business, or fortunate in discovering treasure in the "old cellar," and retired from the ropewalk in early life to commence trading. He was sharp at a bargain, generally paying his workmen in goods at a large advance on cost.

His wife was Jane, a daughter of Joseph Brewster, who in 1727 owned and occupied as a boarding-house the site of the late Isaac Waldron's residence on Congress street. The original house was of two stories. About sixty years after, the first house was removed back and made the ell of the present three-story house* then erected by William Seavey. Col. George Boyd's first residence after marriage was in the John Melcher house, fronting Vaughan street.

They had five sons and five daughters. Mary married Joseph Champney, and died since 1850; Jane married Dr. John Goddard, and died in 1790, aged twenty-seven years; Phebe died young; Abigail, married Capt. Mackay, and afterwards Capt. Samuel Ham, who built the Woodbury mansion; Submit married Hon. John S. Sherburne, and died in 1803, aged twenty-eight years; Joseph died after arriving at years of manhood; George died unmarried; William married a daughter of Capt. Thomas Martin, (and left one son, Capt. George W., now living, and the only descendant who bears the name of Boyd); Supply and Henry Lucas died young.

Submit, his youngest daughter, was born in October, 1774, just before Boyd's departure for England. It was said that the name given to her was intended as his expression of what he regarded the duty of the country. This intimation, however, has been denied, for he made no direct opposition to the Revolution. He preserved a neutrality, that he might retain his lucrative business—but none of his enemies could substantiate a charge of rebellion, disloyality, nor treason against him; neither could the most ardent "minute men" of those "times that tried men's souls," point out a solitary overt act of his, that betrayed hostility to the country of his birth and her noble cause.

*Burnt in 1870.

Col. Boyd did not long personally enjoy his beautiful seat, for it appears that he left for England in an early part of the Revolution, and spent but little of the last twelve years of his life with his family, which remained at the mansion by the mill, or rather at the *White village*, as from their color, the collection of dwellings, store houses and barns, was sometimes called.

In August, 1787, Col. George Boyd sailed from London for his home, from which he had been many years absent. He took with him a handsome coach, and an English coachman named Charles Harrington, who afterwards became the coachman of Woodbury Langdon. His gardener, John Cunningham, (who died a few years since, at the age of ninety-four,) he also sent over from England, at an earlier date. Without probably anticipating its use so soon, he also brought in the same ship with his coach an elegant monument [it may be seen in the north burying-ground], for his grave at some future time, with a place for a marble tablet on which to have recorded his final departure. The vessel had a long passage, and did not arrive at our port until the 8th of October, two days after his spirit had departed. Thus, at the age of fifty-four years, just reaching the scene of his magnificient mansion and spacious gardens in season to occupy a tenement six feet by two, on the opposite side of the way, and to be covered by the cold stones which had accompanied him on his voyage. How fleeting the riches and grandeur of earth. There can now be found scarcely a trace of the treasures of him who was our Crœsus eighty years ago—excepting in that tomb stone!

## RAMBLE XXXIII.

Ropewalks in former times on Islington road, Elm and Middle streets—Present Ropewalk on South street —Improvements in machinery—Longfellow's hempen lines.

"In that building, long and low,
With its windows all a-row
Like the port-holes of a hulk,
Human spiders spin and spin,
Backwards down their threads so thin,
Dropping, each, a hempen bulk."

"SPINNING of street yarn" is the rambler's occupation; it is therefore not out of place for him to give some attention to spinning generally—and in the first place to the most important branch, the stoutest thread, that of Rope Spinning.

The time was, and that not very distant, when the ropewalk was the only imposing factory building any town in New England presented. Our cotton and woollen fabrics were either imported or woven at the homestead—but our ropes required more room for spinning and laying, and the long, long structure was extended out and out until a man at one end looked small as a mouse from the other, and the wheel in the converged distant point like the whirling toy top.

"At the end, an open door;
Squares of sunshine on the floor
Light the long and dusky lane;
And the whirling of a wheel,
Dull and drowsy, makes me feel
All the spokes are in my brain."

With the four hundred per cent. increase of tonnage in the last thirty years, there is now a less number of ropewalks in operation than there were in 1825. The improvements of machinery have enabled a vastly greater amount of work to be accomplished in the same time and space, and have thus rather diminished than increased the number of cordage factories long drawn out.

The first ropewalk in Portsmouth, of which we can find

any trace, was built a few rods east of the present location of the Jail, about where Rock street is, and extended north from the front of Supply Ham's, on Islington street, to the water. After some years the ropewalk was either removed or rebuilt near the same vicinity. The tar-house of the latter was on the spot where the garden of Ira Haselton now is, and was for many years the residence of Robert Bartlett. The ropewalk extended west from this spot parallel with Islington street, about two hundred feet from it, to where Cornwall street now is, This walk was down before the recollection of our oldest inhabitants, but the elevated ridge of ground was visible until the recent improvements have leveled it out of sight. This walk was owned by Mr. Myrick and conducted by George Boyd, a practical ropemaker, who afterwards built a ropewalk on Elm street for a son.

At the time when this walk was in use, there was no bridge to shut out the direct connection of Islington Creek with the river. Ships were built at the west end of the Creek on the south side, opposite the Ham premises. A ship and two schooners have been on the stocks there at the same time. There were also saw and grist mills in the vicinity. The north mill bridge was built in 1764, after which time the mills at the head of the creek were suffered to decay, and ship building in the creek was suspended.

On the spot where the Eastern Railroad depot now is, and extending west to the water, were two ropewalks, both erected before the Revolution. They were in pretty constant use until after the war of 1812. After that time the most northerly walk, belonging to Daniel Wentworth, went to decay. John Underwood kept the other walk (formerly owned by John Hart) in operation for many years after. It was here that the cordage of the Washington seventy-four was made—and many will long remember that procession of eighty sailors which passed through our streets bearing from that walk, on their shoulders, the monster cable of that ship of the line.

There are other recollections of this ropewalk, as the place for public dinners on the 4th of July, in the war of 1812. The room was ample for the most extensive companies. Tables were extended to the length of five hundred feet through the decorated walk, and seven hundred seats were here occupied. We can yet see the processions of 1813 and 1814 moving from the Fire and Marine Insurance office, (now the Atheneum reading room), escorted by the Gilman Blues under Col. Joshua W. Pierce, and the dignified Col. E. J. Long performing the duty of Chief Marshal on both occasions. The orator on one occasion was the then boisterous Capt. William Ladd, and on the next anniversary, the mild and retiring Nathaniel A. Haven, Jr. Rev. Dr. Parker was the chaplain, and Sewall the reader of Washington's Farewell Address. Though some of the yarns spun in this walk in those days might have been immediately picked into oakum by political opponents, yet when such men as Webster, Mason, Sheafe, Cutts and Haven were the spinners, cables were probably laid which held in safety the great Ship of State.

Some sixty or seventy years ago, a ropewalk was erected by John Akerman, on Middle street, extending south from Wibird's hill. This was not much used after 1825, and the last vestige of it has not been seen for more than a dozen years.

On the south side of the South Mill pond is now located the only ropewalk in Portsmouth—in fact the only cordage factory in operation between the Kennebec and Salem, Mass. Our first most vivid impression of that locality was the sight of a ropewalk in flames, in 1814. The conflagration is more vividly impressed from the circumstance that the week previous an Eliot seer had prophesied that on that evening it was to be burnt. The subject was commonly talked of among the boys on that day, and sure enough at seven o'clock in the evening it was in flames. In this case, as in many others, the prophecy doubtless led to its own fulfilment: the incendiary was prompted to the deed by the visionary lunatic. This ropewalk in the time of the war of 1812, was used for the barracks of a portion of the soldiers drafted from other towns for the defence of Portsmouth. Among those who here found quarters, was Ichabod Bartlett (afterward member of Congress), a drafted militiaman from the town of Durham.

The walk was rebuilt after the fire, put in use, and in ten years after it came under the superintendence of Jeremiah Johnson, from Newburyport. From a practical knowledge of his business and strict oversight of his work, he was successful in producing superior cordage, and bore off the first premium in the Mechanic's exhibitions of other States. For three or four years past, in company with John N. Handy, the business of the establishment has been much extended. Another fire in 1854 having swept the factory to ashes—it has since been rebuilt and very desirable improvements made. In our recent walk we spent an hour in its various apartments. The whole building is now about eight hundred feet long, and half that distance it is two stories in height. It is operated by steam.

For thirty years we had not entered a ropewalk, and the improvements in the machinery and modes of operation struck our eyes as the change of things did Rip Van Winkle after his long nap. In this establishment, with thirty or forty men and boys, double as much cordage is now manufactured annually, as the product of all the other walks in Portsmouth when in full operation in former times. In 1855 there were turned out between three and four hundred tons of cordage, of the first quality. Nearly all the ships built here are rigged from this factory—as well as a large number built in Maine and Massachusetts. Among the ships of high reputation owned abroad, built within a few years, and rigged with this cordage, might be named many of the world-renowned clippers. The *Dreadnought*, harnessed in their strong ropes, plunges confidently on in its fearless career—the graceful *Nightingale*, spreads her full wings to the breeze, safe in rapid flight in its strong stays; Thus confidently rushes on with equal speed the *Highflyer* and the *Dashing Wave*; and then comes up that good representative of strong-headed network, the *Webster*—all clippers of the great commercial emporium—and heading a fleet of others is the strong-muscled *Cœur de Lion* of Boston—each bearing aloft the product of the Portsmouth cordage factory. South-end feels just pride in having so important a branch of domestic industry prospering in its midst.

That Rope Spinning is a matter of general interest, Longfellow has most elegantly illustrated in a recent poem, on visiting a ropewalk. He spun out the following hempen threads, and neatly laid them down in a six-line chord:

As the spinners to the end
Downward go and reascend,
Gleam the long threads in the sun;
While within this brain of mine
Cobwebs brighter and more fine
By the busy wheel are spun.

Two fair maidens in a swing,
Like white doves upon the wing,
First before my vision pass;
Laughing, as their gentle hands
Closely clasp the twisted strands,
At their shadow on the grass.

Then a booth of mountebanks,
With its smell of tan and planks,
And a girl poised high in air
On a cord, in spangled dress,
With a faded loveliness,
And a weary look of care.

Then a homestead among farms,
And a woman with bare arms,
Drawing water from a well;
As the bucket mounts apace,
With it mounts her own fair face,
As at some magician's spell.

Then an old man in a tower
Ringing loud the noontide hour,
While the rope coils round and round,
Like a serpent at his feet,
And again in swift retreat
Almost lifts him from the ground.

Then a school-boy, with his kite
Gleaming in a sky of light,
And an eager, upward look—
Steeds pursued through lane and field—
Fowlers with their snares concealed,
And an angler by a brook.

Ships rejoicing in the breeze,
Wrecks that float o'er unknown seas,
Anchors dragged thro' frithless sand;
Sea-fog drifting overhead,
And with lessening line and lead
Sailors feeling for the land.

All these scenes do I behold,
These, and many left untold,
In that building long and low;
While the wheels go round and round,
With a drowsy, dreamy sound,
And the spinners backward go

## RAMBLE XXXIV.

The Old Cellar—Rock Pasture—Myrick's Ropewalk—His departure—The buried gold.

Associated with the early recollections of the men of threescore, is the Old Cellar, with its gradually declining green banks and pool of water. It was on the west side of Ann street, perhaps a hundred feet from the street, and the like distance south-west of the residence of the late William Shillaber. Near the north-west corner, fifty feet distant, was a boulder of several tons, setting high enough above the ground for a seat for the visitor, and extending far enough below the surface to cover,—the boys used to say money,—but the rock was too heavy for them ever to satisfy their curiosity by proving or disproving the fact. In summer around it was the favorite play ground for the Rock pasture boys,—and when frost came, and the ice was formed, here was the skating school for the tyros before they entered upon that scene of active life, the great mill pond. The times have changed, and what was once a cow pasture, is now the site of the Sagamore Mill,—and McDonough, Penn and Lyme streets, with the houses that line them, fill that once attractive open space;—and the house of Daniel P. Drown sits now upon that centre of all attractions, the Old Cellar. We may look with joy upon the progress of improvement, but with some regret at being deprived of the open scenes which gladdened the youthful eye.

As the Old Cellar has been made the subject of a romance by one who can appreciate its early attractions, it would perhaps be interesting to give its traditionary history, which has enough of romance connected with it to make it attractive without a borrowed dress.

Before the Revolution, Rock street was the outskirt of the town,—so decidedly so, that when a map of Portsmouth was made in 1778, it extended only to Parker street in the westerly direction. At that time, and long after, there was no house on the north side of the street between Parker street and Martin's hill. On the site of the residence of Capt. Hussey, was a high rock, which gave to the whole neighborhood the name of Rock Pasture—and from it Rock street took its name. Behind the rock, commencing where Mr. Haselton's stable stands, was a ropewalk, extending west and terminating near Cornwall street.

The whole pasture, from Ann street to beyond the Sagamore factory, it has been said, was purchased by a Mr. Myrick, an Englishman, who was preparing to make a handsome park, and build a house in the vicinity of the river, which then, being unobstructed by a bridge, was deeper, clearer, and more beautiful than it has since usually been. Mr. Myrick had laid out his plans, and the cellar for his house was dug,—that *Old Cellar*,—between the west end of the ropewalk and the river. When he had made progress thus far, the times began to present a squally appearance. Desiring to visit England, he found it very difficult at the time to obtain passage either from this port or from Boston. He found a vessel bound to Jamaica, and knowing the frequent intercourse between that island and the mother country, he took passage. Nothing was ever heard of him after. It was supposed he was lost in some ship between Jamaica and England. Some years after, one afternoon, as John Redding and George Boyd closed work in the old ropewalk above described, Boyd threw off the hemp which had been wound around his body, exclaiming—"There—I will never spin another thread—I'll get my living in an easier way." This remark somewhat surprised the other workmen, as they knew of no means he had for a livelihood aside from his regular trade. He however soon went into business with a mysterious capital, and ever after spun the silken rather than the hempen yarns of life.

It was commonly supposed that when Myric left for England, there being no safe depository for treasure in any American institution, and less safety in attempting to carry it away, he hid his gold beneath this boulder near the Old Cellar, which was a few rods north of the ropewalk,—and that the sudden riches of the ropemaker arose from his discovery of the treasure. This is the tradition of the Old Cellar. It may be true—it may not be in every respect, but such is the tradition.

No one claiming the land, it was held by the original proprietors, and many deeds have been given since, in which those who have had a knowledge of the facts have granted a *quit-claim* in preference to a *warrantee* title.

## RAMBLE XXXV.

Vaughan street—The Old Assembly House—Michae Whidden—Nathaniel Meserve—Stamp Act—George Meserve—Revolutionary scenes—Liberty Bridge—Occupants of the Meserve house—Old trees.

Having rambled several times from Market square to Vaughan street, (until 1778 called Cross street,) occasionally looking up the latter, we will now turn the corner and follow in the track of this narrow though great thoroughfare, through which all the coaches now pass at every arrival of the cars.

But where is the old Assembly House? Sawn asunder, split in two, wheeled to the right and left, and just where we used to enter its large front door, we enter now the centre of Raitt's court; the two houses on the entrance of the court were made from that old Assembly House, which Washington in 1789 pronounced one of the best he had seen anywhere in the United States. How many recollections are associated with it! How often have the white teeth of Cuffee Whipple distinctly shown from its orchestra to the *elite* of the town on the floor below, as he labored with his violin to keep up the mazy dance! Cuffee was not alone, for sometimes that life of the Assemblies, Col. Michael Wentworth would stand by his side and as an amateur give his aid. How often here brilliant stars "strutted their short hour," in illustration of the powers of the histrionic art; and here were the curiosities of art and nature displayed; oft has the note harmonious of the Handel Society here ascended; and here too have audiences in this spacious hall been convened to worship their Creator. It was a large and curious building, the plaything of one who had much experience in building houses. The Assembly Room was the full size of the front of the building, lighted on three sides, with two drawing-rooms, and an orchestra over the entrance. The builder was Michael Whidden, who also built and was the first occupant of the house in Deer street afterwards occupied by Col. Peter Livius and Thomas Martin, and now occupied by George Annable. He also built several other houses in the vicinity, and among these the house on the corner of Deer and Vaughan streets, occupied by John S. Harvey, and the two-story gambrel roof house directly in front of the old Assembly House, now owned and occupied by the family of Robert Gray.

The latter house, could all its old occupants be made to pass in procession before us, and could the incidents which have grown up in their connection be related, would form the subject of an interesting volume, not only of our local, but also in our State and national history.

To understand our story it will be necessary to go back a little beyond the days when Mr. Gray's house was built, which was about a century ago.

At the siege of Louisburg, in 1745, Col. Nathaniel Meserve of this town, a ship builder, rendered essential service in constructing sledges on which the canon were drawn through a deep morass. This service was not forgotten; for in 1749 he was commissioned by the British Government to build a ship-of-war of fifty guns, called the America. He then lived in a house of his own construction next south of the North mill bridge, which has since been called the Boyd house, and now belongs to the Raynes family. The ship was built near where the present Raynes' ship yard now is. As the bridge was not then constructed, the ship might have been built on the pond side in the rear of the Moses house. Col. Meserve acquired much wealth, and was of unblemished reputation. In 1756, he had command of the New Hampshire regiment raised for the Crown Point expedition. To his care was entrusted Fort Edward, which was gallantly defended. In 1758, he embarked with over a hundred carpenters to aid in the second siege of Louisburg. The small pox broke out among them, and all except sixteen died, including the Colonel and his eldest son. He left one other son, George Meserve, who was married to Miss Newmarch, and for them the Gray house was built by Mr. Whidden about the year 1760. Mr. Meserve, when in England in 1765, at the time of the passage of the Stamp act, was appointed agent for distributing the stamps in New Hampshire. Nowhere in the colonies was there a more determined spirit of resistance to the oppression of the mother country manifested than in Portsmouth. Mr. Meserve well knew this, and thereupon, on arriving at Boston, on the 6th of September, (about seven weeks before the law was to take effect,) the excited state of the public feeling induced him to resign his office of stamp master. His resignation was not known here; so the indignant populace, on the night of the 11th of September, placed on the hill in front of the jail a triple effigy, representing Lord Bute, who was father of the bill, Meserve and the Devil. A board was extended from the mouth of the Devil to Meserve's ear, on which was written:

> George, my son, you are rich in station,
> But I would have you serve this nation.

The effigies stood through the day, and in the evening they were carried about the town with much clamor, and then burnt. A week elapsed before Meserve arrived in Portsmouth. He then on the parade made public his resignation. He was joyfully escorted to this house, and from its quiet retreat looked out upon the troubled world around him. The first of November, when the act was to be in force, was ushered in with tolling bells, half mast flags, etc., and at 3 P. M. a funeral procession was formed, bearing the coffin of *Liberty*, etc. On depositing it in a grave, signs of life appearing, the muffled drums beat up a lively air, the tolling of bells was changed to ringing, and the spirit of patriotism was planted yet deeper in many a heart.

The next year, in January of 1766, another scene is presented at this house. The stamp master commission of George Meserve arrives. The jealous people, well knowing that "eternal vigilance is the price of liberty," are in commotion. A delegation of the choice spirits of the times, among them John Davenport, Thomas Manning, George Gains, and brother "sons of liberty," might be seen convened in Vaughan street, and standing sword in hand at the door of this house. The stamp master appears at the door, and their business is made known. He takes from the desk the commission he has just received, gives it up to them, and submits to the administration of an oath by Wiseman Claggett, that he would not directly or indirectly attempt to execute the office. The commission is taken—on the point of a sword it is elevated, and the procession moves down Vaughan and up King street, bearing the trophy, hailed by the shouts of the "sons of liberty." They pass the parade, and proceed to Swing Bridge, on Water street, where they erected a Liberty standard. From that day Swing Bridge received the name of Liberty Bridge, and the motto—"*Liberty, Property, and no Stamp.*"

In this course of events Mr. Meserve was subjected to some losses, without those emoluments of office to which he had been looking. In 1772 he was appointed Collector of this port. Mr. George Meserve had one son, George, and two daughters. One of the daughters, Sarah, was married to James Sheafe (afterwards U. S. Senator and candidate for Governor,) who purchased her father's house and here resided soon after the peace of 1783. Here too he continued to reside for several years after his marriage with his second wife. After Mr. Sheafe's removal to the vicinity of Market Square, another distinguished merchant, Dr. Nathaniel A. Haven, became an occupant, and here resided until the erection of the mansion on High street, in about the year 1800, now occupied by Charles H. Ladd. The next occupant was Hon. Jeremiah Mason,—no less distinguished for his gigantic stature than for his prominence in the legal profession. Here several of his children were born, and the young lawyer who entered here almost a stranger, left it in six or eight years, with a fame not confined to his own State, for his seat on "Mason's Hill." The next tenant was Daniel Webster. Show us a house in New England where two tenants of more powerful minds, of stronger intellects, of more enduring fame, have been under the same landlord in succession. This was the place of his first occupancy as the head of a family—and here, when he visited Portsmouth in after years, would he look back to the place where Grace Fletcher, the early loved and early lost, was the esteemed associate at the domestic hearth. The next resident was Gen. Timothy Upham, distinguished in the field of battle, and in civil life a candidate for the chief magistracy of the State—and discharging with fidelity the various public trusts committed to his charge. The great fire of 1813 made the owner homeless, and Hon. James Sheafe again occupies the premises he vacated twenty years before. When next vacated, Capt. Elihu Brown, who was prominent in the war of 1812, occupied it for a time,—then Dr. Robert L. Thorn, of the Navy, a gentleman of noble spirit and of much prominence, made this his home. It was afterward successively occupied by Major Edward J. Long, Joshua B. Whidden, John H. Sheafe and G. W. Pendexter, not alienating from the Sheafe family until 1839, when it was purchased by Robert Gray. When the house was built in 1760, there was no house on the west side of Vaughan street, from the corner of Congress street to and around the corner of Deer street to where David Libbey now lives.

In the garden planted by Meserve, was a bergamot pear tree, which after enduring the storms of a century, and liberally furnishing to the tables of Meserve, Sheafe, Mason, Webster, Upham, Long, Thorn, etc., its choice fruit, has but just passed to that decay to which all things mutable are destined. In the same garden are two towering sassafras trees, measuring nearly a yard in circumference, which are as old as the house. Who of the thousands who have attended the old North School, from the days of the Revolution to the present time, has not picked up the leaves as they have blown over the fence, and enjoyed their aromatic fragrance, and nutritious, pulp-like taste. Many a time, too, in successive generations, has the feeble knock at the door found the little caller asking the privilege of gathering some of the leaves of the "sarsafax."

Thus we ramble round, stirring up some remembrance of those who have, like the old pear tree, been valuable in their day—and whose memory, like the leaves of the sassafras, still imparts a fragrance to those who take pains to gather them.

## RAMBLE XXXVI.

Doctor Moses—Single tens—Small glass—Congress at Albany—"Dr. Moses's bottle"—Conjuration—His widow.

PEACE to the ashes of our good old friend, the late Thomas Moses, who for so many years was ever ready with his kind attentions at the Bath house, and who led the life and died the death of a Christian, in 1856. We honor his memory, but we only speak of him now as a connecting link for introducing his father, Samuel Moses, the famous barber of the last century, of whom has been told many a lively story. But we cannot at present say much of him either, as our ramble carries us back yet one generation further, to his father, Joseph Moses, familiarly called *Doctor*.

Dr. Joseph Moses was a native of England, an eccentric humorist, who was by trade a house-carpenter, and about one hundred and twenty years ago lived in a house on the corner of Fleet and Congress streets, built on the spot now occupied by Jackson & Co.'s express office. The house was of one story, with two rooms only; one of them was occupied by the father, mother and nine children; in the other the cow was kept, in the yard her hay stacked. Dr. Moses, although in snug quarters, found room to spare; for when one son had learned the trade of a shoemaker, he had a shop parted off in his father's mansion. The house for many years was without a shingle or a clapboard. About the year 1750, when the North meeting-house was shingled, the old shingles were carried to his house, and formed the first outer covering of the Doctor's residence.

The title of Doctor was acquired from this circumstance. He was employed on a job at a place where he frequently found his spirit bottle emptied without his agency. He put a powerful preparation in the bottle, and left it. Soon after the spirit again disappeared from the bottle, and poor Sambo, the black, thought his spirit too was about leaving him. Sambo recovered and was cured of spirit stealing—and his master gave Moses the title or *Doctor*, which he ever after retained.

In those days the General Assembly held their session in a room at what is now the corner of State and Pleasant streets, on the same spot occupied in 1860 as our city government rooms. The Doctor had less respect for the Assembly than he had for the enjoyment of a clever joke. A man from the country one day in pursuit of a place to buy some nails, asked Dr. Moses where he could find some *single tens.* "Go down there," said the Doctor, pointing to the door of ten in council, "and you will find them." The man entered the room, and abruptly said, "Let me have a pound of your single tens." The honorable dignitaries felt deeply insulted, and were about to have the man committed for contempt, when the countryman finding that an imposition had been played upon him, expressed sorrow for the unintential intrusion: moreover pleading that he was directed to call there by a man, a description of whom left no doubt that it was the Doctor.

The matter was now understood; the man was dismissed with an admonition, and a messenger dispatched to summon Doctor Moses before the august body. The Doctor at length appears—the charge is made, the Doctor pleads guilty—and for his contempt of the Assembly is commanded to get down on his knees and ask pardon. The Doctor submits resignedly to the execution of the sentence. In a prominent part of the room he bends on his knees and humbly asks pardon for any offence he may have committed; then rising upright before them he commences rapidly rubbing the dust from his knees, exclaiming in no smothered accents, "*A dirty house—a dirty house!*"

At one time he called on Secretary Atkinson on some

business. The Secretary, agreeably to the custom of the times, tendered the Doctor a glass of wine, in one of those miniature glasses which may now be seen in collections of ancient glass ware. The Doctor emptied the glass, smacked his lips, praised its flavor, and asked the Hon. Secretary how old it was? "Of the vintage of about sixty years ago," was the reply. "Well," said the Doctor," "I never in my life saw so small a thing of such an age."

Dr. Moses became so great a favorite of Hon. Theodore Atkinson, who was a dear lover of humor, that when he was appointed a delegate to the Congress which met at Albany in 1754, he took Doctor Moses with him, nominally as waiter, but really to enjoy his wit. In the evening, when nothing was doing in Congress, the Doctor was sometimes called to the parlor after the punch bowl had been prepared. He would then tell some droll story, and enjoy the treat with the rest. On one of these occasions he became rather too familiar, telling his honorable associate, "You ain't fit to carry garbage to a bear." "Man, you are too bold," said Mr. A. "I cannot receive such a remark from you; you must either recall your words or quit my service. "Well, I will take them back," said the inveterate joker, "*You are fit.*" Nothing more could be said to such a subject.

"Doctor Moses's bottle" is a term applied to demijohns, in use by some of our older citizens to this day. It originated in this manner: The Doctor was employed by one of our liberal citizens to do a job of work. He was on hand very early in the morning, as it was the custom in former times to do two or three hours' work before breakfast. The early attendance pleased his employer, and as a mark of his approbation, he told the Doctor to bring a bottle and he would fill it with some old Jamaica. The Doctor's next appearance found him accompanied with a bottle, which, instead of being of the common junk size, was of five gallons capacity. The unexpected receptacle, being within the bargain, was filled by the astonished employer agreeably to promise, and from that day in Portsmouth the demijohn received the name of "Dr. Moses's Bottle."

The Doctor made some pretensions to necromancy, fortune-telling, or what perhaps in modern days would be called spiritualism. A man from Kittery applied to him one day to know who had stolen a valuable rope. He told him to call in a few hours, and he would make a conjuration. In the mean time the Doctor made inquiry to ascertain who was the worst fellow in Kittery, and one Michael Mahoney was pointed out as a bad fellow. He then wrote with onion juice on a piece of paper, which was invisible until exposed to heat:

"I do not laugh, neither do I joke—
"But Michael Mahoney stole your rope."

The man came for the result of his divination, and he handed him the piece of white paper as the result, which was hid from him, but would be disclosed when he exposed the paper to the heat. The man paid his fee, and when the terrified Michael Mahoney was informed that the spirits had exposed him by writing with an invisible hand, he acknowledged the theft and gave up the plunder.

Doctor Moses, when shingling the Freeman house, which now stands on the corner of Hanover and High streets, fell, and was ever afterwards lame.

There was a school kept in the house on Congress street during the Revolutionary war, by "Marm Moses," probably the widow of the Doctor. Soon after the peace of 1783, Nathaniel Dean, from Exeter, came to Portsmouth, and built the present house, now owned by Jackson & Akerman, which he occupied for about forty years, doing business in his latter days in the brick building now occupied by Thomas Treadwell.

## RAMBLE XXXVII.

Samuel Moses—Samuel, Jr.—Fish story—Shaving—Theodore Moses.

DR. JOSEPH MOSES, the subject of our last ramble, had a son Samuel, a barber, whose shop was located near the theatre, opposite Robinson's store on Bow street, where the blacksmith shop now stands. He was a most excellent man. Although possessing no small share of his father's wit, he chose rather to do those things which led to the spiritual good of his fellow men, than to make sport at the expense of others. He was industrious—and after discharging his duties in his shop in the forenoon, would in the afternoon whirl the spinning wheel—and do his part in supplying the lack then felt of more extensive factories.

Among his sons was one who bore his name and followed his profession—his oldest son, probably. As we pass from Congress into Fleet street, on one of the pave stones a little south of the carriage shop, is deeply cut, "S. M. 1801." Although the wear of nearly sixty years by the constant passers-by has been upon it, yet it still stands distinct—a memento of one who was determined to perpetuate his name—although perhaps not one in a thousand of those who have aided in smoothing that stone, have known whose initials were there chiseled. They were those of this Samuel Moses, 2d—whose residence was in a house near where that stone is placed. That Samuel was a man of small stature, and in purity of life did not walk so much in the footsteps of his father as in those of his grandfather. Among the stories related of him was the device for raising a treat. One morning the change was short, and the means for a treat with a friend did not appear at hand. There was hanging in the shop a fresh cod fish for dinner. He told his companion to retire, and to return after he saw the next person enter, and to call it a *cusk*. Mr. Hill soon coming in to get shaved, remarked to Mr. Moses, "this is a fine cod." "Cod—cod! why sir, that is a cusk." "No, it's certainly a cod." "A bottle of spirit on it," said Mr. Moses, "and we will leave it to the first man who comes in." "A-greed," said Mr. Hill, confident in his correctness. Now enters the companion, as though it was his first appearance, wishing them good morning. "What fish is this?" asked Mr. Moses. "This is a cusk—and capital eating it is too." The treat was paid by Mr. Hill, and the joke as well as the spirit was enjoyed by the confederates.

At another time a stranger applied to be shaved. He asked the price. "Four coppers," was the reply. "I won't give but three." "Well give me three and sit down." The work was speedily dispatched, but the stranger on looking in the glass found that just one-half of his beard on one side, had not been touched. On remonstrating, Moses said that he had taken off just three coppers' worth and would for another copper finish the job. The copper was paid, and the work completed.

Samuel Moses Jr.'s shop was on the lot directly south of Mrs. Alexander Ladd's residence. On the opposite side of the street, where the Messrs. Sise's crockery ware store now is, was also an eccentric man, Mr. John Allcock, who dealt in hardware, groceries, provisions, hats, etc., as his father had on the same spot many years before him. It was John who endeavored to make a speedy sale of chalk on hand, by announcing that it would soon become scarce, as the *chalk-maker* in England was *dead*. One day as he was in his counting-room, looking in a glass which reflected the position of his customers at the counter, he saw a young lady whom he left selecting needles, put several of them slyly in her mouth. After receiving pay for the few she exhibited, he suddenly clapped both hands against her cheeks, saying he liked to pat a pretty girl, bringing the points of the needles to the surface of the skin! It was a rash act, but was doubtless effectual in curing the girl of petty shop-lifting.

Theodore Moses, a brother of Samuel 2d, and grandson of Dr. Moses, is now living in Exeter, in his ninety-third year, and in the full possession of his faculties. He was the oldest "Son of Portsmouth" who returned to the gathering of July 4, 1853. He recently addressed to the Portsmouth Journal a letter, which shows he yet feels a deep interest in Portsmouth. *

---

* EXETER, Nov. 8, 1858.

*Mr. Brewster,—Dear Sir :*

I have read many of the "Rambles" in your papers, some of which have occurred since 1770 to 1779. You refer to the South School House over the lower mill-dam, where I first went to school to Capt. Osborn. They were then building a new school house lower down, —then he moved his school to his own house [No. 19 South street,] a short distance below the new school house. When the school-house was finished, he moved his school there. Mr. Osborn was very excitable. One day he stayed in school and wrote a list of rules, and pasted them up in the room, which had a good effect upon the scholars. He kept school till the Revolutionary war broke out, then he went out in an armed ship with Capt. Thompson, Lieut. Shores, and Lieut. Manning. 'Twas said they discovered a ship in sight in their cruise, held a counsel and concluded not to put away for her,—and they made a song about it in Portsmouth. The school was next taken by a Mr. Holbrook.

You speak of Mr. Clarkson in your "Rambles," who lived down further south. I met him one warm day coming home from school, on Pleasant street, with his hat in his hand —he was quite a large man. Capt. Thomas Pickering, who went in the ship Hampden, I saw frequently at Mr. Tilton's Tavern. Some of the Portsmouth boys went out with him, and he was killed in an engagement. The ship came in under the command of Captain Mead, and anchored in the lower harbor. Capt. Mead came up to town in a barge. I and some other boys asked liberty of him to go down to the ship, and he let us go. When we came up she fired minute guns. The colors were half mast high.

I left my native town the first day of September, 1779. I lived eight years in New Market, then came to Exeter, lived in Exeter and New Market two years longer. Made bricks eighteen years in the summer and hats in the fall, winter and spring. Went into trade in December, 1811, came out 1847. I have lived sixty-six years in one house, on Back street near the Railroad crossing. From a Portsmouth boy in his ninety-third year.

Your humble servant,

THEODORE MOSES.

## RAMBLE XXXVIII.

**Staver's hotel—John and Bartholomew Stavers—First Stage to Boston—Progress of travel.**

On the south-west corner of Court and Atkinson streets stands a large, square house of three stories, which in the ninety years it has stood has been the scene of as varied incidents as any house in New Hampshire. Its more particular history we defer, to give place to incidents which transpired prior to its erection.

When its builder, John Stavers, came to this country, we do not know. We find on the town books that in 1756 John and Bartholomew Stavers paid their first town tax, and it was probably the first or second year of their location. John kept a public house for ten years in Queen street, bottom of State street, at which place the sign of the "Earl of Halifax" was displayed. Queen street afterwards bore the name of Buck street, and then of State street. It extended from the water to Fleet street, and continued the name of Queen street until it reached King, which is now Congress street.

It was from Mr. Stavers's stable that the first stage chair was run regularly from Portsmouth to Boston. The event was one of scarcely less interest than the opening of a railroad or the launching of a "Great Eastern" of modern times. There was then no other regular coach for passengers run from any town this side of Boston. We have before us one of the bills of the day, dated Portsmouth, April, 1761. In comparison with the present speed of travel the bill is a curiosity. Here it is:

"*For the Encouragement of Trade from Portsmouth to Boston.*

A LARGE STAGE CHAIR,

With two good horses well equipped, will be ready by Monday the 20th inst. to start out from Mr. *Stavers*, inn-holder, at the sign of the Earl of Halifax, in this town, for Boston, to perform once a week; to lodge at Ipswich the same night; from thence through Medford to Charlestown ferry; to tarry at Charlestown till Thursday morning, so as to return to this town the next day; to set out again on the Monday following; it will be contrived to carry four persons besides the driver. In case only two persons go, they may be accommodated to carry things of bulk and value to make a third or fourth person. The price will be *Thirteen Shillings* and *Six Pence* sterling for each person from hence to Boston, and at the same rate of conveyance back again; though under no obligation to return in the same week in the same manner. ☞Those who would not be disappointed, must enter their names at Mr. *Stavers* on Saturdays, any time before nine o'clock in the evening, and pay one-half at entrance, the remainder at the end of the journey. Any gentleman may have business transacted at Newbury or Boston with fidelity and despatch, on reasonable terms.

As gentlemen and ladies are often at a loss for good accommodations for travelling from hence, and can't return in less than three weeks or a month, it is hoped that this undertaking will meet with suitable encouragement, as they will be wholly freed from the care and charge of keeping chairs and horses, or returning them before they had finished their business."

After a month, "several stages having been performed with satisfaction," notice was given that *five* persons could be carried; that in future it would leave on Tuesday instead of Monday morning, and arrive back on Saturday night.

In November, 1762, notice is given that the "Stage Chaise" will run, except in bad weather, through the winter; fare $3.00.

As an evidence of the speed of those times, we notice the arrival of a special express from Boston, with important news, which left Boston at 11 o'clock one day, and arrived at Portsmouth at 2 o'clock the next afternoon.

On one occasion, January 1764, the Charlestown and other ferries were so frozen, that the Post was obliged to pass round by Cambridge, riding not far from one hundred miles in circuit.

The promised four-horse carriage was not completed till May, 1763. Here is the advertisement:

"THE PORTSMOUTH FLYING STAGE COACH

Is now finished, which will carry six persons inside; runs with four or six horses; each person to pay 13s. 6d. to Boston, and 4s. 6d. to Newbury. Sets out from the Sign of the Earl of Halifax, every Tuesday morning between 7 and 8 o'clock, goes thro' Newbury to Boston, and will put up at inns on the road where good entertainment and attendance are provided for the passengers in the coach. The subscriber, master of the stage coach, is to be spoke with from Saturday night to Monday night, at Mr. JOHN STAVERS', innholder, at the sign of the Earl of Halifax. *Bartholomew Stavers.*"

Bartholomew, the first regular stage driver north of Boston, was the father of Capt. William Stavers, now of Portsmouth. His family lived at one time on Pierce's island. He was strongly allied in feeling to the mother country, and regarding the movements of the Revolution as a rebellion, for which those who engaged in it would be subject to the halter, in December, 1774, he left for England. His son William was born in February following. The father and son never saw each other. He had one other son, Andrew, who died young. His wife, Mrs. Martha Stavers, died in this town February 19, 1792.

The history of John Stavers and the "Earl of Halifax" and "William Pitt" hotels have enough of interest for a separate ramble.

## RAMBLE XXXIX.

Earl of Halifax hotel—Meetings of Royalists—Mob assault—Mark Noble injured—Staver's escape—John Langdon—French fleet—Distinguished visitors—Lafayette—Louis Phillippe—Washington.

Before us on the south-west, as we stand at the intersection of Court and Atkinson streets, is the ancient three story mansion, now, although very well preserved for a building in its ninetieth year, possessing no very inviting aspects. When it was erected, buildings of three stories were few and far between. So late as 1798, of the six hundred and twenty-six dwelling houses in Portsmouth, eighty-six were of one story, five hundred and twenty-four were of two stories, and only sixteen of three stories. The general style of building large houses up to the time of the Revolution was with gambrel roofs—but so far as our investigations have extended but few of that class were built after the Revolution. So when the reader wishes to pick out the old houses which have stood for eighty years, he may safely regard the gambrel roof houses as older than the American Constitution.

Many of the present age have doubtless passed this old building on Court street without regarding it any more worthy of note than a hundred others in the city, and but few know that it has historical associations which entitle it to pre-eminence.

In our last ramble was given some account of John and Bartholomew Stavers, who more than a century ago came to Portsmouth from England, and by close application to business acquired property. John was an inn-keeper. His first hotel was on Queen street, under the sign of the "Earl of Halifax." Having acquired a sufficient sum to warrant the enterprise, in 1765 he purchased of Hon. Theodore Atkinson this lot directly in front of the Atkinson residence (the old house now half demolished.)

In 1770 the new hotel was completed, and thrown open for the accommodation of genteel travellers. On a high post which was planted near the north-east corner of the hotel, was put up the favorite sign of the "*Earl of Halifax*," which had become as necessary as the proprietor's name to give popularity to a hotel, which was then to Portsmouth what the *Revere* is now to Boston, and the *St. Nicholas* to New York. Such spacious accommodations for man and beast. In proof of the latter, is the stable now standing in the rear of the house, on the corner of Jefferson street, a marvel for its capacity even in these times. It was the stable not only for the horses of the travellers, but also of those that bore the "Flying Stage Coach" once a week to Boston and back, and the repository of that rare vehicle every week from Saturday night to Tuesday morning.

In the upper room of this hotel the Masonic meetings of St. John's Lodge were for several years held. The Grand Lodge of New Hampshire also met here. But these were not all the exclusive meetings held in the hotel. Mr. Stavers being an Englishman by birth, the distinguished travellers from abroad put up with him, and the hotel was in some degree regarded as under foreign influence. In 1775, when the troubles with the mother country began to assume a threatening aspect, the "Earl of Halifax" hotel was regarded with a jealous eye. It continued to be made a place of resort by those who had for years frequented it, and as the transactions of the ruffled and laced government officials in the back rooms were little understood by those out of doors, no very good construction was placed upon them. Whether or not a tory spirit was nurtured there, is not for us at this day to say;—but frequently as the spirits in the decanters became depressed and the spirits around the table became correspondingly elevated, the noise from the company would sound rather too loyal to the listening patriots. It was a day when the light of the Revolution began to gleam in the distance, and it must have been a matter of no small anxiety with the officers of the crown to show to their sovereign a loyal deportment, or put at risk not only their emoluments of office, but also peril their necks.

These private meetings at the "Earl of Halifax" hotel were regarded with a jealous eye by the Sons of Liberty, and one day as a company of recruits was passing down the street, the leader, Capt. Hopley Yeaton, threatened that if any one looked out from the hotel, the windows should be smashed. None appeared, and the company passed on. The threat was probably given for a pretence to assail the hotel; for, a few days after, a mob gathered around the premises, and an axe was heard cutting at the foot of the sign-post. The irritated landlord, Mr. Stavers, gave an axe to his black slave, and commanded him to warn the invader, and cut him down if he did not desist. The slave dare not disobey one whose word was law—and gave a blow directly upon the head of Mark Noble, which brought him to the ground. Noble survived—but was an insane man for the forty years he afterwards lived. The mob soon collected around, the black fellow retreated, the sign was brought down, and a general assault was made with stones and brickbats upon the house. Every window on the street was broken in, the house was left in desolation, and the visitors escaped as they could find opportunity.

The affrighted slave immediately disappeared. Search was long made for him, and at length in a large rain water tank in the cellar, which extended nearly up to the ceiling, he was found standing up to his chin in water. Mr. Stavers did not feel safe within the reach of the mob, so taking a supply of gold in his pocket, he hastened by the back door to his stable, bridled his little black mare, and without waiting for a saddle, made a speedy exit through Jefferson street, for some place of safety, (where, he knew not,) until the excited feelings of the populace should subside. It was soon noised abroad that he had fled, and two men went on horseback in pursuit. After passing through Greenland they came within hail of him, and called upon him to stop. This quickened his pace, and he was soon, by a bend of the road, out of their sight; and turning suddenly into a barn in Stratham, open by the road side, his pursuers were permitted to go ahead. In Stratham he quartered for a fortnight with William Pottle, Jr., a man who had usually supplied his hotel with ale.

The affair soon put the town in commotion, and John Langdon, with other leading patriots of the day, repaired at once to the Hotel. As Langdon entered the north-east parlor, one of the mob had just raised a chair to dash in pieces an elegant mirror. Langdon seized the man's arm and holding him firmly said—"Stop, young man, you must have a dash at me first—you may perhaps be doing more harm than good."

By judicious management, Capt. Langdon quieted the excited feelings, saved the house from being demolished, and through his influence in due time Mr. Stavers was induced to return.

After returning to Portsmouth, he was seized by the committee of safety, and conveyed to Exeter jail. He was opposed personally to taking up arms against his own countrymen, but willingly took the oath of allegiance, and was released on the assurance that he would in no way oppose the effort to procure independence. Mr. Stavers soon had all suspicions of toryism removed, and enjoyed that share of confidence and support to which as a good citizen he was entitled.

The ravages of the mob had been of material injury to Mr. Stavers, and he did not immediately repair his hotel. The windows were for some time boarded up, and many of the distinguished officers of the Revolution have feasted in those rooms with scarcely a pane of glass in the windows. At length the hotel was fitted up—the old sign retouched, and the name of "*William Pitt*" took the place of "*Earl of Halifax.*" This sign was placed against the side of the building and remained there until about fifty years ago. This sign gave the name to *Pitt* street.

Now comes another scene. It is 1782, the French fleet is in our harbor, and eight of the principal officers in white uniforms, take up their quarters at the sign of "William Pitt." Who is this young and handsome officer now entering the door of the hotel? It is no less a personage than the Marquis LAFAYETTE, who has come all the way from Providence to visit the French officers who are here boarding. Here was the scene of their happy meeting, which was enjoyed with all that enthusiasm which characterizes the habits of the French. Forty years elapsed between this and LAFAYETTE'S last visit to Portsmouth, which changed his raven locks to gray hairs, and his buoyant step to the infirmities of age.

Who is this alighting from his coach, dressed with so much taste and attended by his servants—to take up his quarters here? It is one whose name stands out on the Declaration of Independence, like the pencilings of a thunderbolt on a clear sky—JOHN HANCOCK truly. Here, too, is the place where ELBRIDGE GERRY, RUTLEDGE, and other signers of the same immortal instrument, have found a cordial welcome. And General KNOX, that stalwart man, who was two officers in size and three in lungs, here many times found such a resting place as his heavy frame required.

Who are these three young men with their servant, standing at the door politely bowing and asking, on the recommendation of Gen. Knox, for accommodations? It is in the time of the French Revolution, and here stand three sons of the Duke of Orleans—LOUIS PHILLIPPE and his two brothers. The hotel is full and the future King of France bows and retires, to take quarters with Governor Langdon. Louis Phillippe ever remembered that visit to Portsmouth. When on the throne in France, he made enquiry of a Portsmouth lady who had obtained an introduction, "Is the pleasant mansion of Governor Langdon still standing?"

One scene more. It is 1789: General John Sullivan, the President of New Hampshire, and his Council, are here convened. There, coming down Pitt street, on foot, is the noblest guest that ever honored any American hotel by his presence. He enters this very door, and GEORGE WASHINGTON, President of the United States, here makes his final complimentary visit to our State authorities. This is the last spot where the father of his country personally complimented our State, through its official dignitaries. That circumstance, if no other of the interesting incidents connected with the history of the "Earl of Halifax" and "William Pitt" hotel, should give value to its ancient frame so long as it may stand. As a note of its past history, the picture of William Pitt, the friend of America, should be again restored over the door, that the interesting events of the old hotel may be kept in lasting remembrance.

---

## RAMBLE XL.

Scenes on Market square—William Pottle the Tory—Whipping of a woman at the town pump.

HERE we are again on Market square, near where was once the old State House. You can see exactly where the State House stood, for this pavement, the obtuse angle of which extends into the street from the front of

Robert Gray's shop, terminates abruptly just where the west steps of the State House door used to stand.

It is the 16th of December, 1774. Here are assembled on the Parade some hundred individuals from other towns, as well as our own citizens. It is an important time, not only in the country abroad, but also immediately at home. The town has been in excitement for several days past, in consequence of an express from Boston, stating that two regiments of red coats were coming to take possession of Fort William & Mary. The Sons of Liberty, spurred on by the news, have just stolen a march, captured the fort, and taken away a hundred barrels of powder. The news spreading abroad has brought into town these strangers, who to-day are holding council together on the momentous issue. The Governor and Council are also in session, and give assurance that they know nothing of either troops or war ships visiting Portsmouth. As one after another comes into town on horseback, a person approaches, who, in the view of many, has shown too little opposition to the oppressions of the mother country. It was stated in a former ramble that when the landlord of the "Earl of Halifax" fled, he found quarters in Stratham for a fortnight with William Pottle, Jr., the brewer.

The man who now appears on horseback is Pottle himself. Some one points him out, exclaiming: "There is a tory—there is an enemy to his country—see how he looks!" Said another: "There is a man who says he will join Gen. Gage in fighting against his country, whenever called!" The voice of Deacon Boardman of Stratham is now heard: "Gentlemen, this villain has appeared an open enemy to his country; he has held mock meetings, when we have held meetings to choose delegates to Congress; he has opposed sending provisions to the poor in Boston; he has opposed the effort to suppress the use of tea. He ought to be made to sign an acknowledgement and ask pardon of this body." Another voice exclaimed: "I would not give one farthing for his acknowledgement; hiss and drive him out of town; that is the best treatment he deserves!"

A loud *huzza* is now raised, and Pottle, putting spurs to his horse, soon separates himself from the company; but instead of leaving town he only retires to a more quiet street, and afterwards is seen near the Bell tavern. Deacon Boardman is again upon him, and addressing a company collected: "Gentlemen, this man has conducted in such a manner that we ought no more to use his malt, than we do tea. For my part I am determined I will not; I will not drink his beer, good as it is, made of tory malt."

Pottle is hissed, and again disappears under the pressure of the populace. On church hill he is overtaken, pulled from his horse, roughly handled, and then put upon his horse and pursued until out of town. But Pottle is soon back again, and subjected to further rough treatment before finally taking refuge at his home in Stratham.

Such is an illustration of the feeling existing in those times. While it is a wonder to many that the public generally were for independence, the wonder under the excited state of things was greater that so many submitted themselves to the greater danger they incurred from opposing the strong popular current of patriotic spirit which stirred the sons of liberty in that eventful period.

Let the scene change for another of a different character, in the same vicinity, which occurred ten years earlier. It is a cold day in January, 1764. A woman, who had entered a shop in the house on the corner where the dining-room of the Franklin house now is, was seen to secrete beneath her hood-cloak a pair of children's shoes. When she left the shop, the person who saw the act informed the keeper. Out he rushes: "Stop thief! stop thief!" Goodman Newmarch, who lived in the house next east of the Bell tavern, rushes out, seizes the running woman, and she is borne over the way to the house of Hon. Hunking Wentworth, Justice of the Peace, resident next west of the North church. The evidence is produced, the culprit is found guilty, and is sentenced to be publicly whipped! The whipping post was the town pump. Here her hands are tied up to staples, her shoulders and back are bared, and the sheriff applies the cat-o'-nine-tails! Think of such a scene ever occurring on Market square! The newspaper of the next week calmly reports the event as follows:

"Last Friday one of our female pilferers received a flagelation at the whipping post, who had a great number of spectators to see this good work performed; and it is hoped that others, who so justly deserve it, will soon be brought to the same place to receive their deserts."

In contrast with the corporal punishment so common a century ago, when even the public whipping of a white female was looked upon with complacency, we see the good influences which houses of correction and places of reformation are now exerting upon society.

---

## RAMBLE XLI.

Residences on Middle street—Sketch of the eccentric Shepherd Ham—Middle street church site.

On Middle street, for some years after the Revolution, there were but five two-story houses between the present location of the Academy and Wibird's Hill. Sheafe Griffith occupied one on the site of the residence of E. F. Sise, on Haymarket Square. Col. Joshua Wentworth, a house on the present site of that of Mrs. Henry

Ladd. Jonathan and Joseph Shillaber occupied two other houses a little west on the same side of the way—not far from the houses of John P. Lyman and Rev. Dr. Peabody. A few one-story houses were also scattered on the same side. On the opposite side of the street, there was no dwelling between the Langdon house, now the residence of Samuel Lord, and Wibird's hill. State street, west from the Middle street church, was not opened until about the beginning of this century.

For many years the western terminus of State (then Broad) street, was opposite the rocky site of Shepherd Ham's premises, who occupied the gore of land on which the sightly Middle street church and its neat chapel have been erected.

Only sixty years ago, this locality was regarded so far on the outskirt, that the lady of John Pierce had some objection to his building that elegant mansion on Haymarket Square, on account of its great distance from the centre of Portsmouth. At the time when it was built, in 1800, not one of the houses on the opposite side of the street or above it, was erected. The hay scales were erected in front about the same time—and on the rocks a little further off were the shanty of Shepherd Ham, in front, and a little to the north and west, his stables and sheds for his vehicles. The premises of the eccentric old gentleman (whose real name was William, but was so generally called *Shepherd*, that it was by many regarded as his real name), extended so far into the desired location of the street then about to be opened, that his barn was exactly in the way and forbade the opening. Some roguish young men, who wished to see the street opened, and had no fear of the law or of the owner, one night pulled out a few props which supported the barn, and the next morning it was a heap of ruins, and State street was soon after opened to Mason's hill.

William Ham was in his younger days a king's surveyor. While New Hampshire was a royal province, it was the custom for a surveyor to pass through the forests and put a certain mark, called a broad arrow, on such trees as would make masts for the royal navy. These trees must not be cut for any other purpose. Having on one occasion marked some trees already cut down, the people resented it, and he fled to Portsmouth for safety. The Revolution shortly after destroyed his office: but he retained his silver-laced badges, and his tory feeling of dignity, to the day of his death.

The "Bloomer costume" has awakened visions of Shepherd Ham's petticoat trousers. If the reader will imagine a pair of corduroys of no particular color, or if they must be colored, say a faded snuff color,—each leg of which is large enough to cover a man's body, but so short as only to reach just below the knee,—he will get some idea of petticoat trousers; and if he will think of white dimity well worn, and not very well washed, he may have a clear idea of another pair. But to get an image of the wearer, we must add a pair of long, loose boots of coarse leather, dusty or muddy, according to the weather—varied occasionally by shoes of similar neatness—with or without stockings, just as it happened. Add also a kind of frockcoat with broad skirts, so long as to reach the knees, vest carelessly buttoned or open, bandanna neckerchief, long beard and ill-looking hat,—and we have a full-length portrait. The whole style of his dress was the shabby genteel.

After the loss of office, he ran coaches, and let horses and carriages for several years, and had, for those days, quite a fair share of business; but his peculiarities, one of which was closeness, ripened and increased, so that he neither shod his horses nor repaired his carriages. As a matter of course, they could not be let very well. And when let, his horses were not always sure to be obedient. In one case, a young gentleman with his lady joined a party to have a good time at Greenland. Shepherd's horse had been accustomed to stop at the Globe tavern at the Plains; and as nothing would induce him to go further, they had to be content with stopping there also. His house, except a room or two where he lived, was filled with old saddles and harnesses, old sleighs that had the rickets, dilapidated coach bodies, and chaise, whose broadcloth lining made food for moths, while the cushions afforded excellent lodgings for a large colony of mice. Old wheels, rusty axles, and parts of carriages, filled the sheds and adorned the yard; while the stable sometimes contained a few old horses. Most of the horses, however, were commonly out to grass, or at least had gone up the road to look after it. Their owner in his oddity, or, as some said, insanity, would often refuse to let any of them,—and as to selling them, that was utterly out of the question. Of course, horses, carriages and owner, all grew old together; and his buildings likewise. The horses, by exposure, became long haired and woolly; their tails and manes full and shaggy, and tangled and matted with burdock burrs. In a storm, especially a snow storm, the old man would be out driving home his shabby, ill-conditioned beasts; and the more violent the storm, the greater became his solicitude to get them together. The neighbors, as they looked from their windows, when the roads were deserted by travellers because the weather was bad, would exclaim, "There goes the careful Shepherd with his flock." And in good truth he spent half his time in looking them up and getting them together, only to have them stray again. His old rickety stable doors could not detain them long, after they chose to go; and he had too much regard for horses' rights to tie them in a barn that was bare of hay and provender.

These horses, as well as some others belonging to truckmen, were in those days continually roaming about the streets, an annoyance to men and the dread of women and children,—and sometimes they might be seen in odd positions. When the steeple of St. John's church was in course of erection, a hanging stage was affixed, which was raised and lowered by a tackle; and one morning when the workmen came they found the staging raised high in air, and one of those stray horses standing quietly upon it near the belfry—raised there, out of mischief, by some of the roguish boys.

Shepherd's house, black and ragged with age and weather, stood in its last days among the most elegant mansions in the town, forming as whimsical a contrast to other buildings as he did to other men. And among his other notions, he was greatly concerned lest some person might break in while he was absent, and steal his treasure. He was a bachelor, and for many years was without a female domestic. His bedding did not require much attention, for as "the fur which warms the monarch, warmed the bear," so was he made warm by the use of the dressed skins of his departed horses for a nightly covering.

As his strength failed and his house afforded him but a poor shelter, a brother, Robert Ham senior, persuaded him, after much ado, to leave his premises and go to his house, (the house now occupied by his grandson, Asa Ham.) He went only on the condition that he should carry his *valuables* with him. He did so, and filled a room with old rubbish, in the midst of which stood his bed. There as he lay or sat in his sickness he could see strings of old sleigh bells, assortments of old rusty harness buckles, some old bridles and stirrups, with old horse shoes enough to keep off the witches. There, too, was his bureau, with locked drawers, in one of which was found, after his death, more than a bushel of old tobacco quids. And seeing this trumpery, he seemed comparatively happy, except when troubled with the fear that something might be stolen while he slept.

He was in this exactly like other misers, except that their guineas or dollars took the place of his belts and buckles. And like others, too, though he held his treasure so strongly, yet at last (in November, 1809, at the age of seventy-five,) death loosened his grasp, and he passed away from his toys leaving them to "heirs he knows not who."

Odd as our subject was, he found a few companions who used to visit him at his domicil, especially on Sundays. And as he did not attend church for many years, the little knot that gathered round him was styled his meeting. Hence when any Sunday loafer was questioned as to his place of worship, he would reply that he had been to "*Shepherd Ham's meeting*," the same as saying that he had idled away the day.

The lot of land descended to Robert Ham junior, who sold it to the Baptist Society in 1828. and on this rock their handsome church edifice was built. As the advance of Christianity smooths the rugged paths and hides the rough places, so have the improvements here hid the unsightly spot which for many years was the rough, but now pleasant western prospect of State street.

---

## RAMBLE XLII.

**Sagamore Creek—Origin of name—Residences—The Bridge—Lear the Hermit.**

A SAIL down the river, and a visit to the Shoals, is a pleasant excursion, but a sail to Little-harbor and thence up Sagamore creek, presents greater attractions to the lover of the picturesque. Passing down the western channel of the river, and under Newcastle bridge, the first object which attracts the curious eye is the romantic mansion now occupied by Mrs. Cushing, formerly the residence of Governor Wentworth. The style of its architecture, as we have already stated, would be a poser for any builder to decide. Without any particular height, size, order or front, the appearance of the mansion, from the river, in connection with its romantic situation on the point, is agreeable. After passing the point on the Piscataqua on which this mansion is situated, we enter the beautiful inlet, extending up several miles, which bears the name of Sagamore creek.

As we pass up its broad channel, and mark the outlines of the green banks on either side mirrored in the unruffled surface, we have an opportunity to answer the inquiry often made but not so often answered—"from what does the creek derive its name?"

When the discoveries were first made of our country, it was found that in the northern parts, (where the severity of the winters rendered the residence less inviting than at the south), there were no large collections of Indians together, and their government was rather more of the patriarchal than monarchical kind; that is, some family commonly took a precedence above the others, of which the oldest son had absolute government over the region,—and this governor received the title of *Sagamore*. When the English commenced their settlements, there were twenty locations of these Sagamores between Kennebec river and Connecticut; the first at Kennebec, second at Casco bay, third at Saco, fourth at Piscataqua, fifth at Merrimack, etc. On the Piscataqua were many families under the Sagamore, extending up the several streams of the river,—and on this Creek it is supposed the Sagamore resided.

History informs us that such places as they chose for their abode were usually at the falls of great rivers, or near the sea-side, where there was any convenience for catching such fish as every summer and winter used to come upon the coast: at which times they used, like good fellows, to make all common; and then those who had entertained their neighbors by the sea-side, expected the like kindness from their friends higher in the country: and they were wont to have their great dances for mirth at those general meetings. With intercourse of this kind were the affairs and commerce carried on between those who lived in the interior and those who were seated on the sea-coast about the havens and channels that issued into the sea, where there used to be at all times, clams, muscles, bass and sturgeon, of which they used to take great plenty, and dry them in the smoke, and keep them the rest of the year.

So as we pass up the beautiful creek, we cannot but admire the good taste of the aborigines in selecting this location for their head-quarters; nor does it require any great stretch of imagination to see the red men seated on the banks, roving in the woods, plying their paddles, perched upon the elevated rocks which are met with on the shores, or encircling the domicil of their respected Sagamore.

On the north side of the creek, after passing the Cushing farm, and the pleasant seat of T. S. Coffin, we approach that of Mrs. Martine, which has recently been purchased by Clement March. It was at this house that Louis Philippe with his brothers, when on a visit to Portsmouth in 1798, spent a week to enjoy the beautiful scenery*. In this same house was the eccentric Estwick Evans born; and here the author of "Resignation" found scope for the range of her imagination, and gathered her landscape sketches. We next approach the site selected by Abner Greenleaf, the first Mayor of Portsmouth, for

---

* In an account of Louis Philippe's tour in the United States, in 1797–8, published at the time of his death, we find this extract:

"Talleyrand was busy in making purchases for the West India market, and wishing to visit the lumber contractors in Maine, the Princes joined him. They left Boston in a covered wagon, and passed some days at Newburyport, riding up one bank of the Merrimac to Haverhill, and returning by the other. Journeying northward, the Princes were for a week guests at the Martine farm, on the borders of Sagamore creek, near Portsmouth The Martine homestead is still standing, and some flowers sent from its gardens to the Tuilleries soon after Louis Philippe had ascended the throne, were acknowledged by an autograph letter. At Gardiner they accepted the hospitality of Gen. Henry Dearborn."

his residence. From this place, in 1850, the city extended the bridge over the creek. Next after passing the bridge is the farm of Spencer Holmes. On the south side of the entrance to the creek is the Sheafe farm, which the heirs have recently sold to Edmund Davis. It extends west of the bridge. Next on the south of the creek comes the farm of James Moses, which has been in the family for two centuries. Then we arrive at the old Beck farm, on which Gideon of the Gazette was born. It is now owned by John Johnson. At the head of the creek on the south, is the farm of John Elwyn, on which his grandfather, John Langdon, was born, and in this beautiful locality were early nurtured those principles of liberty, which shone so brightly in his after years.

A little west of Sagamore bridge, on the south side of the creek, may be seen the spot where lived and died one of the most singular men of the age. No one has been more deserving the title of *hermit.* His name was BENJAMIN LEAR. He died on the 17th of December, 1802, aged 82.

For more than twenty years, Mr. Lear dwelt entirely alone in a hut, which scarcely any one would have thought decent for a barn. He made his own garments, which were in fashion peculiar to himself. He tilled his land, milked his cows, and made his butter and cheese; but subsisted principally on potatoes and milk. Owing, no doubt to his simple and temperate mode of living, he exhibited, at the age of eighty-two, a face freer from wrinkles, than is generally seen in those of fifty.

The farm on which he lived, and which he owned, was of sufficient extent and fertility to have supported a large family, with proper management, in a comfortable manner; but he had long imbibed the idea that he should live to need and spend the whole. He always spoke of the town, where he made his appearance once or twice a year, as the *Bank*, the ancient name of the place, which he had heard his grandmother use.

His mother lived to be more than a hundred years of age, and died in the cottage, which her son inherited from his parents. When she was at the age of one hundred and two years, some people visited her on a certain day, and while they were with her, the bell was heard to toll for a funeral. The old woman burst out in tears, and said, "O when will the bell toll for me! It seems to me that the bell will never toll for me. I am afraid that I shall never die."

Mr. Lear, although repeatedly invited and urged to repair to some of his neighbors to spend the winter months, where he might be comfortable, always declined, alleging that he had every thing he wanted. He would not suffer any one to spend a night in his house to take care of him, even in his last illness. For several weeks he had been in a very feeble state of health. On the evening before his death, the cold was so extreme that the mercury fell to four degrees below zero. In the evening he was so well as to be laying out his business for the ensuing spring; but in the morning he was unable to rise. He had his senses; but soon expired. Almost any one else would, in similar circumstances, have been totally frozen long before morning. According to his usual custom, he was without a shred of linen on his back; but was clad in an old tattered cloth garb, and his only covering for the night, besides, was a small ragged blanket, and his bed was a parcel of straw! He was of an inoffensive disposition towards his fellow-creatures; but with the means in his hands, he denied himself of almost every comfort of life.

The cellar of the hermit's residence is near the shore, and the underpinning of his barn, a few rods distant, when we last saw it remained undisturbed. The apple trees, which used to yield him fruit, are still on the spot, though age has placed its rough hand upon them, and decay has entered their heart.

## RAMBLE XLIII.

Slavery in Portsmouth—Their standing—Cyrus—Prime Fowle—Cuffee Chase—Sambo Stevens—Peter Warner—Negro elections—King Nero—Black court—Continuance of slavery.

In the days when slavery was common in New England, Portsmouth had a large proportion of the slaves held in the State. There were in this town, in 1767, one hundred and twenty-four male and sixty-three female slaves. Their masters were generally kind to them, and they were permitted not only to enjoy their own social meetings, but were aided in sustaining a mock government among themselves.

There were negroes of distinction then, and there was nearly as much *ebony* as *topaz* gloss on the face of society. Among the top of the negro quality in former times, was Cyrus Bruce, for many years the waiter on Gov. Langdon. There could scarcely be found in Portsmouth, not excepting the Governor himself, one who dressed more elegantly or exhibited a more gentlemanly appearance. His heavy gold chain and seals, his fine black or blue broadcloth coat and small clothes, his silk stockings and silver-buckled shoes, his ruffles and carefully plaited linen, are well remembered by many of the present generation.

Some of the blacks were good mechanics. The parlor of the house of the late Richard Hart, on Russell street, was handsomely finished by Cæsar, a house slave. Prime Fowle was the pressman of the first paper printed in New Hampshire. Through long service in bending over the press, he was bent to an angle of about forty-five degrees. He mourned the loss of his mistress and called her an old fool for dying. At funerals, it was the custom for the negroes of the family to walk at the left hand of each white survivor, among the chief mourners. At the funeral of Mrs. Fowle, Prime should have gone on the left of his master, but he went on the right. His master whispered, "Go the other side." Prime did not move. His master touched him and whispered again, "Go the other side." This was too much. The old peppery negro sputtered out, as loud as he could, "Go tudder side ye sef, ye mean jade."

Cuffee Chase, brother of Dinah Whipple, was of a resentful spirit, and could not easily forgive an injury. His master's horse bit him one day, and Cuffee in return deprived him for several days of his food, and had almost starved the animal before the family discovered the cause of his failure. The slave of Rev. Joseph Stevens, of Kittery, had a better apology for a similar act. His master, as he saw him picking some bones for dinner which had been already well trimmed, said to him, "Nearer the bone the sweeter the meat, Sambo." Not long after, he was sent to the pasture with the horse of a visiting clergyman, which he tied to a pile of rocks. To a reproof for the act, Sambo replied, "Nearer the bone, the sweeter the meat—nearer the rock, the sweeter the grass, massa."

Jonathan Warner had several slaves, among them Peter. One day Peter's hat being the worse for wear, he asked his master for a better covering for his head. "If you will make a rhyme, Peter, you shall have a new hat," said his master. This was discouraging to Peter, for he was never guilty of such a thing in his life. He left in a very thoughtful mood, and at length resolved to get assistance in his difficulty. He goes to the office of Wyseman Claggett, and states his case, "What is your name?" asked the counsellor. "Peter Warner, massa."

"Peter Warner—threw his hat in the chimney corner,"

said Mr. C. playfully. "There is your rhyme, now go and get your new hat." Peter went home, repeating the rhyme all the way, and hastened to the parlor. "Massa, I've got the rhyme," said he, much elated. "Well, say it."

"Peter Warner—took off his hat and threw it—in the fireplace."

Peter received his hat, his master remarking that it was nearer to a rhyme than he expected of him.

Some slaves had intellect somewhat inferior to Peter's. Dinah, a slave in the family of Samuel Ham, on Freeman's point, could not count five. In planting corn, she would put in the hole three kernels, and then two. She could count no higher.

The slaves were permitted to hold their social meetings, and had a mock government of their own, as above stated. For many years they held their annual elections in June, usually on Portsmouth Plains. They elected a King, (who was also a judge,) a Sheriff and Deputy, besides other officers, and closed their election by a jolly time. They went up from town in procession, led by their King, Nero, the slave of Col. William Brewster. It happened that Nero was not one who in any respect could be called a calf, and even his legs were wholly divested of any alliance to that name. The full dress in small clothes required some filling in the back of the silk stockings, to give a proper contour to the person of the King. As the procession was moving on, an observing black hastily leaves the ranks, runs forward, and bowing to the King, somewhat damps his glory by the information that his calf "has got afore."

If any black was guilty of any crime which was regarded disgraceful to the ebon society, he was duly tried and punished. Nero's viceroy was Willie Clarkson, a slave of Hon. Peirse Long. A report comes that Prince Jackson, slave of Nathaniel Jackson of Christian Shore, has stolen an axe. The Sheriff, Jock Odiorne, seizes him, the court is summoned, and King Nero in majesty sits for the examination. The evidence is exhibited, Prince is found guilty, and condemned to twenty lashes on the bare back, at the town pump on the parade. There was a general gathering of the slaves on such occasions; and the Sheriff, after taking off his coat and tying up the convict to the pump, hands the whip to his deputy, Pharaoh Shores, addressing the company, "Gemmen, this way we s'port our government"—turning to his deputy—" Now, Pharaoh, pay on!" After the whipping was over, the Sheriff dismissed the prisoner, telling him that the next time he is found this side Christian Shore, unless sent by his master, he will receive twenty lashes more. Prince, however, did not reform; for, soon after, he was found guilty of larger thefts and brought under the cognizance of the county court.

There is one other story told of a trial which took place here by the court of Nero, which is probably true, but for the truth of which we have no voucher. It was this: A culprit was under trial, when the old North clock, which regulated so many matters the last century, struck the hour of twelve. The evidence was not gone through with, but the servants could stay no longer from their home duties. They all wanted to see the whipping, but could not conveniently be present again after dinner. Cato ventured to address the King: "Please your honor, best let the fellow have his whipping now, and finish the trial after dinner." The request seemed to be the general wish of the company, so Nero ordered ten lashes, for justice so far as the trial went, and ten more at the close of the trial should he be found guilty!

No general emancipation law was ever passed in this State, but most of those who were here held as slaves at the time of the Declaration, or during the war, were emancipated by their owners. A considerable number, however, who had grown old in their masters' service, refused to accept their freedom, and remained with their masters, or as pensioners on the families of their descendants during their lives. And until the two or three last returns of the census of the United States, some slaves have always been returned in New Hampshire.

## RAMBLE XLIV.

### The Association Test of 1776.

THE Declaration of the Independence of the United States was well ascertained to be the voice of the people, before it was signed in the Congress at Philadelphia on the 4th of July, 1776. On the recommendation made by Congress, March 14, 1776, the signatures of the people were obtained to an obligation to oppose the hostile proceedings of the British fleets and armies. The fullness of the returns gave the signers of the Declaration assurance that their acts would be sanctioned and sustained by the country. We give below a document from the Secretary of State's office, which shows all the names of the citizens of Portsmouth in 1776, and the position in which they stood in regard to the Revolution. It will be seen that while four hundred and ninety-seven signed the Association test, thirty-one were either absent or refused to sign. Of the latter, fifteen were reported as "being notoriously disaffected to the common cause." The Test list is headed by the name of Meshech Weare. We have arranged the names alphabetically, for convenience of readers.

*To the Selectmen and Committee of the Town of Portsmouth:*

COLONY OF NEW-HAMPSHIRE,
In Committee of Safety, April 12th, 1776.

In order to carry the underwritten Resolve of the Hon. Continental Congress into execution, you are requested to desire all Males above twenty-one years of age (luanticks, idiots, and negroes excepted,) to sign to the Declaration on this paper; and when so done, to make return hereof, together with the name or names of all who shall refuse to sign the same, to the General Assembly, or Committee of Safety of this Colony.

M. WEARE, *Chairman.*

In Congress, March 14, 1776.

*Resolved,* That it be recommended to the several Assemblies, Conventions, and Councils, or Committees of Safety of the United Colonies, *immediately* to cause all persons to be *disarmed,* within their respective Colonies, who are *notoriously* disaffected to the cause of America, or who have not associated and refuse to associate, to defend by arms, the United Colonies, against the hostile attempts of the British Fleets and Armies.

Extract from the minutes.

CHARLES THOMPSON, *Sec'y.*

In consequence of the above Resolution, of the Hon. Continental Congress, and to shew our Determination in joining our American Brethren, in defending the Lives, Liberties, and Properties of the Inhabitants of the United Colonies:

We the *Subscribers,* do hereby solemnly engage, and promise, that we will to the utmost of our Power, at the Risque of our Lives and Fortunes, with Arms, oppose the Hostile Proceedings of the British Fleets, and Armies, against the United American Colonies.

Amos Abbet
William Abbott
William Adams
Simeon Akerman
Nahum Akerman
John Akerman
Joseph Akerman
Walter Akerman
Barnet Akerman
Benjamin Akerman
Joseph Allcock
William Appleton
Samuel Aris
James Arnold
Benjamin Austin, Jr.
Jona. Austin
Edward Ayers
Thomas Ayers
George Ayers
Thomas Ayers
Joseph Ayers
Perkins Ayers
Jonathan Ayers
John Ayer
Samuel Ball
Peter Ball
Samuel Ball, Jr.
Charles Banfill
Joseph Banfill
John Banfill
Tobias Banfill
John Bartlett
Joseph Bass
Samuel Beck
Andrew Beck
John Beck
John Beck, Jr.
William Beck
Samuel Beck
Joseph Benson
Thomas Bickford
Henry Bickford
Benjamin Bigelow
Abner Blasdel
Samuel Bowles
Thomas Bowles
Joseph Boyd
Joshua Brackett
Caleb Brewster
David Brewster
William Brewster
Moses Brewster
Daniel Brewster
Samuel Briard
John Briard
Joseph Brotten
Benjamin Brotten
John Broten
Edm. Butler
James Byan
David Call
Benj. G. Carter
Henry Carter
Samuel Cate
Samuel White Cate
William Cate, Jr.
Richard Champney
Benjamin Chandler
William Chiles
Jeremiah Claney
Supply Clap
Thomas Clark
Joseph Clark
Josiah Clark
John Clarke
James Clarkson
Philaneon Colbdor
John Collins
Richard Cotten
William Cotton
William Cotton, Jr.
Nathaniel Cotton
Thomas Cotton
Joseph Cotton
Joshua Crocket
Caleb Currier
Thomas Currier
Samuel Cutts
A. R. Cutter
Samuel Dalling
Theodore Dame
George Dame
Joseph Damrell
Ruben Danil
Eliphalet Daniell
John Davenport
Edmund Davis
Daniel Davis
John Davis
Edward Dempsey
John Dennett
Ephraim Dennett
Jeremiah Dennet
Nathaniel Dennett
John Dennett
George Doig
Richard Dolly
James Drisco
Samuel Drowne
John Dudley
John Dury
James Dwyer
Abraham Elliot
Richard Elliot
Stephen Evans
Richard Evans
Daniel Evans
James Fall
Richard Falpey, Jr.
Moses Feren
Mark Fernald
Gilbert Fernald
Richard Fitzgerald
Gershom Flagg
Nath'l Folsom
Nath'l Folsom
Luke Foster
Michael Fouler
James Frisbee
Michael Frost
John Frost
Rendal Furnald
John Furnald
William Furnell
Robert Furniss
Thomas Gaines
George Gains
William Gale
John Gardner
Wm. Gardner
Henry Gardner
George Gebon
William Gibbs
James Gooch
John Gooch
Nathaniel Gookin
Daniel Grant
John Grant
John Greenleaf
Alex. Greenlan
John Gregory
Nath'l S. Griffith
James Grouard
Ezekiel Gumdier
Wm. Gunnison
John Gunnison
Josiah Haines
Samuel Hall
George Ham
Samuel Ham
Samuel Ham, Jr.
Ephraim Ham
Timothy Ham
William Ham
William Ham, Jr.
Joseph Ham
Samuel Ham
Thomas Hart

George Hart
George Hart, Jr.
James Hart
John Hart, 3d
John Hart, Jr.
Daniel Hart
Richard Hart
Edward Hart
Robert Hart
William Hart
Richard Harvey
James Haslett
Matthew Haslett
Samuel Haven
Samuel Haven, Jr.
Thomas Hayley
Hugh Henderson
Dennis Hight
James Hight
Elisha Hill
James Hill
Samuel Hill
Charles Hodgdon
Benjamin Hodgdon
Phineas Hodgdon
Thomas Hodgson
Abiah Holbrook
Joseph Holbrook
Robert Holmes
Jeremiah Homes
William Homes
George S. Homans
John Hooker
John Hooper
Leaverett Hubbard
Enoch Huntress
Jonathan Huntress
Samuel Hutchings
John Hutchins
George Hull
William Hunt
William Hunt
Joseph Jackson
Clement Jackson
Hall Jackson
George Jackson
Samuel Jackson
Richard Jackson
John Jackson
Daniel Jackson
Daniel Jackson, Jr.
Nathl Jackson, Sr.
Nath'l Jackson, Jr.
Eben'ezer Janvrin
George Janvrin
William Jenkins
Alexander Jones
James Jones
James Jones
Joshua Jones
Peter Kennison
George King
George King, Jr.
James P. King
Richard Kitsson
Temple Knight
Wm. Knight
Paul Laighton
Samuel Langdon
Samuel Langdon, Jr.
William Langdon
John Langdon

Richard Langdon
Joseph Langdon
John Langdon
John Langdon
Daniel Lang
Mark Lang
John Lang
James Lang
Henry Lang
John Lang
Nathaniel Lang
Josiah Leach
Joseph Leach
Nathaniel Lear
Benjamin Lear
Samuel Lear
Tobias Lear
Thomas Leigh
Joseph Leigh
John Leina
John Lewis Jr.
George Libby
Jeremiah Libbey
Pierse Long
John Lord
Joseph Lowd
Edward Lowd
Joseph Low
Daniel Lunt
David Maclure
John Mackmahawn
Benjamin Mackay
Peter Man
Thomas Manning
Clement March
Thomas Marden
Israel Marden
John Marden
James Marden
George Marshall
George Marshall, Jr.
John Marshall, Sr.
John Marshall, Jr.
Obdenor Marshall
Willia m Marshall
Thomas Martin
William Martin
Francis Massuerre
George Massey
Hugh McBride
A. McIntyre
James McInter
Thomas Mead
Stephen Meeds
John Melcher
John Melcher
James Melcher
Nathaniel Melcher
Nathaniel Mendum
Benj. Miller, Jr.
Moses Miller
Richard Mills
Jacob Mills
John Moffatt
Richard Monson
Thomas Moses
Theodore Moses
Samuel Moses
James Moses
Nadab Moses
John Moses
Aaron Moses

Joseph Moulton
Timothy Mountford
Nath'l Mucharmore
Robert Neall
Mark Nelson
William Nelson
Leader Neson
Benj. Newmarch
John Noble
Mark Noble
Joseph Norris
Samuel Norris
John Norton
Henry Nutter
Valentine Nutter
Henry Nutter
Samuel Oakes
Thomas Palmer, Jr.
William Palmen
William Parker
William Parker
John Parker
Benj. Partridge
William Patridge
William Pearry
Thomas Peirce
Thomas Peirce, Jr.
John Peirce
Daniel Peirce
Noah Peirce
Philip Pendexter
Edward Pendexter
John Penhallow
Samuel Penhallow
R. Wibird Penhallow
A. Pepperill
William Peverly
Kinsman Peverly
John Pickering
Nath'l Pike
John Pike
John Pike
Thomas Pillar
Ezekiel Pitman
Joseph Pitman
John Pitman
Noah Pitman
John Pope
James Priest
G. Purcell
Benjamin Quint
Jonathan Quint
Benjamin Reed
George Reed
John Reid
William Richards
Robert Robertson
Thomas Ransom
Moses Ross
Nehemiah Rowell
Charles Rundletts
Thomas Sawyer
Jonah Savage
John Savage
Henry Seaward
Giles Seaward
Shackford Seaward
Joseph Seaward
John Seaward
Mark Seavey
John Seavey
Thomas Seavey

Samuel Servise
Joseph Simes
Nathaniel Shannon
Ruben Shapley
Richard Sharman
Joseph Shaw
John Sherburne
Henry Sherburne
Thomas Sherburne
Andrew Sherburn
Thos. Sherburne, Jr.
William Sherburne
Nathaniel Sherburne
John Sherburne
George Sherburne
D. Sherburne
Sam'l Sherburne
Nath'l Shurburne
Edw'd Shurburn
John Sheafe, Jr.
Jacob Sheafe, Sen.
Samuel Sherref
Jona. Shillaber
Joseph Shillaber
Peter Shores
Peter Shores, Jr.
James Shores
James Shores, Jr.
William Shores
John Showers
Samuel Slade
Ruben Snell
Keith Spence
Wm. Stanwood
John Stavers
Cotton M. Stevens
James Stoodly, Jr.
Gupey Stoodley
James Studely
James Swett
David Swett
John Swett
Stephen Sumner
Richard Tarlton
James Tarlton, Jr.
Samuel Thompson
E. Thompson
William Thompson
John Thompson
Thomas Thompson
Jacob Tilton
Daniel Towle
Jacob Treadwell
Nath'l Treadwell, Jr.
Charles Treadwell
W. E. Treadwell
Nath'l Treadwell
Samuel Tripe
Richard Trusdel
William Trefthen
John Tuckerman
John Tuckerman, Jr.
Joseph Tucker
George Turner
John Varrel
William Vaughan
William Walden
John Walden
Thomas Walden
George Waldron
Gideon Walker
Joseph Walker

Wm. Walker
Daniel Walker
Mark Walker
Tobias Walker
Samuel Walker
Tobias Warner
Nahum Ward
Richard Ware
Samuel Waters
Charles Waters
George Waters
Samuel Waterhouse
Timothy Watson
Meshech Weare
Joseph Weeks
Benjamin Welch
William Welch
John Wendell
George Wentworth
Joshua Wentworth
H. Wentworth
John Wheelwright
Michael Whidden
Joseph Whidden
Samuel Whidden
J. Whipple
John White
William White
Richard White
P. White
Nathan White
James Whiteaker
Zebulon Wiggin
John Williams
Richard Wilson
William Wilson
Joseph Winkall
Richard Woods
Moses Woodward
William Yeaton
Robert Yeaton

Pursuant to an order to us directed by the Committee of Safety of this State, we have waited on every person in town, and have tendered them the association for signing, and do herewith return the said association, and the names of those who have refused to sign the same, viz.

Noah Parker
Isaac Rindge
Stephen Weeks
Chase Freeze
Jos. Stacy Hastings
Theodore Atkinson
James Sheafe
Stephen Little
William Torrey
William Hart
Maj. Samuel Hale
Cotton Palmer
John Peirce
Moses Noble
John Eliot
John Moore
Thomas Armet
Alford Butler
Eleazer Russell
Samuel Gardner
George Jaffrey
Mark H. Wentworth
Daniel Warner
Jona. Warner
John Sherburne
Samuel Waters, Jr.
John Campbell
Richard Tucker
Giles Pickett

Daniel Rogers, absent, at Nottingham; Peter Pearse, absent, at Newington.

STATE OF NEW-HAMPSHIRE,
Portsmouth, 14th August, 1776.
By order of the Committee.
H. WENTWORTH, *Chairman.*
JOSEPH SIMES,
GEORGE GAINS,
WILLIAM LANGDON, } *Selectmen.*

While some of those who refused to sign were English in sentiment and too strongly attached to the mother country to rebel, others there were who were willing that a revolution should take place, but would not risk the chance of their offices or business by taking a part in the rebellion, fearing the consequences, should it prove a failure. Nearly all who held office under the crown refused to sign the test. The case of Jonathan Warner may be that of some others. Warner was a Commissary under the crown, and of course classed with the tories. In his keeping were some of the munitions of war, which the patriots needed. The Sons of Liberty, before whom the sign of the Earl of Halifax fell, waited on Warner, and demanded the keys of the store house, which was on Church hill, where Robinson's store now stands. With all the sternness of an official he said: "What right have you to make such a demand? The keys are my private property, I will not give them up to any body; but if you *break in my door*, what can I do?" The hint was taken, the door broken open, and the munitions of war removed. The Commissary did not perhaps regret the proceeding, by opposing which his reputation as an officer did not suffer with his sovereign. The next day he met one of the patriots, and remarked: "What do you think! they broke open my store last night, and *I should not be surprised* if they do it again to-night."

---

## RAMBLE XLV.

Capt. Thomas Pickering—Capture of Fort William & Mary—Langdon—Sullivan—Scarborough's boat conflict—The Hampden—Death of Pickering.

Just north of the South mill bridge, at the corner where stands the house of the late Benning Morrill, and extending over the land where Josiah Folsom formerly lived, was a house of large dimensions, in which resided a man of high spirit, born for the revolutionary age in which he lived. Capt. Thomas Pickering was little over thirty years of age when the contest with the mother country began to assume an open aspect. As Portsmouth held an elevated position in resistance to the usurpations of England, so among her sons could be selected some who bore prominent parts in the struggle, and among them none more prominent than Capt. Pickering. Intrepid, daring, he could never overlook an insult, nor bow to oppression. His antipathies were strong—when once fixed nothing could remove them. His father had been cruelly cut to pieces by the Indians while on an eastern expedition in the Indian war, and the hatred of the son to all Indians was so great that he could hardly resist attacking any copper-face who came within his reach. One day two peaceable Indians came into his residence near the mill. He entered the door, went to the yard—his mother knowing what was coming, bade them run for their lives. They ran up Water street, with the Captain in full pursuit. Finding he could not gain upon them, when near the South Church hill he threw his axe, which passed between them, the handle touching one of their shoulders. Such was the spirit of the man whose exploits in other directions should be, although they have not yet properly been, made a part of our local history.

In 1774, an order was passed by the King in council, prohibiting the exportation of gunpowder and military stores to America. The information was received by the committee of safety in this town, by express. Capt. Pickering, knowing that no time should be lost, called at once privately on his intimate friend, Major (afterwards Governor) John Langdon, and invited him to accompany him to fort William & Mary, at Newcastle, to take a glass of wine with Captain Cochran, its commander. "It will not do," said Maj. Langdon with his usual caution, mistaking the nature of the visit, "it will not do under the present state of public affairs to take such a step." When Capt. Pickering fully disclosed to him his design, with the remark that if twenty-eight like themselves could be obtained to join them, he would undertake to lead in the capture of the fort, Maj. Langdon heartily gave his assent to be his companion.

The company was soon made up, the plan of operations being arranged in the most secret manner. On a favorable night in the month of December, by the light of the moon which lacked but three or four days of being full, the boats were manned with the adventurous company, and before midnight they landed at a place not far from the fort. The fort at that time was much smaller in dimensions than at present. The ramparts on the west were of turf, and of sufficient inclination to make the walls more easy of access than at the present time.

The company landed unperceived by any one, when Pickering in advance of the main body scaled the ramparts of the fort, and seizing the sentinel with his muscular arm, took his gun, and threatened death if he made the least alarm. Signals of success were given to the company, which soon had charge of the sentinel, while Capt. Pickering entered the quarters of Capt. Cochran, and before he was fairly awake announced to him, that the fort was captured and he was a prisoner!

Cochran surrendered, and gave his sword to Capt. Pickering, who politely handed it back to him, observing, he was "a gentleman and should retain his side arms," and turned to leave him. As he turned, Cochran thought he had the gallant Pickering at his advantage, and aimed a blow at him with a sword, which Pickering parried with his arm, and then, without deigning to draw his trusty sword, he felled the miscreant to the ground with his clenched hand. He was then secured.

After the work was accomplished, the patriots returned to Portsmouth, and, elated with success, were disposed to visit Governor Wentworth and other loyalists, but Major Sullivan and George Frost of Durham, Dr. Bartlett of Kingston, Major Langdon and others of Portsmouth, addressed them, dissuading them from their purpose, and they again visited Newcastle and brought off fifteen of the lightest cannon.

Early in the morning the gunpowder in the magazine was put on board the gondolas. It all passed through the hands of Maj. Langdon and Samuel Drown, half brother of Capt. Pickering. Part of it was carried to Durham Falls, where Maj. Sullivan resided, put under the pulpit of the old meeting house in Durham, on the site of the one which was taken down in 1848, and afterward stored in a magazine which Capt. John Demeritt of Madbury had constructed in his cellar, and was afterward (excepting such part of it as Capt. Demeritt reserved for the use of his company), sent to Cambridge. Samuel Hall of Portsmouth, the grandfather of the present Samuel Hall, of Sagamore road, had the charge of its transportation to that place.

Capt. Eleazer Bennett, of Durham, who died in 1851, aged one hundred and one years and six months, was one of the company which captured the fort. The following are his own statements of this expedition of Americans against British soldiers, which, though attended with no bloodshed, was a very bold and daring affair. If the war had not followed, it must have doomed all who took part in it to the fate of rebels. It occurred six months before the battle of Bunker Hill, and four months before the battle of Lexington. It was recorded in the British Annals as the first action of the rebels against British soldiery, preparatory to the war of the Revolution.

Capt. Bennett states that "on the 15th of December, 1774, he was in the employ of Gen. Sullivan in his mill at Packer's falls, when Michael Davis came up from Durham falls and told him that Sullivan wished him to come down and go to Portsmouth, and to get any body he could to come with him. He could not get others to go, but went himself. The party consisted of about a dozen men. Their names, as far as he could remember, were Major John Sullivan, Capt. Winborn Adams, Ebenezer Thompson, John Demeritt of Madbury, Alpheus and Jonathan Chesley, Peter French, John Spencer, Michael Davis, Edward Sullivan, Isaac and Benjamin Small, and the narrator. They took a gondola belonging to Benjamin Mathes, who was too old to accompany them, and went down the river from Durham to Portsmouth. It was a cold, clear, moonlight night. Stopping a short time at Portsmouth they were joined by John

Langdon with another party. They then proceeded to the fort in possession of the British, at the mouth of the Piscataqua harbor. The water was so shallow that they could not bring their boat to within a rod of the shore. They waded through the water in perfect silence, mounted the fort, surprised the garrison, took the captain and bound him, and frightened away the soldiers. They found in the fort one hundred casks of powder and one hundred small arms, which they brought down to their boat, again wading through the water that froze on them, and made their way back to Durham. The arms were found to be defective and unfit for use."

The following extract from a letter appeared in the N. H. Gazette of December 23, 1774:

"*December* 16, 1774.—We have been in confusion here for two days, on account of an express from Boston, informing that two regiments were coming to take possession of our fort. By the beat of the drum two hundred men immediately assembled and went to the castle in two gondolas, who on their way were joined by one hundred and fifty more, and demanded the surrender of the fort, which Capt. Cochran refused, and fired three guns, but no lives were lost; upon which they immediately scaled the walls, disarmed the captain and his men, took possession of ninety-seven barrels of powder, put it on board the gondolas, brought it up to town, and went off with it to some distance in the country. Yesterday the town was full of men from the country, who marched in in form, chose a committee to wait on the Governor, who assured them he knew of no such design as sending troops, ships, etc. This morning I hear there are one thousand or fifteen hundred on their march to town. The Governor and Council sat yesterday on the affair, and are now meeting again. The men who came down are those of the best property and note in the Province."

Governor Wentworth resorted to extreme measures. Summoning the Council, he deprived Dr. Bartlett and Dr. Thompson of their commissions as Justices of the Peace, and Major Sullivan and Major Langdon of their commissions in the militia, and issued a proclamation to that effect.

While the powder was in Capt. Demeritt's possession, a brother of his besought him imploringly to surrender the powder to the royal authorities—assuring him that unless he did so he would be hanged as a rebel; but he told him that a crisis was at hand, when a struggle for liberty would ensue, and that it was his unalterable purpose, come life or death, to be on the side of liberty.

Daniel P. Drown, a nephew of Capt. Thomas Pickering, once related a trifling incident which transpired in connection with the history of this powder, which is worth mentioning. In the autumn of 1799 or 1800 Mr. Drown was at Major Demeritt's in Madbury, and as he was about leaving the house in pursuit of gray squirrels with his rifle, (formerly the sporting piece of Sir William Pepperrell,) the Major requested him to wait. On returning from the house he gave him about two charges of powder, which the Major said was a part of the powder which Mr. Drown's father assisted in taking from the fort, and bid him be sure that it did execution. It did so, and he returned to Portsmouth rich with a good bunch of squirrels, but richer with the gratification of telling his father the story.

In 1775, when the Scarborough ship-of-war, commanded by Capt. Barclay, was in the lower harbor, he seized some of our fishing craft, while he was at the same time supplying himself with such provisions as our market afforded. The vessels seized were laden with provisions, which were sent by Capt. Barclay to Boston, for the use of the King's forces. This so excited the indignation of Capt. Thomas Pickering, that he determined that the Scarborough's provision boat should not again approach our wharves. Capt. P. resided near Pickering's mills, and the shop of his half brother, Samuel Drown, was opposite Long wharf, where Jefferson street intersects

Water street. When the boat was coming up the river, Capt. P. entered Mr. D.'s shop and enquired of him "where he kept his musket, and whether he had any ammunition on hand?" Being informed that the musket and cartridge box filled with ball cartridges was under his bed, said P., "I want them." "For what purpose?" asked Mr. Drown. Said P., "I am determined that Capt. Barclay's boat shall not approach the town for a supply of provisions again," and hurried off after the musket, etc., which Mrs. Drown, his sister, delivered to him. On returning, he met Samuel Hutchings, the father of the late Samuel Hutchings, apothecary, and requested him to accompany him to a wharf, on which was a pile of boards, at the same time informing him of his purpose. The boat was soon seen approaching, and as a guard with muskets always accompanied the boatmen, Pickering anticipated a battle, and requested Hutchings to stand behind the boards, as there was no need of his exposure to the shot from the boat, and to hand him the cartridges and ramrod as fast as he fired. When the boat had approached to within a suitable distance for the balls to take effect, Pickering fired one ahead of the boat, but the boat proceeded on her course. Pickering then directed his shot immediately to it. He now received shot in return from the boat; but so quickly were his shot thrown that some of the men on board placed themselves out of P.'s sight; the others plied their oars with great dexterity and were soon out of harm's way. Capt. Pickering never learned whether any of his shot took effect, though from appearances he supposed they did. He was, as well as Mr. H., unharmed. After that the Scarborough's boat did not come to town for provisions.

Capt. Thomas Pickering afterward had command of the Hampden, twenty-gun ship, and was killed in a severe engagement with a heavy letter-of-marque, in March, 1779. He was never married. John, his oldest brother, was the owner of the South mill, the ownership of which and of the whole of the land bordering on the water from the mill to the Point of Graves was early in the Pickering family.

Capt. Cochran, who had command of the Fort, was a native of Londonderry, in this State. He married Sarah, a daughter of Zechariah Foss, who kept a tavern, about ninety years ago, in the house which was afterwards owned and occupied by John Weare, on the spot where the stable of the Franklin House now stands. Capt. Cochran soon left with the adherents to the mother country, and took up his residence at St. John's, New Brunswick, where he spent the remainder of his days, with his family. His youngest daughter was the wife of Charles Hardy of this city.

A small affair, but a good comment not only on the strict surveillance of correspondence by the patriots of the Revolution, but also on their gallantry, is shown in their reception of foreign refugee letters. Capt. Cochran, after removing to St. John's, sent some letters to his old friends here, and one to his aunt, the widow of John Gains, containing a piece of ribbon as a memento of friendship. The intercepted letters were all brought before Congress and read; of that Congress John Langdon was a member. To him the ribbon was entrusted, and on his return to Portsmouth he called on the old lady and politely delivered it.

Mr. Adams, page 248 of the Annals, notices the removal of the powder, etc. from Fort William & Mary, but his version of the affair conflicts in some respects with the above, which we gather from recollections of it as given to Daniel P. Drown by his father, whose wife was the sister of Capt. Thomas Pickering, who was really the projector and leader of that achievement, and not Gen. Sullivan, to whom Mr. Adams gives the honor of it.

John Pickering and Thomas Pickering, brothers, came

from England at the early settlement of the country. All the Pickerings of Newington and Greenland were descendants of Thomas Pickering, who made a settlement on Great Bay in Newington more than two centuries ago.

John Pickering located at the same time at the south part of Portsmouth. Not one of his descendants now bears the name of Pickering. The late Isaac Nelson was a son of the sister of Capt. Thomas Pickering, whose history this ramble records.

## RAMBLE XLVI.

**Major Samuel Hale—Latin grammar school in State street—Patriotism—First Province school.**

As the bad travelling forbids a walk more distant, we will just step down by Exchange Buildings, and standing at the stone post on State street, gather up a few reminiscences. On the west is the site of the old Rockingham Bank, now occupied by the new Custom House, and a little to the east is what for half a century had been the high school house. In the last century one whose residence was on the site of the Rockingham Bank, passed this spot to that school house, for as many years as the children of Israel were journeying from Egypt to the promised land.

Although the teacher, and nearly all of his host of scholars have now passed away, yet to his instructions, his example and devoted life, may be attributed as much that has tended to build up Portsmouth and give it character, as to any other source—with due deference to the pulpit.

As the subject of education, schools and school-houses, is at this age occupying the public mind, it may not be out of the way to call the attention of the younger members of the community to this able and devoted teacher of the Latin grammar school of Portsmouth, in former times. We refer to the venerable and much respected Major Samuel Hale. Born in the year 1718, he graduated at Harvard College in 1740. He commanded a company of New Hampshire provincials at the expedition to Cape Breton in 1745, and soon after returning from the siege of Louisburg, in 1748, was engaged as instructor of the school which was kept on the spot where the present brick school house is located, on State street. It was, we think, a large, one-story, wooden building, much like the old school house formerly on school street. He continued this occupation for nearly forty years, with great ability and effect. He imparted instruction to several thousand scholars, fitted a large number for college, and lived to see many of his pupils afterwards numbered among the distinguished men of the country. At Major Hale's school, John Langdon, Woodbury Langdon, John Peirce, and the old stock of Havens, Sheafes, and most of our distinguished merchants were educated. Those of his scholars who were destined for a liberal education were prepared for college under his tuition, and it was remarked that he never offered a candidate for admission to college who was rejected.

Early in life he became a member of the South Church, and was highly respected for his piety, integrity, learning and talents. He died July 10, 1807, at the advanced age of eighty-nine years. A conspicuous headstone to his memory is erected in the North burial ground. The epitaph thereon, written by J. M. Sewell, is still quite legible.

As an instructor of youth, he was not only remarkably fond of the employment, but his fame in the regions of the Piscataqua, was equal to that of his cotemporary, Master Lovell, in the metropolis of New England.

He was a warm friend of the American independence, and though living in the midst of political sentiments very different from his own, he early took a decided part in opposition to the tyrannical proceedings of England towards her colonies. Before the commencement of hostilities, he was a moderator of the town meeting, on a certain occasion, when several resolves were passed strongly expressive of the feelings of the true sons of liberty. The abettors of the royal prerogative spared no pains to impress upon his mind what they, no doubt honestly, thought would be the consequence. Not long after this, from the peculiarly gloomy aspect of the provincial affairs, and from the representations which were continually rung in his ears, he came to the conclusion, that the leading patriots would soon end their days at Tyburn. Such were his feelings when he declined signing the Association Test. However, he soon rose superior to those fearful apprehensions, and was a strenuous asserter, and an active promoter of the liberties of his country.

Soon after the declaration of independence, he was appointed one of the judges of the court of common pleas for Rockingham county, and held it with dignity until the adoption of the state constitution in 1784.

Major Hale had four sons and two daughters. Elizabeth married Capt. Ebenezer Thompson, and Mary married Thomas Sheafe. His sons, Samuel and William, were merchants and ship owners; in the latter years of their life the former resided in Barrington, and the latter in Dover. Thomas also resided in Barrington, and John was a bachelor lawyer in Portsmouth. All are now dead. Hon. Samuel Hale, formerly of Portsmouth and now of Rollinsford, was the son of Samuel Hale, of Barrington.

Forty years before Major Hale commenced his school, there was a province free school ordered by the Assembly to be kept in Portsmouth, which in the act is called "A free scool for righters, reeders and Lateners." To support this school Portsmouth was assessed £21, Hampton £10, Exeter £8, Dover £8, and Newcastle £3. This law passed May 10, 1708. By the following order of the

Assembly, passed six months after, it appears that the school arrangements had not then been completed:

PORTSMOUTH, 16 Nov. 1708.—Notwithstanding the pious law of the Governor, Council and Assembly of this province, in raising a free Grammar School for the province, to be kept in the town of Portsmouth, being the head of the government, and their good provision for the maintenance of a master, the Council are now informed that there is no provision made by the town of Portsmouth for a school-house for the receipt of the master and scholars.

*Ordered*, that the selectmen of the town of Portsmouth be notified of their neglect herein, and that they forthwith provide a suitable house for the said school to be kept, that the scholars may not lose their time, within three days next coming, upon the penalty of fifty pounds to be levied upon their persons and estates, as other fines, to be brought through the treasury to be expended in building of a good school-house for the future service: that the aforesaid good and religious act of the Assembly be not evaded or eluded.

## RAMBLE XLVII.

New Custom House and Post Office—Former Custom Houses—Eleazar Russell—His peculiarities—Collector and State Postmaster—His death.

So our fair city is having a public building erected, on which our tax payers may look without feeling that their eyes are feasted at the immediate expense of their pockets. The new Custom House is a noble structure, perhaps adapted to what Portsmouth is to be, rather than what it now is: a place where the business of entering and clearing a thousand ships a year may be accomplished, and in the Post-Office under the same roof the letters of fifty thousand inhabitants can be received and delivered with the greatest facility.

Previous to occupying the present rooms of the Custom House, which have now been in use over forty years, Col. Joseph Whipple was Collector, and transacted the business in the office adjoining his residence, (now the mansion of the heirs of the late Jacob S. Pickering,) on State street. Many years previous the office of the Collector was in Merchants' Row; and yet further back, for many years, probably from the Revolution up to 1798, the business was transacted in a more antiquated building, and by an antiquated man, yet further North on Market street.

Eleazer Russell, whom we now introduce to the reader, occupied as his residence and as the Custom House, a building on the south side of the ferry landing, exactly on the spot where the stone store now stands. This building was also the first Post Office, as Mr. Russell was the first postmaster in New Hampshire. Here all letters addressed to New Hampshire were deposited, to be sent for from other towns. For some years this was the only Post Office in the State. Being on the orchard of President John Cutt, it was probably erected in his day, and might have been the "new ware house" which is referred to in his will of 1680. Mr. Russell's mother was Margaret Waldron, a grand daughter of President Cutt, and the property around the ferryways and up Russell street (which took its name from his family) came to him by inheritance. Market street then terminated at the ferryways; and the land between Russell street and Bachelor's lane (now Green street) was Russell's orchard, with a few house lots on the west near Vaughan street.

Have you a vessel to clear? brush up and put on your best coat, for although the house with its little diamond windows and carpetless floor is nothing to command extra respect, yet the occupant is a man of bows, and so dignified that you may feel awkward if to a rough address you are conscious of a rough exterior. A knock at the door brings at once to your view a spare man somewhat advanced in life, of sharp countenance, with a cocked hat and wig, a light coat with full skirts, a long vest with pocket pads, light small clothes, with bright knee buckles, and more ponderous buckles on his shoes. Your business is asked; and if it is not his hour for breakfast or dinner, the clearance papers are soon prepared. The way of delivery of the papers is rather peculiar, and is a specimen of house clearance which allowed of no hanging on in the old Custom House. The fee stated and paid—the official, with the papers yet in his hand, steps to the door, opens it, and with a bow gives up the papers; and with a wish for a prosperous voyage, closes the door and the interview.

Eleazer Russell was a bachelor. He had a brother Benjamin who died on the coast of Africa, and four sisters, all of whom died single. Three of his sisters resided with him for many years. He was a man of strict integrity and regular habits. Nine o'clock was his hour for retiring, and no invasion of his prerogative would he permit. One evening Col. Clapp called for a social hour, and from the interest of the interview did not mind the flight of time. Mr. Russell, however, did. It was a splendid evening, and Mr. Russell invited the Colonel to the door to see the stars. They looked but a moment, when following his office routine, he bid the Colonel good night, closed the door, and left him to admire the stars, while he retired. There was an apparent lack of courtesy in this proceeding, but it may be a question whether a fixed, correct habit should not be as much respected as the feelings of those who encroach upon it. At another time, he invited some mechanics in his employ to dine with him. As soon as the meal was despatched, he rose and addressed his guests: "Joiners, I have done with you."

While he was courteous to his neighbors, he always expected respect to his most trivial rights. "*Leave is light*," said he one day, touching a neighbor on his shoulder, who had put some fence boards on his side of the street, without asking permission. Attention to these three words would doubtless add to the peace of many neighborhoods.

His house was glazed with diamond glass, the windows opened on hinges, and the space between the inner and outer walls was so capacious as to allow fuel, after being split for the winter fire, a depository in closets beneath the window stools. Such was the only Custom House in New Hampshire in the early days after the Revolution; and such the individual who sat at receipt of customs.

Mr. Russell built the Market-street House (now owned and occupied by C. W. Walker), in 1788, for his own occupancy. He kept his office in it for a few years, but died before removing his sisters into it. His property he gave to Daniel Waldron, a nephew, whom he had brought up and watched over with fatherly care.

Eleazer Russell did not bear the title of Collector, but that of Naval Officer; he performed, however, all the duties of Collector. He held several important offices under government, among them that of sole Postmaster of New Hampshire, the duties of which he performed with faithfulness and ability. He was one of the Sandemanian brotherhood, full of Christian love, and his domestic relations are spoken of as the most harmonious and happy kind.

He was always in great fear of small-pox and of foreign epidemics. When a vessel arrived and the papers were carried to the Custom House, he would receive them with the tongs and submit them to a smoking before he examined them.

When the yellow fever appeared in Portsmouth, in

1798, it first broke out in his neighborhood. His fear of contagious diseases no doubt tended to hasten his end. For although he did not take the fever, he died on the same week in which one of his sisters and another female died of it at his house. His death occurred on the 18th of September, 1798, at the age of seventy-eight years, and he was buried in the North burying-ground.

We have thus brought forth in our ramble an indistinct daguerreotype of one of our old citizens, of whom we can find no public record before made, except the single line which records his death and age.

## RAMBLE XLVIII.

The Buckminster house—Occupants—Nathaniel Warner's disappointment—Lettice Mitchel—Wyseman Clagett—The marriage—Domestic troubles—Sketch of life—Official acts—Character.

There is little need of travelling over the regions of imagination to get a touch of the romantic. Were the history of the past in Portsmouth fully written, as brought forward in the reminiscenses of our old mansions which have numbered their century of years, there would be enough to make several interesting volumes. Almost every old house has its traditionary story, as yet unwritten, and in time destined to pass into forgetfulness. Perhaps it were better that some should so pass.

The house on Islington street, nearly opposite the Academy, where Mrs. Tompson has for several years kept a boarding-house, has recently been made a new house, by its present owner, George Tompson, who has shown excellent taste in carefully preserving its original exterior appearance. It was for many years the residence of Col. Eliphalet Ladd, and of his widow, afterward the wife of Rev. Dr. Buckminister. Before Ladd's removal to this town it was at different times occupied by Clement Storer, Daniel R. Rogers and John Wendell, the father of Abraham, Isaac and Jacob. About eighty years ago it was owned and occupied by Nathaniel Nichols, who then owned and improved the distillery which stood on the spot where the Concord depot is now located. He was the uncle of Rev. Dr. Nichols, late of Portland. The house was built in 1720 by Daniel Warner, who came from Ipswich, Mass. His son, Jonathan Warner, was born here in 1726.

Prominent among the belles of the time, a lady of great beauty, was Miss Lettice Mitchel (a daughter of Dr. Mitchel, who then resided in the house No. 19, South street), to whom Nathaniel Warner was engaged, and for whom his father designed this good structure, which (with all its antique fixtures) has ever been a public ornament. Mr. Warner made a voyage to Europe for his health, leaving his lady-love to shine in the brilliant circle of which she was a prominent star, intending on his return to make her the occupant of this large house.

In that age the appendages of royality extended to this side of the Atlantic. The officers of the crown were decked in such regalia as simple republicanism would now look upon with astonishment. In 1758, there was a new officer located in Portsmouth, who bore the title of King's Attorney. His name was WYSEMAN CLAGETT. The King's Attorney was a single man, and made quite an excitement in the first circles. Among all the ladies, none was so attractive as the beautiful Lettice Mitchel. She was pleased with the attentions given her, but she had pledged her affections to another. The officer of the King, in his glorious apparel, was, however, to the mother too strong an allurement, and her persuasion overcame her daughter's better feelings, and in the year 1759, at the early age of eighteen years, before the return of Mr.

Warner from Europe, she was united in marriage to Wyseman Clagett. Warner returned—he could love no other—and he died, it is said, of a broken heart.

We will now introduce the reader to another house of historical interest, next east of the Cutter house, now owned and occupied by Miss Leavitt. It was for some years occupied by her father—previously by John Abbott, about fifty years ago by J. Tufts Pickering—and for twenty years before that time by George Doig, a painter. This house was formerly occupied for several years by Wyseman Clagett, who removed to this place from the Hart house, corner of Daniel and Penhallow streets, after the fire of 1761. But this house was far from being the scene of that happiness which Lettice's mother had anticipated for her. The King's Attorney, in his official capacity, was in the main just, but his decision was marked with that severity which made him a terror to evil doers, and even to some who did well. In his domestic relations, all his decision and severity were brought into requisition. Being congratulated by a companion for having married a fortune, he replied, "I have not married a fortune, sir, I have only married one of Fortune's daughters, a Miss-Fortune." This early prophetic idea he seemed to carry through life. He would permit nothing to be done in the house without his special order and direction; and if everything was not to his liking, the most violent demonstrations would be made. The washing and fresh sanding of a room without his order, has been met with a command for the servant to scatter mud or snow over the floor. For putting vinegar on the table in a cream pitcher instead of a cruse, his wrench of the table cloth scatters the whole contents of the table on the floor. The idea that his wife's affections rested on her first love, was a source of constant irritation to him, and brought with his other rough treatment the taunt,—"This is to pay Warner's debts." Two of their children were sent to school for a quarter, but attended only a week. Mrs. Clagett called on the teacher to pay for the quarter. The teacher declined receiving full pay. "You must take it," was the reply, "or I shall never dare to see his face again." Thus, through fear, she was in a constant state of unhappy bondage. They had eight children, six sons and two daughters. Judge Clifton Clagett of Amherst, was one of them. Wyseman was born in Bristol, Eng., in 1721, and died at Litchfield, N. H., in 1784. His lady lived six years a widow, and afterwards married Simon McQueston, and died at Bedford in 1827, aged eighty-five.

In the discharge of the duties of his office, the King's Attorney was loyal to his sovereign; but when the British Parliament passed the "Stamp act," and other oppressive laws against the rights of the Colonies, he was among the foremost to remonstrate. With Warner, Adams, Rindge, Hale, Peirce and Sherburne, he was appointed by the town "to give particular instructions to Representatives" (Dec. 2d, 1765). In these instructions they complain of the Stamp act and the danger of *liberty.*

He was a most persevering searcher out of petty offences against the dignity of the crown and peace of the province. There was no escape for the violater of the law, and the statutes against small offences were executed in their utmost rigor. In common parlance the word "Clagett" became synonymous with the word "prosecute," and "to be Clagetted" meant the same thing as "to be prosecuted."

There is one anecdote related of the King's Attorney which would seem to indicate, that however just he might be in administering for the King, he could swerve a little when self-interest and irritation prompted. There was one day a load of wood on the parade for sale. The man would not part with it for the sum offered. The Attorney, in a state of irritation, went home, and told one of his servants to go and insult that man, and report what he said or did. The man did as he was told—for none who lived with him dared do otherwise. The irritated teamster, with an oath and a threat, shook his goad at the man. A complaint was at once made, the man summoned before the King's Attorney, charged with using profane language. He appeared trembling before the throne which Clagett had erected in his office, on which, in his judicial wig, he presided with magisterial dignity, with the clerk's seat on one side and the sheriff's on the other. The poor man begged his honor's pardon and asked forgiveness. "I heartily forgive you," was the reply. The man began to retire. "Stop, stop, sir—*I* forgive you, but the *law* don't. You are found guilty of profanity, and fined five dollars." "Oh dear, sir, my load of wood, which I brought in to raise the means for paying my taxes, will not sell for so much, and I have nothing else—what shall I do!" "Your case," said the King's Attorney, "is indeed a hard one, and in pity for you, you may drive the load of wood into my yard, and I will make up the balance of the fine myself." The *favored* man left his wood as directed.

As every Quixote has his squire, so Clagett had in a town constable, an associate of congenial spirit. At times they were low in purse. One day the constable called, to see if he could find a job. "Nothing to do—and what is worse, nothing to eat," said the King's Attorney. The constable goes into a hotel in Water street, and finding two sailors with their bowls of toddy on a table, he takes up one bowl and drinks it off. The sailor of course applies his fists to him. The constable retires, and has the sailor arrested for assault and battery, and summoned before the Attorney's throne. A sufficient fine is imposed to put them in funds for the day.

Many like anecdotes are told of him, but these are sufficient to show the man, and excite the wonder of the reader that one of so pure character, sound morals, and excellent political standing as his son, the Hon. Clifton Clagett, should have had such a parentage.

The coat-of-arms, now in possession of the family, shows the ancestry of the "Clagett family" four generations back of Wyseman, commencing with Robert Clagett, of Malling, Kent, Eng., and in the descent is said to be connected to some of the nobility.

His father, Wyseman Clagett, was a barrister at law—occupied a large estate at Bristol, called the Manor of Broad Oaks, had a mansion with twelve chimneys, lived in style, kept a coach and not less than eight servants. He died bankrupt.

Hon. Charles H. Atherton, of Amherst, who was personally acquainted with Wyseman, the son, says:—

"His person was tall and robust, his countenance stern and severe, with a strong brow, devouring black eyes, and a voice like Stentor himself. He also had a peculiar convulsive twitch of the mouth, by which it was drawn to the ear, as if he would engulph it, accompanied by a strong muscular motion of his bushy brow, and a snap of the eye, appalling to the beholder, and indicative of anything but placidity and mildness. With this forbidding exterior, however, he was a wit, fond of conviviality and not insensible to the charms of female beauty.

"When he moved to Litchfield, he was the proprietor of a fall-back chaise, which went to decay, and was never replaced, an indifferent pony became his only aid for travel. When on horseback, as the writer has seen him, with his full bottomed white wig, his cocked hat, still retaining some remnants of its gold lace, and his coat bearing evidence of its antiquity, as well as of the original excellence of its texture, he exhibited a striking picture of dilapidated importance."

The children sustained an unexceptionable respectability in life.

## RAMBLE XLIX.

Eliphalet Ladd—Early life—Family—The Hercules—The Archelaus—Buildings—Portsmouth Aqueduct—The challenge—His death and character.

SPRING has returned. The face of nature,—in the promise of the swelling bud, in early creeping grass, in the growing warmth of the sunshine, and in the return of the feathered songsters,—now extends invitations for all to come forth, and enjoy those charms which were not lost with Eden. All these the rambler can richly enjoy,—but it is his more peculiar province to walk in the scenes of the past, and thus endeavor to give interest to the existing localities which meet every eye. To say that our present walk is to the *Portsmouth Journal office* block, in Ladd street, would convey the idea of a very limited ramble, and perhaps of an unsightly termination. But as it takes the circuit of nearly a century to reach the point, some scenes of interest may arise.

On the morning of the 25th of January, 1761, the old hotel of James Stoodly, on Daniel street, was burnt on the spot north of the Post Office, where a like structure was afterward reared, and long known as the mansion of Elijah Hall. At the same fire a barber's shop was consumed, and Wiseman Clagett's residence (the Hart house,) in the immediate vicinity, was torn in pieces, his property much damaged and many things stolen. The sight of such a fire was then a rare occurrence—its brilliancy was seen in neighboring towns, and its light shed far out upon the ocean.

Between Portsmouth and the Shoals its light shone upon one adventurous boat, in which, before the dawn of day, a young man of seventeen years was bearing to those isles some articles for traffic with the islanders. At the time when a general scarcity prevailed from the failure of crops, and the energies of the young men were aroused to do what they could for a living, this juvenile merchant, then an inhabitant of Exeter, began in this small way his career in the arts of trade. As he looked back upon the illumination from his small craft, little did he then think that his own prosperity and that of the terrified town, were destined in after years to rise together; or that the time would arrive when the largest merchant ship of the last century that the Piscataqua floated, would be passing over the same ocean track, from his own ship yard. But young men have only to expect great things, live accordingly, and they will receive them.

In a day or two the adventurer returns with his load of fish, and passes through to Exeter. The events of the next thirty years of his life mostly transpired in that town. In 1772 he married a lady of Berwick whom he met at her brother's house in Portsmouth, Miss Abigail Hill, who was a true helpmeet. To her good management, he used in his latter days to attribute at least three-fourths of his wealth. Ten children were added to their household—William, Henry, Alexander and Eliphalet. Four of his daughters were married. Rev. William F. Rowland, of Exeter, Capt. Samuel Chauncy, John P. Lord, and John Langdon, Jr. of Portsmouth, were their husbands. Two of the children died in youth.

When about sixteen, he went with some civil engineers on a professional expedition to Crown Point. At that time Vermont as well as the western part of our own State was a wilderness. The company mistook their way, and were several days in the woods without provisions. At length they were driven to the necessity of eating horse meat and raw pumpkins. The meat relished well, and the pumpkins were as palatable as ripe melons usually are. In after life when the children at his bountiful table were disposed to find fault with any provision, he would remark that if they could but once have an appetite for horse meat or raw pumpkins, no complaint would be heard.

In business matters, the thirty years spent at Exeter exhibited all the various changes which are attendant upon men of enterprise, whose motto is, "nothing risk, nothing gain." Three times he regarded himself a man of wealth, and as many times he was reduced to his last dollar, before his removal to Portsmouth in 1792, and to the occupancy of the Tompson mansion near the Academy, which so long bore his name.

In the time of the Revolution, Col. Ladd built a twenty gun ship, called the *Hercules*. The enemy, well posted up in all the movements of the rebels, had a knowledge of the building, and in a Halifax paper was inserted an advertisement, giving notice that a ship of twenty guns, then on the stocks on the Piscataqua, would be sold at auction in Halfax on a day designated. Two British frigates were put on the watch, and the Hercules was captured and sold at Halifax on the very day advertised!

He accomplished, what was a marvel in his day, the building of a monster merchant ship of nearly *five hundred* tons. The *Archelaus*, the Leviathan of sixty years ago, was built at Exeter, and was three years in being completed. She afterwards became the property of Mr. Scott of Boston, and was lost, we have been told, on Cape Cod. Among the articles received in payment for the ship was a *cord* of coat buttons, which Col. Ladd, being in the hardware and variety line, no doubt turned to good account. But a stock of one hundred and twenty-eight cubic feet of buttons could not be at once disposed of. Some remained on hand until in the war of 1812 there arose a great demand for bright ball buttons for military use. They were scarce, could not be imported, and an advance of several thousand dollars was at once made on the stock which remained on hand in his sons' store.

Among his real estate enterprises was the removal of the large house which now stands on Bridge street, facing Hanover street, from Exeter—also the barn, next south, recently taken down by George Tompson, to give place to his new one. Col. Ladd opened the street which bears his name, and built the block of buildings in which our office is located. At the fire of 1802 the whole block was burned. He immediately rebuilt it, and the eastern tenement which we have occupied for a third of a century, was fitted for a store for his own occupancy. The trap-hatch for taking in his goods is still under our press.

He also built the three stores on Market street, from the corner of Ladd street to that now occupied by J. Woodman Moses. Into one of these stores he removed and continued his business until his death. In the erection of that symmetrical structure now used as the Piscataqua Exchange Banking house, he was the principal architect.

But what should, more than any of the above matters, keep him in remembrance, is the active part he took in supplying Portsmouth with one of the greatest luxuries we have,—a luxury which few places in the world so liberally enjoy, and of which none can boast a superior quality—pure water.

In 1797 a company was formed and incorporated under the name of the "Portsmouth Aqueduct Company." Eliphalet Ladd, Samuel Hill and Thomas Chadbourne were managers, who in person broke the ground at its commencement. They purchased the invaluable springs at the Oak Hill farm, about two and a half miles from Market Square, and in two years the water was brought into town, through logs, and into immediate use in two hundred families. The stock of the company was divided into one hundred shares, and such sums only were assessed as were necessary to commence the work, and the balance of expense paid from the income. The whole direct assessments ever made have amounted to only eighty-two dollars on a share. There were some eight or ten years when the income was devoted to meeting expenses, but for many years it has been so good property that the shares have been sold as high as three hundred dollars. Col. Ladd made a personal survey of the track of the aqueduct from the fountain into town; and so confident was he of his accuracy as an engineer, in levelling, that he erected an upright pipe in front of his mansion, cut it off at a particular height, and said, "thus high the water will rise." When it was let into the logs, it rose exactly to the point he designated, not varying an inch.

But it is the real benefit of the public generally, more than the pecuniary benefit to the aqueduct proprietors, that we take into view, when we bring into remembrance those who have bestowed upon Portsmouth blessings which are now many leagues in length, and flow in upon a thousand households every hour.

The springs (which from their flowing in winter bore the name of the "warm springs" more than a century before an aqueduct was extended from them,) are inexhaustible—they have never diminished in the least in the greatest drought. An analysis of the water shows it of unsurpassed purity. Who can duly estimate the blessing!

Of the sons of Col. Ladd, were William Ladd, the great apostle of peace, and two of our most distinguished and successful merchants, Henry and Alexander Ladd—gentlemen of education and enterprise, whose impress has been felt upon our public institutions.

In the strong party times near the close of the last century, it was almost impossible for any man who took an active part in public affairs to avoid coming in collision with political opponents. Col. Ladd was not disposed to mince matters in such discussions, and drew upon himself the ire of a distinguished ship master, a leader of the opposition, who felt himself so much aggrieved that nothing short of pistols were looked to, to heal the breach.

The challenge was borne to Col. Ladd by Gen. Clement Storer. It was presented in due form, in the presence of his son William, whose disposition at that time partook more of the belligerent than of that peace spirit which in his latter days made him conspicuous on both sides of the Atlantic. The challenge was read—the place of meeting designated was the island, that has since become the Navy Yard. Looking up to the second, Col. Ladd said, "Tell Tom—— he is a dirty fellow." "What! do you mean to insult me by such a message," said the dignified General. "And you are another," was the only response.

The General withdrew somewhat irritated. After he had retired, young William Ladd, feeling somewhat stirred by the occasion, said, "Father, I'll fight him." "Set down, Bill, set down; why, hang the fellow, it is as much as a man's life is worth to go over the river on such a day as this." The meeting did not take place.

Col. Ladd died on the 24th of February, 1806, in the sixty-second year of his age. The record of his death is accompanied with a sketch of his character: "Having always led a life of assiduous industry, his example excited the emulation of others, and the industrious were certain of receiving his approbation and encouragement. In sentiment too independent to be biased by flattery, he neither condescended to it himself, nor permitted it in others. Though cautious in the formation of his opinions he was not obstinately tenacious of them, and he adhered to them no longer than they were believed correct. He possessed a degree of fortitude rarely attainable, which enabled him to bear the frowns of adversity without being depressed, and the smiles of prosperity without being elated. Whether success or defeat attended his undertakings, he remained calm and equable, acknowledging in all that befell him the hand of God, and reposing unlimited confidence in the justice of providence. As he was a lover of his country, he extended a liberal hand for the encouragement of all works of public utility; and as he was a professor of the Christian religion, he strove to extend its influence, by discountenancing and repressing vice and irreligion, and by animating others to the practice of piety and virtue."

As here we sit, perhaps in the very spot where Col. Ladd once sat devising plans which gave business to those around him,—and from the small pump by our side flows at command that clear stream from a pure fountain several miles distant, brought by him to our chamber recesses—how can we do better than to invite the thousands in Portsmouth when they read this sketch to fill one goblet of that sparkling fluid, and drink with the rambler, "*The Remembrance of Col. Eliphalet Ladd.*"

---

## RAMBLE L.

Frenchman's Lane—The French fleet three months at Portsmouth—The murder—Their laundry at the Creek.

'Twas a brave old spot, and deep was the shade
By the fast locked boughs of the elm tree made,
Where the sun scarce looked with his fiery eye,
As he coursed through the burning summer sky,
Where breezes e'er fanned the heat flushed cheek,
Old Frenchman's Lane, up by Islington Creek.

Most lovely the spot, yet dark was the tale
That made the red lips of boyhood pale,
Of the Frenchman's doom and the bitter strife,
Of the blood stained sward and the gleaming knife,
Of the gory rock set the wrong to speak,
In Frenchman's Lane, up by Islington Creek.

*Shillaber.*

ONE event in the American Revolution tended to give for several months a lively interest to Portsmouth. It was the arrival in our harbor, in August, 1782, of a portion of the large French fleet which a few months previously had received hard treatment from the English, in the West Indies. We can find in the papers of the day two simple notices only of the event. The N. H. Gazette of August 18, 1782, says: "On Thursday last, an eighty-gun ship, and two seventy-fours, and a thirty-two gun ship, belonging to the French fleet, arrived in our harbor." We find no other record made of them until November, when in a severe thunder storm it is said that the eighty-gun ship of the French fleet was struck by lightning, and four men killed. The Annals of Portsmouth give only the latter item. Though passing events of that time were deemed of little account, they are not forgotten by our aged inhabitants, and from the store of their memory we will endeavor to restore a picture which would otherwise soon pass into oblivion.

The squadron of French vessels, of which three were eighty-gun ships, eight were seventy-fours, one forty, two thirty-twos, and a cutter of fourteen guns, arrived in Boston on the ninth of August. This fleet, bringing in with them six prizes, enrolled about ten thousand men as officers, soldiers and marines. This was rather too much for Boston at that time, and so five of the fleet left the next week and anchored in Portsmouth Harbor, where they remained over three months. For that time over two thousand Frenchmen were in our neighborhood, many of them boarding in town, and all of them at times enjoying opportunities for coming on shore. An old lady whose father kept the first boarding-house in the place at the time, has told us many illustrative incidents of French manners. The dress of the officers was white. In the attic of the hotel (the Stavers' house on Court street) was a large meal chest. They would sometimes complete their toilet in the morning by rolling over a few times in that chest, for the lack of the white powder to which they were accustomed.

There were two regiments of marines; the uniform of one was white, the other white turned out with blue. They were under the order of the Marquis de Vaudreuil. The State legislature, then in session in Portsmouth, gave a public dinner in honor of the Marquis, and balls were also given at the Assembly House, by the citizens. There were public rejoicings, by ringing of bells, firing of guns, etc., on the birthday of the dauphin of France, and indeed for three months Portsmouth became quite of the French *ton*.

"Do you recollect the incident of the death of the Frenchman at the Creek?" said we the other day (in 1856) to an old gentleman of eighty-five. As well as though it happened yesterday," said he. "Living near the place, I was early on the spot; my father and myself were the first who reached there, after the man who made the discovery." This venerable old gentleman was Richard Fitzgerald.

Before the year 1792, Islington road, now commencing at the Creek and extending direct to the Plains, was not opened. The Plains road curved round near the head of the Creek, and along the present track of the Eastern railroad, (called Frenchman's lane,) it crossed the present road to White's road, and so passed from the pound to the Plains.

While the French fleet was here, they made the Creek, in the vicinity of where the stocking factory lately stood, a place of much resort. Here was a brook of fresh water, here were frogs in abundance, and here the washing for the fleet was generally done. Six or seven large boilers might have been seen by the side of the brook, with fires burning beneath them, and the laundry process going on in a style more extensive than Portsmouth has witnessed since. And here, too, after the washing was over, might be seen kettles of seven or eight buckets capacity, filled with soup, in which birds, fish, meat and frogs, with a good addition of flour loaves, made up an epicurean dish, which would require the nicety of a French taste duly to appreciate.

In connection with the eating was usually some drinking, and in the neighborhood, a few rods west of the residence of True M. Ball, was the Rackley house, of no better reputation than it ought to have had. It is supposed that from some quarrel at this house the murder was committed. It was in the month of October,* before daylight, a person in the neighborhood, in passing near the turn of the lane, saw something white, which he supposed to be a bag. On touching it with his foot he found it a dead man! Much terrified, he ran to the houses of some of the neighbors, and our informant, with his father, were the first on the spot. There lay, with his head on a flat stone, a young man between twenty-five and thirty years of age. He had on white pants and a Guernsey jacket, white with dark spots. His head was half severed at the neck, and there were marks of a blow by a stake on the cheek. He lay there as the pasture boys drove their cows by, and was then removed to the tan yard, where an inquest was held. The plank on which he was laid was kept in the tan house for many years. Although soaked for months in the brook, the marks of the blood were not washed out. And for half a century after the event, the boys as they fearfully stood on the flat rock near the turn in the lane, fancied, in a slight discoloration, that the blood remained there still. It was imagination; but it excited a horror for the event in many a young mind.

An investigation showed that two men called on a Frenchman, boarding at the north end, and invited him to walk with them. He was sitting in his shirt sleeves, while the landlady was mending his jacket. In haste to accompany them, he took the jacket as it was, with the needle still remaining in the half mended rent; and by

* It appears from an entry in a manuscript "Weather Register," kept at the time by Dr. Brackett, that the Frenchman (named John Dushan) was killed on the 23d of October, 1778, four years previous to the time of the visit of the French fleet. The entry is recorded in Ramble LXXVI. page 44, Second Series. We give the story, however, as written by the author.

the circumstance of finding the needle there he was afterwards readily identified. The party went over to Christian Shore, (which at that time had only six houses, occupied by R. Jackson, N. Jackson, N. Dennett, R. Shortridge, T. Ham and S. Walker), and passing through Sherburne's woods came to the head of the Creek. A stake taken from a fence, was found near the spot, with which he was knocked down. The perpetrators were never arrested. The funeral was attended by about one hundred and fifty French officers and sailors, and he was buried in the North cemetery, directly inside of where the gate formerly opened. Here his devoted companions would gather from day to day, and make crosses over his remains.

Thousands of Frenchmen had just fallen in the battle which drove the fleet to our harbor—and tens of thousands have since passed as ignobly away in the campaigns of Napoleon—but neither we nor our fathers saw them, and of course their wholesale fall is esteemed of less consequence in the local account than the tragedy which has given the name to *Frenchman's Lane*, the first full record of which has been left to form the subject of our present ramble.

Frenchman's Lane is the spot which has had a second memento, for the lovers of home. Here were landed from the cars on the fourth of July, 1853, a thousand of the sons of Portsmouth. Here were they marshalled, welcomed, and like a triumphal procession from hence entered the streets where they once joyfully rambled, and on the scenes which were indelibly stamped on their minds in earlier days.

"And Frenchman's Lane has passed away,
No more on its sward do the shadows play;
The pear trees old from the scene have passed,
And the blood-marked stone aside is cast,
And the engine's whistle is heard to shriek,
In Frenchman's Lane, up by Islington Creek.

But true to ourselves, we shall ever retain
A love for the green old Frenchman's Lane,

And its romance, its terror, its birds and bloom,
Its pears and its elderblow's perfume—
And a tear at times may moisten the cheek
For Frenchman's Lane, up by Islington Creek."

## RAMBLE LI.

Richard Fitzgerald—His residence—Interview with Com. Hull—His garden—The old rose bush—Love of flowers—Death of husband and wife same day.

Now that Frenchman's Lane has been opened to us, and its early scenes been made a matter of history, we will turn our ramble to the house in that neighborhood in which the narrator of the events of nearly seventy years ago was born, and in whose memory the tragic scene was deeply imprinted through life.

The last week in November, 1858, Islington street presented the solemn spectacle of a funeral, in which were two hearses in succession, bearing to their last resting place the remains of a husband and wife, who after a pilgrimage together of forty-five years, had together on the same morning, gone upon that long journey from which no traveller has yet returned. It was a realization of the idea of the Scottish bard, touching indeed as the mere fancy of the poet, but deeply thrilling in the reality of this finale:

John Anderson, my jo, John,
We climb the hill thegither;
And many a canty day, John,
We've had wi'ane anither;
Now we maun totter down, John,
But hand in hand we'll go,
And sleep thegither at the foot,
John Anderson, my jo.

Mr. Richard Fitzgerald, at the age of eighty-seven, died in the house which his grandfather built, and in which he and his mother were born. This house of two stories, on the west corner of Anthony and Islington streets, is among the antiquities of the west end of the city. It presents a good exterior, showing that it has been occupied by those who have had a proprietorship in it. The timber with which the frame of the house was made, was cut in 1724, from a forest back of it. It was built by Mr. Mead, whose daughter, here born, married Richard Fitzgerald, a tailor, father of the last occupant. Richard Fitzgerald, Jr., was here born in September, 1771, and occupied the rooms which were his birth place and that of his mother, extending to some years over the long limit of a century.

Mr. Fitzgerald was a man of some irritability as well as of independence, free to express his opinions without regard to persons. At the time when Commodore Isaac Hull had the command of our Navy Yard, (the renowned Commodore Hull whose "Victory" has been danced at every ball for the last forty years,) there was occasion for iron as well as copper work for a ship-of-war at the Navy Yard, and Mr. Fitzgerald was among the workers in iron. One day the Commodore looked into Mr. Greenleaf's copper foundry, next east of the Stone church, and found Mr. Fitzgerald roughing out some iron work for a future finish. The Commodore, in his way, turning the rough pieces of iron with his cane, remarked, "What bungling fellow has been at work here?" The son of Vulcan was a little touched, and turning his face up to him who had looked down his thousands, replied: "I don't know what bungling fellow you mean; you may have bungling fellows in your ships, but there are none here. That is just as much as you know about it." The Commodore thought best to make no reply to an old man of the revolutionary stock, and retired. A day or two after he returned to the shop again, and finding Mr. Fitzgerald surrounded by the well finished pieces of shining iron, each neatly adapted to its purpose, the Commodore, touching them with his cane, remarked: "O, this looks finely." "That is just what I told you the other day," said Mr. Fitzgerald, "we have no bunglers here." The Commodore, instead of being displeased, replied with an oath, "You are a good fellow for standing up for your craft."

Mr. Fitzgerald was never of a roving disposition; content to stay at home, he never but once entered a rail car or a stage coach. By his first wife, who died about fifty years ago, he had six children, most of whom arrived to mature age, but have all been dead for the last twenty years. It is not long since that Mr. Fitzgerald presented to us a handsome cluster of damask roses, from a bush in his garden, which seventy-six years ago he transplanted there with his own hands from the Banfield garden, then a few rods in the rear of where the Journal office is now located. When removed, the bush was well grown, and had probably borne roses before the Revolution. The bush has had his personal care during three-quarters of a century, and when we last saw it, but little more than a year since, it was promising flowers still in its old age. He had a better opportunity for watching the nature of the bush than any professed naturalist. He found that it usually bloomed for six years in succession; then it took a season of rest, dwindled and ceased to bear for three years, and on the fourth it usually came out in fresh vigor, and bloomed again for another six years.

The garden spot which he used to cultivate when a boy, he dug personally every successive year from the age of ten to eighty-six. And during the last summer he might have been seen bending over the soil he loved, with his hoe in hand, banishing the weeds against which he ever felt an enmity. "Stones must grow," said the old gentleman, "for I have picked all the stones out of the garden every year for seventy years, and yet I find a few more every spring." The garden was always a pattern of neatness; and even in the little blacksmith's shop in the garden, the smoke seemed to ascend without blacking the ceiling.

He tilled the soil and cultivated the flowers with a feeling which was above that of mere love of labor, or its pecuniary rewards. A true lover of nature, age rather increased than diminished his admiration of her works. The old gentleman, when bending beneath the weight of years, would hold up some common flower or leaf, and admire in its structure the wisdom of Him who created all things. And that old rose bush: although its flowers came the same year after year, they were as fresh and beautiful in his eye, as when he first beheld them. We have received bouquets from younger hands, but from none with a more feeling sense of the beauty and richness of the gift than he expressed when he last gave us a bunch of beautiful roses from his old bush.

The last three days of their lives, Mr. Fitzgerald and his wife (who had been suddenly paralyzed,) were both insensible, and both died the same morning, without a consciousness of each other's condition. She (having been born on the dark day, May 19, 1780) was seventy-eight years of age; and he had reached the age of eighty-seven.

Thus have passed away the last of the family, and there was none of its members to continue the occupancy of a spot which has so many years been literally a *family home*. The venerable old gentleman, who gave us an account of what he witnessed of the Frenchman's Lane tragedy, and many other incidents in his recollection, which have been of interest to ourselves and our readers, has passed into that cemetery where he has from time to time followed his household. He and his partner have now gone to the presence of Him, on whom, during the latter years of penury and infirmity, they placed their hope. The experience of his providential care richly repaid them for their trust; and not the least is that singular mercy which has not left one to mourn for the loss of the other.

## RAMBLE LII.

**Washington's tour to New Hampshire in 1789—His own account.**

EVERY age has some epoch from which events before and after are dated. Among the epochs of Portsmouth in the past century may be ranked the year of the great fire in 1813, the year of the yellow fever in 1798, the year when Washington visited Portsmouth in 1789, and the year of the declaration in 1776. These events made so deep impressions upon the participators in the scenes, that all minor events are frequently dated as so many years before or after their occurrence.

Washington was inaugurated President on the 30th of April, 1789, and soon after attended the first session of the first Congress at New York, which closed on the 29th of September. A few days after its close, attended only by his two private secretaries and servants, he left New York on a tour through Connecticut and Massachusetts to New Hampshire. In nine days he reached Boston, and in seven days after arrived in Portsmouth, which was the eastern termination of his tour.

With our readers we will now ramble over the streets of Portsmouth in company with Washington, revive some of the old scenes, and enter some sketches which the page of written history has not yet presented. It is a matter of no little satisfaction for us to stand aside awhile, and let our honored guest give his own account of that visit, made in his private diary at the time, but never before this given in print. With deep interest was it first listened to at our Temple, when in 1858 Edward Everett, in his silver tones, read it to a Portsmouth audience, among whom were some who almost seventy years ago, were witnesses of the scenes. Mr. Everett, at our request, has furnished us with the extract in full.

## FROM WASHINGTON'S PRIVATE DIARY, 1789.

SATURDAY, 31st Oct.

Left Newburyport a little after eight o'clock, (first breakfasting with Mr. Dalton,) and to avoid a wider ferry, more inconvenient boats, and piece of heavy sand, we crossed the river at Salisbury, two miles above, and near that further about; and in three miles came to the line which divides the State of Massachusetts from that of New Hampshire. Here I took leave of Mr. Dalton and many other private gentlemen,—also of Gen. Titcomb, who had met me on the line between Middlesex and Essex counties, corps of light horse, and many officers of militia; and was received by the President of the State of New Hampshire, the Vice President, some of the Council, Messrs. Langdon and Wingate of the Senate, Col. Parker, Marshal of the State, and many other respectable characters; besides several troops of well clothed horse, in handsome uniforms, and many officers of the militia, also in handsome (white and red) uniforms, of the manufacture of the State. With this cavalcade we proceeded, and arrived before three o'clock at Portsmouth, where we were received with every token of respect and appearance of cordiality under a discharge of artillery. The streets, doors and windows were crowded here, as at all other places; and, alighting at the Town House, odes were sung and played in honor of the President. The same happened yesterday at my entrance into Newburyport, being stopped at my entrance to hear it. From the Town House I went to Colonel Brewster's tavern, the place provided for my residence, and asked the President, Vice President, the two Senators, the Marshal and Major Gilman to dine with me, which they did; after which I drank tea at Mr. Langdon's.

NOVEMBER 1st.

Attended by the President of the State, (General Sullivan,) Mr. Langdon and the Marshal, I went in the forenoon to the Episcopal church, under the incumbency of Mr. Ogden; and in the afternoon to one of the Presbyterian or Congregational churches, in which a Mr. Buckminister preached. Dined at home with the Marshal, and spent the afternoon in my own room writing letters.

MONDAY, 2d.

Having made previous preparations for it, about eight o'clock, attended by the President, Mr. Langdon and some other gentlemen, I went in a boat to visit the harbor of Portsmouth, which is well secured against all winds, and from its narrow entrance from the sea, and passage up to the town, may be perfectly guarded against any approach by water. The anchorage is good, and the shipping may lay close to the docks, etc., when at the town. In my way to the mouth of the harbor, I stopped at a place called Kittery, in the Province of Maine, the river Piscataqua being the boundary between New Hampshire and it. From hence I went by the old Fort (formerly built while under the English government) on an island which is at the entrance of the harbor, and where the lighthouse stands. As we passed this Fort we were saluted by thirteen guns. Having lines, we proceeded to the fishing banks, a little without the harbor, and fished for cod,—but it not being of proper time of tide, we only caught two,—with which, about ten o'clock, we returned to town. Dined at Col. Langdon's and drank tea there with a large circle of ladies, and retired a little after seven o'clock. Before dinner I received an address from the town, presented by the Vice President; and returned an answer in the evening to one I had received from Marblehead, and another from the Presbyterian clergy of the State of Massachusetts and New Hampshire, delivered at Newburyport—both of which I had been unable to answer before.

TUESDAY, 3d.

Sat two hours in the forenoon for a Mr. ——, painter, of Boston, at the request of Mr. Brick of that place, who wrote Major Jackson that it was an earnest desire of many of the inhabitants of that town that he might be indulged. After this sitting I called upon President Sullivan and the mother of Mr. Lear; and, having walked through most parts of the town, returned by twelve o'clock, when I was visited by a clergyman of the name of Haven, who presented me with an ear and part of the stock of the dyeing corn, and several small pieces of cloth which had been dyed with it, equal to any colors I had ever seen, and of various colors. This corn was blood red, and the rind of the stock deeply tinged of the same color. About two o'clock, I received an address from the Executive of the State of New Hampshire, and in half an hour after dined with them and a large company at their Assembly room, which is one of the best I have seen anywhere in the United States.

At half after seven I went to the Assembly, where there were about seventy-five well dressed and many very handsome ladies, among whom (as was also the case at the Salem and Boston assemblies) were a greater proportion with much blacker hair than are usually seen in the southern States. About nine I returned to my quarters. Portsmouth, it is said, contains about five thousand inhabitants. There are some good houses, (among which Col. Langdon's may be esteemed the first,) but in general they are indifferent, and almost entirely of wood. On wondering at this, as the country is full of stone and good clay for bricks, I was told that on account of the fogs and damp they deemed them wholesomer, and for that reason preferred wood buildings. Lumber, fish and potash, with some provisions, compose the principal articles of export. Ship building here and at Newburyport has been carried on to a considerable extent; during and for some time after the war, there was an entire stagnation to it, but it is beginning now to revive again. The number of ships belonging to this port are estimated at —.

WEDNESDAY, 4th.

About half-past seven I left Portsmouth quietly and without any attendance, having earnestly entreated that all parade and ceremony might be avoided on my return. Before ten I reached Exeter, fourteen miles distance. This is considered as the second town in New Hampshire, and stands at the head of the tide-water of the Piscataqua river, but ships of three hundred and four hundred tons are built at it. Above (but in the same town) are considerable falls, which supply several grist mills, two oil mills, a slitting mill and snuff mill. It is a place of some consequence, but does not contain more than one thousand inhabitants. A jealousy subsists between this town (where the Legislature alternately sits) and Portsmouth, which, had I known it in time, would have made it necessary to have accepted an invitation to a public dinner; but my arrangements having been otherwise made, I could not.

The above is President Washington's own account of his four days visit at Portsmouth, and presents the town as seen by him. Now for a view of President Washington as seen by our citizens.

## RAMBLE LIII.

Washington's Visit to Portsmouth—Committees—Reception—Reply to town address—Attendance at church—Dr. Buckminster's address—Fishing—Little Harbor.

A VISIT from a person so distinguished and beloved, had he come without the insignia of office, would have created no little enthusiasm,—but a visit from its first President, when the young Republic had been organized scarcely half a year, occasioned to the community a thrill of ecstacy which vibrated through every heart; an outburst of joy due from a grateful populace to one to whose skill and superior virtues, they owed their happiness. There was a mixture of novelty, of joy, of patriotic enthusiasm, felt by every heart. The committee of twelve appointed in town meeting to superintend the reception, consisting of Richard Champney, Elisha Hill, Joseph Akerman, Peter Coues, George Hart, Jacob Walden, Richard Billings, James Hill, Samuel Drown, Edmund Sargeant and John Wendell, Jr., were among the most active of our public men, and very efficient in putting everything in order. The old watch house, which had stood on the south side of the Parade for many years, was taken away,—a stage was erected near the corner of Mr. Pearse's store east of the State House. The committee appointed to address the President was composed of our leading men: Messrs. John Pickering, John Parker, A. R. Cutter, Jonathan Warner, Joshua Wentworth, John Langdon, George Gains, Jeremiah

Libbey, James Sheafe, John Peirce and Woodbury Langdon.

The reception of the President at the State line, and his progress, is given in his private Diary. The President, at Greenland left his carriage, in the occupancy of Col. Tobias Lear, and mounting his favorite white horse, he was there met by Col. Wentworth's troop, and on Portsmouth Plains the President was saluted by Major General Cilley, and other officers in attendance.

From the west end of the State House, on both sides of Congress street and into Middle street, the citizens were arranged in two lines in the alphabetical order of their occupations. And on the east side of the Parade ground, the children of the schools, with diamond shaped cockades on their hats from which a quill projected, were arranged near the State House. The different schools were designated by different colored cockades.

The President at his entrance received a federal salute from three companies of artillery under the command of Col. Hackett. The streets through which he passed were lined by citizens; the bells rang a joyful peal, and repeated shouts from grateful thousands hailed him welcome to the metropolis of New Hampshire.

On his arrival at the State House, he was conducted through the west door to the Senate Chamber, by the President and Council of this State, and took his station in the balcony on the east side. Here the town address to the President was delivered by Judge Pickering. In it, after giving Washington a most cordial welcome to New Hampshire, and congratulating him on his election, he expressed the deep gratitude of the public to him, "who with a magnanimity peculiar to himself under the smiles of heaven, defended the rights and gave birth to the empire of America." The address further says: "Permit me to add, the grateful sense we entertain of our high obligations to you, sir, as a town, for our security from that devastation which was the fate of so many other seaports in the Union, and would probably have been ours, had not the enemy, by your wise and spirited exertions, been driven from the capital of a neighboring State, and compelled to seek an asylum, for a while, within their own dominions." The address closes with a reference to the depression of our commercial interests by the war, from which we were happily recovering,—and by an expression of gratitude to a kind providence for the restoration of the President's health.

The President made the following reply:

*To the Inhabitants of the town of Portsmouth:*

GENTLEMEN: I am forcibly impressed with your friendly welcome to the metropolis of New Hampshire, and have a grateful heart for your kind and flattering congratulations on my election to the Presidency of these United States.

I fear the fond partiality of my countrymen has too highly appreciated my past exertions, and formed too sanguine anticipations of my future services. If the former have been successful, much of the success should be ascribed to those who labored with me in the common cause—and the glory of the event should be given to the great Disposer of events. If an unremitting attention to the duties of my office, and the zeal of an honest heart can promote the public good, my fellow citizens may be assured that these will not be wanting in my present station.

I can claim no particular merit, gentlemen, for the preservation of your town from the devastation of the enemy. I am happy, if by any event of the war, your property has been preserved from that destruction which fell but too heavily on your neighbors; and I sincerely condole with you for the loss which you have sustained in navigation and commerce; but I trust that industry and economy, those fruitful and never-failing sources of private and public opulence, will, under our present system of government, restore you to your former flourishing state.

The interest which you take in my personal happiness, and

the kind felicitations which you express on the recovery of my health, are peculiarly grateful to me; and I earnestly pray that the great Ruler of the Universe may smile upon your honest exertions here, and reward your well doings with future happiness.

G. WASHINGTON.

On the stage opposite the balcony, in front of the store of Mr. Pearse, was an amateur band, which sung three appropriate odes, composed by Jonathan M. Sewall. In the band were Mr. Dame, Mr. Sparhawk, the poet, and others.

ODE FIRST.

[*Full Chorus.*] Behold he comes! Columbia's pride,
And nature's boast—her fav'rite son,
Of valor—wisdom—truth—well tried—
Hail, matchless WASHINGTON.

[*Recitative.*] 'Tis gratitude that prompts the humble lay,
Accept, great chief, what gratitude can pay.

[*Air.*] Let old and young—let rich and poor,
Their voices raise, to sing his praise,
And bid him welcome o'er and o'er.

[*Chorus.*] Welcome matchless WASHINGTON!
Matchless as the deeds you've done.

[*Recitative.*] From north to south, from east to west
His fame unrivalled stands confest.

[*Air.*] This, this is he—by heaven designed,
The pride and wonder of mankind.
United then your voices raise,
And all united sing his praise.

[*Chorus.*] Welcome matchless WASHINGTON!
Matchless as the deeds you've done.

ODE SECOND.

He comes! he comes! your songs prepare,
The matchless chief approaches near,
Each heart exults! each tongue proclaims,
He's welcome to Hantonia's plains.
[*Chorus.*] Welcome! Welcome! Welcome! Welcome!
Welcome to Hantonia's plains.

Those shouts ascending to the sky,
Proclaim great WASHINGTON is nigh!
Hail nature's boast—Columbia's son,
Welcome! welcome WASHINGTON.

Let strains harmonious rend the air,
For see the godlike hero's here!
Thrice hail—Columbia's fav'rite son,
Thrice welcome matchless WASHINGTON.

The third ode sung was a patriotic effusion to the tune of "God save the King."

Then the whole of the troops, under the command of Major General Cilley, passed him in the review, horse, foot and artillery, and the line of officers, every officer saluting as he passed. The troops and the procession marched down Pitt street to Stavers' hotel, and there separated; the President having been conducted to his lodgings at Colonel Brewster's (whose hotel was on the site of Richard Jenness's residence) by the President and Council of the State, the Hon. Mr. Langdon, and John Parker, Marshal of this district, escorted by a company under arms.

In the evening the State House was beautifully illuminated, and rockets were let off from the balcony.

On Sunday, Washington, accompanied by President Sullivan, Hon. John Langdon, and his two secretaries, attended divine service in the morning at Queen's chapel, and in the afternoon at the North Church. The President was conducted to his pew, attended by the Marshal of the district, and two Church Wardens, with their staffs. [The Marshal's staff is now in possession of Rev. Dr. Peabody.] On this uncommon occasion both houses of worship were crowded with spectators. At the Queen's chapel several pieces of music, suitable to the occasion were well performed by the choir. The Rev. Messrs. Ogden and Buckminster, in well adapted discourses, paid just and beautiful eulogiums on the numerous virtues of this distinguished personage. Dr. Buckminster did not introduce his sermon as usual, by announcement of his text, but by an address to the people, congratulating them upon the safe arrival of the President of the United States. The address is so singular in its character, so patriotic and so eloquent, that it is entitled to preservation in our pages. The President's seat was in the wall pew of Hon. William Whipple, signer of the Declaration, next to the pulpit on the south side. His seat was facing the side of the pulpit, and his eyes were fixed upon the minister during the address.

## REV. DR. BUCKMINSTER'S ADDRESS.

To take notice of the events of providence which deeply interest the views and feelings of a people, cannot be unsuitable at any time or place. You will not, then, think it improper, that, on this sacred day, and from the desk devoted to the purposes of religion, I should take occasion to congratulate you, my dear brethren, upon the safe arrival of the PRESIDENT of the UNITED STATES to this metropolis.

No event, of this nature, could be more highly pleasing to the hearts of a free and grateful people. You have, doubtless, made it a matter of your devout acknowledgment to Him by whom you believe all events ordered. and without whom no sparrow falls to the ground.

We see the MAN whom heaven designed as the principal instrument of accomplishing one of the greatest revolutions in the nations of the earth; of whom the event has proved that GOD said, as of Cyrus: "Thy right hand will I uphold, and I will go before thee, and make the crooked places straight; I will break in pieces the gates of brass, and cut in sunder the bars of iron."

We see the MAN endued by him "from whom cometh down every good and every perfect gift" with that rare assemblage of qualities which unites the jarring interests, views and affections of an extensive continent; who, when the cruel hands of tyranny and unjust usurpation had formed chains and shackles to bind us at their pleasure, at the call of his country, cheerfully stepped forth, in the first place of danger, to oppose their measures, to guide and direct our efforts, to defend our liberties.

We see the GENERAL, who, with a cool, intrepid bravery, faced every danger; with unexampled firmness sustained every discouragement; and, with persevering magnanimity, surmounted every obstacle of a long and unequal war; and under the auspices of an indulgent Providence, procured for us peace, liberty and independence.

You see the MAN who shared with your fathers, your brethren and sons, the fatigues and perils of many dangerous battles;

who sympathized with them in their sufferings, and mingled his tears with yours in your various losses.

We see the MAN, who, having fought our battles, and defended our liberties, nobly retired to private life, claiming only his share, with the multitude of his brethren, in those privileges which he had secured to them. But heaven had not yet accomplished all its purposes by him. Leading you to form a new constitution of government, to unite the interests and resources of the extended States—he who has the hearts of all in his hands, with an unanimity that is unparalleled, led three millions of people to make choice of him as their chief magistrate, and place him at the head of this rising empire.

We see the MAN who bowed obedient to the voice of GOD, thus expressed by the people; who sacrificed every private consideration to the wishes of his country—leaving his beloved retreat again to immerge in the cares and duties of public life, at a time when they are peculiarly embarrassed. May heaven reward him for his generous sacrifice with blessings greater than earth can give—may he find support proportioned to his burdens; and may that "wonderful counsellor by whom kings reign, and princes decree justice," make him distinguished in the cabinet as he has been in his victories.

We now see this illustrious PATRIOT, like the father of a great family, visiting the various branches, to bless and to be blessed, to start the tear of joy and awaken mutual congratulations. He comes, not attended with mercenary guards, like kings and emperors who hold their dignity by hereditary descent; who even fear where no fear is; he comes, not in the triumph of military parade, to show the spoils and laurels he hath won; but he comes triumphing in the confidence and affections of a free and grateful people, who, under GOD, hail him the deliverer of their country, and the protector of its liberties.

It has been pleasing to see with what anxious emotions his arrival has been expected from place to place, how every exertion has been made to smooth the way before him, how all ages and characters have united to bid him a hearty welcome and testify the joy they felt at the honor of a visit. What can be more pleasing than the efforts of human nature, however imperfect, to express a grateful remembrance of past benefits and a lively sense of present favors. May the illustrious PRESIDENT long live to receive fresh testimonials of affection from a free people, and to be the instrument, in the hand of GOD, of fresh blessings to the undeserving. Too much respect, that falls short of religious homage, cannot be paid to one to whom we are so much indebted;—were this offered, he would say with the angel in the book of the Revelation, "See thou do it not, I am thy fellow servant, and of thy brethren that have the testimony of Jesus; worship God."

Whatever distinctions there may be among mankind, however indebted we may be to an earthly benefactor, "We have all ONE FATHER, for GOD hath created us, there is none in the heavens that may be compared to him, there is none among the sons of the mighty that may be likened to Jehovah." Permit me, then, my brethren, to take occasion, from this auspicious event of a kind Providence, to excite your expectation and solicit your preparation for the approach of that glorious character "who is the brightness of the father's glory, and the express image of his person;" who is so infinitely exalted that it is the crowning excellence of the most dignified human character to be his servant and disciple. This I shall do by calling your attention to that sublime demand of the royal poet,

"Lift up your heads, O ye gates, and be ye lifted up ye everlasting doors, and the King of glory shall come in. Who is this King of glory? The Lord strong and mighty, the Lord mighty in battle."—*Psalms* 24: 7, 8.

With this passage of Scripture as a text, Dr. Buckminster then commenced his sermon. In it there is but little reference made to the President. Towards the close he said:

We venerate the benevolent conqueror in the cause of liberty; we love the man whom heaven has made instrumental of bursting the bands of oppression, vindicating the oppressed, and delivering from temporal enemies; and shall we not more highly venerate and love that glorious conqueror who subdues spiritual enemies, delivers the soul from oppression and blesses with the liberty of the sons of God?

We hail welcome the saviour of his country; we wish in every proper way to testify the grateful emotions of our hearts; and shall we not much rather hail welcome *the Saviour of the world*, and testify our higher obligations for his infinite merits?

When on Monday the President went on an excursion down the harbor, his barge was rowed by seamen dressed in white frocks. They were accompanied by another barge containing the amateur band, who gave occasional displays of their musical powers. Of those two fish taken, Washington drew one from the water. Zebulon Willey, who was fishing in the vicinity—finding them toiling in vain, had hooked a cod, and coming along side, handed his line to the President, who drew up the prize. This was a good pull for *Zebulon*, for the President gave him a silver dollar,—and the story was a golden one for him ever after. And who had a better right to such a reward than he who by name inherited the right to "dwell at the haven of the sea." The boats landed at Little Harbor, where the company passed the residence of Capt. John Blunt,* and proceeded to the seat of Col. Michael Wentworth, then in the height of his glory, who gave the company a magnificent reception at the old Governor's mansion. From this point they returned to town by carriages.

The calls upon President Sullivan at Stavers's hotel, and on Mrs. Lear in Hunking street, we speak of in other rambles. As the walks of Washington were probably in the narrow streets at the south part of the town, it is not surprising that he should comment on the "indifferent" appearance of the wooden houses. The impression he received of ours being a "foggy" and damp atmosphere

* This, if the family tradition is correct, was not the first meeting of Capt. John Blunt with Washington. When Washington crossed the Delaware, (an event which has called forth the painter and the engraver beautifully to illustrate,) there was much floating ice. When the General took his boat, he saw some danger, and said, " is any one here who is well acquainted with the river?" Some one replied, "Here is Capt. Blunt, who is familiar with the navigation." Capt. Blunt had been regularly coasting for some years between Portsmouth and Philadelphia, and was nearly as well acquainted with the Delaware as with the Piscataqua, and at the personal invitation of Washington, "Capt. Blunt, please take the helm," he stepped on board and was the navigator of the boat in which the prints represent "Washington crossing the Delaware."

was not correct. It appears that Washington left town on Wednesday morning, not Thursday as stated in the Annals. In about a fortnight after he reached New York.

## RAMBLE LIV.

Gardner and Hunking streets—The old linden—The Lear house—Tobias Lear, Washington's private secretary—Washington's family—Washington's visit to Mrs. Lear—Memorials of the President and his lady—Tobias Lear's political life.

How few now-a-days stroll from Water street through Gardner's Arch, around Col. Gardner's old mansion, and up Hunking street to Water street. We must say that, until recently, a quarter of a century has elapsed since taking that short circuit, which affords sufficient material for an interesting ramble, to us if not to our readers.

Nearly in front, a little south of the Gardner house, is one of the handsomest ornamental trees in Portsmouth—a noble Linden of a hundred years. The trunk of the tree for ten feet from the ground is about twelve feet in circumference. It rises to the height of sixty feet, spreads out symmetrically, and when looked upon in July it appeared as fresh and vigorous as a young tree, and covered with its rich yellow bloom, imparted fragrance to the whole neighborhood. Such a tree on Market Square would be the pride of our city.

Secluded as it is, and till recently unknown to us, yet near its shadow is a spot once made memorable by the presence of President Washington. Properly to explain will require a short historical sketch.

In that ancient, hip-roofed, two-storied, yellow dwelling, near the east end of Hunking street, which although more than a century old is yet in good order, and a handsome house, in 1760 was born Tobias Lear, the son of

Captain Tobias Lear. The father was a shipmaster, and was owner of the Jacob Sheafe farm at Sagamore Creek. The son was liberally educated, and graduated with honor at Cambridge in 1783. At this time Gen. Washington, who had just retired from the field of war, to his fields of grain and the comforts of domestic life, found the need of a private secretary to aid in his extensive correspondence, and also of a tutor for the two children of Parke Custis, whom he had adopted. He stated his wants to Gen. Lincoln, of Boston, who with Rev. Dr. Haven, of Portsmouth, recommended Tobias Lear as a suitable person. He at once took up his residence in Washington's family, and close attention to the duties of his position endeared the relation which Washington held to him until the close of his life, which occurred sixteen years after. Among the papers of Dr. Haven is a letter from Gen. Washington, written some months after Mr. Lear's introduction, stating that he had deferred replying until he had ascertained that Mr. Lear had all of those qualities for which he was so highly recommended—of which he was then fully satisfied.

Washington, it is well known, was a man of strict punctuality in all engagements: this Mr. Lear well understood. When Mr. Lear once apologized for tardiness by attributing it to his watch being wrong, it was sufficient; but when a second failure was attributed to the same cause, Washington replied—"Mr. Lear, you must get a new watch, or I must get a new Secretary." From that day the sun and watch were probably always together, as we have no tradition of any other failures. Washington having no children of his own, Col. Lear was as a son in the family, and enjoyed such acquaintance at the domestic hearth at Mount Vernon as no other one probably possessed. At the final scene, when Washington was upon his death bed, Col. Lear was the chosen attendant, and by him was administered such help as could be given in the hours of his suffering. It was the letter of Tobias Lear that communicated to President Adams, and through him to Congress, the information of Washington's death. President Adams's reply to Mr. Lear closes by saying;

"I pray you, sir, to present my regards to Madam Washington and all the amiable and worthy family, and assure them of my sincere sympathy with them under this great affliction. I feel also for yourself, as you have lost in Gen. Washington a friend not to be replaced."

When Washington visited Portsmouth in 1789, he was accompanied by Col. Lear. Washington entered the town on horseback, and Col. Lear rode in an open carriage next following. As they passed on, many, from his position and dignified appearance, mistook the Colonel for the President, and bestowed upon the Secretary that honor which was meant for the "Father of his country." While here, Washington expressed a desire to visit the home of Col. Lear, which was then occupied by his mother and Samuel Storer, who was a dry goods merchant, (doing business at the corner of Hanover and Market streets, where the McIntire block was afterwards built,) and whose wife was a sister of Col. Lear.

On the morning of a pleasant day, Washington sent a note to Madam Lear, informing her of his intended visit, and at the same time making a request that he might see all the children. In due time, the President on foot might be seen coming down Hunking street. After he entered the Lear mansion, a crowd such as has never since been seen there, gathered around the door. In the south-west parlor he was introduced to and cordially greeted every member of the family—the venerable mother, her children, and her grand-children. Of the latter might be seen a bright little girl of three or four years, sitting upon his knee and giving him a kiss. No other lady now living in our state can probably bring up a like reminiscence. That lady, Miss Mary L. Storer, still occupies the mansion. There is also a babe presented, who has been christened "George Washington." The President places his hand gently upon the infant's head, and expresses the wish that he may "be a better man than the one whose name he bears." There are probably but two individuals now living in the country who can say that they have thus been under the hand and received thus the personal blessing of our country's father—these two are Washington Irving and Admiral George Washington Storer.

The room in which Washington was received remains now with the same paper on the walls, and the same chairs, (made of cherry wood raised in the garden,) and other furniture, except the carpet, which were then used. There are also in the room three china mantle ornaments, a bird on a branch, a peasant with a bouquet, and a lass in a basque of modern cut, with flowers. These ornaments were taken from Washington's own mantle, and forwarded by Martha Washington "for the children." There is a worth imparted to these trifles, by the circumstances, which renders them invaluable. The parlor, fashionable in its day, having for seventy years remained untouched by the change of fashion, is now a matter of interest to visitors, aside from the associations of Washington's visit.

But there is one other relic of deep interest we saw here, which probably has no like elsewhere. A piece of black satin, of eight by ten inches, is framed and glassed, and around the edge, just inside the frame, is a piece of narrow white taste. It was wrought about the commencement of the century, in a handsome manner, in Roman letters, by the lady who then sat upon Washington's knee, and now exhibited the work to us. The words were the composition of her grand-mother,—the mother of Col. Tobias Lear. The inscription tells its own story.

"*This is work'd with our Illustrious and beloved General*
GEORGE WASHINGTON'S HAIR:

Which covered his exalted head;
But now enroll'd among the dead,
Yet wears a crown above the skies,
In realms of bliss which never dies.

*This is work'd with Lady*
MARTHA WASHINGTON'S HAIR,
*Relict of our beloved General.*

I pray her honor'd head,
May long survive the dead;
And when she doth her breath resign,
May she in heaven her consort join.

*This hair was sent to Mrs. Lear,*
*By her good friend Lady Washington.*"

In 1798, when Washington accepted the command of the provincial army, Mr. Lear was selected as the military secretary, with the rank of Colonel. After the death of Washington, his papers remained in the custody of Col. Lear for several months. In the strong political excitement of the time, a charge was made that Lear had endeavored to obtain the favor of Jefferson by suppressing some letters which had passed from Jefferson to Washington, said to charge him with belonging to "an Anglican monarchical, aristocratical party." In Randall's Life of Jefferson, just published, Col. Lear is ably vindicated, and the aspersion which had for some time rested upon him, is removed.

The division of parties then was by the terms federal and republican—Col. Lear was of the latter, and Washington of the former party. When Jefferson came into office, as a grateful token of respect to the memory of Washington, as well as of friendship to a political friend, he appointed Col. Lear Consul General at St. Domingo; and afterwards, in 1804 we think, he was appointed Consul General at Tripoli, and together with Com. Barron negotiated peace with the latter power.

He remained in Algiers about eight years—the last few months accompanied by his son. When in 1812 the Bar-

bary powers declared war, he was allowed but a few hours to leave the country, and then returned to Washington.

He was afterwards appointed Accountant in the War Department, in which office he died very suddenly on the 10th of October, 1816, at the age of fifty-six years. A more full account of the life and extensive correspondence of Washington's most intimate associate should be given to the public than has yet been entered upon any published history.

Col. Lear was three times married. His first wife was Mary Long, daughter of Hon. Pierse Long, and sister of the late Hon. George Long, of Portsmouth. She died in Philadelphia in 1795. They had but one child, who bore the name of Benjamin Lincoln, who died in Washington in 1831, leaving but one child, a daughter, born after his death, now the wife of Wilson Eyre, of Philadelphia, and the only descendant of Col. Lear. In the recent law-suit for the papers of Col. Lear, this grand-daughter established her claim, and now has them in her possession. The contestants were the children of Com. Henley.

Col. Lear's second wife was Miss Custis, niece of Martha Washington; on her decease he married Miss Henley, sister of Com. Henley,—both of whom died without issue. The widow of Col. Lear died in 1856 at Washington. The widow of B. Lincoln Lear, now the widow Derby, is at present [1858] residing in Italy.

## RAMBLE LV.

Andrew and James Clarkson—The Pretender's ensign—The tan yard—Rev. John Murray.

One of the most spacious old houses south of the south mill bridge was taken down in 1835. Its location was some rods west of the Haven School House, in the rear of the residence of Francis Marden, Esq. It was gambrel roofed, facing the street, and about a hundred feet back from it, leaving a handsome green spot in front, and a gravel walk to the door through two rows of trees.

A century ago it was occupied by Andrew Clarkson and his brother James. They were natives of Scotland and men of distinction. Andrew was born about the beginning of the last century. He was educated in the Protestant faith, and was a Presbyterian, but infatuated in his youth with the delusion which possessed many of his countrymen at that time, he enlisted under the banners of the pretender, and was an ensign in his army. After the defeat of the army, many of the prisoners were treated as rebels. Mr. Clarkson came to this country in the year 1717, and brought with him the colors belong-to his company. He settled in this town as a place of safety, being then about seventeen or eighteen years of age, and became a teacher in one of the public schools. He boarded at the house of William Cotton, a tanner, at the south part of the town. Mr. Cotton died whilst Mr. Clarkson was a member of his family, and left a widow and six small children. Mr. Clarkson married the widow, who was several years older than himself, took charge of the tan-yard, and acquired by means of it, a handsome property. He often spoke of the early transactions of his life with regret, but said he thought at the time, that his conduct was justifiable.*

* Mrs. Elizabeth Clarkson, wife of James Clarkson, died March 10, 1746, aged fifty-eight. Walter Clarkson, son of James and Elizabeth, died April 28, 1789. These two items are copied from grave stones in the Cotton burying ground. They are contiguous to that of William Cotton, Jr., the tanner, who deceased in 1717, in his thirty-eighth year. William Cotton, Jr. was a man of property, and made liberal provision in his will for his widow, Elizabeth, who also possessed some property in her own right. He left two sons and four daughters, his wife to have all the personal estate, etc., for the bringing up of their children, and all the profits and income of all his estate, until the eldest son John came to the age of twenty-one years, when he was to have, with his mother, each of them during her life, half of the homestead and tanyard; and he to have two-thirds of various other parcels of property, paying out to his sisters two-thirds of £400 as they became of age, and to have all the homestead at his mother's decease. He succeeded to the place, and dying 1759, left two sons and five daughters by his wife Mary, and by his second wife, two sons, Clement

As early as 1745, James was moderator of the town meeting which elected him a Representative. For twenty years he was moderator of nearly all the town meetings, while his brother Andrew shared with him occasionally the honor of being a Representative. Andrew, while holding that office, died in 1765. In 1763, after the State House was built, the North parish refused the use of their church for a town meeting; James Clarkson was elected moderator on the door step, and then, by vote, the door was broken open and the election went on in the church as usual.

It is probable that Andrew left a son of the same name, as our informant well recollects one Andrew Clarkson, an extensive tanner and public man, residing there since the time of the Revolution. He describes him as a portly man. He also recollects their slave, Will Clarkson. Capt. Hugh Clarkson was of another family.

There was in olden times not only a scarcity of carriages but also of wheels. Messrs. Clarksons' team might be seen passing frequently through the town, without any wheels,—two shafts attached to the sides of the horse, the ends dragging on the ground, made up the dray on which their hides and leather found conveyance to and from the yard.

The wife of James Clarkson died in 1746. In 1762 he married Mrs. Sarah Holland of Boston, a lady of *spirit.*— Rev. Jonathan Parsons of Newburyport, in 1770, married Lydia, the widow of Andrew Clarkson.

Very honorable mention is made of the Clarkson hospitality by Rev. John Murray, and our town books give record of their honorable offices year after year. Mr. Murray, however, was never informed of the home preliminaries for reception by the family of James Clarkson,

and Joel, and three daughters under age. John Cotton's eldest son William was a tanner, and subsequently occupied the house and tanyard, west of and adjoining the Chauncy house. He became feeble minded, and his two sons-in-law, Drown and Stavers, were appointed his guardians in 1790. He died in 1791. His wife Catharine died in 1803.

on his first visit to Portsmouth, in 1773. Mrs. Clarkson was not of the most amiable disposition—and while her husband's great delight was in visiting and administering to the wants of the poor—hers seemed to be in thwarting his efforts. "Now Mrs. Clarkson," said her husband, "what shall I give you for a good reception to the new minister, Mr. Murray?" She proposed as the condition a full suit of thread lace for an apron, a cap and square handkerchief. It was assented to, and a dinner worthy of his standing was provided, at which the lady presided. Dinner was no sooner over, however, than the restraint was removed, and she very freely gave her opinion of her guest. "My good woman," was the reply of Mr. Murray, "it is not you that hates me, it is the devil in you."

About the year 1779, James Clarkson died. The next week, when some friends were making his widow a visit, she dropped dead upon the floor. Mr. Clarkson left no children,—and here we will drop the scene, as the family of this good man disappears.

## RAMBLE LVI.

Pierse Long—Early history—Revolutionary sketch—Family.

THE successor as occupant of the Clarkson house was one who has been overlooked by the annalist, but who is more deserving of honorable notice than many who have passed away. We refer to Hon. Pierse Long, who spent many years of his life and its closing hours in the mansion, which, after his death in 1789, was known as the Chauncy House.

Pierse Long (the father of Col. Pierse Long of Revolutionary memory) was born in Limerick, Ireland, about the commencement of the eighteenth century, and served an apprenticeship with one who did business with America; and by him was sent out with goods, the manufacture of Ireland, to this town, in the year 1730. For the more convenient sale of goods, he opened a store in State (formerly Buck) street, and continued receiving consignments from Ireland of both ships and goods, for the purpose of purchasing cargoes of lumber and such other articles as the country produced that suited the West India market; to which islands the ships carried and sold their cargoes and took freights of sugar, cotton, etc., for London. This was the usual course of business from year to year, during Pierse Long's lifetime. Two years after his arrival in America, he married Abigail Sheafe, of Portsmouth or Newcastle, and by her had three children: Abigail, Pierse and Mary. Pierse Long, the senior, died in 1740, leaving two children, Mary and Pierse; Abigail having died previously, and single. Mary, also, was never married, and died at the house of her nephew, George Long, about the year 1800.

Pierse Long, Jr., (afterwards Col. Long), was born in 1739. He received instruction in the elements of education from the celebrated teacher, Samuel Hale. At the age of fourteen, Pierse was apprenticed as a clerk to Robert Trail, an emigrant from Scotland, and a distinguished merchant of Portsmouth. At the close of his apprenticeship, Pierse Long was established in business by Mr. Trail, as a shipping merchant, which he continued to prosecute with success until the war of the Revolution. In this Mr. Long took an early and decided part, and in 1775 was chosen one of the delegates to the first provincial Congress, convened at Exeter. In this office he continued for some time, acting also about this period as one of the Committee of Safety for Portsmouth, and was engaged with Langdon, Pickering, Drown, and about forty other citizens, in surprising and capturing the fort at the mouth of Portsmouth harbor.

Pierse Long continued to fill different offices under the then province and town until May, 1776, when the Provincial Legislature appointed him to the command of the first New Hampshire regiment, with Mooney as Lieut. Colonel; Hodgdon, as Major; Noah Emery, paymaster; Edward Evans, chaplain; James M'Clure, adjutant; captains, Hilton, Sanborn and others. This regiment continued in the service of the Province until July 15, 1776, when it being determined by the general government to receive into the service no more provincial troops, it was disbanded, but immediately re-enlisted into the continental service, under Pierse Long as Colonel and commander.

This regiment continued to be stationed at the forts around Portsmouth harbor (a company in Portsmouth being stationed near the Old South) until October, 1776, when it received orders to march to the Canada border, near Lake Champlain. It reached there safely in about twenty days; and reporting for duty to Gen. St. Clair, Col. Long was assigned to the command of Fort Independence, across the Lake, with his own and Col. Carleton's regiments; and at the same time was made Brigadier General, by brevet. The Lake being closed with ice during the latter part of the fall, the winter and part of the spring, nothing of note occurred until about the middle of June, 1777, when the English flotilla of many guns advancing by water, to be joined by Gen. Burgoyne, with ten thousand English, Canadians, tories and Indians, by land, it was determined by Gen. St. Clair, in a council of officers, to abandon his position with his small army of three thousand men, and retreat with the American flotilla up through Lake George, towards Fort Edward. Col. Long was entrusted with the command of the flotilla, consisting of one schooner of sixteen guns, one of ten, and several smaller crafts, with orders to blow up the vessels to prevent their falling into the hands of the enemy,—which was accomplished after they had disembarked his own and Col. Carleton's regiment at Skensborough. Leaving Skensborough, the troops proceeded on towards Saratoga, and the next day (July 6) Col. Long, with his command, was overtaken at Fort Ann by the British ninth regiment, under the command of Col. Hayes. An action ensued, in which the British were beaten, and retreating left the field in possession of the Americans. At about this time, the period for which the troops had enlisted having expired, they all asked and received their discharge, officers as well as men, excepting Edward Evans, chaplain; Noah Emery, paymaster; and Lieut. or Col. Meshach Bell, and Col. Long's servant, James Mullen. These, with Col. Long, continued on to Saratoga, and there volunteered their services to the commander-in-chief, and assisted in the capture of General Burgoyne and his army. Col. Long being ill, arrived in Portsmouth December 6, and continued confined to his house for six months with the disorder usual to camps; nor did he entirely recover till a year had expired. As soon as he had sufficiently recovered his health he resumed his mercantile pursuits, but at the same time suffered from attacks of the gout, and sometimes could not move without the aid of crutches.

In 1784 he was appointed by the State of New-Hampshire a delegate to the old Congress, which post he filled through three or four successive years, till 1786. From the year 1786 to 1789 he was elected State Senator or Councillor, and in 1788 was delegate to the convention to adopt the present constitution, and gave his influence and vote for its reception by New Hampshire. When Washington was chosen President, he appointed Col. Long Collector of the Customs at Portsmouth; but before he had taken possession of his office, he was found dead in his bed. He retired in apparent health, but died without any previous warning, of (as it was supposed) gout in the stomach, at the early age of fifty, April 3,

1789. His remains are interred in the lot in the Proprietors' burying ground, belonging to his son, at the western end of the granite monuments. Col. Long was a handsome, portly man, of unblemished christian character, amiable and courteous, a correct merchant and a good soldier.

Col. Long was twice married. The only child by his first marriage was a son, George, and by his second wife two daughters, Mary and Abigail. Abigail married George W. Prescott, and died at St. Bartholomews. Mary married Col. Tobias Lear, private secretary to Gen. Washington, and died of yellow fever in the family of Gen. Washington, at Philadelphia, in 1795. The sisters were remarkable for their personal beauty. George Long, the only son of Col. Pierse Long, was born July 4, 1762. He received instruction from Samuel Hale, the instructor of his father, Col. Long. His mother dying when he was an infant, the early care of him fell chiefly to his grandmother. It is not probable that he was apprenticed to any merchant, as the Revolutionary war breaking out when he was but twelve years of age, most commercial business was suspended. He was a successful ship master till 1789, when he left the sea for mercantile pursuits at home, and acquired much wealth. He carried an almost youthful vigor to the close of his life. He died in 1849, at the age of eighty-seven. His surviving children [in 1858] are Com. John Collings Long, now of the U. S. Navy, Samuel Pierse Long, Mrs. Charles Tappan and Mrs. Henry H. Ladd.

The history of the later occupants of the old house will be given in another ramble.

## RAMBLE LVII.

Charles Chauncy—Family history—His interest in the Revolution—Anecdotes —Character—Descendants—Charles W. Chauncy—Finale of the old house.

In 1791, two years after the death of Col. Pierse Long, the old mansion on South street, noticed in our last ramble, came into the possession and occupancy of Charles Chauncy, great grandson of President Charles Chauncy, of Harvard College.

Probably no family in Portsmouth can trace its pedigree beyond that of the Chauncy. Chauncy de Chauncy came into England with William the Conqueror in 1066, from Chauncy, near Amiens in France. The female branch goes back directly to Charlemagne and Egbert, about the year 800. The descendants occupied the estates in England, making but one change, up to the birth of President Chauncy in 1592, who, experiencing some severe persecutions under Bishop Laud, emigrated to Plymouth in 1638. He was inaugurated as the second President of Harvard College in 1654. His son Isaac, born in 1632, was the father of Rev. Dr. Charles Chauncy, who was born in Boston in 1705, and died there in 1787. A Street, a Place, and a Hall there bear honorable remembrance of the latter in their names.

Charles Chauncy, who in 1809 died at the house in South street above referred to, was the son of the minister of Boston. After graduating in 1748, being prevented by feeble health from studying for the ministry, he entered the counting room of his uncle, Sir Wm. Pepperell, at Kittery. In 1756 he married Mary Cutts of Cutts' Island. She died in 1758, leaving no children. In 1760 he married Joanna Gerrish of Kittery, daughter of the proprietor of Gerrish's Island. She remained his companion to nearly the close of life, dying but three months before him. They are interred in the Cotton burying ground. His grand-daughter, Mrs. Eliza Porter, wife of Lieut. John Porter of the Navy, represents him as a superior man in talents, attainments and moral excellence. She gives a graphic description of him, as she used to see him in that old mansion:

"I remember my grandfather as a small, very erect old gentleman, of quick movement, wearing a cocked hat, small clothes, and black silk hose, with diamond knee buckles. I have a faint impression that he was in the army during the war of the Revolution, from his being sometimes called captain, and from an old sword, a military coat and buff vest, with which the grandchildren amused themselves in playing old soldier; but of this I am not certain. I know that he was much interested in political affairs, and with fearless independence expressed his opinion in speaking, and writing for many papers in Boston and in Portsmouth. It was a part of my daily duties to read the papers to him, scarce a word of which I could comprehend. When I read anything of his own writing, he would become very impatient and say, "how you drawl that out; it is a stirring article and should be read thus;" and he would then read it out with such vehement tones and gestures, without looking at the paper, that I would be nearly frightened out of my wits, and run off to my grandmother, or aunt, to inquire what he meant by 'stirring articles.' 'Tory and Federalist and Republican,' how he would read without seeing the paper!

"He was a devout Christian and strict in enforcing religious observances in his family. He read and instructed us in the Scriptures during the evening, and repeated with much ease and solemnity, passages from the psalms, which he required me to commit to memory, and took great pains to instruct me in reciting them. He wrote with great vigor and conciseness, and often with eloquence. The promptness with which he used his pen caused him to have many applicants for public speeches, etc.*

"He was liberal in his charities and detested ostentation; frequently refusing to aid, by public subscription, persons to whom he would send a generous private donation. He complained if his table was not abundantly spread, that there would be nothing left for the poor. Many a needy pensioner mourned the cessation of his bounty, when too generous a confidence in the integrity of others had curtailed the provisions made for age and infirmity. I felt an unconscious pride steal over my heart when walking with him, as I noticed the respect and reverence with which every one greeted him. Even the children would cease their play as he approached, saying, 'here comes the squire,' and stand aside to doff their hats, or bob their courtesies, as he passed."

The children of Charles and Joanna Chauncy were:

Charles, born April 22, 1761; died Sept. 10, 1789, aged twenty-eight. He was esteemed for his piety and exemplary deportment; but having been too assiduous in the pursuit of mental acquirements, he became insane at the age of sixteen, and continued so until a week before his death.

Isaac, born Jan. 14, 1763. He was captain of the ship Columbia, of Portsmouth, N. H. She was cast away on a reef of rocks, near Marshfield, Mass. The Captain was

* John Ball, for ten years the City Missionary of Salem, was a native of Portsmouth, and died in Salem in January, 1859. About three weeks before his death, in a letter addressed to the editor of the Portsmouth Journal, he speaks thus of Charles Chauncy:

"Your Rambles I continue to read with interest. In regard to 'Old Squire Chauncy,' as the boys called him when I was a boy, I would say, we all respected and loved him, because he always had a kind word for us whenever we met him. I often think of the tablet on his tombstone in Cotton's burying-ground, which is in Latin. The first three letters on it are—H. S. E.—and some one who knew him, no doubt, (whether he was a wag or not,) scratched on the marble next to the above letters so as to read, 'Hon. South Ender.' I remember the old gentleman had a word ready for every one. He was one day walking from his house up town, and passing along he heard a passionate old woman belching forth anything but gentle remarks. The Squire looked over the fence and said, 'What is the matter old lady, this morning?' 'Why,' she replied, 'they are unloading that hay near my garden, and the pesky grasshoppers will eat up all my cabbages; what shall I do, Squire?' 'O,' said he, 'catch 'em and yoke 'em,' and walked on. I love to think of the good old man."

sick at the time and was confined to the cabin. He and fourteen of the crew perished March 11, 1792. He was about to be married.

SARAH, born Feb. 12, 1765; married John Moore, shipmaster, of Portsmouth, N. H. Their children were, Statira, who married Peter Shores; Joanna Chauncy, who married William M. Shackford; John, who married Caroline Blunt; Almira Chauncy, who was a preceptress at Exeter, N. H.

The fourth child of Charles Chauncy was SAMUEL CHAUNCY. He was born May 12, 1767. He was from his boyhood a mariner. At an early period he commanded a ship belonging to Col. Eliphalet Ladd. Afterward he became joint proprietor with Col. Ladd's sons, Messrs. Henry and Alexander Ladd. He ever evinced much prudence and intelligence as a commander, and was successful as a supercargo. In 1795 he married Betsy, the second daughter of Col. Ladd, and occupied a house on Daniel street, near where W. M. Shackford now resides. In about 1799 their only living son, Charles William, was born. In 1807 Captain Chauncy purchased a beautiful location on the southerly side of Islington street, fronting Ann street. Here he erected a large three-story dwelling-house, and commodious out-buildings—the present seat of the family of the late Captain Lewis Barnes.

After this time he relinquished his marine pursuits, to enjoy the pleasures of domestic ease. The life of a landsman, he soon discovered, was not congenial with the requirements of his health, morally and physically. About the year 1815, he sold his pleasant dwelling-house to Capt. L. Barnes, and removed to a valuable farm and country seat owned by Mrs. Ladd in Stratham, some ten or twelve miles from Portsmouth, in the hope of finding advantages for health in a change of situation. Here, surrounded by the comforts of life, with leisure for reading and social intercourse, and the visits of friends, in agricultural pursuits he hoped to find contentment and health. But he still looked to the ocean as his home, where "rocked on the billows of the deep," he might hope to find rest for his unsatisfied, diseased mind. Under the impression that his circumstances demanded an increase of income for future support, on the 17th of March, 1817, he took command of the Hannah in Portsmouth, and set sail for Bremen. In October, intelligence came that Capt. Chauncy had ended his life by suicide, aged fifty-one. Mrs. Chauncy, a lady of very noble qualities, died Nov. 17, 1821, at the age of forty-five years.

Elizabeth Hirst, the fifth child of Charles Chauncy, was born July 11, 1769. She married Jeremiah Clark, of York, Me. They had one child, Eliza C., who in 1815 married Lieut. John Porter, of the United States Navy, brother of Commodore Porter. He died at Watertown, Mass., 1831.

Joanna was born in 1772. She was married to Edward Parry, for many years a merchant of Portsmouth, and died suddenly in June, 1800.

Lucy was born Oct. 20, 1773. She was married to Capt. William Yeaton, of Portsmouth. They removed to Alexandria, and were living there in 1817.

Their other five children all died young.

The only descendant of the oldest son of President Chauncy, who bears the name of Chauncy, is Charles William, the son of Samuel, born in 1799. He graduated with honor at Harvard College in 1819, and took the degree of M. D. from the same institution in 1822. After some years absence in Europe, he commenced successful practice in Portsmouth in 1827, and was also popular as a lecturer. In about the year 1834 there was a vacancy in the lecture room of the Berkshire Medical College, by the temporary absence of one of the professors. Dr. Chauney was invited to fill the chair of the absentee during the lecture season. He entered on the duties of the chair very successfully, but suddenly became deranged, in the midst of a lecture. He was soon apparently restored, though he did not complete the course of lectures. On his return home, his mind, after a time, gradually failed, from the disease in his mental organs. He declined all professional business, from the consciousness that he was not competent to attend to it. After trying the effects of a sea voyage, and on his return residing on his fine estate in Stratham, he was sent, first, to the Massachusetts General Hospital and afterwards to the Insane Retreat in Concord, N. H., where he now is, the mere wreck of what he once was.

As the old mansion has now disappeared, so has passed away from our locality that ancient name, which has been distinctly traced by the unwearied William Chauncy Fowler through thirty generations.

There are some marks of the cellar yet left, and those tan pits which a century ago, and even since the house was vacated by the Chauncys, have been brought into use, can yet be seen. About the year 1812 an adventure took place in the ruins which for a long time gave a name to the locality. A sailor, in his new blue dress, was wandering about the yard, when in passing over the decayed covering of a pit for liming skins, he slipped in. It was not long before he was seen among his fellow-privateersmen in Water street, with much more the appearance of being in white French uniform, than in the true blue. "Well Jack, where have you been, said the wonder-stricken ship-mates. Better acquainted with white sand than with lime, and with the technicalities of the sea coast than of the tan yard, he replied—"Blast me, if I haven't been capsized in a *sand pan.*" There was a hearty laugh all around, as well as a general treat—and for many years the old locality bore the name of the "*Sand Pans.*" In 1835 the old mansion was demolished, but long will remain its remembrance.

## RAMBLE LVIII.

Market Square in 1789—First store of three stories—Knight's house—The robber discovered—Inspection of travellers and goods.

MARKET SQUARE as it is, is a great improvement on what it was seventy years ago, when President Washington, from the balcony over the eastern door of the State House, was formally received by the citizens of Portsmouth. At that time the premises of Stephen Pearse's father extended on a line with the present market twenty-five feet west into the Parade, as then called, and twelve feet north into Daniel street. The old State House, standing opposite, left the Parade no wider than the street now is in front of the Exchange Buildings. The road was very narrow on the north of the State House,—and between the State House and the North Meeting House was a rough ledge of rocks, over which no carriage could pass. Market and Daniel streets were only about as wide as Ladd street now is. There was then no bank house nor market house. Directly in front of where the Rockingham bank now is, in the middle of the street, was a brick watch house, ten feet square, which, after standing there twenty-eight years, was looked upon, as some now look upon our market house, as not very ornamental, and was taken down just before Washington arrived, and the ledge on which it stood levelled. Between the North Church and the new Custom House site stands the first building of *three stories* which was erected for a store in Portsmouth, now owned by William S. Hadley. At the time of its erection by Daniel Austin, in 1800, there were only fifteen three storied houses in Portsmouth, most of which had been erected but five years. In 1811 Mr. Austin sold the property to Gen. Asa Dearborn, who afterwards disposed of it to Joshua Wentworth, who made it his place of business for several years.

On the spot where Col. Hadley's hotel recently stood, was the residence of William Knight—a large two-story house, end to the street, entrance to front door from a yard on the south. The original stable was taken down in 1857.

Madam Knight was the daughter of John Moffat. She lived here in that aristocratic style which in latter days is more rare. Although within a stone's cast of her place of worship, her chariot, with two horses would be in requisition to take her to the door. John Moffat had two other daughters. One of them was Mrs. Sherburne, the mother of Governor Langdon; the other was the lady of William Whipple, a signer of the Declaration of Independence.

Madam Knight died over sixty years ago. The house was then occupied by Capt. Robert O. Treadwell; next by Hon. Benjamin Penhallow, Dr. Lyman Spaulding, then by John Elkins, and after by Hadley & Clark.

There is one feature in the position of the property around Market Square, which goes far to disprove the idea that unentailed real estate will soon pass out of a family. The Jacob Sheafe estate, extending from Daniel street down the east side of Market street, has been in the family one hundred and sixty years—the opposite corner, owned by Stephen Pearse, where he has personally been in business for himself sixty-five years, was the residence of his father, and grandfather, Jotham Odiorne, who owned it more than a century ago. The Rogers property has been in the family a longer period, and the land on which John N. Handy's stores, west of the Athenæum, are now located, has come down without deed through six generations. The property next west to the corner has been in the Peirce family for a century at least; and the Gains property for a hundred and thirty years. There is also land near by, the seat of Charles H. Ladd, which has descended regularly in the family from

John Tufton Mason, the proprietor of the title to New Hampshire.

One other mark of stability in this vicinity is the fact, that the location of Albert Badger's tin shop, in Daniel street, has been used for the same purpose for at least seventy years. Mr. Norry manufactured his tin ware there before John Badger, father of Albert, came to Portsmouth.

While we are on Market Square we will relate a little incident which took place here in 1770. Near where the Athenæum now stands was the barber's shop of Peter Mann. His apprentice was a dashy young man, named Samuel Chandler. There had been many store robberies made in the previous year,—Mr. Cutts missed his dry goods—Mr. Penhallow his wares, and Mr. Griffith his watches. Search was made, but no traces could be discovered. One morning in January, George Dame came into the shop to be shaved. In his jocose way he said to Mr. Mann, "so you have been stealing more goods, have you?" It was received of course as a joke. Sitting down in the chair, as young Chandler was arranging to shave him, he said—"Do tell me, Sam, what you did with the goods." Chandler was seized with trembling, and could not shave him. Suspicion at once falling upon him, he was arrested, confessed his crime, and in the attic of the State House he disclosed a stock of valuable goods which he had stolen from time to time, intending when of age to open shop, without being troubled with the credit system. Chandler was banished from the town.

In those times, before the discovery of inoculation, every precaution was taken to prevent the introduction of small pox here. Mr. Dame, above referred to, had an office somewhere near the Pound, where all travellers and packages from Boston had an inspection and smoking, if deemed necessary, before they were permitted to pass.

## RAMBLE LIX.

Auburn street Cemetery — First training field — Cotton's burying ground — Execution of Ruth Blay — Duel by Frenchmen — Laighton's poem.

THE Auburn street Cemetery, now arranged with that good taste which places it at a far remove from the repulsive features of an antiquated grave yard, is a place of quiet resort and one of the pleasantest walks the city affords. A map readily directs any visitor to such locality as he may be desirous to visit. The fast growing trees begin to give a shade which in some parts is almost equal to that spread over it by nature two centuries ago.

It may not be generally known that this spot was designated for a burying ground about a hundred and fifty years before it was fully used for that purpose. Our town records show, that on the 5th of June, 1671, "It was agreed with Goodman William Cotton to fence the town's land that lyeth by Goodman Skates, for a trayning place, to cutt down all the trees and bushes and to clear the same from said ground by the first of April next, and for his soe doeing he and his heirs shall have the above feeding and use thereof as a pasture only, for twenty years—and the said land shall still remayne for a trayning field and to bury dead in."

It was on this spot that Capt. John Pickering's company were instructed in military tactics. What a sight would that company now be, once more marshalled in their puritan uniforms,—no modern display would be more attractive. After Goodman Cotton's twenty years expired, and a few more years had elapsed, the "trayning field" was a privilege granted to the pastor of the South Parish, where he might pasture his cows, etc.; and eventually, by a vote of the town, it became the property of that parish.

In 1711 it was voted to enclose the burying place in

the common land or training field, adjoining to William Cotton's. It was also voted that the training field be enclosed. This vote was not carried into effect; for ten years after, in 1721, the town resolved that the vote respecting the fencing of the burying place at the training field be put in force this year. This was the Cotton burying place.

In 1735, the town voted to grant the use of the training field to Rev. Mr. Shurtleff for a horse pasture during his ministry. A similar vote was passed in 1752, just before Rev. Dr. Haven was settled, giving the use of the field to the next minister who should be settled over the South Parish.

In the course of Dr. Haven's ministry, the training field at the Plains was given to the Province, and the South road field was left to the undisputed occupancy of the pastor, and was called the Minister's pasture. After Dr. Haven's death, about fifty years ago, a vote was passed in town meeting, giving the field to the South Parish. About the time of building the Stone Church the land was transferred by the Society to the Trustees of the Charity Fund, who in 1830 founded what is called "The Proprietors' Burying Ground," but now more generally known by the more euphonious name of "*Auburn Cemetery.*"

There are two scenes connected with this spot which have a more harrowing effect than the contemplation of a hundred quiet graves.

On that most elevated spot on the north side of the Cemetery, just above the row of tombs, a gallows was once erected—and there, amid a thousand spectators, on the 30th of December, 1768, an unfortunate girl was hung—a poor, misguided girl, of better conscience than many who have marble monuments with gilded inscriptions to perpetuate their memory.

In August, 1768, Ruth Blay, of South Hampton, was

indicted for concealing the death of an illegitimate child, whereby it might not be known whether it were born alive or not, or whether it was murdered or not. The English statute prescribed the penalty of death for this offence. This blood written law was not repealed even in this state till 1792, when a milder punishment was substituted for that of death. The exordium of Attorney General Clagett in the above prosecution is still remembered for its pompous solemnity. "He called heaven to witness, that he was discharging a duty that he owed his country, his King and his God."

An old lady who was present at the execution of Ruth Blay, said—as Ruth was carried through the streets, her shrieks filled the air. She was dressed in silk, and was driven under the gallows in a cart. Public sympathy was awakened for her, and her friends had procured from the Governor a reprieve, which would have soon resulted in her pardon—for circumstances afterwards showed that her child was probably still-born, and she was not a murderer. The hour for her execution arrived, and the sheriff, not wishing, it is said, to be late to his dinner, ordered the cart to be driven away, and the unfortunate woman was left hanging from the gallows, a sacrifice to misguided judgment. If we are rightly informed, she was a girl of good education for her day, having been a school-mistress. The indignation of the populace can hardly be conceived when it was ascertained that a reprieve from the governor came a few minutes after her spirit had been hastened away. They gathered that evening around the residence of Sheriff Packer, (the locality of Richard Jenness's house,) and an effigy was there erected, bearing this inscription:

Am I to lose my dinner
This woman for to hang?
Come draw away the cart, my boys—
Don't stop to say amen.
☞Draw away, draw away the cart!

May this last execution in Portsmouth, which occurred ninety years ago, long remain the last on our annals.

Ruth was buried a rod or two from the north side of where the pond now is,—and was the first one for whom the soil of that Cemetery was broken, ninety-seven years after it was designated as "a place to bury the dead in."

It is a remarkable incident that this spot so early selected for the repose of the dead, should, before being appropriated to that purpose, be made the scene of a public execution and of the only fatal duel of which we have any record.

Ruth Blay was the last, but not the only individual who has been executed in Portsmouth. In 1739, Dec. 27, Sarah Simpson and Penelope Kenney were executed for the murder of a child. In 1755, Eliphaz Dow of Hampton Falls, was executed for murder. Thomas Packer was the High Sheriff at the three executions—in 1739, 1755 and 1768.

Albert Laighton has devoted a few pages in his valuable volume of poems, just published, to the remembrance of the Ruth Blay tragedy:

In the worn and dusty annals
  Of our old and quiet town,
With its streets of leafy beauty.
  And its houses quaint and brown,—

With its dear associations,
  Hallowed by the touch of time,—
You may read this thrilling legend,
  This sad tale of wrong and crime.

In the drear month of December,
  Ninety years ago to-day,
Hundreds of the village people
  Saw the hanging of Ruth Blay;—

Saw her clothed in silk and satin,
  Borne beneath the gallows-tree,
Dressed as in her wedding garments,
  Soon the bride of Death to be;—

Saw her tears of shame and anguish,
  Heard her shrieks of wild despair,
Echo thro' the neighboring woodlands,
  Thrill the clear and frosty air.

When at last, in tones of warning,
  From its high and airy tower,
Slowly with its tongue of iron,
  Tolled the bell the fatal hour;—

Like the sound of distant billows,
  When the storm is wild and loud,
Breaking on the rocky headland,
  Ran a murmur through the crowd.

And a voice among them shouted,
  "Pause before the deed is done:
We have asked reprieve and pardon
  For the poor misguided one."

But these words of Sheriff Packer
  Rang above the swelling noise:
"Must I wait and lose my dinner?
  Draw away the cart, my boys!"

Fold thy hands in prayer, O woman!
  Take thy last look of the sea;
Take thy last look of the landscape;
  God be merciful to thee!

Stifled groans, a gasp, a shudder,
  And the guilty deed was done;
On a scene of cruel murder
  Coldly looked the Winter sun.

Then the people, pale with horror,
  Looked with sudden awe behind,
As a field of grain in Autumn
  Turns before a passing wind;

For distinctly in the distance,
  In the long and frozen street,
They could hear the ringing echoes
  Of a horse's sounding feet.

Nearer came the sound and louder,
  Till a steed with panting breath,
From its sides the white foam dripping,
  Halted at the scene of death;

And a messenger alighted,
  Crying to the crowd, "Make way!
This I bear to Sheriff Packer;
  'Tis a pardon for Ruth Blay!"

But they answered not nor heeded,
  For the last fond hope had fled;
In their deep and speechless sorrow,
  Pointing only to the dead.

And that night, with burning bosoms,
  Muttering curses fierce and loud,
At the house of Sheriff Packer
  Gathered the indignant crowd,—

Shouting, as upon a gallows
  A grim effigy they bore,
"Be the name of Thomas Packer
  A reproach forevermore!"

The other tragedy occurred fourteen years after. We find it nowhere recorded, but have it as it was related by a man who said his father was the witness referred to. In 1782, when the French fleet was lying in our harbor, a man from Little Harbor was crossing the path which led through this field, when he saw a boat with several men row up the cove,—the men came on shore and up into the field. He was about leaving, but they beckoned him to remain. He did so. Two men dressed like officers were soon engaged in combat with swords, and one of them fell mortally wounded and soon expired. A piece of gold was given to the witness by the duellists, whether to keep him silent or to reward him for standing by to see fair play, does not appear. The corpse was taken on board, and the boat was soon in the stream.

These are the melancholy legends of the Auburn street Cemetery.

# RAMBLE LX.

William H. Rindge—Noble act of an unknown sailor—Mrs. Sigourney's sketch—Disclosure at death.

JOHN P. RINDGE died in May, 1852, in his eighty-second year. The death of this aged citizen brings to our mind the remembrance of his son, WILLIAM H. RINDGE, who, in the discharge of a disinterested act of benevolence, perilled his own life to save that of a child, and taking the deed as its own reward, sealed it in his own bosom, and never disclosed the fact until on his death bed, five years after.

It was at the great fire in the city of New York, in 1835, that a mother was seen in the streets frantically shrieking for her babe, which had been left in the upper story of a building enveloped in flames. The young sailor heard the mother's voice, rushed through the flames, in a few minutes returned with the child in his arms, gave it to its mother, and in an instant disappeared. Much enquiry was made for the noble sailor at the time, and calls through the public prints for information respecting him, were without effect. The circumstance was commented upon in the papers of the country, and while nothing was disclosed respecting the individual, the pen of Mrs. Sigourney narrated the thrilling scene as follows, under the title of "The Noble Sailor."

It was a fearful night;
The strong flames onward spread
From street to street, from spire to spire,
And on their treasures tread.

Hark! 'Tis a mother's cry,
High o'er the tumult wild,
As rushing toward the flame-wrapt home,
She shrieked, "My child! my child!"

A wanderer from the sea,
A stranger marked her woe,
And in his bosom woke
The sympathetic glow.

Swift up the burning stairs,
With daring feet he flew;
While sable clouds of stifling smoke
Concealed him from the view.

Fast fell the burning beams
Across the dangerous road,
Till the far chamber where he groped,
Like fiery oven glowed.

But what a pealing shout
When from the wreck he came,
And in his arms a smiling babe,
Still toying with the flame.

The mother's raptured tears
Forth like a torrent sped;
But ere the throng could learn his name,
That noble tar had fled.

Not for the praise of man
Did he this deed of love;
But on the bright, unfading page,
'Tis registered above.

We well recollect frequently meeting, soon after, a young man of retiring manners, who was suffering under consumption. At length in June, 1840, the disease had made such progress that his life was evidently soon to close. It was not until almost the final moment of his life, that he disclosed the fact that the cold which brought on the disease was contracted at the time he rescued that child from the flames. Where is the high-reared monument of this noble sailor? Humanity asks the question —for he periled his own life to save that of a fellow- being. By that successful exertion a life was saved, although his own life, at the interesting age of twenty-three, was sacrificed by the effort. Let such noble deeds be held in lasting remembrance.

## RAMBLE LXI.

William Brewster—Display of dauntless bravery at New York—The fatal disaster on ship-board—A model of self-devotion.

On Hanover street, in the rear of our office, there is now a block of buildings which covers a site where the residence once stood of one of the most noble-spirited boys of our town. William Brewster possessed in an uncommon degree a spirit of boldness, enterprise and daring, yet modestly retiring from the praise which was justly due to him for his labors in the cause of humanity. so forward was he to fly to the relief of the suffering, that his own personal safety was ever, in his estimation, of secondary importance. The consciousness of having performed his duty was all the reward he sought. Numerous instances might be given, illustrating his character,—such as exposing his own life to rescue the drowning, where others dared not venture, etc., but we shall only advert to two instances, which are borne in the recollection of many of our citizens.

In May, 1811, while he was in New York, the first officer of the brig Fame, a great fire commenced in Chatham street, which destroyed over a hundred houses. The flames at length communicated to the lofty steeple of the Presbyterian church, at the head of Beekman street. At this moment, with the flames above the reach of the engines, when destruction not only to the church but also to a vast amount of property in the neighborhood seemed inevitable, there was seen ascending the lightning rod an intrepid young man bearing a bucket of water. The fearful height was attained, and the flame was quenched. He sought not to be known, and refused a reward when it was tendered to him. He replied to the tender, I have done no more than my duty. The vessel with which he was connected sailed in three days; and another individual, named Knapp, had the address to claim the reward which young Brewster so nobly refused.

As an evidence of his unobtrusive and modest turn of mind, the following extract from a letter, which he wrote to his mother, is subjoined. It was dated at Gustavia harbor, in St. Bartholomew's, June 17, 1811: "You have, doubtless, heard of my little exertion in arresting the progress of the fire in New York, which I should not have mentioned, had I not seen it published in a Charleston paper. I hope my conduct on that occasion gave you satisfaction."

In an ode written by John Lothrop of Boston, for the anniversary of the Massachusetts Charitable Fire Society, is preserved an honorary memorial of this brave and meritorious youth.

See on the sacred temple's spire
  The impious demon's ruthless hand,
While half the city sinks in fire,
  Has fixed the wildly blazing brand.

His red right arm, with mighty power,
  Launched the fell instrument of woe;
And lo, a desolating shower
  Pours on the humbled roofs below!

Aghast, the trembling crowds survey
  The sparkling torrent from on high!
Ah, what can now the ruin stay,
  Unless some aid divine be nigh?

While yet they gaze, behold, with speed,
  The dauntless BREWSTER eager springs;
Angels! who noble actions heed,
  Uphold him with your guardian wings!

He swiftly mounts on Franklin's rod,
  The steeple's smoky height ascends,
Nobly preserves the house of God,
  And calms the fears of virtue's friends.

Such was the deed, that lately saved
  Our sister city's beautéous domes!
The champion's image is engraved
  On hearts secure in peaceful homes.

On the 18th of October, 1811, this young man lost his life in a distressing calamity which occurred at Bombay Hook. The vessel with which he was connected as mate, on board of which were thirty casks of powder, took fire and blew up, destroying all on board except one boy. In this closing calamity, the intrepidity which marked his whole course of life, was also nobly displayed. The boy stated that he saw the mate, just before the explosion, throwing water upon the binnacle. Destruction seemed inevitable, and he had opportunity, by taking to the water, to save his own life,—but he sacrificed it in the hope that he might do some good to those who were on board. Thus he left the world only three days before arriving at the age of manhood, in this act of humane self-devotion.

The place of his early home, the house of Capt. William Brewster on Hanover street, which was taken down in 1848, has ever awakened pleasant emotions in our memory, and we cannot see the last ruins pass away without some record of the worth of that dauntless young man.

## RAMBLE LXII.

Paved street in 1780, by an old lady—Location of buildings on the east and west sides—Dearborn's school—Dedication of his academy.

In a recent ramble we gave a sketch of Market street in 1789, when Washington visited Portsmouth. That account was read in 1853 by the widow of Capt. William Brewster, (for several years a resident in Philadelphia,) of the age of eighty-five years, and in the full enjoyment of her mental faculties. She was the daughter of Deacon Noble and the mother of that disinterested young man referred to in our last ramble. In a book published in New-York more than forty years ago, in connection with an account of the noble and generous deed of her son, is a high comment on the exemplary religious character of the mother. It is gratifying to know that she is (in 1859) still living at the age of 91, although her faculties do not retain the strength of earlier years. In 1853 she addressed to us a letter in her own hand, in which she says that she is a constant reader of the Portsmouth Journal. Seeing in one of its numbers an account of Paved street in olden time, she thought she could remember ten years further back than that article, and wrote down the following interesting recollections, which are copied from her manuscript:

"At the entrance of Paved street from the Parade stood at the right hand Daniel Rindge's double house, with an open fence around it. Next to the house stood a store; then the *old* Rindge house (very much decayed) with two doors front. The boys called it the haunted house. Next stood Benj. Dearborn's house, end to the street, with a shop in it, where Mrs. Dearborn kept some articles to sell. The room over the shop Mr. Dearborn occupied as a school room, where he accommodated a large number of scholars. Judge Pickering's house came next, end to the street, with an office in it. Next stood Madam Wibird's large brick house, with a shop in the end. Madam Wibird occupied the whole house herself, with a woman to wait upon her, besides a number of servants in the kitchen. At her decease the property all went into the hands of Mr. John Penhallow. Next to the house there was a lot of land fenced in, and a store next to it; then a large house fronting Spring hill, occupied by Mr. William Gardner. At the decease of Madam Wibird, Mr. Penhallow moved his family into the old mansion house.

"On the left side of Paved street from the Parade there was a large building occupied by a family of the name of Armit, who came from England in the time of the war, and at its close moved to Barrington. Next came a long string of very old one-story buildings owned by Robert Fowle—his printing establishment was in it. John Melcher was apprenticed to him. He occupied one part as a dwelling house, had a woman, a relative, with him, and an old negro man named Primus (whom I well remember) to wait on him. Next stood a one-story house; then an open yard where a large oak tree stood, and Peter Mann's large double house, end to the street, with two shops, one occupied as a school room—the sign over the other was "pies, cake and ale sold here." Mr. Mann was a barber, and had a shop on the Parade for his business. Then came Deacon Noble's large two story house, end to the street, with a shop in one end, where Mrs. Noble traded during the war; next a paved yard, and then Mr. Joseph Simes's and Capt. Mountford's houses, both situated with the end to the street.

"A few recollections of Mr. Dearborn's school in 1780: Mr. Dearborn taught the first school in Portsmouth for misses, in a large room in his own dwelling house. The scholars brought the Spectator and the Guardian and such books as they had, until suitable books for reading could be procured from Boston. Mr. Dearborn wanted to get up a class in grammar, but could only prevail upon *six* scholars to join. Many parents thought it an unnecessary branch for misses to attend to. The grammars were obtained from Boston; I have mine still, bought in March, 1781.

"Mr. Dearborn, full of energy and enterprise, determined on raising a building on a lot he owned, back of his house. He went on rapidly and soon had a noble academy under way. When it was completed Dr. Haven delivered an elegant address in honor of the occasion, in the North Church, and Mr. Sewall wrote an ode. The scholars were all present. The next day they were introduced into the new Academy. Mr. Dearborn soon had assistant teachers, all the branches were attended to and the school was in a flourishing condition, when Mr. Dearborn left all for Boston. He was a very good man, and his departure was much regretted by the inhabitants of Portsmouth. I shall always revere and cherish his memory."

## RAMBLE LXIII.

Market street—Dearborn's residence—Its builder—Romantic incident.

The desolating fires of 1802, 1806 and 1813, have changed the aspect of Portsmouth, by removing many of the structures of which but few men now living have a remembrance. At the close of the last century, neither Penhallow street, Jaffrey's court, nor Commercial avenue, had been opened; and the whole centre of the square encompassed by Paved, Bow, Chapel and Daniel streets was occupied as gardens and orchards connected with the few mansions which stood on the south and west sides of the square. On the corner of Daniel and what is now called Market street, was the large two-story double house of Daniel Rindge. Around it, on the south and west, was an open fence with large capped posts. Market street then was not much wider than Ladd street now is, and Daniel street was only twenty feet wide. Next north of the Rindge estate came three or four two-story wooden stores, in which Messrs. Henry Haven, Nathaniel A. Haven, Nathaniel Dean, and others carried on business.

Then, on the site of the building now occupied by the Mechanics and Traders' Bank, was a two-story house, with a shop in the basement and a dwelling-place over it. Its end was to the street, and it extended back some distance. The house for many years afforded the place of abode and the school room of Benjamin Dearborn, where grammar and the other higher branches not introduced into the public schools, are taught. Here, too, young females (for whom no provision was made by the public for their instruction) were collected, and received that education which fitted them for ornaments to society. From a hundred to a hundred and twenty of both sexes were sometimes convened for instruction in that school room, —which is spoken of in a previous ramble.

In this house, too, when not engaged as auctioneer, Mr. Dearborn employed many of his hours in studying mathematics and the mechanical powers. Here were projected and first introduced to the public, the world renowned "Dearborn's Patent Balances." Here, too, before the power printing press had been put into operation in this country or in Europe, the ingenious Dearborn, convinced of the practicability of such a machine, spent no small labor in maturing plans which did him credit for design; and although he was not successful in the completion, was doubtless of use to those who afterwards matured the great invention of the power press. In this house, too, was a hall for dancing; and many a merry hour has been spent there by those who now, like the old violin to which they moved, are unstrung and silent, and leave us to hear the tale only as an æolian whisper from the distant time. We have something more to say of the Dearborn mansion, the early history of a part of which, never before submitted to print, has induced us to make this sketch.

About the year 1750, a gentleman of property from London, with an only daughter, about seven years of age, came to this country, and taking a fancy to this locality, purchased the lot of land and erected a house for his own occupancy and use. Whether the wife of Mr. Robinson died in England, or soon after their arrival here, we know not; but the care of the daughter Mary (or *Molly*, as she was nicknamed, agreeably to the custom of the time), fell upon him, and she received such an education as fitted her for a good station in society. They were without relatives on this side of the Atlantic, and their associates being few, were of course more firmly confided in. Before Mary arrived at womanhood, her father's health failed, and in his anxiety to provide for her future, he made a will, putting all his property in trust of a friend for his daughter's support, to pass into her own hands on her marriage, should she marry to the liking of the guardian. If she did not so marry the man of *his* choice, the property should all belong to the guardian.

In due time a suitor won the heart of Mary, but through the gold glasses by which the executor viewed the property, he could not see that perfection in the lover which warranted his assent. So Mary took her lover, and the guardian took the property. Thus, by the unwise provision of her loving father, the daughter was deprived of her rightful property on becoming the companion of one who depended upon his daily toil on land, or on fishing on the coast, for a livelihood. Many years did the patient wife spend in her humble situation. At length she became a poor widow. The skill in fine needlework she had early acquired was eventually brought into requisition to make and repair the nets of the fishermen; and her skill in cookery, becoming known, was frequently called into exercise when an epicurean party wished for a chowder of the choicest kind.

Thus employed, the unfortunate and virtuous widow passed more than her three score and ten, living on the resources of her honest industry. As infirmities crept on, at the age of seventy-five she was provided for by the town, and the records of our almshouse state that after a residence there of seventeen years, on the 8th day of October, 1835, died Mrs. Molly Driscol, a native of London, aged ninety-two years.

The father, the daughter, the husband, and the guardian are now but dust, and the house has for more than fifty years been in ashes. We will not further disturb the embers, or give life to the coals which for many years burnt in the bosom of the unfortunate Mary Driscol, the remembrance of whose latter days is still fresh in the minds of many of our readers.

## RAMBLE LXIV.

Jefferson Hall—Its school scenes—First public female school, Montague's—Only town grammar school, Taft's—The first Sunday school.

ONE more return to Market Square, and to one of the scenes which our grandmothers remember with the deepest interest. It is to the opening of the first public female day school in Portsmouth. For one hundred and sixty years our town had not regarded the education of females of sufficient public interest to make any appropriation for public schools for them. Those who were able sent their girls to private teachers; those who were not, gave only home instruction. In 1784, when the return of peace awoke the attention of the public to many neglected things, not the least in importance among the new enterprises was the provision for a public school for females. The place selected for the school room was the large chamber of Mr. Grouard's house and hat store, which was on the same spot on which the Brick Market now stands. The house was old, of two stories, and faced the south. The teacher selected was Mr. Montague, a name revered by the grandmothers of the present generation. Never since has Jefferson Hall (which embraces in its limits the very site of the old school room) been filled with a happier company than on the day that school was opened. The girls from eight years and upwards flocked in from the east and from the west, from Christian Shore and from below the South Mill. From all accounts Mr. Montague was an excellent teacher, imparting the rudiments of learning in so impressive a manner that those of his scholars now living, regard that one year's instruction received from him, worth more than any five years' instruction received from any of the private teachers of that day. Mr. Montague's services were continued but one year. He was preparing for the ministry in the Episcopal church, and from the avails of this year's labors he procured the means for visiting England to complete his preparation. Mr. Butler then took the school: but failed in keeping up an interest in the scholars. At the end of his six months the school was given up! And so far as we can learn, for the succeeding *thirty years*, until 1815, there was no public provision for any regular school for the education of females—if we except the opportunity offered them in the summer months of attending in the boys' school rooms, two hours a day, from six to seven in the morning, and from five to six in the afternoon, on four days in the week, to receive instruction from the boys' teachers in reading, writing and arithmetic.

There have been good private schools for girls always sustained, from the days of Benjamin Dearborn in the last century; and those who had the means have enjoyed the advantages of good education. But it was not until the district system was introduced in 1815, that boys and girls were placed on an equal footing in our public schools.

It has been found that the education of girls is as important as that of boys; and that in capacity for acquiring some of those higher branches which were rarely presented for their study in former times, the preponderance is in favor of the young ladies. Look in upon our female high school of 1859, and see every one of its hundred and twenty seats filled with scholars who have passed the lower branches,—every one with her Latin grammar,—algebra and geometry going off as a pastime, and history and moral philosophy a regular treat, and then question the importance of female education.

What a change in public sentiment! And what an amount of gratitude will be felt for those who have bestowed their influence and their means in producing this great mental elevation of the female sex. The dark ages are not quite so distant as we usually date them. Think of our fathers after the Revolution, awakening to an eighteen months' experiment of the public education of females, and then for thirty years retiring again into that darkness over which their progenitors had plodded for a century and a half!

There are too many novelties in the early history of the boys' schools in Portsmouth to present them in this ramble.

While on the spot of the primitive female public school, we are reminded of the second occasion when that same spot was occupied by a school, in which the writer was enrolled. The devastating fire of 1813 having swept away all but the walls of the old brick school house in State street, Jefferson Hall was furnished with seats, school commenced—and here that venerable apostle, Master Taft, and his fondly attached scholars, were gathered for a year, until the ruins were restored. Master Taft had been one of Washington's Life Guard, and in nobleness of character seemed to emulate his high example. If he ever erred, it was from having too much urbanity in his disposition.

Up to 1815, Mr. Taft's was the only public grammar school in Portsmouth. The district system was that year introduced—eight grammar schools were at once established, in which girls and boys had equal privileges of seats, and all the old teachers were laid aside. If there was ever anything that touched the school boy's heart with sorrow when he again stood on Market Square, it was to see the venerable Master Taft, in the possession of the full dignity of his manly virtues and classic learning, and uncontaminated by any of the follies of life, compelled from penury to take the humble position of clerk of the Market—the learned companion and guard of Washington bending his naturally upright and manly form, and daily performing the menial duties of his office! The boys felt it—but they had not the means to do for him as their hearts dictated.

Again, for a third time, children are gathering for instruction in the same locality where the girls attended their first public school in 1784, and where the town grammar school for boys closed in 1815. It is now 1818—it is the Sabbath, and in Jefferson Hall is the first Sunday School of the town. There is no parcelling off into sects, or sexes, or complexions. The moral wants of all are equally regarded, and the Bible is the great text book. That town school is a matter of history.

We will not attempt a further sketch, for there is enough in the recollections of those *three schools* to carry the imagination of the reader in a more extensive ramble than we present, when he again paces Jefferson Hall, or passes its uncomely exterior.

---

## RAMBLE LXV.

Gardner's Arch—Gardner family—William Gardner's history—Sacrifices in the Revolution—His appointment and removal—Thomas Manning—Gardner's character.

PORTSMOUTH has but one arched street—and the name of *Gardner's Arch* is as familiar to the old and the young, as Portsmouth Plains or Market Square. At the south-east corner of Gardner street stands the mansion of Major William Gardner—built originally by the Wentworth family, it was for several years occupied by Ichabod Nichols, father of the late Rev. Dr. Nichols of Portland, and was purchased by Major Gardner in or about the year 1792.

Major William Gardner was born in 1751. His father, John Gardner, was a tailor, whose house was in Buck (now State) street, on the spot where Mayor Morrison now resides. John had six sons—David, Christopher, (who died at Goshen, N. H.) William, (the subject of this article) John, Samuel (the father of Mrs. Abraham Wendell, also of John Gardner now residing on South street, and of Samuel, the printer, who—of the firm of Peirce & Gardner—was publisher of the N. H. Gazette), and Benjamin (the father of Andrew Gardner); and one daughter, Frances, who married Benjamin Drown.

Major Gardner was brought up to mercantile pursuits. His business education was obtained in the counting room of Col. Joshua Wentworth, at the corner of Vaughan and Hanover streets. At some period of the Revolution he was an acting commissary, and furnished the army with supplies.

In a dark hour of the Revolution, there was a lack of blankets, and a requisition from the head commissary was made for them. There were none then in Portsmouth, but Major Gardner understanding there was such an article as was needed in the hands of a merchant at Newburyport, went there to make a purchase for the government. The merchant, (we think his name was Titcomb,) was desirous to sell, but said he, "the government is already so much in debt to me, that if the revolution is not carried, I am a ruined man. I cannot *trust the government* any further." After some conversation he said, "if Major Gardner will take them on his own *personal* note, he can have them." It was for a large amount,—but the soldiers needed them, and without delay the stock was taken up on his own account, and the army supplied.

When Major Gardner applied to government in after years for his pay, he found the treasury bankrupt, and himself a heavy sufferer for his patriotic services. His sacrifices for his country led Washington afterwards to appoint him Commissioner of Loans for this section. Major Gardner built the arch-house, and the room over the arch he occupied as a "U. S. Loan Office." There was transacted business on not quite so extensive a scale as the Rothschilds', but he was the medium of many investments which have been productive of good incomes to many in our State. His office also embraced that of Pension agent.

When Adams took the Presidential chair, there was a wide sweep of public officers, to give place to political friends. Among those who were removed in Portsmouth in 1798, was Major Gardner. This ostracism was not expected, nor received in a very submissive spirit. It was a mark of ingratitude which embittered his feelings against the Administration. Had you been walking near the arch on that day, you might have seen the

Major with axe in hand, extending his arm from his window, and staving that Loan Office sign into a hundred pieces. Its remains kindled a Republican fire at the south end, which for years made it the seat of the anti-Adams party.

The feeling was not wholly confined to political meetings. It invaded the social circles, and embittered the hearth-stones At a social gathering where Major Gardner and his lady were guests, some remarks were dropped reflecting on the Republican party. He at once turned to his lady. "Mrs. Gardner, take your bonnet—it is time to go," was the quick decision of the hater of John Adams.

About this time the New Hampshire Gazette, under John Melcher, was too much in favor of the federal party to suit him, and strictures on some of the Republican leaders appearing therein, Major Gardner was much offended. A nephew of his, Samuel Gardner, was at that time apprentice in the office. Major Gardner went into the office, and said to his nephew—"Sam, take your hat, and quit this place." He did so. Several years after Samuel Gardner was one of the publishers of that paper. In the mean time the "Republican Ledger" was established here, as the exponent of the radical doctrines of the party, and was continued until the election of Jefferson, in 1802.

Capt. Thomas Manning, whose mansion fronts Liberty bridge on the south side, was a man of sympathizing sentiments, and in some respects of the spirit of Major Gardner. They both despised ingratitude, were both of the same political tenets, patriotic in their feelings, and generous in their subscriptions for party purposes. They were both men of strict punctuality, and required the like virtues in those they dealt with. One illustrative anecdote we will give.

Capt. Manning was rich, and would loan money on

good security. He had accommodated his friend, Abel Harris, and the time of payment had gone by a few days. Meeting him in the street, in his abrupt way he said—"Harris, come down and settle your note." In as abrupt a manner the reply was, that he would see him to Guinea first. "Then I will sue you as soon as I can put my hand on the note," said he passing rapidly on. Mr. Harris knowing his fixedness of purpose, soon turned round and called him back. "I'll come half way." It was agreed,—they met. "Capt. Manning, it is no use for two such hot heads as you and I to quarrel—I will come down and settle this afternoon." "Very well." At the hour, the money was ready and the note asked for. "Mr. Harris, I don't want this money—you can have it as long as you wish—only be *punctual* when the pay day arrives." Harris paid the interest, and kept the loan.

Major Gardner had his office restored to him after Jefferson's election, in 1802, and retained it as long as the office was continued. A new sign appeared on the Arch, and remained there, we think, nearly to the time of his death, which occurred on the 29th of April, 1833, at the age of nearly eighty-three years.

For many years before his death Major Gardner was confined to his house by a disease in his eyes, which resulted in blindness. But with his sight he did not lose his interest in public affairs and in the matters of his own town. For public dinners, he would always buy his ticket, to be used by some one who was not able to purchase. He gave encouragement to the young in various ways, delighting to know that he was contributing to their happiness. He was the patron of that model juvenile military company of forty years ago, "The Gardner Whites." At the formation of the Apprentices' Library, Major Gardner was the donor of many valuable books. He ever contributed freely for every public purpose brought before him.

In the midst of the turmoil of public excitement men can scarcely free themselves enough from the mists of prejudice to discover whether they are led on by sentiments of patriotism, or personal feeling. At this stand-point of half a century, it is plain to discover that much of the party rancor which divided our citizens and even families of the nearest kin, grew more out of the appointment of this man or that man to office, than from any danger the country incurred by this or that public measure of the administration.

Major Gardner, though in party times he showed strong political prejudices, was one of the most honorable and respected of our citizens, one of the most generous friends to the cause of humanity—a model of courteousness of manners, and of disinterested, active and ardent benevolence. That Arch was worthy of preservation in more enduring form, to perpetuate the memory of a true patriot and devoted friend to his country in the season of its greatest peril,—but in 1858, after this sketch was written, it has been removed, and become among "the things that were."

---

## RAMBLE LXVI.

Daniel Webster—His residence in Portsmouth—His last visit to Portsmouth—Public reception at Jefferson Hall—Meeting at the Cameneum.

DANIEL WEBSTER, in 1807, became a resident of Portsmouth, and looking upon this as his future location, he arranged for those domestic relations which make a residence a home; and in June 1808, was married to the tenderly beloved Grace Fletcher, who remained his partner for nineteen years. They occupied first the house now owned by Robert Gray in Vaughan street. In the fire of

1813, they were residents of a house on Pleasant street, in front of Richard Jenness's mansion. This house was burnt, and Mr. Webster suffered a heavy loss. He afterwards occupied the house next north of the residence of Charles H. Ladd, on High street. Mr. Webster's office was on the west side of Market street, over the store now occupied by Mr. Stavers.

Mr. Webster came not among us as a *young* lawyer.—Though but twenty-five years of age, his noble form, his manly boldness and his maturity of mind, readily commanded the attention and respect of more advanced years. His influence was not only felt in the court-room, but as a citizen he was ever looked to for counsel; and to the calls of philanthropy no ear was ever more open or hand more free. Here were developed those peculiar qualifications which afterwards exhibited him as the statesman who would do honor to any nation. It was while residing here that his own State placed him in the council of the nation; and at a time, too, when the elements of politics were burning more fiercely than they have since. The confidence reposed in him was found not to be misplaced, and after serving one term he was re-elected. In 1816, after a residence in Portsmouth of nine years, he removed to Boston. After Mr. Webster left Portsmouth he visited this place several times, but only once had he a public reception. That was given on the 17th of May, 1844. It was on the occasion of the return of the New Hampshire delegates from the Baltimore Convention which nominated Henry Clay for the Presidency. The reception was given in Jefferson Hall. Here he met those of his old friends who had survived, and the greeting was cordial with the citizens of his former place of residence.

Twenty-eight years form a portion of time in which one generation gives place to another—the boy becomes the man—and manhood retires into the shade of years.

His return at that period seemed to him almost a realization of Irving's fine conception of the change of scene which meets the eyes of one who had slept through an age. As the concourse gathered around him, he could see here and there a countenance with which he was once familiar—though time had furrowed the full cheek and age had blanched the dark locks upon which he used to look. This number, however, was so comparatively small, that he could not address them as his audience. '*Your fathers—were my associates and my friends,*' was the expression prompted by the scene. His speech on that occasion was marked with much feeling and patriotic sentiment. It was delivered in that slow, distinct and impressive manner, which enabled every one to understand and remember. Addressing the presiding officer of the meeting, (Hon. I. Bartlett,) he said:

"I hardly know whether personal or political friends in any other part of the country, could at this time have induced me, even briefly, to address them in a public manner. I have deemed it a duty incumbent on me to decline addressing public assemblies; for the business of popular addresses seems to devolve more justly upon younger men who are coming forward among us, and on whom the responsibility of sustaining the purity of our political institutions must rest. Nevertheless, visiting as I do the town in which I spent many years of the most active portion of my life, when your fathers, occupying the places you now fill, were my associates and friends, I should do injustice to my feelings not to respond to the call that has now been made."

Mr. Webster here went into an extensive discussion of the politics of the day. He closed his address with this remark:

"The future is not within our power—no one knows what is assigned to his lot: human life is uncertain, human destiny is unknown—but we have a country which will be spared for future generations: human life is short, but institutions of government should be made to endure: the creatures of to-day may be of but small importance—but this Constitution of the greatest Republic in the world, extending over so vast a territory, from its effects on the prosperity and happiness of untold generations, has a value incalculable. However it may happen to us—however it may be with the events which are beyond our control—let us see to it that the basis of our free institutions, so long as left in our keeping, is sacredly preserved."

Mr. Webster here sat down, amidst the most hearty cheering.

On the evening of the day, Mr. Webster met at the Cameneum those of his old townsmen, their wives, their sons, and their daughters, who wished a social introduction. Here he stood, not as the statesman or the politician, but as the citizen, the neighbor, the old townsman, who after a long absence had returned to greet his friends. The scene was one of touching interest. The house was well filled. Much of the life which animated the meeting could not number in years his absence. Here and there the bright visage which met his eye reminded him of his fond and beautiful daughter, the first here to greet him as a father, who though long reposing in the tomb, was never buried from his thoughts. Here, too, were some of the intimate associates of the bosom companion of his early life, and the associations which arose from this circumstance were not among the least vivid in his recollection. In the senate-chamber he could contend with and unquailingly overcome the most powerful opponent; but no truly great man is so powerful as to overcome the tender sympathies of the heart. In one portion of his short and feeling address he said,—"The nine years of the most active portion of my life spent here, are treasured in my heart with my dearest, my most enduring recollections." It required not words to interpret what was passing in his mind; tears trickled down his cheek and checked his utterance. The imagination of the audience needed not much effort to see passing before him the long procession of his old associates in his various relations in society, who were now resuscitated. After a momentary pause, he went on, expressing in the most feeling manner his warm attachment to the institutions of his native State, and his gratitude for the good feelings which had ever been manifested toward him by our citizens.

After a social hour was spent in receiving and reciprocating the courtesies of those present, Mr. Webster retired amidst the cheers of the audience. This was Mr. Webster's last visit to Portsmouth; and the recollection of it should be preserved.

---

## RAMBLE LXVII.

Stoodley's hotel—Masonic hall and ball room—Etiquette of the last century.

PREVIOUS to the Revolution, there was a hotel kept by Col. James Stoodley in the house afterwards the mansion of his son-in-law, the Hon. Elijah Hall, opposite the Post Office in Daniel street. Mr. Hall married Elizabeth Stoodley. William Stoodley, her brother, married a sister of the late Capt. John McClintock. Capt. Nathaniel Stoodley, of the revenue service, was William Stoodley's son.

The third story of that house was thrown into an arched hall, and used for masonic purposes, as well as for public dancing parties, before the Assembly House in Vaughan street was erected. Here might be seen Col. Michael Wentworth in all his glory, as well as the leading bucks of the day, with the belles of the town, engaged in the mazy dance, and quenching their thirst at the liberal punch bowl. Merry days were those ; but we would not raise the curtain which would disclose the unwritten history of some of the popular follies which were the characteristics of those times. Suffice it to say, that however much imperfection reigns, the moral standard is much higher now than it was in high life in Portsmouth, in the last century. This remark, however, has no special application to this respectable locality.

Few of those who daily spend a half hour around the Post Office for the opening mail, now ever cast a glance at the once leading hotel of Portsmouth, or look to those windows of the yet spacious attic for the bright eyes which used to peer out there,—those of the beautiful lady of John Hancock among them,—or listen for the sound of the violin, which now unstrung is laid aside, silent as all those who once were moved by its stirring touches.

The violin was sometimes accompanied by the tambourine; and doubtless here, as afterwards at the orchestra of the Vaughan-street Assembly Rooms, the gallant Colonel Michael Wentworth might be seen in his red coat, embroidered long vest and small clothes, directing the dance, and industriously plying the bow of his own favorite violin. Assemblies in those days were not quite so republican as they have become in later years. Etiquette was so strongly adhered to, that no man could be admitted without the proper dancing dress. Small clothes only were admissible. An officer of some standing in the army appeared in his full costume, but was denied the privilege of the ball room because he wore pantaloons. In that attic hall might be seen, what five years ago would have been esteemed a much greater curiosity than at present—the belles with *hoops*. Who knows but the next change of fashion may make us familiar with the full dress small clothes, and full bottomed wigs ; and as to hats, why they only need their broad brims of the present day tied up in a triangle to restore the style of our great grandsires.

In the year 1761 there was a house occupied by Mr. Stoodley, of similar construction, burnt on the same spot. The present house was soon after put in its place, and was continued for many years as a tavern, noted in the almanac for a dozen years as the stopping place for travellers in journeying from Boston for Maine.

When Mr. Stoodley died we know not. In 1785 his widow had married Mr. McHurd, who continued the house for boarders. Not long after it came into the possession of Hon. Elijah Hall, who here spent his latter years. The house sets far into the street, but until within a few years it had a yard fenced in front.

## RAMBLE LXVIII.

Decorations of Market Square—The Packer house—Deacon Penhallow—The Langdon and Thompson houses—Great elm—The old man's sketch—Sandemanian church—Brimstone hill.

Market Square is the grand centre of attraction for epicures, and the diverging spot for a walk to either point of the compass. The green trees now so thrifty on the Square have an enlivening effect. In the landscape, they add much to the beauty of the new church, and to the good architecture of the Piscataqua Exchange Bank opposite, and the Rockingham Bank, which eclipses every business building on the Square. It is raised sixteen feet higher than the other exchange buildings. The second story has spacious rooms for public offices—the third is an Odd Fellow's Hall. It has arched iron window frames, and the whole building is covered with mastic. The first building of the kind in Portsmouth. The new Custom House also stands forth in much beauty—but its elevation above the surrounding buildings has a rather depressing effect upon those in the neighborhood.

As we pass from Market Square down Pleasant street, we meet with various sites of local interest. Many remember the appearance before the fire of 1813 of the spot on which is now Ex-Mayor Jenness's residence. In front, on Pleasant street, was a stone wall higher than the present iron fence, and on that wall an open fence. There were many stone steps to pass over before the front door was reached. The house was of two stories, of a dark color, and the whole of the premises had more the appearance of a castle than of a common dwelling. More than a century ago, in 1735, and how much earlier we know not, the Packer family owned and occupied these premises. Here High Sheriff Thomas Packer lived in 1768, when he executed Ruth Blay—and in front of these premises that night the effigy was displayed.

Mrs. Packer was fond of making extensions to her domicil, and therefore, it is said, when her husband was absent from home on any long journey, he would find some addition to the house on his return. The house was thus so enlarged that it became desirable for a public house. Sheriff Packer died in 1771. The family soon after vacated the premises, as we find that in the time of the Revolution it was the family residence of Hon. John Langdon. When he vacated it, the widow Purcell removed from her family residence, (the house now occupied by Samuel Lord, Middle street,) and here opened a boarding house. Capt. Purcell had seven daughters; one became the wife of Capt. Thomas Manning, another the wife of Major William Gardner. He also had two sons. Only one of the nine "who filled that house with glee," is now living. In 1786, Col. William Brewster, who occupied the Bell Tavern, changed residences with Mrs. Purcell, and here Col. Brewster opened a genteel boarding house. In 1789, President Washington was quartered at this house, during the four days he remained in Portsmouth. It was afterwards occupied by John Greenleaf. At the time it was burnt in 1813, that good schoolmaster, Deacon Enoch M. Clark, who married Mr. Greenleaf's only daughter Mary, was the occupant. Goodness, more than learning, was the requisite for schoolmasters in those days. Deacon Clark was the master of the school in School street for many years, had frequently a hundred scholars, but had never himself studied the English grammar! The "three R's" were all he was able to manage, reading, writing and arithmetic. There was one other "ah!" sometimes brought out by way of respiration, when the double-headed ferrule or the cowhide were brought into free use. But early recollections are taking us into a wrong track.

In the house on the corner south, resided the good Deacon Samuel Penhallow and his prim lady. The shop in front had a variety of goods such as the public needed. It was here that Rev. Dr. Buckminster boarded when he commenced his ministry in 1779. Mrs. Lee, a daughter of Rev. Dr. Buckminster, in a graphic sketch of the inmates of this house, presents a picture of life in the last century. She says:

"They dwelt in a small, plain house, one little parlor of ten feet square containing all that was requisite for their comfort. The deacon himself tended a little shop in front of the parlor, filled with needles, pins, tape, quality binding, snuff,—that most common luxury,—with a small pair of scales to weigh a copper's worth. The deacon always wore a full suit of very light drab broadcloth, with white cotton stockings and silver knee buckles, and a full bottomed white horse-hair wig, always powdered. His exquisitely plaited ruffles were turned back while he was in the shop, under white sleeves or cuffs, and a white linen apron preserved the purity of the fine drab broadcloth. His solitary mate sat in the little three-cornered parlor, whose fireplace was an afterthought, and built in the corner; the bricks forming successive little shelves, where various small things could be kept warm. There she sat all day at her round table with needle-work, dressed in an old fashioned brocade, with an exquisite lawn handkerchief folded over it, and environed with a scrupulous neatness, where the litter of children's sports never came."

As we pass down Pleasant street, the prospect which opens from the front of Rev. Dr. Burroughs' mansion (which Washington regarded the handsomest in Portsmouth,) over his field to the pond, and the green banks and the thrifty elms on the opposite shore, are inviting to the eye, and create a desire to see *that* bridge which will one day make the Elwyn fields the most desirable building lots in the city.

On the premises of the late Dr. Dwight, adjoining the sidewalk, is one of the largest elms in the city. Its girt is about sixteen feet, and its wide-spread limbs give the wayfarer a refreshing shade on a sultry day. It is a memorial of times gone by. As we stand by it, an aged man approaches, whose birth-place was near that spot more than ninety years ago. "Perhaps, Mr. Fernald, you can recollect when this tree was young?" He raised his head as the thought of former years came over him, and refreshing his recollection replied:

"No I do not: it was about a foot in diameter when I first knew it. Then there were no houses between those on the corners of Pitt and of Gates streets. In this gully you see under the tree extending east, the water at every high tide flowed from the river to the mill pond. Canoe bridge, near the dock on Washington street, admitted small boats from the river to pass, at high tide, under this tree to the pond. This left us below on an island, which at times horses would have to wade through two feet of water to approach. There was a foot-path made of large stones where the walk now is, which could be well crossed by day, but was a dangerous road by night. These two houses (Rev. Dr. Burroughs' and Dr. Dwight's) were built in 1784, the year after the peace. One was built by Gov. John Langdon, the other by a ship-master I sailed with. I know it well, for I aided by holding the surveyor's lines in laying out the ground for the foundations of Capt. Thomas Thompson's house and barn, which were afterwards Dr. Dwight's. Then the Sandemanian meeting-house was standing on the spot where Dr. Dwight's barn now stands, and was taken down to give the barn place. It was a story and a half building, occupying half as much again ground as the barn now does. It had no pews, but was provided with seats. I have heard Noah Parker preach there, and seen J. M. Sewall scattering the hymns of his own composition among the audience. The meeting-house was built in Vaughan street for this society, when this house was taken down."

The old gentleman stated that he well remembered the erection of Rev. Dr. Langdon's house, (now occupied by the family of John K. Pickering,) and Col. Oliver Whipple's, (on the spot where William Petigrew's house now stands.) All the houses were alike, of two stories, with gambrel roofs, and were built by Hopestill March of Dover, a mulatto. At that time the land on which Joseph Haven afterwards erected his mansion was his father's orchard. "But O!" said the venerable man, "what a change there has been since the Revolution!" The old gentleman passed on his way, and we on our ramble.

From what the name of "Brimstone Hill" was derived, we have never been informed. There is nothing volcanic about that sound primeval granite, which has been undisturbed since the creation, and promises to remain. Sometime early in the present century that open rough lot was purchased for six or seven hundred dollars. The sum paid for it at compound interest would amount now to ten thousand dollars. There are many other spots in the city eating up their value, which would long ago have been a source of profit if brought into use.

But where is the Pleasant Street Church? Like the Sandemanian, that too has disappeared! Those familiar walls, that tower, the large arched windows, the wide doors, the desk, the pews, the orchestra, have all within a few months departed! Of all that made it a temple, not one stone is left upon another! Another ramble has touched upon its history.

---

## RAMBLE LXIX.

Rev. Dr. Haven—Settlement and residence—Manufactures—Revolutionary anecdotes.

PASSING down Pleasant to Gates street, we come to the former residence of Rev. Dr. SAMUEL HAVEN, who came to Portsmouth in 1752, from Framingham, Mass., and was settled over the South church. He soon selected a site for his residence, and probably before his marriage in 1763 erected the house on Pleasant street, at the head of Gates street, now occupied by the family of his grandson, the late Nathaniel A. Haven, Jr. having always remained in the family. About thirty years after, it was remodeled, and early in the present century it underwent a change, from a two-story gambrel roof to a three-story structure. In all the alterations, several rooms have remained undisturbed. This feature must be as pleasant for keeping in remembrance esteemed ancestral relations, as the wide spread elm in front, in a more open manner, is an agreeable memento of former days—days when the numerous children with which the Doctor was blessed were players around the homestead, and planting those little twigs—a fit family emblem—which in after years imperceptibly became the overhanging trees in front of this Pleasant street residence.

In some letters of Dr. Haven before us, we learn that

he first received an invitation to settle in Medway, Mass. in April, 1751. This he declined, because the call was not unanimous, and because the salary offered was inadequate "to sustain ye dignity or afford me leisure to perform ye duties to which you would call me, which are well-becoming and absolutely incumbent on ye minister of Christ." He also declined a call, made in February, 1752, to settle in Brookline, from a lack of unity in the call. He adds, "nor may it be impertinent just to mention to you the very agreeable union that appears in the vote of a distant church, by which I am invited to labor in another part of Christ's vineyard."

This latter invitation was from the South church in Portsmouth. The salary offered was "Seventy pounds sterling money yearly." This call he accepted. While in his acceptance he regarded their unanimity, peace and love above any other inviting circumstance, "yet I would by *these* represent to you how much I confide in your generosity and christian kindness to afford me some further *assistance* for my comfortable support in your service. And as *wood* will be a very chargeable article in this populous town, so your generous allowance of eight or ten cords annually, or its equivalent in money would be, though to you an inconsiderable expense, yet to me a very valuable kindness."

He was settled May 6, 1752. As the history of his long pastorate is fully given in Rev. Dr. Peabody's sketch of the South church history, we will only give such matters as are not there stated.

How the item of wood in the salary was settled, does not appear; but probably some of the members of the church and parish were influential in causing the vote to be passed which gave him the use of the training field for his horse and cow pasture, which is spoken of in another place.

That it was difficult to raise even the small salary

agreed upon, may be inferred from the fact that at Dr. Haven's decease there was due to him $289.26. His receipts show that his salary was paid in small sums as it could be collected.

In looking over Dr. Haven's early account book, it will be found that he purchased considerable wood, and he often balances his accounts with hay, corn or meal, probably raised in his own garden or field; and in 1783 a shoe bill has often these words recurring, "To your son's shoes, *your upper leather*, or *your leather*;" and then credited by "One bushel and a half of salt," made, probably, at his own salt works.

During the Revolutionary war, Dr. Haven was a genuine "son of liberty," giving the whole weight of his character, influence and exertion to the American cause. When the news of the battle of Lexington reached Portsmouth, he sat up a good part of the night with his family making bullets. And when, in the course of the next year, an alarm was given in the night that the enemy were approaching, he shouldered his fowling piece, and went with his parishioners to share in the toils and dangers to which they might be exposed.

His brother-in-law, Mr. Appleton of Boston, visiting Dr. Haven, they rode to Greenland to see his brother, John Haven, who resided there. On returning home the horse stopped to drink at a brook which then ran across the road, the bits were broken, and losing all command of the animal, they were both thrown into the stream, and the horse there left them. Thoroughly wet, they proceeded to the first house, where dwelt a parishioner of Dr. Haven's, a militia captain. He had no clothes to offer his worthy pastor but his regimentals, and so accoutred in them he walked home, exciting the wonder of all he met, and no less the dismay of his own family, at the fear of sudden mental aberration; but an explanation in due time showed that even the preacher of peace might under peculiar circumstances be justified in assuming the militant armor.

There are some tangible evidences left of the patriotism of the clergymen who espoused the cause of their country in the days of the Revolution. We have some documents which show that while the Rev. Dr. McClintock and his sons were in active service, the father prominent in the battle of Bunker Hill, no less devoted was Dr. Haven in preparing for the manufacture of an article so essential to carry on the warfare. Read the following certificate, signed by two physicians of Portsmouth, given only two months before the Declaration:

"This may certify that we, the subscribers, by the request of the Rev'd Dr. Haven, have examined a quantity of saltpetre made by him, and have weighed off three hundred and eight pounds, which we judge to be sufficiently pure and dry.

"Portsmouth, May 13, 1776. J. BRACKETT,
HALL JACKSON."

That this was not the close of the saltpetre business we have evidence in the following copy of an agreement, made the week after:

"May 18, 1776. Mutually agreed between the Rev'd Dr. Haven and Messieurs Lang and Melcher, yt the said Haven will deliver up to them his salt petre works for space of one month, yt he find one-half of the wood and potash, and all the utensils; yt he find them collectively one-half pint of rum per day, or one pitcher of cyder, and his horse to hale the nitre earth; and that they, said Melcher and Lang, render to said Haven half the produce of said saltpetre.

"N. B. It is understood that said Haven advance what money is necessary for pott ash and wood, to said Lang and Melcher, and take his pay in saltpetre; that he take off all the saltpetre, and pay them at the market price; and likewise that they count one month from said Haven's return from his intended journey."

The place of manufacture was the then vacant lot north of Dr. Haven's residence, afterwards owned by Edward Parry. Earth from beneath the old South church, from the cellar on which Benjamin Akerman afterwards built a house on Islington near Cass street, and from other localities, was taken for the manufacture. Thus while some clergymen took the field in defence of their country, others were quietly, but not less effectively, turning the soil into the means of national defence.

---

## RAMBLE LXX.

Old North church—Rev. Dr. Buckminster—Last service—Pew occupants in 1812—The Vane's appeal.

It was in the old North Church, and the time but a few weeks since, [March 1854,] that the afternoon service was closed with the hymn—"When I can read my title clear," sung in good spirit by the choir.

The deep sentiment no doubt was felt by many of those in attendance; but with some it had also the effect of bringing back the recollections of former years,—recollections which rise unbidden now that the walls of the old Church are so soon to be prostrated, and in their fall close from the view all that is left of the cherished associations of by-gone years.

It was to 1812 that we were carried back. Again the heavy pulpit with its sounding board, appeared on the west side of the church; (it was a meeting house then;) gallery above gallery again appeared, and the long spiral rod was extended from the chandelier to the almost dizzy height of the blue ceiling. The pews of the house again were divided off into their varied shapes and sizes. The place of the organ and its pipes was filled by human organs, and the place of the stoves and their pipes was a blank, for neither were permitted there. There were three porches for entrance—on the north, south, and east. The latter opened to the broad aisle; and here the reverend pastor, Dr. Buckminster, always entered, decked in his canonicals, his robe and bands,—his tri-cornered hat in hand. He was the object of veneration for man and boy, maid and matron; none looked lightly upon him; all felt some personal relation to him, for scarcely one of his parish could not either say he officiated at my wedding or at my baptism.

It was at that season, the last of May, when nature was in its liveliest attire without, that the venerable and dignified pastor entered for the last time the house, and that pulpit which he had regularly filled for thirty-three years. There were evident signs of indisposition resting upon him, yet he went through the services in his accustomed fervent manner, and the reading of the closing hymn seemed a foreboding utterance of those great events which were soon to await him. The few now alive of those who heard, are witnesses to the deep feeling with which he read,

"When I can read my title clear,
To mansions in the skies;
I'll bid farewell to every fear,
And wipe my weeping eyes."

Nor will they soon forget the scene which another month presented, when the pulpit, the chandelier and the galleries were draped in black, and the deep feeling with which Rev. Dr. Parker uttered the sentiments of his own heart and those of the parishioners, on the loss of one who had enjoyed their mutual estimation. Many weeks did that drapery remain, but much longer did the people mourn their loss. He was the last pastor who has been called home. The four pastors who have since been settled, Messrs. Putnam, Holt, Clark and Moore, are now [in 1854] all living—showing but one death in a pastorate of seventy-five years.*

* Rev. Edwin Holt died at Madison, Indiana, June 12, 1854, soon after this was written.

But as we cast our eyes around the church "as it was," and in imagination retrace the aisles and glance at the pews, how few of the persons who were present in 1812, or even of their families, are now to be found here. There are some interesting reminiscences of that day which should be recorded before they forever pass from remembrance.

The pulpit was on the centre of the west side of the house. We pass from it on the right and glance at the wall pews. First is that of Hon. William Whipple, a signer of the declaration of independence, which his widow then occupied. Washington and James Monroe have been seated here. Next that of Hon. Hunking Penhallow, for many years State Councillor. Hon. Isaac Waldron's came next; then Joseph Clark's; and in the south-west corner was Col. Eben Thompson's. The next on the south side was occupied by the venerable John McClintock, who looked to our young eyes like an old man then; but a further pilgrimage of forty-five years was then in store for him. Then came the pew of Madam Adams, which her son Timothy Farrar occupied. Then followed the pews of Jacob Cutter, James Rundlett and Daniel Webster. That of the latter distinguished statesman occupied the spot where the pulpit afterwards stood. Next was the pew of Mrs. Sargeant, then that of Colonel Joseph Whipple, and the spacious pew in the south-east corner was occupied by Gov. John Langdon. The next four on the east side were occupied by Nathaniel Dean, Capt. George F. Blunt, Capt. Nathaniel Folsom and Col. William Brewster. Passing the entrance to the middle aisle the other wall pews on the east side were occupied by the families of Jacob Sheafe, William Hill, Daniel R. Rogers and Joseph Akerman.

Rev. Israel W. Putnam, D. D., died at Middleborough, Mass. Rev. Rufus W. Clark is settled at Albany, N. Y. Rev. Henry D. Moore removed to Portland, Me. Rev. Lyman Whiting was installed here Nov. 1, 1855, and in Dec. 1858, asked dismission, and removed to Brooklyn, N. Y.

A double pew in the north-east corner was occupied by Hon. John Goddard. Capt. William Rice and Peyton R. Freeman occupied the two next, on the north side. After passing the entrance by the bell porch, they were occupied by John Peirce, Stephen Pearse, Elisha Hill, James Winkley, Richard Hart and Oliver Briard. Richard Tibbets and Thomas G. Berry occupied the pew in the north-west corner; and the several pews extending thence to the pulpit were occupied by William Garland, Misses Slade, Madam Treadwell and Daniel Austin. This completes the circuit of the wall pews.

Entering the middle aisle from the east, we see on our right the pews of Capt. William Furber, Peter Wilson, John P. Lord, Edward Cutts, (his was lined with bright scarlet cloth,) John Langdon, Jr., Benjamin Penhallow, John B. Hill, Portsmouth Female Asylum, and on the corner in front of the pulpit, was Edward Parry's. Following the aisle around north to the starting point, we find those of Isaac Smith, Langley Boardman, John F. Parrott, Aaron Lakeman, Benjamin Akerman, John Hill, Robert Yeaton, Sarah Gregory, Jeremiah Dennett, James Hill and Simeon Stiles. In the centre of the northern pit pews were those of Enoch M. Clark, Mrs. Greenleaf, John Bowles, Amos Tappan, Nathaniel T. Moulton, J. Plumer Dennett, Ammi R. Hall and Daniel Pinkham.

Beginning again at the east entrance of the middle aisle, we pass around the south pit pews occupied as follows:—by John Penhallow, Rev. Dr. Buckminster's family, John Melcher, William and Theodore Chase, Edward J. Long, Henry Ladd, Samuel Chauncy, William Vaughan, the sexton, Mr. McIntire, Charles Peirce, John Salter, Mrs. Spence, Job Harris, Elisha Whidden, John Gouch, Tobias Walker, William Neil, Josiah Folsom, Hannah Leigh. In the centre of these were the pews of Joseph Bass, Nathaniel Fernald, R. Cutts Shannon, Nathaniel Brown and Samuel Brewster. The latter pew was regularly occupied by the same family from the erection of the house in 1712 to the change of 1837.

The gallery pews were also taken up by old standard parishioners. Among these we recollect the pews of John March, Daniel Davis, George Fernald, Nathaniel Jackson, John Nelson, John Staples, William Whidden, William Furber, Robert Holmes, Ebenezer Rowe, Nathaniel Dennett, Timothy Ham, Robert Ham, Barnet Akerman, George Tetherly, William Moses, Mark Adams, George Walker, George Hart, Nehemiah Green, Thomas Peirce, John Reding, sen., Timothy Ham, jr., and Samuel Akerman.

Among the regular occupants of pews in the gallery was Richard Fitzgerald. He once said to us that his parents told him that he first went to meeting with them in April, 1774. He was present on the day when the services were last performed in the church, in April, 1854, in his gallery seat, from which he was scarcely ever absent of a Sabbath,—thus completing eighty years' attendance.

There were but few regular occupants of the upper gallery except the inmates of the almshouse, and a full representation from all the colored population of Portsmouth.

The three deacons, Amos Tappan, Job Harris and A. R. Hall, took their seats in front of the pulpit, facing the audience. No boy smiled when he passed a deacon in those days. A fixture, almost as stationary as the minister, was the sexton, William Vaughan. For twenty-five years he was in regular attendance in that capacity. The heavy bell he could manage like a plaything, while some men of double his strength could with difficulty set it. Order was a requisite he could never dispense with, and if boys were seen to behave rudely in meeting, the sharp countenance of the old gentleman was upon them, and if not at once quiet, his firm hand was found marching them to the pulpit stairs.

There rise before us such a host of early recollections of the spirits of the past, that we must break short our story that they may be quietly allayed. It is not strange that the contemplated demolition of the only thing on earth in which they held a common property should have disturbed their repose. But old things must pass away and all things become new.

When the old North church was built in 1712, it was symmetrical in form, the steeple being in the centre of the front. An enlargement on the west side was afterwards made. The Vane bore the date of 1732, when it was put up. It was not gilded until 1796. When destined to come down in 1854, the Vane is thus personified, to enable it to tell its story. Hardened by long exposure, tenacious of life to the last, the man of the spire whirls around with every breeze. He sees in the garden a few rods to the north-west, an aged oak of two centuries, which is the only visible object older than himself. Listen to his appeal.

I can't come down—I can't come down!
Call loudly as you may!
A century and a third I've stood,
Another I must stay.

Long have I watched the changing scene,
As every point I've faced,
And witnessed generations rise,
Which others have displaced.

The points of steel which o'er me rise,
Have branched since I perched here—
For Franklin then was but a boy,
Who gave the lightning gear.

The day when Cook exploring sailed
I faced the eastern breeze;
Stationed at home, I turned my head
To the far western seas.

I've stood while isles of savage men
Grew harmless as the dove;
And spears and battle axes turned
To purposes of love.

I looked on when those noble elms
Upon my east first sprung,
And heard where now a factory stands,
The ship-yard's busy hum.

When tumult filled the anxious throng,
I found on every side
The constant breezes fanned a flame,
And freedom's fire supplied.

*William and Mary's* fort I've oft
Through storms kept full in view—
*Queen's Chapel* in the snow squalls faced,
And west—looked *King street* through.

*Fort Constitution* now takes place
To meet my south-east glance;
The shrill north-easters from *St. John's*
Up *Congress street* advance.

In peace I once felt truly vain—
For 'neath my shadow stood
The man whom all the people loved,
George Washington the good!

I've seen—oh, may I ne'er again!
  The flames thrice round me spread,
And hundreds of familiar homes
  Turned to a light ash-bed.

But why recount the sights I've seen!
  You'll say I'm getting old—
I'll quit my tale, long though it be,
  And leave it half untold.

The fame of Rogers, Fitch, and Stiles,
  And Buckminster—all true;
And later men, whom all do know,
  Come passing in review.

Their sainted souls, and hearers now—
  Your fathers—where are they?
The temple of their love still stands—
  Its mem'ries cheer your way.

Till that old oak, among whose boughs
  The sun my first shade cast,
Lays low in dust his vig'rous form,
  A respite I may ask.

This little boon I now must crave—
  (Time's peltings I will scorn)—
*Till coward like I turn my head,*
  *Let me still face the storm.*

## RAMBLE LXXI.

Revolutionary meeting at North church—Resistance against the importation of Tea.

THE old North Church has some political as well as religious reminiscences. Before the Court House was built, all town meetings were held there; and in the times of the Revolution, some public meetings on the affairs of the country. We find the following account of a PORTSMOUTH TEA PARTY, held in that place, not to drink, but to discontinue the use of that beverage at a time when the spirit of the colonies required it. That there was a patriotic feeling in that party, the resolutions show. At a meeting of the freeholders and other inhabitants of the town of Portsmouth, held at the North meeting-house December 16, 1773, for the purpose of consulting and advising upon the most proper and effectual method to prevent the receiving or vending of teas sent out by the East India Company, Samuel Hale was moderator, and the following among other resolutions, were passed:

*Resolved,* That it is the natural right of men, born and inheriting estates in any part of the British empire, to have power of disposing their own property either by themselves or their representatives.

*Resolved*, That the act of the British Parliament, levying a duty on teas, landed in America, payable here, is a tax whereby the property of Americans is taken from them without their consent.

*Resolved*, That every virtuous and public-spirited freeman ought steadily to oppose to the utmost of his ability, every artful attack of the Ministry to enslave the Americans.

*Resolved*, That the power given by Parliament to the East India Company, to send out their teas to the colonies, subjected to the payment of duties on being landed here, is a plain attempt to enforce the Ministerial plan, and a direct attack upon the liberties of America, and that it is an indispensable duty of all true-hearted Americans to render this effort abortive.

*Resolved*, That in case any of the Company's tea shall be brought into this port, in order for sale, we will use every method necessary to prevent its being landed or sold here.

*Resolved*, That whoever shall directly or indirectly promote, or in any way aid or assist in the importation of any of the East India Company's tea, or any teas subject to the payment of a duty here, by an act of the British Parliament, shall be deemed an enemy to America.

*Resolved*, That the proceedings of this meeting be published and sent to every considerable town in this government, and that a committee be appointed to correspond with them, and also with the several committees in the other governments.

Therefore, *Voted*, That Hon. John Sherburne, John Pickering, Esq., George Gains, Jacob Sheafe, Samuel Cutts, Esq., Samuel Hale, Esq., and Capt. John Langdon, or any three of them, be a *Committee*, for the purposes aforesaid.

In the early days of Rev. Dr. Buckminster, before other denominations arose in Portsmouth, the pews in the upper gallery of the North Church were generally occupied. One who attended the meeting when the revolutionary war was in progress, gave us a *pungent* illustration of the spirit of the women of that day. He entered a family pew in the gallery, with some other children, under the charge of his grandmother, to witness the ordination of Mr. Buckminster, in 1779. Some male intruder had entered and taken possession of her usual seat in front. Not heeding her request to remove, she took a ball from her pocket, and taking out a pin of the largest size, deliberately gave one thrust at his arm; in a moment he sprang out of the pew, and she was left undisturbed to her devotions. Such was the spirit of the mother of that distinguished patriot, George Gains, of Revolutionary memory.

---

## RAMBLE LXXII.

Town security against foreign paupers—Orders for strangers to leave—Promptness of town officers—Who built the forts.

The citizens of Portsmouth in old times, although not very aristocratic, were yet very choice in having such men for citizens as would be able to support themselves. The following town records show that emigrants had much more difficulty in obtaining a residence in former times than at the present day:

"1686, July 20. The Selectmen gave a warrant to the Constable to warn John Kelley, Peter Harvie, John Reed, Mis Stocker, before the selectmen to give an account of their being in towne, and for Harvie's entertaining strangers without liberty.

"July 24th. John Kelley being examined for bringing his wife and two children into town without leave, was warned by the Selectmen to give security for saving the town from any charge of himself and wife and children, or to depart. He then promised he would within a week. Peter Harvie being questioned for entertaining his sister and two children, said he would get security speedily. So did Mis Stocker and John Reed the licke.

"July 30. The Selectmen then appointed Goode Chasely that shee should remaine in this town but a fortnight from this day, being no inhabitant.

"Aug. 27. It was ordered that Peter Harvie do no longer entertain his sister and her two children in his house, in penalty of the law for so doing; and that she forthwith repair with her children to Boston from whence she came, or otherwise to be convaied by the constables from town to town till shee come thair.

"Then ordered that John Reed do forthwith hire himself out to service by the year, or otherwise must expect to be put out by the selectmen according to law. Then ordered that Jacob Lavers give security for his two servants the time they reside with him.

"1692, Dec. 29. The selectmen being informed that wido Markwell being in town contrary to law and order, have issued out a warrant to John Snell constable, to warn her to go out of the town to the place from whence she came—also to forewarne them that entertain her, not to entertain her any longer without good security to save the town harmless from all charges that should accrue thereby, on penalty of paying 5s. per month for every month.

"Roger Thomas makeing request to the inhabitants for admission to be an inhabitant in the town, their answer was they would not doe it without he gave good security to save them harmless from all charges—he providing none, the selectmen in behalf of the towne did then warn him forthwith to return to the place from whence he came."

They had a way of securing attention to business by town officers in old times, which might be profitably adopted in the modern:

"May, 1692. It was agreed that every one of the Selectmen are to meet together on the first Thursday of every month—if any selectman shall fail to appear at time and place, unless providentially hindered, shall pay five shillings unless the major part of the selectmen shall see fit to remit the same. The time of meeting is one o'clock—if any come after the hour to be at the mercy of those selectmen there met together how much to be abated."

The records of old times in Portsmouth show who built the early Forts on our coast.

"In 1666, June 19. At a general towne meeting, for the better carrying on of the fortifications at Fort Poynt, it was consented unto and voted, that every dweller and liver in the towne above sixteen years of age, whether house-holder, children, servants or any other residing in the towne, shall and doe here promise to worke at the same one whole weeke betwixt this and the last day of October next ensuing, and shall appeare on such days as they shall have notice given them from time to time untill they have accomplished their severall sayd weekes worke, and to be allowed out of their subscriptions three shillings per day, and to be at the Fort by seven o'clock in the morning and to give over at six in the evening, to begin on the Great Island and so round by Sandy Beach, and thence through the whole towne."

## RAMBLE LXXIII.

Newmarch and Billings' house—Bell tavern—Melcher house—Waldron's—Jenny Stewart's—Mary Martin's—John Francis—The privateer adventure.

JOHN NEWMARCH, merchant, son of Rev. Mr. Newmarch of Kittery, purchased about half of the first meeting-house erected below the South mill, and removed it to the premises on which now stands the lofty three-story brick edifice called Congress Block; where it remained in a state of sound preservation until 1846. At that time, Samuel E. Coues purchased the estate, and the house was sold to Frederick W. Rogers, who took it down, and of the lumber erected a cottage, which is now standing in Jackson street.

Mr. Newmarch occupied his house from the time of his marriage. After his decease, one of his daughters, who was married to Richard Billings, succeeded her father in the proprietorship and occupancy of the homestead. Mr. Billings was a clerk to John Hancock, and his old master used to honor him with a call when he visited Portsmouth. Here Mr. Billings departed this life Dec. 9, 1808, aged 75; and Mary, his wife, Nov. 8, 1815, aged 78. Their only son, John, and his wife, owned the property till 1819, and he died shortly after that time.

During a long series of years, Mr. Billings occupied the southerly corner room of the house as a store, and it was continued by him till the time of his decease. His stock in trade consisted principally of flax, chalk, spinning wheels, corn brooms, tobacoo, Dutch smoking pipes, coffee and tea, (as was indicated on a long white sign board suspended at the door.) He had also beneath the back shelves a few blue kegs of what gave men the *blues*. There was also a goodly quantity of brass cooking utensils; but nothing was so conspicuous and attractive as the pewter ware, which was exposed to the view of every passer-by. Those memorable shining great platters, white and bright as a Spanish dollar, and that variety of Spanish pipes, with stems varying from the length of a finger to that of an arm; the pipes fantastically arranged in those huge plates, then placed on the turn-down window shutter, (which served the office of a shelf on the outer side,) are objects of too memorable attraction to be forgotton by those who were then children, who would gaze in front, first at the loaded mammoth dishes, then at the old gentleman, to see him raise his three-cornered hat to adjust his wig, with one hand, while the other was employed in profusely supplying himself with delicious macaboy. Mr. Billings' gentlemanly affability ever led him to deal out some pleasing past-time expression to his young spectators, and often some happy little joke, which was ever gratefully received. The business part of the building was subsequently occupied many years, and until it was torn down, as a broker's office, by George Manent. Some of the diamond glass windows remained until the building was demolished.

Within a few years the old Bell Tavern has undergone many mutations. The building was erected in 1743, by Paul March, who married a daughter of Mr. John Newmarch, then an occupant of the Billings' house. Mr. March was a merchant, and at times has filled the large yard in the rear of the tavern with hogsheads of rum and molasses. An old lady born in the Gains house, adjoining the Bell Tavern, who died a few years since, stated this as a rich sight a hundred years ago.

The Melcher house, on the corner of Congress and Chestnut streets, facing Vaughan street, was formerly a gambrel two-story house, like that in which the Express office is now kept. It belonged to the Boyd estate. Seventy years ago it required three or four steps to reach the door—the road in that place has been filled that much since. Between 1780 and 1790 it was occupied by Robert Gerrish, and in it was the printing-office in which he printed the New Hampshire Mercury.

Directly east of this house was the bake house of Robert Metlin. Metlin lived to the age of one hundred and fifteen years, and died in 1789. He used to walk to Boston in a day, the distance was then sixty-six miles—buy his flour, put it in a coaster, and then return the third day. This feat was last done when eighty years of age. On the same spot now lives Benjamin Carter, over eighty years of age. He was formerly a baker, and has still in his house the first cracker he made, in 1792.

In 1851, in the process of repairing the two-story wooden dwelling house on the southerly corner of Islington and Parker streets, and next easterly of the brick mansion of the late Robert Rice, a large beam was taken from the building, on which was chalked the name of "Daniell Remark, John Thompson, — Holms, J. Thomas, — Stephens, John Thomas, 1696."

Inquiries have been made of many of the persons most noted for acquaintance with the early history of

Portsmouth, but none impart any information respecting the erection of this building. The above date doubtless shows when the house was erected, and the names of some of the builders.

There was found carefully imbedded in the masonry a three quart stone jug, with a sound cork stopper, containing about a pint of red liquid, of a sweet flavor, but the life of the original spirit which was probably there, when the playful masons sealed it up in the bricks one hundred and fifty-five years ago, had escaped. Around the chimney, under a hearth, several bushels of salt were taken out, which was in a compact state, and retained much of its original strength.

It was formerly owned by a family bearing the name of Stewart; it afterwards belonged to a descendant, and was called "the Jenny Stewart house" for many years. It is situated on a ledge of large extent, which prevented facilities for obtaining water on any part of its garden lot. Its well was consequently made in the street on the side opposite the house, and remained in use as a well until nearly fifty years since; it was then filled up to give a gate passageway for the house now occupied by Cpat. Wm. Parker.

The formation of wells in the public roads of Portsmouth for the convenience of private families, was not uncommon in olden times. About the year 1715, Joseph Brewster, who owned and occupied for boarders the Waldron house on Congress street, had his well before his front door on the opposite side of the street, which remained there for nearly a century. Similar cases were common in the early settlements of Portsmouth. The well opposite the Episcopal chapel, fifty years ago was in the front yard of Abraham Isaacs—the northern side of State (then Buck) street being the south edge of where the covering of the well may now be seen.

There are older houses in Portsmouth, but no one so

aged could be found, in 1843, which had so well preserved its original external appearance as that on the hill in Islington street, occupied by Miss Mary Martin. The land was purchased by her great grandfather, in 1710, and the house was soon after erected. So that it had stood about one hundred and thirty-two years. It was never clapboarded or painted. Its weather-beaten sides stood the rude buffeting of many a tempest, in proof that plain boards will outstand the age of man even without the application of preservatives. The forest was near it when it was reared,—the branch of the river on its front was unobstructed by a bridge,—and at the head of the creek was a grist and a saw mill in operation. On the south-east, the eye could pass unobstructed to the islands in the river; and in nearly the same direction could be seen the only meeting-house in town, which later than that day, it was voted in town meeting, "shall continue the town-meeting house forever!" How have the obstinate descendants of our worthy sires rebelled against their mandates!

Though Anthony street does not come up to the Fifth Avenue houses, it can claim some residents who are as industrious and as happy as those who dwell in palaces, without half the care and anxiety attendant on high life. There are some localities here, too, which have a historic interest. See this two-story dwelling on the east side of the street, numbered four from Middle street. It sits high, is capacious, and although somewhat dilapidated in appearance, bears marks of once having been a desirable residence. Now for its history.

At the early part of the war of 1812, some American vessels managed to carry on trade, although at no small risk of the owners, for even American flags would not always give protection when any cause of suspicion or doubt arose in the minds of the privateersmen. A vessel belonging to Messrs. Nathaniel A. and John Haven of this port, had made a successful voyage, but before reaching home was overhauled by a southern privateer. Not being satisfied with her papers, she was seized as a prize, and the officers taken on board the privateer. The vessel was manned, and ordered for a port in South Carolina or Georgia. Among the crew was a colored man, bright and active, who was retained on board to aid in taking the vessel into port. This man was John Francis. He not only knew every rope in the ship, but he knew also where the treasures below were concealed. Watching his opportunity, he brought from below the gold for which a cargo had been sold, and in the tub on deck, from which the masts were occasionally slushed, he buried it from sight beneath the greasy mixture which was rarely stirred up. He made himself useful, and aided in bringing the vessel into port. On arriving at the wharf he was permitted to leave. He told them he was poor, and asked permission to take that old slush tub, as the grease would raise him a little change for a day or two. The modest request was granted. He might be seen with that old tub on his shoulder, marching on shore, an object of merriment if not of pity. But John cared for neither. He soon put matters in good trim; fifteen thousand dollars in gold were deposited in the bank, and he notified the owners of the vessel that that sum was subject to their order. In due time the whole amount was realized by the owners, and in gratitude for his faithfulness, the Messrs. Haven built this house for John Francis, and here were spent many years of the life of this honest and devoted negro. "Domestic relations" being unfortunate, Francis went to New Orleans, and the last we heard from him he was there in a trusty clerkship. Whether dead or alive, the reward of his honesty is visible to all who pass through Anthony street.

## RAMBLE LXXIV.

Market street—Bow street—Penhallow's garden.—Penhallow family—Theatre.

SIXTY years ago next north of Dearborn's combined shop, house and academy, was the mansion of Judge John Pickering. Connected with the Penhallow mansion, which came next, was a large garden extending back over the land now bearing the name of Penhallow street. The Boyd premises were on the corner of Bow street; next was the residence of Joseph Haven, about in the position of the north corner of Penhallow street; the bookstore of Mr. Sparhawk was next east; then a small range of stores belonging to Daniel Rindge; and a little east of where Gerrish's foundry now is, was the Portsmouth Theatre, a large, two-story building, the eastern side bounded by the Wentworth garden. Around this garden the brick wall was then extended as it has been seen in later years.

There was a theatrical company in Portsmouth near the close of the last century, composed of young men of Portsmouth, with occasional assistance from other places. Their performances were given in the theatre on Bow street. The amateur performers were literary men from twenty to twenty-five years of age. There were no female performers, but the most delicate young men, in flowing robes and curls, personified the ladies. On that spot, before the scenery furnished by a home artist, the gratified audiences of the day would listen to such actors as E. St. Loe Livermore, Charles Cutts, Samuel Elliot, George Long, George W. Prescott, Tilton, Haven, Cutter, Sheafe and others, who in this school fitted themselves for more gracefully discharging the courtesies of after life.

The fire of 1806 destroyed the theatre, with the warehouses around it, as well as that more valuable edifice, the Episcopal church.

From the Episcopal church there was opened on the west a fine and extensive garden prospect, which was preserved, although gradually becoming more limited, for years after. The Wentworth house, the Jaffrey mansion, the residence of Elijah Hall, and the buildings already described, flanked the opposite edges of the picture, while directly south of the church the oldest brick edifice in Portsmouth, the residence of Jonathan Warner, made no unimportant feature in the landscape at the close of the last century.

The mansion owned by John N. Frost, on Market street, was formerly the boarding-house of Mrs. Noah Parker. Directly opposite, where Mr. Payne now keeps, was the store where Benjamin Penhallow commenced business. He one day saw a lady of Gloucester, who stopped at Mrs. Parker's, on her way to Portland. He sought an introduction, and in due time was married to Susan, the daughter of Col. William Pearce of Gloucester. They were visited by a young lady, Miss Harriet Pearce, daughter of David P. of Gloucester—and Hunking Penhallow took her as his helpmeet. When Miss Mary Beach of Gloucester, was afterwards on a visit to Mrs. Hunking Penhallow, she was first seen by Thomas W. Penhallow, who became her husband. This matrimonial alliance with Gloucester made him acquainted with his second wife, who is a half sister of the late Hunking Penhallow's wife. Little did that lady who stopped here for a few hours in her journey, think that that day's results would be a matter of so much interest in so many families, both of Gloucester and Portsmouth.

## RAMBLE LXXV.

Deer street—Why so named—Houses of Newmarch, Collings and Fitch—Christian Shore—Tradition of the Beehive.

Of the collection of old houses on the west side of Market street, the second north of Deer street, built in garrison style, is the house where a lady was once killed by lightning. It was on the second day of June, 1777. Mrs. Catharine Clark, who had been married but one week, was expecting company. In the afternoon, there came up a heavy shower. After the force of the shower had appeared to pass away, she went into a back room, put her head out of the window to observe the clouds, and was instantly killed by a flash of lightning. It is a remarkable circumstance, that this is the only case on record of fatality from lightning within the limits of Portsmouth. In 1782, some Frenchmen were killed by lightning on board of a vessel in our river.

This building on the north of Deer street, near the corner of Market street, was once a public house, with the sign of a *Deer*. This gave the name to the street.

Passing up Deer street, see that old house on the north side. The chimney presents to every passer-by the record of its age, "1705." It was built in that year by John Newmarch. The next house, long the residence of the venerable Richard Hart, was built in 1737, by Capt. John Collings, the great grandfather of Com. J. Collings Long, of the Navy. There is yet in the house some of the original furniture. We have seen there recently a wine bottle stamped "J. Collings, 1736," which has stood the use of over one hundred and twenty years, and is yet as good as new.

That house in which Simeon Stiles recently lived on High street, was the residence of Rev. Jabez Fitch, who preached at the North Church from 1724 to 1746.

Passing a variety of places of historic interest, we find ourselves on Christian-shore, or as now called, North Portsmouth. We cannot learn why it ever received the name of Christian-shore. Previous to the building of the mill-bridge in 1764, there were only three or four houses on that side of the river. There was the Jackson house on the point, the Ham house on Freeman's point, one or two near where the hay scales now are, and the large Dennett house, sometimes called "the beehive," on an elevation west of the old school house. The latter mansion is more than one hundred and forty years old. Of its early days, when the boys from Christian-shore passed round the head of the creek to attend school on the South road,—and of the troubles which arose when the boat was not at hand to pass the river in the evening,—and of the hundred other little incidents which might be brought up, we will say nothing, although tradition is full. We will give only one sketch relating to the "beehive" or Dennett mansion.

One of the ship masters employed by Sir. Wm. Pepperell was Capt. Colby, who married Lydia Waterhouse. More than ninety years ago she became a widow, and afterwards was married to Ephraim Dennett, and resided at the above old mansion on Christian-shore. Years rolled on, and she again found herself a widow. Like a good housewife, in those days when no factories were in operation, she kept her flock of sheep, and attended to the various processes of converting their product into cloth; and her fame extended beyond the limits of the town. Near the house is a good spring which still flows on as of old. It was a time for wool washing. Laying aside the widow's weeds, dressed in a leather apron, a man's broad brim hat, and other apparel to match, she was washing her wool at the spring, when a stranger on horseback approached, and inquired for the residence of the widow Dennett. Nothing daunted, she pointed to the house, directed him to the front door, while she stepped round and entered the back way. He was not long in waiting before the lady of the house in comely apparel appeared. The gentleman introduced himself as John Plummer of Rochester. He had heard of her good reputation, said perhaps it was too soon to come a courting, but would ask the privilege in proper time of proposing himself to her favorable consideration. In due time Judge Plummer came again, and they were married. They lived happily together many years, and their grave stones in Rochester record the ages of each at about ninety years.

Whether he ever inquired who it was he found washing wool at the spring, we have never been informed. If the events at the well where Rebecca was found were of sufficient importance to be perpetuated, there is certainly enough of the primitive simplicity in the meeting at that spring to keep it in lasting remembrance by the descendants of that respectable family. To us, whenever we pass the premises—or are reminded of its history by seeing the elevated old mansion even across the mill-pond, there ever appears the vision of the Judge on his horse, and the industrious widow disguised under her broad-brim and leathern apron.

## RAMBLE LXXVI.

Three generations of trees—Lombardy Poplar—Sycamore—Elm and Maple.

The thrifty trees which line our walks in every direction, some of noble dimensions, we are prone to look upon as stationary, while the lives of the passers-by may be fleeting like their shadows. But the experience of Portsmouth has shown that the durability of most of our ornamental trees scarcely equals that of the age of man.

A century since, a few elms were put out here and there, nearly all of which have been thrifty and are now falling,—prematurely in most cases, from trimming their cumbrous trunks to the ideas of the public taste in the accommodation of our side-walks. It is with great regret that we behold the departure of these giants of a century. The elms once extending from the Market along in front of what are now Exchange Buildings, were very thrifty, affording a continuous shade to the walk and to the dwellings. The fire of 1813 destroyed them. The mournful appearance of their charred limbs among the standing chimnies on the morning after the fire, will not soon be forgotten.

More than twenty years elapsed after the Revolution before there was any systematic effort made for planting ornamental trees in our streets. In 1792 or 1793, Gov. Langdon introduced the first Lombardy poplars, and put them in front of his residence. They were so thrifty and elegant that they became very popular with the public, and not only did they find place in front yards, but the citizens were stirred up to give them place in all of our most public streets. Before six years had expired, rows of them were seen on both sides of Pleasant street, —on the east side from what is now Court street to the old South Church; a row on the south side of Jaffrey (now Court) street, east from the then new mansion of John Peirce; also on Broad (now State) street, east from where the Rockingham house is located; a row nearly the whole extent of Deer street on the north side,—and in front of some of the residences on Islington street. These trees were generally purchased in Boston at a high price, put out with care and well boxed. Portsmouth for some years was indeed a *popular* place, verdant and thrifty.

But beauty soon fades. The trees ran up to an elegant taper for a time; but the frost or the lightning in a few years nipped their tops. Their decapitated trunks, shorn of every vestige of beauty, sending out a seven fold number of new shoots, had more the appearance of the fabled hydra than of the product of Eden. In twenty years they gradually, as by common consent, began to disappear, except in the borders of grave yards, where they seemed left to show the downward progress of beauty.

In their places the more hardy sycamore or button wood were seen springing up in long extended rows in the peaceful thoroughfares of Portsmouth. These for some years were all the rage; the smooth bark, the grateful shade, the lively green, all made the change highly prized. But there is no rose without its thorn. It was found in a few years that the sycamore had other than human lovers. When passed under in the evening, myriads of caterpillars, attached by gossamer cords to the leaves above, would light upon the shoulder or meet directly the face of the traveller. By day they returned again to their verdant retreat, and revelled around the leaves, making such network of them as to put human skill at defiance. The sycamore, thus losing its reputation by its bad company, and then its foliage and life by the like means, in twenty years received sentence of death, which was speedily executed. The French guillotine was scarcely more speedy. Street after street was swept, until hundreds of sycamores with noble and apparently healthy stocks, were corded up as if of no account. And now, with the Lombardy poplar, has the sycamore almost entirely disappeared.

But shade trees the public must have, and past experience has led to more care in the last selection. The elm and the maple have been extensively planted in all our principal streets in the course of the last twenty-five years, by the public spirit of individuals in some cases, but more generally by the Portsmouth Tree Society, of which our late lamented townsman, Samuel R. Cleaves, was the projector, and a most efficient and useful member.

Among the oldest elms now standing is that on Pleasant street, at the head of Gates street, in front of the residence of Mrs. E. W. Haven. Its age is about four score. A young school boy picked up the little twig as he went from his house to Major Hale's school, one morning; he placed it carefully away till school was dismissed at noon, and then planted it on the spot where it now stands. The tree is now of gigantic size, its branches completely over-shadowing the street. He who planted it was more than eighty years among us, and, doubtless, as he looked on its increasing branches year by year, was reminded often of the early associations of its history, as he was when a few years since he related the circumstance to us. That gentleman was the venerable William Haven, son of Rev. Dr. Haven.

## RAMBLE LXXVII.

The three Episcopal churches, of 1638, 1732 and 1808 —Richard Gibson, Arthur Brown, John C. Ogden, Joseph Willard, Charles Burroughs, William A. Hitchcock, rectors.

In the attic of the blacksmith's shop on Bow street, next in front of St. John's church, is the upper half of an arched window, which was prepared for a square frame. The glass is eight by ten, four panes wide. Through this window is thrown some light on the subject of the present ramble.

The first edifice erected for public worship in Portsmouth was an Episcopal church. It was erected prior to the year 1638, on the south-east corner of the twelve acres of glebe land, near where the late Charles Robinson's house now stands. The parsonage house stood near the site of the late John K. Pickering's house. The Rev. Richard Gibson was the first minister, and continued in the office until the year 1642, when he was summoned to Boston to answer to the charge of marrying and baptizing at the Isles of Shoals. The laws of Massachusetts colony forbade the practice of clerical duties by ministers of the Church of England. For these offences, on presenting himself at Boston, he was taken in custody, in which he continued for several days, till at length he made a full acknowledgement of all he was charged with, and submitted himself to the favor of the court. Whereupon, as he was a stranger, and was to depart the country in a few days, he was discharged without any fine or other punishment.

In 1732, a new church was erected nearly on the ground where St. John's church is now standing. It was called Queen's chapel, in honor of Queen Caroline, consort of George II., who gave the books for the altar and pulpit, the plate, and two elegant mahogany chairs, which are still in use every Sabbath, in the chancel, by the rector. The names of many respectable individuals are to be seen among the benefactors of the church. Doctor Benjamin Franklin was one of them, and a proprietor.

The Rev. Arthur Brown was rector of the church until the day of his death, in June, 1773. He was buried under the western entrance of the church. From this time to 1780, only occasional services were had, when the Rev. John Cosens Ogden became their pastor, and continued to the year 1793. The parish was incorporated Feb. 15, 1791, by the name of St. John's church. The Rev. Joseph Willard was ordained by Bishop Provost, in New York, in 1795, as rector of St. John's church. At Easter, 1806, he resigned, and removed to Newark, in New Jersey.

Among many candidates for the vacancy in this church

after the present handsome edifice had been erected in 1808, was Rev. Charles Burroughs, who was invited by the unanimous vote of the parish to be their minister. He was admitted to the order of Deacons by the Rt. Rev. Bishop White, Dec. 10, 1810. On Wednesday, May 20, 1812, he was admitted to the order of Priests by the Rt. Rev. A. V. Griswold, Bishop of the Eastern Diocese. The next day Rev. Mr. Burroughs was inducted rector of St. John's church. This office Rev. Dr. Burroughs filled with much ability until March, 1857, when, after forty-seven years of constant service, he tendered his resignation, which he would not reconsider, although invited by the unanimous vote of the church. The present rector (1859) is Rev. William A. Hitchcock. He was ordained in April, 1858.

The old church, built in 1732, was on the present site. It was of wood, a little smaller than the present church, with a steeple like that on the old South. The belfry was on the western end, with a bell of about six hundred pounds, which was brought from Louisburg at the time of its capture in 1745, and was in that year presented by the officers of the New Hampshire regiment to this church. There were two entrances, the one on the west, the other on the south. The vestry room was under the stairs on the west side. There were two rows of high arched windows, the window frames being square. One of them may now be seen in the front of the attic of the blacksmith's shop on Bow street, above referred to, the only remains of the old edifice within our knowledge. The centre of the wall pews on the north side was raised above the rest, a heavy wooden canopy built over it bore the royal arms, and red plush curtains were festooned around it. A good representation of the canopy may be seen in the portico over the front door of the residence of the late Dr. Dwight, on Pleasant street. Previous to the Revolution this pew was called the Governor's Pew. Two chairs were in it, presented by the Queen for the Governor and his Secretary. After the Revolution these trappings of royalty were taken down, and in the place of the Lion and the Unicorn, a sign in gold letters, in 1790, designated it as the "Wardens' Pew." In 1796, Col. Thompson, who then owned the Dwight house, bought the Wardens' pew, and took down the canopy and trimmings. That canopy was probably used in the erection of the portico of that house.

President Washington, on his visit here in 1789, with his Secretary, Tobias Lear, occupied this pew, and those chairs furnished by the Queen of England for her royal Governors, were filled by men who were ready to place royalty beneath them. Gen. Washington's appearance at church was said by those present to have been truly elegant. He was dressed in a complete suit of black silk velvet—coat, vest and small clothes—with black silk stockings and brilliant shoe buckles, etc., and being an Episcopalian, he joined in all the church services.

The font of St. John's church was taken by Col. John Tufton Mason at the capture of Senegal (in Africa) from the French in 1758, and in 1761 was presented by his daughters, Sarah Catherine and Anna Elizabeth Mason, to St. John's church. It is of Porphyritic marble, of a brownish yellow color, veined, and undoubtedly African. The height from the ground is three feet three inches, the base being twenty inches in length, eleven in width, and five in thickness. The pedestal with mouldings, which support the bowl, is twenty-three inches high. The whole is an oval; the bowl sufficiently large for the immersion of an infant, being thirty-eight and a half inches in length, thirty inches in breadth, and about twelve inches deep. At present, the interior is coated with a white cement, a portion of which divides it in the middle into two parts. On this barrier of cement is fastened a flat brazen cover, which opens from either end to the centre. This cover bears in a Latin inscription the donors' names, etc.

A silver christening basin, presented A. D. 1732, by Queen Caroline, consort of George II., is used for holy baptism, being placed upon the font.

When the church was burnt, on the morning of Dec. 24, 1806, this font, with the communion tables, bible and prayer books, were among the few articles saved, (through the personal effort of the late Alexander Ladd, and another gentleman, who entered the body of the church when on fire,) and are in the present church, which has been elegantly remodeled internally within a few years, and the font has been placed within the chancel rail, in a conspicuous position.

## RAMBLE LXXVIII.

Opening of Middle street—The naming of Congress street—Thomas Manning—Houses on Congress street—Jail history—The keeper's story.

In 1737, George Jaffrey for £70 sold to the town a road three rods wide, which leads from the country road "from Portsmouth up to Islington," running "south-westerly from the front of Dr. Ross's house." This was the opening of Middle street. It appears from his deed and other documents, that the settlement at the head of the creek around the mills then bore the name of *Islington.*

Previous to the Revolution, when the old State House was on what is now the west side of Market Square, the street extending west as far as where the Academy now is, was called *King* street. As above this point there were but few houses, the *road* here commenced—and hence the road to Islington became a continuation from

King street. And since that road has by denser settlement become a street, the old name of John Gilpin's renowned avenue has been continued from the same point.

Portsmouth at the time of the Revolution had many devoted patriots, and among them was an energetic shipmaster, who was a leading spirit of the day. He was the life of Water street, and a hospitable citizen. Where he led, there was ever a host to follow; when he spoke, his words were with effect. Leaving the thousand and one incidents which might go to make up the biography of a true son of liberty, we will refer to only one for our present purpose. The declaration of Independence had just been made, and on the State House steps it had been read with interest and cheered with enthusiasm. Everything pertaining to royalty was then as distasteful as taxed tea. Who is that throwing up his hat in King street near the western steps of the State House?—and why are those cheers by the group around him? It is THOMAS MANNING, and his words are, "*Huzza for Congress street!*" From this moment the street's name was changed, and to this day the great thoroughfare of the city bears the name of Congress street. This one incident, if no other, should embalm the memory of Thomas Manning.

Dr. Ross, above referred to, married a daughter of Gov. George Vaughan, and occupied the March house, on the spot where George Chesley's house now stands. The next east was the Furber house, taken down a few years since. In this house Doct. Nathaniel A. Haven commenced housekeeping. Next east, on Mr. Hackett's site, was the residence of Capt. Thomas Simpson eighty years ago. There was no curb to the well in the rear, and one winter afternoon Mrs. Simpson slipped in as she was drawing water; and was drowned. Alfred W. Haven's house was erected by Dr. William Cutter about forty-seven years ago. The house opposite, owned by

Col. J. W. Peirce, was built by William Sheafe about 1785. He removed from the Wentworth residence on Pleasant street to this house.

Portsmouth Academy was erected in 1809. Two one-story huts were removed to give it place. The mansion of George W. Haven was erected by his father, John Haven, in 1800. The house occupied by Oliver P. Kennard, on the opposite side of the street, is at least 150 years old. It was formerly the Eagle tavern. In 1719, in the time of the great snow storm, there was a child born in this house. The depth of the snow forbade any entrance for the doctor and the nurse except through a chamber window, and thus they entered.

Capt. William Parker's house, fronting Parker street, was built by William Seavey, about 1790. It was proposed at that time to straighten Islington street from the parade to Martin's hill. Col. Wentworth offered all the land needed for $200. The frame of Seavey's house remained several weeks awaiting the town's decision. The town would not act, and so the house was put up, and the bend in the street from the academy to the jail made permanent. It was the residence of John Penhallow after the fire of 1806. Afterwards that of John P. Lord. Before it was built there was but one house between the academy site and Anthony street.

The brick house of Capt. Andrew Hussey, next east of the jail, was built by Joshua Haven, in 1812. The cellar was dug from a solid rock. On this spot was an elevated rock, which for many years gave the name of "Rock pasture" to this vicinity. The house next west of the jail was built by Samuel Brewster in 1795. The house of Ammi R. H. Fernald was built by his father in 1797, and Aaron Lakeman's the same year. At that time the house next west on the north side of the street was Barnet Akerman's, west of Martin's hill.

The Jail was built in 1782; the stone cells about fifty

years after. Before the old jail was burnt in 1781, this site was purchased for a new jail. The eastern half of the lot was bought in 1779 by Major Gains, as commissioner for Rockingham county, of John and Samuel Penhallow, for £2000—then about $400. The name of the first keeper was Barker. The next was Eben. Chadwick, who left there about the year 1800. Then Timothy Gerrish was keeper until 1815. His son Andrew had charge until 1835; Winthrop Pickering until 1837; George W. Towle to 1856; and since that time it has been under the charge of Joseph B. Adams.

About a century ago, when the Portsmouth Jail was kept by Tobias Lakeman, some Quakers were imprisoned to await their trial for some breach of the laws against heresy. He showed them great kindness; he even went so far as to let them go to their homes, on their mere promise to return in season for the trial. They kept their word, and the humane jailor received no detriment. Emboldened by this, he suffered a "gentleman" debtor to depart in like manner on a like promise. He came not back. The debt for which he was arrested was large; and the law stripped the jailor of his property, dismissed him from his office, removed his family from the county house, and made his children penniless. They sought and earned an honest living; but he became insane, quite harmless, but unfitted for doing any business.

And now began his wanderings. He was but the wreck of a man; but this wreck, like that of a noble ship, showed what the man had been. We well recollect his appearance when nearly ninety years of age. Slight and thin, once erect, but now bent a little by age; his gray locks covered with a flexible round hat, whose depending brim shaded and almost hid his face; his apparel old, but neat and trim, worn but not ragged; with a strong staff strongly grasped, and with a step nervous but not feeble, he trod the highway with the air of a gentleman, and made the journey backward and forward between Ipswich (his native place) and Portsmouth, three or four times a year.

He was friendly by nature, and now that he could no longer do friendly acts, he could at least make friendly visits. And so he did. He had lived in Hampton, N. H. —he had relatives in Ipswich, and he had friends all the way—for every Quaker was his friend in particular. At their door he knocked often but never in vain. He needed not to ask for food or shelter; the best of board was good enough, but not too good for him. The men whom he befriended lodged him—their children also rose up and called him blessed.

This simple story needs no moral; the moral is in the story. The good old man loved nature and loved man—he enjoyed the sight of both—and though insane was not unhappy. At last, just as one winter set in, he returned from his usual journey feebler than usual—and when the spring returned the pilgrim was missing from the road—the Friends inquired for him—but the way-worn traveller was at rest.

## RAMBLE LXXIX.

**Gov. Vaughan's residence — North burying-ground — Buildings on Market Square.**

In retracing some of the ground already passed over, we find some matters of historic interest worthy of preservation. That old house on the corner of Deer and Market streets, where Mrs. Chase of late years has kept a boarding-house for sailors, one hundred and sixty years ago was the property and residence of Lieut. Gov. George Vaughan, the predecessor of the first Gov. John

Wentworth. In the year 1702, a deed was given by John and Elizabeth Vaughan of a lot of land to Michael Whidden, between this house and his bakehouse, which was then the next house north of it. George Vaughan was the second son of William Vaughan, mentioned in the will of Richard Cutt as his son-in-law.

At the seige of Louisburg, in 1745, Mr. Cutt, an officer from this section, met with a kinsman from the mother country who bore the name of Cutts. The name was adopted from that date by the families here.

With those who died of the small pox at the time of Col. N. Meserve's decease at Louisburg, in 1758, was Col. John Hart. He was the owner of the land now used as the North burying-ground, and it did not become town property until 1753, little more than a century ago, when Col. Hart sold it to the town for £150, on condition that it should be kept for a burying-ground. There had been some interments previously made there, but the Point-of-Graves had been the principal place of the early interments. One grave stone has been found here of a person who died in 1632.

We neglected to mention in our account of Market square at the time Washington visited Portsmouth in 1789, that on the spot next south of the North church, where Austin's three-story house was afterwards erected, then stood the gambrel-roofed house which is now occupied by Benjamin F. Webster, No. 2 Court street. In this house the first number of the Portsmouth Oracle was printed by Charles Peirce, in 1793.

The residence of John Peirce, a two-story ell house, was on the spot where William Simes's store now stands. The Peirce family resided here about a century, until the erection of the mansion No. 1 Court street by John Peirce, in 1799.

Next east of the Peirce premises on Market Square, sixty years ago, was a one-story shop, occupied by Penhallow & Dame, next was the two-story store and house of John Nelson, then a passage way to the back yard. On the east side of the Athenæum premises stood the large two-story house of John Melcher, whose land extended around the corner into Market street. These buildings were all destroyed in the fire of 1802, which commenced in the New Hampshire bank, on the site of the Piscataqua Exchange, burning the Market house, and extending around to High street and down Market street, including Ladd street.

---

## RAMBLE LXXX.

Peirce family—Sketches of Joshua, Daniel and John.

In 1666, Daniel Peirce of Newbury, Mass., with his son Joshua Peirce, became interested in land in New Jersey. They owned a large part of Perth-Amboy, for which they paid eighty pounds. The son Joshua died in Woodbridge, N. J., in 1670, and Daniel, the father, in Newbury, in 1677. Joshua had one son born in 1670, whose name was Joshua, and was the progenitor of the Peirce family in this town.

Joshua Pierce came to Portsmouth about 1700, and was married to Elizabeth Hall of Greenland. He opened a large retail shop in his residence on the corner of Market square and High street, and here did much business in this way; he also carried on a very considerable fishery at Canso, was concerned in navigation, owned several ships, and did a great deal of business. He brought up a large family in credit, and left a good estate. He was a very active, industrious man, and in the course of his life held the several offices of town clerk, parish clerk, proprietors of Portsmouth commons' clerk, selectman, representative, and for many years before his death was a member of his majesty's council, and also recorder of deeds for the province; all which offices he held with credit to himself and gave general satisfaction. He was respected as an honest and useful man. He died about the year 1743, and left four sons and five daughters, viz.: Joseph, Joshua, Daniel and Nathaniel, Sarah Winslow, afterwards Sargeant, Anna Green, Mary Moore, Elizabeth Osborn and Margaret Green.

His son, Daniel Pierce, was born May 1709, received a liberal education, and had a degree at Harvard College in 1728. Married Anna, daughter of John Rindge, about the year 1743. In the earlier stage of his life he did some business in trade, as appears by his papers, but for this manner of life he had no relish. He was a principal acting magistrate in Portsmouth many years, was appointed recorder of deeds for the province instead of his father, which office he held as long as he lived, and was a member of the king's council for New Hampshire several years. He was a man of very great natural parts as well as acquired abilities, but had no turn for any kind of business that required constant application. He was well versed in history, a great theologist, had considerable knowledge of law, and once studied it with a design to appear at the bar, but he thought the practice of law was inconsistent with the character of an honest man, which was the reason he discontinued his studies.*

* From a file of Ames' Almanac kept by Daniel Peirce we copy the following historical memoranda, entered by him:

1744, June 3. There was a smart shock of an Earthquake; it lasted two minutes.
June 4. War was proclaimed against France.
1745, Jan. 1. The Town Clock was set agoing this day.
Feb. 25. The Rev. Mr. Whitfield came to town and preached for Mr. Shurtleff, and the next day for Mr. Fitch.
Mch. 23. The forces raised in New-Hampshire to go on the expedition against Cape Breton, sailed from Piscataqua. The regiment commanded by Col. Samuel Moore.
July 5. By an express from Boston we have the agreeable news of the surrender of Louisburg confirmed. It was on the 17th June.
Mch. 30. The new bell put up at the Church, which was bought at Louisburg by the officers of the New-Hampshire regiment and presented.
1755, May 8. Eliphaz Dow hanged for murder.
July 12. Portsmouth Work-house raised.
" 14. Hay-Market raised.

He was also a good geographer, had likewise a great mechanical inclination, and worked very ingeniously with his own hands. He was exceedingly fond of company, and was also very severe when he had imbibed prejudice against any person. One who knew him well, said: "I affirm he was the most honest man I ever knew before or since his death. And with all his good qualities he had something in his natural disposition that may be said to have been very obstinate, and was besides rather too arbitrary. He was a man of genius and a truly original character." He died Dec. 5, 1773, and left three children, viz.: Ann (who married Thomas Martin), died in 1811; John, died in 1814; and Joseph, died in 1812, unmarried; he had another son named Joshua, who died very young.

John Peirce, the eldest son of Daniel, who succeeded him in the occupancy of the homestead, was born in 1746. He received his mercantile education in the counting room of Daniel Rindge, and being early entrusted with the charge of the property of his uncle, M. H. Wentworth, and with the management of affairs relating to Mason's patent, he found enough to occupy a large portion of his time. In 1791, and for several successive years, he was an active and efficient member of the State

Mch. 18. At 4 o'clock this morning we were roused by an Earthquake. It came with a roar like thunder and shook terribly. It was immediately repeated, and both shocks held a considerable time, more than two minutes.
Dec. 31. Baptized this year at the South Parish 47. Buried in whole town 85.
1765, Sept. 12. Effigies of a stamp master hung up all day at the hay engine, in the evening carried through the town by the mob and then burnt.
1766, Jan. 9. A grand mob compelled G. Meserve to surrender his commission.
Mch. 14. Barrell's ship drove from the wharf and overset on Waterhouse's Island.
Apr. 14. An Express, which came on purpose, arrived about noon, and brought the agreeable news of the Repeal of the Stamp Act.
1767, Oct. 8. Began paving the street leading from the Parade to Spring Hill.
1768, Sept. 28. Troops arrived in Boston to keep them in order.
1770, July 5. The Trustees of Dartmouth College met again at the Governor's, and concluded to place it at Hanover.
Sept. 24. Mr. Whitfield preached yesterday in the afternoon, and this forenoon in Mr. Haven's meeting-house.
" 25. Mr. Whitfield preached this forenoon at Mr. Langdon's meeting-house to a full audience, from the 15th Luke and 2d verse.
" 30. About noon Edmund Davis brought the shocking news that Mr. Whitfield died this morning at 6 o'clock at Newbury.
Oct. 3. Geo. Meserve, Esq. and family went to Boston to-day in J. Hart's stage coach.
1772, July 14. Went to Long Lane to view a new road to Rye.

Legislature. He was the principal agent in erecting Piscataqua bridge in 1794, and in the construction of the turnpike to Concord. He was Loan Officer during John Adams' administration, and for many years had charge of an insurance office. Always open, honorable and correct in his conduct, and liberal in his charities, he enjoyed the respect and confidence of men of all parties. He died on the 14th of June, 1814. His wife was Mary, daughter of Peter Pearse. Their children were Mark W., who married Margaret Sparhawk; Samuel, who died young; Joshua W., who married Emily Sheafe; Ann R., the wife of Rev. Dr. Burroughs; Mary O., died young; and Daniel H.

---

## RAMBLE LXXXI.

Langdon family—Tobias—Family genealogy—Samuel—Woodbury—John—The Revolutionary services of John Langdon.

As those three lofty trees near Breakfast hill have in past years stood out prominently above the forest, and been landmarks from the ocean, so with a few associates, on the horizon of our local history stands out that devoted patriot, the friend and associate of Washington—JOHN LANGDON—who as President of the first United States Senate, declared the vote of the nation which elected Washington as President and Adams as Vice President of the United States, and administered to them their oaths of office.

At the head of Sagamore creek, a short distance east from Sagamore road, is the spot where once stood the house in which John Langdon was born. The farm is still in the family, owned by his grandson, John Elwyn. The old house of the Langdons, in which lived Capt.

Tobias Langdon, and in which his seven sons and two daughters were born, stood where the little farm house now stands: burnt about 1741. Gov. John Langdon, then a babe, was, it is said, thrown out of a window upon a snow bank. The next house was a good two-story dwelling, nothing at all antique, and in it lived and died his father and mother, John and Mary Langdon. Thomas Elwyn lived there a good deal, and even in the winters. He built a new summer kind of house at the western end of the old one. John Elwyn pulled down the old portion, and let Chandler E. Potter haul to town the newer part, which now stands on State street and is occupied by Dr. E. B. Goodall. Mr. Elwyn then built the present little farm house on the old place, but with a larger and better cellar.

Capt. TOBIAS LANGDON was born on this farm, which came to him from his grandfather. His first commission of ensign is from James II. He died in 1725 aged sixty-five years His wife was Mary Hubbard. They had seven sons and two daughters.

2. *Joseph*, their first son, was born 1694 and died 1767—a ship carpenter—his wife was Mary Banfield. *Samuel*, born in 1699, died at Rye in 1725—a cooper—his wife Hannah Jenness. *William*, died 1770—a tanner—his wife Sarah Partridge. *Mark*, died 1773—a carpenter. *Richard*, a seaman. Tobias—a cooper—his wife Miss Winkley. *John*, born 1708, died 1780—his wife Mary Hall. *Mary*, married George Peirce.

3. The children of Capt. JOSEPH LANGDON were one son and three daughters. *Samuel*, a farmer, born in 1721, and died in 1779—his wife was Hannah Storer of Wells. *Mary*, born 1725, died in 1807—wife of Amos Seavey. *Hannah*, wife of James Whidden. *Elizabeth*, wife of James Seavey.

4. The children of Capt. SAMUEL LANGDON were two sons and five daughters. *Elizabeth* died young. *Mary*, born 1751, died 1836—wife of Joseph White. *Samuel*, born 1753, died 1834—married Lydia Brewster. *Anna*, born 1755, died 1790, wife of James Whidden. *Joseph*, born 1758, died 1824—his wife Patience Pickering. Elizabeth, born 1761, died 1831—wife of Andrew Sherburne. *Hannah*, born 1766, died 1812—wife of Edward Gove.

Capt. Samuel Langdon, and his son Major Samuel Langdon, in December, 1774, were engaged with that band of patriots who removed the stores from the fort at Newcastle. Major Samuel Langdon, on the 22d of May, 1777, took the charge of four teams loaded with gunpowder, to be delivered at Cambridge. In February, 1778, he had charge of two teams from Portsmouth to Valley-Forge, Penn., with clothing for the army, and delivered them at Washington's head quarters.

5. The children of Rev. JOSEPH LANGDON, who preached at Newington twenty years from 1788, were four daughters. *Mary*, born 1791, wife of Amos S. Parsons. *Elizabeth*, born 1795, wife of Samuel Whidden. *Temperance*, born 1797, wife of Joseph L. Seavey *Hannah*, born 1805, died 1839, wife of Capt. Samuel Langdon. [The latter, a son of Samuel and Lydia Langdon, now occupies the homestead at the junction of the Lafayette and South roads.]

3. The children of JOHN LANGDON, who married Mary Hall, were two sons and four daughters. *Woodbury*, *John*, *Mary*, (married Storer, Hill and Mc Cobb,) *Elizabeth* (married Barrell,) *Martha*, (married Barrell, next Simpson, next Gen. James Sullivan,) and *Abigail*, (married Goldthwaite.)

WOODBURY LANGDON was born in 1739. He was a merchant, a member of the old Congress, Judge of the Supreme Court, and a firm patriot, devoted to the cause of his country. His wife was Sarah, daughter of Henry Sherburne. Their children were *Henry S.*, *Sarah*, wife of Robert Harris, *Mary Ann*, *Woodbury*, *Caroline*, wife of Gov. Eustis of Boston, *John*, *Joshua*, *Walter*, *Harriet*, and *Catharine*, wife of Edmund Roberts. In 1781, the house of Woodbury Langdon was burnt on the spot on which he afterwards erected as his residence the spacious edifice now called the Rockingham House. He died in 1805, at the age of sixty-six years.

JOHN LANGDON, born in 1739, on the family farm on Lafayette road, attended Major Hale's school. The distance forbade his going home to dinner, and a corn bread luncheon was his usual repast. After a mercantile education in the counting room of Daniel Rindge, he entered upon a seafaring life, but was driven from it by the Revolutionary troubles. He married the only daughter of John Sherburne, (she was the sister of Judge John S. Sherburne.) They had but one child, Elizabeth, who married Thomas Elwyn. John Langdon early took a decidedly American stand. In another ramble is given some account of his aid in the capture of the fort at Newcastle, and also of his quelling the riot at the Pitt street hotel. In 1775 and 1776 he was a delegate to the general Congress. He also took command of an independent company of Cadets, and was present at Burgoyne's surrender. He served in Rhode Island with a detachment of his company, and was present when Gen. Sullivan brought off the American troops. He was a member and Speaker of the Provincial Legislature in 1776 and 1777. When the news of the fall of Ticonderoga reached Exeter, where the Legislature was then in session, John Langdon, the Speaker seeing the public credit exhausted and his compatriots discouraged rose and said:

"I have a thousand dollars in hard money; I will pledge my plate for three thousand more. I have seventy hogsheads of Tobago rum, which will be sold for the most they will bring. They are at the service of the State. If we succeed in defending our firesides and our homes, I may be remunerated; if we do not, then the property will be of no value to me. Our friend Stark, who so nobly maintained the honor of our State at Bunker Hill, may safely be entrusted with the honor of the enterprise, and we will check the progress of Burgoyne."

It is well known that from this noble offer sprang the gallant little army of Stark's that covered itself with glory at Bennington.

John Langdon was a Judge of the Court of Common Pleas in 1776, but resigned the next year. In 1778, he was agent under Congress for building ships of war, and was Continental agent for supplying materials for the America 74. In 1779, he was President of the New Hampshire Convention for regulating the currency; and from 1777 to 1782, was Speaker of the New Hampshire House of Representatives; in 1780, he was a commissioner to raise men and procure provisions for the army, and June 30, 1783, was again elected delegate to Congress. In 1784 and 1785, he was a member of the New Hampshire Senate; and in the latter year, President of the State. In 1788, he was delegate to the convention which framed the Constitution of the United States. In March, 1788, he was elected Representative in the New Hampshire Legislature, and Speaker in the House, but took the office of Governor, to which he was simultaneously chosen. In November, 1788, he was elected a member of the Senate of the United States, became the first presiding officer of that body, and was re-elected Senator in 1794. Later in life, he was nominated for Vice President, but declined on account of age. From 1801 to 1805 he was Representative in the New Hampshire Legislature; in 1804 and 1805 was Speaker; and from 1805 to 1808, and 1810 and 1811, was Governor. The degree of LL. D. was given him by Dartmouth College in 1805. He died in Portsmouth, Sept. 18, 1819.

Gov. John Langdon was never a man of severe study. In literary, scientific and legal acquirements, or in oratorical powers, he was not a great man. But his deserved popularity arose from a disinterested devotion to the interests of his country—sacrificing his property and risking his life in the cause of liberty. He was a good business man; ever judicious, he looked danger calmly in the face, and generally overcame it. The influence of his example was as powerful as the tongue of eloquence.

In the Association Test of 1776, the name of John Langdon appears three times. One was the father of Gov. John Langdon, and the other a cousin, son of William Langdon.

The mansion on Pleasant street, now the property of Rev. Dr. Burroughs, was built by Gov. Langdon in 1784, and occupied by him until his death, in 1819.

## RAMBLE LXXXII.

Badger's Island—The Seventy-four America—John Paul Jones—Progress of building—Description—Difficulties—Its final history.

A Ramble or two among some of the islands in our harbor before we part with our readers. And first to Badger's, formerly Langdon's Island, where master William Badger built a hundred ships, reserving the hundredth to bear his own name. But all this great fleet has not so much historical interest as the building of one other vessel on that island about eighty years ago.

On the 9th of November, 1776, the American Congress ordered the building or purchase of three ships of seventy-four guns, five of thirty-six, one of eighteen, and one packet. Under this order, the keel of the America was laid soon after at Badger's Island, in our harbor. The island was then owned by John Langdon, who was the agent for supplying material, and it bore his name. The America was, in her time, the heaviest ship that had ever been laid down on the continent for which she was named, and she was, also, the first ship of her class ever built by the Confederated Colonies after their rupture with the mother country; and moreover, the only one of the three seventy-fours authorized that was built, or even begun upon. A year and a half after she was authorized, on the 29th of May, 1778, the Marine Committee reported in favor of making her a two-decker, carrying twenty-eight twenty-four-pounders on the lower battery, and twenty-eight eighteen-pounders on the upper deck—in the whole fifty-six guns. This suggestion appears, however, not to have been adopted, and we learn nothing more about the ship until the 23d of June, 1779, when it was resolved in Congress, "that Robert Morris should be authorized to take measures for speedily launching and equipping for sea the America, then on the stocks at Portsmouth, N. H.;" and on the 26th, John Paul Jones was unanimously elected to command her.

Jones proceeded to Portsmouth about the end of August, and found the America—instead of being ready to be launched, as he had supposed—was not half built; and there was neither timber, iron nor any other material for finishing her. Money would not have procured the necessary articles of equipment and men before winter; but money was wanting; for the Navy Board at Boston had otherwise applied the funds which the Minister of Finance had destined for the America, and he found it impossible to make the necessary advances. The business was, however, begun immediately, and some progress made in construction before winter. It was a service not suited to his impatient temper, and Jones says that the task of inspecting her construction was "the most lingering and disagreeable service he was charged with during the period of the Revolution."

As soon as the enemy had advice that there was a prospect of the America's being finished, various schemes were suggested for her destruction, intelligence of which was sent in cypher to Portsmouth by the Minister of Marine. Jones applied to the government of New Hampshire for a guard to protect the vessel, and the Assembly voted to comply with his demand. None was however furnished, and on the second alarm sent by General Washington, the master builder, Mr. Hackett, and his associate were prevailed upon to mount guard with a party of carpenters by night. For some time Jones paid this guard himself, and took command of it in turn with the master builders. Large whale boats with muffled oars, full of men, came into the river, and passed and re-passed the America at night without daring to land.

When the birth of the Dauphin of France was officially communicated to Congress in the summer of 1782, several of the States celebrated the event with public rejoicings, and Jones seized the opportunity to "testify the pleasure and gratitude"—as he expressed it—"which he really felt." At his private expense he had artillery mounted on board the America. She was decorated with the flags of different nations, displaying in front that of France; fired salutes as often as the forts, and thirteen royal salutes at a toast drunk at a public entertainment, and afterwards continued a *feu de joie* until midnight. When it became dark the vessel was brilliantly illuminated and displayed fire-works, which had a very fine effect, for it was a very dark night. All the inhabitants of the town and its vicinity were assembled on the banks of the river, and testified their admiration by every possible show of applause. On the anniversary of our independence the same year, Jones, who was fond of show, made a similar rejoicing.

The America had only single quarter galleries, and no stern gallery; and both stern and bows were made very strong, so that the men at quarters might be everywhere under good cover. The plan projected for the sculpture, expressed dignity and simplicity. The head was a female figure, crowned with laurels. The right arm was raised, with forefinger pointing to Heaven, as appealing to that high tribunal for the justice of the American cause. On the left arm was a buckler with a blue ground and thirteen silver stars. The legs and feet of the figure were covered here and there with wreaths of smoke to represent the dangers and difficulties of war. On the stern, under the windows of the great cabin, appeared two large figures in bas-relief, representing tyranny and oppression, bound and biting the ground, with the Cap of Liberty on a pole above their heads. On the back part of the starboard quarter gallery was a large figure of Neptune, and on the larboard gallery was a large figure of Mars. Over the great cabin, on the highest part of the stern, was a large medallion, on which was a figure representing Wisdom surrounded by danger, with the bird of Athens over her head. The danger surrounding Wisdom was probably emblematically expressed by flashes of lightning.

The America was fifty feet six inches in extreme breadth, and measured one hundred and eighty-two feet six inches on the upper gun deck. Yet this ship, though the largest of seventy-four guns in the world, had, when her lower battery was sunk, the air of a delicate frigate, and no person at the distance of a mile could have imagined that she had a second battery.

But Jones was not destined to command this beautiful ship, whose construction he had watched and guarded. At the close of the summer of 1782, the Magnifique, a seventy-four gun ship belonging to the French Squadron under the Marquis de Vaudreuil, was lost by accident in the harbor of Boston. Policy, and perhaps equity, rendered it expedient for Congress to present to France their solitary ship-of-the-line, and a resolution to that effect was passed on the 3d of September. Other motives may have had their weight in making this disposition of the America. Thus passed out of their hands the only ship-of-the-line of the Revolution.

This resolution was the more disappointing to Jones as this was the *tenth* command of which he had been deprived in the course of the Revolution. He continued, however, to urge forward the launch with the utmost energy. The difficulties were great. Langdon's Island was small, and between the stern and the opposite shore, Church hill, which was a continued rock, the distance did not exceed one hundred fathoms. From a few feet above the stern, a ledge of rocks projected far into the river, making an angle of twenty degrees with the keel; and from a small bay on the opposite shore, the flood tide continued to run with rapidity directly over this ledge, for more than an hour after it was high water by the shore. It was necessary to launch the ship exactly at high water, and to give her such a motion as would make her pass around the point of the ledges of rock without touching the opposite shore—then a difficult matter. When everything was prepared, Jones stood on the highest part of the prow, or gangway that ascended from the ground to the bow of the ship, a position where he could see her motion, and determine by a signal the instant when it was proper to let go one or both of the anchors that hung at the bows, and slip the end of the cable that depended on the anchor fixed in the ground on the island. The operation succeeded perfectly to his wish, and to the admiration of a large assembly of spectators.

Thus was the America launched, with the flags of allied France and America displayed from the poop. After seeing her safely moored, Jones the same day (Nov. 5, 1782) delivered her to the Chevalier de Martigne, who had commanded the Magnifique. The next morning he set out for Philadelphia. Jones highly commended the perseverance of the master builder, Major Hackett, who had never seen a ship-of-the-line when he drew her plan; and who had no more than *twenty carpenters* at work at any time while her construction was in progress, and says, the workmanship on her was far superior to any before seen in naval architecture. For the main facts in the above account we are indebted to a correspondent of the Boston Journal.

After various adventures and cruising in the French navy, she was captured by the British in Lord Howe's engagement of the 1st of June, 1794. Cooper so says in his Naval History, but some doubt the fact. John Elwyn, who has looked into the history of this famous vessel, says that on the first of June, and in a list of the English Royal Navy in 1799, she comes up with two others after this fashion, from which it looks as if the

English did not bear in mind that she was not a French-built ship. Why they changed her name is that they had already a sixty-four gun ship America; and as the real Impetueux, exactly the counterpart of the America, was burnt at Portsmouth soon after they got in there, they called our Piscataqua ship the Impetueux after her. In this English list we read thus:

"Le Sanspareil of eighty guns, L' Impetueux of eighty guns, Le Pompee of eighty guns; the two first ships were among those taken by Lord Howe in 1794, and the last by Lord Hood at Toulon; they may be considered as the three marine rivals. The stern of the Impetueux is extremely beautiful; it is executed by the French in their best manner. Before she came out of the dock in 1796, the Prince of Wales crest was added to it. She was originally L' Amerique, and was named after the Impetueux that was burnt in Portsmouth harbor."

The Impetueux, under her new name, held the highest possible reputation, and was sometime commanded by Sir Edward Pellew. "She was afloat we believe in the last war, and we have reason to think is now a large fifty gun ship of the Queen's, with her name back again, and is still afloat. She was in the Pacific a few years back, near the same time as the Congress, also built here, and just about her bigness. Be she the same ship through all this," says Mr. Elwyn, "she was an honor to Piscataqua shipwrights and to our coast oak."

## RAMBLE LXXXIII.

River scenery—Peirce's Island—Navy Yard Island—Trefethren's — Shapley's — Salter's — John Salter—The cautious ferryman—Close.

A RAMBLE of an hour from town can find you either on the rough seashore at Newcastle, or at the opposite shore of rock-bound Kittery Point. The scenery on either route is of the most varied, lovely and agreeable kind; and the historic associations of these ancient towns are such as to give them attraction, were they divested of all other.

In passing over Portsmouth bridge, those who know the depth of water and the strength of the current, cannot but admire the skill by which it has been constructed over the Piscataqua, at a place where it is more than a fourth of a mile in width. After nearly forty years' use, rendered by recent improvements stronger than ever, it may now be regarded as permanent. How would the head swim, in looking down the dizzy distance, were all the water to be removed, leaving the traveller elevated between sixty and seventy feet above the ground! Yet he goes over without fear, and without danger, while the great iron horse by his side drags his long train after him, as easily and as safely as the eel glides through the water.

The road from the Portsmouth bridge to the Navy Yard, bordered by well cultivated land, in some parts deeply shaded by trees, and in others well lined with a newly built village, affords a fine variety of scenery. From the tasteful seat of Mr. Traip, by the Whipple cove and ancient garrison house, and by the beautiful summer retreat of Rev. Daniel Austin, to the Point bridge, there is a constant succession of inviting landscapes opening as you advance.

From the elevation a few rods from the road, just before entering upon the Point bridge, is presented the grandest panorama in the vicinity: on the east the winding and green banks of Spruce Creek are traced to a considerable extent; further in the distance Agamenticus stands out with scarcely less importance than the more distant mountains of our own State. As we turn around, Portsmouth, the Navy Yard, the various islands in the harbor, forts Sullivan and Washington, Newcastle, fort Constitution, the several light houses, the Shoals, and the white sails bending to the breeze, sprinkled over the vast blue ocean—altogether present a scene which invites you to look about again and again.

Peirce's island was once the property of Dr. Renald Fernald, one of the first settlers of Portsmouth. We have a deed from Thomas Fernald, son of the Doctor, dated in 1688, conveying what is now Peirce's island and One Tree Island. It commences in this manner:

Know all men by these presents that I, Thomas Fernald of Kittery, in the province of Maine, in New England shipright, being ye eldest lawfull begotten son of Reginald Fernald, doctor, deceased, many good considerations and causes mee thereunto moovinge, and especially in obedience of ye commands of my honoured father and mother at their deceases severally, and ye great and ardent love and natural affectious and respect which I have and bear unto my dearly beloved and loveing sister Sarah, some time the wife of Mr. Allin Loyd, mariner, deceased, and now the wife of Mr. Richard Waterhouse of Portsmouth in ye province of New Hampshire in New England, tanner, have given, granted, etc. unto my said sister Sarah all and whole that part of ye Island commonly known by the term or name of ye Doctor's island, whereon the now dwelling house of ye said Waterhouse standeth, together with a little island near thereunto, and ye land bounded, together with the said little island as followeth, viz: on the one end with some part of ye same island, being at ye narrowest part or place there and commonly known by ye name or terme of ye Mast cove or Bass rock cove, and on the other end near unto which is the aforesaid little island, bounded only with the water leading to that part of Portsmouth aforesaid commonly called Strawbury bank, and one side, together with ye sd little island bounded with ye channel of ye river Piscataqua, and on ye other side with a branch of ye said river leading unto and from that part of said Portsmouth called Little Harbour, which said tract of land or ground, together with all the privileges, properties, conveniences and appurtenances therein, thereon, or thereunto belonging, concerning or any manner or waye appertaining, woods, under woods, rivers, wells or waters, earth, stones, gravel and sands, and fishing, fowling, hunting and hawking, and whatever else is, will or may be profitable or pleasant in or upon my premises, unto my said sister Sarah, her heirs, executors, administrators or assigns forever, etc.

Waterhouse resided on the island, and for many years it bore the family name.

The island on which the Navy Yard is located, containing about sixty acres, was once called Fernald's island.

It was purchased of Capt. William Dennett, by the United States, in 1806, for a Navy yard. The price paid was $5,500. It was a place for drying fish and had but one house upon it.

Next south is a large island, on which fort Sullivan was garrisoned in the war of 1812. It has in late years born the name of Trefethren's island. The Narrows are between this and Peirce's island.

Shapley's Island and Goat Island, (both of which now belong to Thomas E. Oliver of Newcastle,) it is said, were purchased by Reuben Shapley for two hogsheads of Tobago rum. The former contains nine acres, the latter three. On the south side of Shapley's Island, on Frenchman's Point, is the grave yard where those who died belonging to the fleet, when it laid in our harbor, were buried. As the bank washes away, their remains are from time to time disclosed.

There are in Portsmouth harbor more than a dozen other islands of various sizes, adding much to the beauty of the water landscape as viewed from various points. As seen from the Auburn cementery, the most prominent is Salter's island, a handsome swell of land, on which is a house sitting very pleasantly in the basin on the east, near Frame point, where the Newcastle bridge connects with Portsmouth. It was for many years the residence of Capt. John Salter, (the father of the late Capt. John Salter,) who died in 1814, at the age of seventy years.

Capt. Salter was engaged in foreign commerce before the Revolution. He once left this port for England in a vessel in which was a large number of boxes of Spanish dollars. Encountering a storm about Christmas time, he was driven on the rocks at the mouth of the Kennebec river. His vessel was got off some damaged, and he went into a neighboring harbor where he was compelled to remain until March. During all this time he was unable to send a communication to or receive a word from Portsmouth, and no notice of the disaster was received here until the vessel arrived in London. This was not ninety years ago. At that time there was no communication along the coast, except such as was made by vessels. Such a disaster would now be made known to the owners here in six hours by mail, and in as many minutes by telegraph.

One event in the early life of Capt. Salter, although not of much importance, shows his calculating cast when a boy. A stranger of some show and bluster, one day called at Frame point, and, desirous of visiting Newcastle, asked the boy to row him down. Nothing was said about pay, and so the young ferryman, to test his liberality, landed him on Goat island on the way. The man supposing, as the boy wished he should, that he had reached Newcastle, jumped on shore. Bowing to the lad, he said, as he ascended the beach, "I shall pay you when we meet in town some day." The boat was put off speedily. The stranger looking around soon discovered himself the sole inhabitant of the little island, and called, "Young man, come back." The cautious boatman, however, with a "Perhaps we shall meet in town some day," left him, a Robinson Crusoe on his Juan Fernandez.

Here, reader, the Rambler will take leave of you.—His endeavor has been, to present a panorama of six passing generations, fast blending, like dissolving views, into each other. From the devastations of time, enough has been rescued to make up a life-picture, which otherwise, in its detail, would never have been restored. The Rambler has been enabled to introduce those who have accompanied him, to some townsmen and relatives with whom they had little previous acquaintance. They have been found in their original dwellings, their places of business, or houses of worship—and, it is hoped, the introduction will endear us more to those in whose paths, while in life, we are now treading, and whose silent track we are fast following to where we all shall have a better knowledge of each other—where the scenes of the drama of life will pass in review in more vivid colors, and their mysterious impress on eternity be more fully disclosed.

# INDEX OF NAMES.

All the names used in the Rambles are intended to be printed in this index, except the list noted below, to which the reader can easily refer. By all the names, we mean only the general names of families. The same name may occur several times on one page, but only one reference is made.

For a list of Landholders in Portsmouth in 1657, see page 27.

For names of Residents in Portsmouth, Rye and Greenland in 1678, see page 62.

For Pew Occupants in 1693, see page 66.

For Tax Payers in Portsmouth, in 1727, see page 160.

For Association Test, giving names of Citizens in 1776; see page 215.


Abbott, 34 235
Adams, 54 71 77 119 121 122 125 126 221 224 236 269 308 309 328 330 356 362
Addison, 100
Akerman, 48 129 171 185 258 326 328 329 330 355
Alden, 92 94 96
Aldrich, 109
Allcock, 187
Allen, 56 83 132
Amazeen, 87
Ames, 360
Andros, 55
Annable, 133 177
Appleton, 152 165 324
Armit, 299
Atchinclass, 165
Atherton, 145 236
Atkinson, 86 94 95 107 to 112 116 165 183 184 192
Ault, 18
Austin, 35 127 286 329 358 373
Avery, 80
Ayers, 42

Babb, 76
Badger, 288 367
Bailey, 108
Baker, 87
Baldwin, 18
Ball, 248 282
Banfield, 80 252 363
Barclay, 223 224
Barefoot, 86
Barker, 54 356
Barnes, 283
Barrell, 361 364
Barron, 271
Barter, 93
Bartlett, 39 170 172 220 222 313
Bass, 116 124 329
Baxter, 95
Beal, 18
Beach 343
Beard, 35
Beck, 80 208
Belcher, 77 121
Belknap, 55 71 73
Bell, 278
Bennet, 126 221
Benson, 80
Bergen, 132
Berry, 18 41 80 329
Bigelow, 165
Billings, 41 64 258 336 to 338
Blay, 290 to 293 318
Blunt, 89 to 93 266 283 328
Boardman, 198 199 329
Bodge, 117
Bond, 68 70
Bowles, 165 329
Boyd, 133 164 to 168 170 175 178 338 342
Brackett, 18 41 152 248 325
Bradford, 73 159
Brakin, 18
Branhall, 162
Branscomb, 70
Brattle, 37
Brewster, 71 73 74 76 133 162 167 212 255 262 295 to 298 318 328 329 339 355 363
Briard, 329
Briames, 80
Brick, 256
Brooks, 30 88 132
Brown, 104 111 113 117 130 181 329 350
Bruce, 210
Burgoyne, 154 155 277 278 364 365
Buckminster, 54 234 255 262 263 265 319 327 329 332 333
Burroughs, 22 127 320 321 351 362 366
Butler, 304
Bute, 178

Cabot, 60
Camocks, 18
Campbell, 91
Canney, 18
Card, 86
Carlton, 277 278
Carter, 118 338
Cate, 76 125
Chadbourne, 18 242
Chadwick, 356
Chamberlain, 55
Champlain, 16
Champney, 167 258
Chandler, 288
Chase, 92 155 211 329 357
Chasely, 334
Chatherton, 18 41
Chauncy, 240 274 275 280 to 285 329
Chesley, 221 354
Cilley, 259 262
Claggett, 145 179 211 234 to 238 239 291
Clay, 312
Clapp, 231
Clark, 129 284 287 319 327 328 329 344
Clarkson, 188 212 273 to 275
Cleaves, 349
Coe, 18 41
Colby, 345
Collings, 344
Columbus, 9

Cochran, 219 220 222 225
Coffin, 207
Colman, 88
Cook 332
Cooper, 18 371
Copeley, 116 141
Corbett, 34
Cotterill, 24
Cotton, 42 43 80 82 83 108 273 280 289 290
Coues, 132 147 258 336
Cragie, 165
Cranfield, 55 69 86
Crocker, 129
Cromwell, 35 92
Crosby, 124
Crowther, 18 41
Cummings, 34
Cunningham, 168
Currier, 35
Cushing, 105 125 205 207
Custis, 268 272
Cutter, 48 113 137 165 235 258 328 342 354
Cutler, 124
Cutt, 21 24 26 28 29 to 40 55 59 65 79 151 158 165 230 358
Cutts, 130 171 280 288 329 333 342 358

Dalton, 255
Dame, 261 288 359
Daniel, 32 33 79 96 97
Danielson, 97
Davenport, 179
Davis, 87 93 208 221 330 361
Dean, 185 301 328
Dearborn, 207 286 298 to 302 305
Deering, 108
DeMerritt, 221 223
Dennett, 70 71 78 135 162 249 329 330 345 375
Derby, 120 127 272
Doig, 235
Doughty, 34
Dow, 292 360
Downing, 159
Drake, 28
Driscoll, 303
Drown, 52 152 174 220 223 224 225 258 274 276 307
Dushan, 248
Dudley, 56
Dwight, 320 321 351 352

Earle, 162
Edson, 124
Ellins, 18
Elliott, 26 137 342
Elkins, 287
Elwyn, 208 362 to 364 371 372
Emerson, 69 92 93 94
Emery, 30 48 277 278
Eustis, 364
Evans, 85 207 277 278
Everett, 254
Eyre, 272

Fabyan, 50
Farrar, 328
Fenton, 106
Fernald, 18 21 24 41 320 329 330 355 374
Fitch, 77 332 344 360
Fitzgerald, 58 64 247 250 to 253 330
Fletcher, 33 38 162 180 311
Flint, 93
Folsom, 218 328 329
Forbes, 124
Foss, 76 225
Fowle, 132 210 299
Fowler, 285
Francis, 341
Franklin, 143 350
Freeman, 39 83 116 185 329
French, 221
Frost, 87 88 89 90 125 220 343
Fryer, 26 32 60
Furber, 37 91 329 330 354
Furrell, 18

Gage, 198
Gains, 131 133 134 135 136 179 217 225 258 287 333 334 338 356
Gardner, 118 267 307 to 311 318
Garland, 329
Gerrish, 52 87 280 338 342 356
Gerry, 196
Gibbins, 41
Gibbons, 18
Gibson, 350
Gilman, 95 116 255
Goddard, 18 118 167 329
Goe, 18
Goldthwaite 364
Goodall, 38 363
Goodwin, 166
Gorges, 14 18
Gouch, 329
Gove, 363
Graffort, 78 79 80 83 84
Gratton, 124
Grant, 129
Graves, 80
Gray, 177, 181 198 311
Green, 330 360
Greenleaf, 82 83 93 159 207 251 319 329
Greenwood, 147
Gregory, 320
Griffith, 165 200 288
Griswold, 351
Grouard, 304
Gunnison, 93

Hackett, 259 354 368 371
Hadley, 286 287
Haines, 24
Hale, 33 122 227 228 236 276 279 332 333 349 364
Hall, 48 87 115 221 239 315 317 329 330 343 359 363 364
Ham, 14 162 167 170 201 to 205 212 249 330 345
Hammond, 55
Hancock, 102 105 117 196 316 336
Handy, 91 172 287
Hardy, 225
Haselton, 166 170 175
Harrington, 168
Harris, 140 310 329 330 364
Hart, 31 35 129 151 152 165 170 210 235 239 258 329 330 344 358 361
Harvey, 177 334 335
Hatch, 147
Haven, 15 96 118 132 133 145 146 147 152 171 180 227 256 268 290 300 301 321 to 326 340 341 342 349 354 355 361
Hayes, 21 132 278
Henderson, 165
Henley, 272
Herd, 18
Hill, 89 187 240 242 258 328 329 364
Hilton, 32 104 277
Hitchcock, 351
Hoddey, 78
Hodgdon, 277
Holbrook, 188
Holland, 274
Holmes, 76 208 330 338
Holt, 327
Hood, 372
Hooker, 127
Howard, 30
Howe, 371 372
Hubbard, 24 363
Hull, 37 251
Hunking, 34 65
Hunt, 87
Huntress, 129
Hussey, 175 355
Hutchings, 224

Irving, 270
Isaacs, 339

Jackson, 76 162 182 185 212 249 325 330 345
Jaffrey, 43 65 69 76 82 86 117 118 141 165 343 353
James, 18
Janvrin, 52 69
Jefferson, 271 309 310
Jeffries, 118 159
Jenness, 262 291 312 318 363
Jocelyn, 18
Johnson, 18 80 117 172 208
Jones, 18 41 76 132 163 368 to 371
Jose, 31 65

Kaise, 162
Keais, 38 84 124
Kelley, 135 334
Kennard, 355
Kenney, 292
Keyes, 159
King, 108
Kittredge, 118
Knapp, 296
Knight, 18 65 159 287
Knox, 196

Ladd, 21 30 118 132 133 147 151 154 171 180 187 201 233 234 241 to 245 279 283 287 312 329 353
Lafayette, 196
Lake, 34
Lakeman, 329 355 356
Laighton, 292
Lambert, 52
Lamprey, 163
Lamson, 122
Lane, 18 21 50
Lanes, 159
Langdon, 65 74 77 138 139 153 162 165 168 195 197 201 208 219 220 222 225 227 240 243 255 256 257 258 259 262 276 287 318 321 328 329 333 347 361 362 to 366 367
Lander, 41
Lang, 325
Langstaff, 18
Larkin, 117
Laud, 280
Lavers, 335
Lear, 208 209 256 259 266 to 272 279 352
Leavitt, 235
Lee, 319
Leigh, 116 329
Lewis, 26 28
Libbey, 181 259
Light, 162
Lincoln, 268 272
Livermore, 144 to 149 342
Livius, 132 133 166 177
Longfellow, 173
Long, 147 171 181 212 272 275 to 280 329 342 344
Lord, 132 201 240 318 329 355
Lothrop, 296
Louis Phillippe, 197 207
Lovell, 227
Lovet, 80
Lowe, 52
Loyd, 374
Lyman, 165 201
Lynn, 34

Macpheadris, 140 to 143
McClintock, 152 315 325 328
McClure, 277
McCobb, 364
McDonough, 164 165
McHurd, 317
McIntire, 269 329
McMaster, 165
McQuestion, 236
Mackay, 167
Macklin, 64
Mahoney, 185
Maloon, 129

Manent, 337
Manning, 179 188 309 318 354
Mann, 288 299
March, 65 90 128 129 130 207 321 330 338
Marcy, 49
Marden, 273
Markwell, 335
Marsh, 154
Martin, 37 87 132 165 167 177 340 355 361
Martine, 65 207
Martigne, 371
Mason, 10 13 18 to 21 24 32 107 131 132 133 171 180 181 288 352 361
Matthews, 18
Mattone, 31 32
Mather, 71
Mathes, 138 221
Maxwell, 139
Mead, 188 251
Melcher, 167 299 309 325 329 338 359
Meloney, 76
Mendum, 159 163
Meserve, 177 to 181 358 361
Metlin, 338
Millie, 117
Mitchel, 234
Moe, 76
Moffatt, 132 133 151 154 165 287
Montague, 304
Monroe, 328
Moody, 33 37 58 60 64 69 80
Mooney, 277
Moore, 18 283 327 328 360
Morrill, 218
Morris, 367
Morrison, 129 307
Morse, 162
Morgan, 34
Moses, 80 129 178 182 to 188 208 242 330
Mountford, 299
Moulton, 329
Mullen, 278
Mullineaux, 155
Munden, 50
Murray, 274 275
Mussell, 26
Myrick, 166 170 175 176

Neal, 18 129
Neil, 65 329
Nelson, 52 226 330 359
Newmarch, 64 65 178 200 336 338 344
Newt, 18
Nichols, 234 307
Noble, 80 92 125 128 194 298 299
Norry, 288
Norton, 18
Nowell, 130 166

Odiorne, 144 151 152 153 212 287
Odlin, 95
Ogden, 255 262 350
Oliver, 90 91 375
Onion, 76
Osborne, 52 188 360

Packer, 165 291 to 293 318
Palmer, 41
Partridge, 65 68 80 82 363
Parshly, 76
Parsons, 91 274 364
Parker, 117 119 to 127 144 163 171 255 258 262 321 327 339 343 355
Parrott, 139 329
Parke, 163
Parry, 48 284 326 329
Patterson, 52
Paul, 159
Payne, 343
Peabody, 96 201 262 323
Pearne, 165
Pearce, 343
Pearse, 83 84 151 152 258 261 286 287 329 362
Peirce, 83 117 132 151 152 159 171 201 227 236 259 287 307 329 330 347 355 358 359 to 363
Pellew, 372
Pendexter, 181
Pendleton, 24 26 28 32 35
Penhallow, 42 43 80 148 149 163 165 287 288 299 319 328 329 342 343 355 356 358
Pepperell, 88 89 107 223 280 345
Perry, 139
Petigrew, 49 321
Peverly, 18
Phipps, 42 43 80 to 82 84 142
Philbrook, 80
Philbrick, 157
Pickering, 22 26 28 31 41 42 49 to 61 65 68 80 82 83 108 162 165 188 218 to 220 223 to 226 230 235 258 259 276 289 298 321 333 342 350 356 363
Pincomb, 50
Pinkham, 329
Pitman, 103
Plaisted, 42 43 45 65 78 79
Plummer, 135 145 346
Pocahontas, 11
Porter, 147 281 284
Pottle, 195 198 199
Potter, 17 363
Powhatan, 11
Pray, 159
Prescott, 89 279 342
Pring, 9 10
Provost, 350
Prowse, 52
Puddington, 41
Purcell, 100 318
Putnam, 327 328

Quincy, 102

Rackley, 248.
Randall, 85 271
Rand, 18
Raymond, 18
Raynes, 133 166 178
Reding, 175 330
Reed, 334 335
Remark, 338
Rice, 329 338
Rindge, 79 159 165 294 298 301 342 360 361 364
Roberts, 364
Robinson, 49 92 218 302 349
Rogers, 42 44 45 69 93 133 135 234 287 328 332 336
Ross, 51 353 354
Rowland, 240
Rowe, 41 330
Rundlett, 328
Russell, 21 230 to 232
Rust, 124
Rutledge, 196

Salter, 41 329 375 376
Samson, 80
Sanborn, 277
Sargeant, 258 328 360
Scott, 102 129 241
Seavey, 18 26 28 167 355 363 364
Sewall, 122 171 227 261 300 321
Shackford, 74 75 283
Shannon, 329
Shapley, 375
Sheafe, 21 41 51 70 79 86 91 102 105 106 145 146 164 165 171 180 181 208 227 228 259 268 276 287 328 333 342 355 362
Sherburne, 18 24 39 41 52 73 74 80 90 140 158 159 165 to 167 236 249 287 333 363 364
Shillaber, 174 201
Shipway, 33 37
Shores, 188 218 283
Shortridge, 103 249
Shurtleff, 92 to 95 290 360
Sibson, 159
Sigourney, 294
Simes, 91 217 299 358
Simpson, 292 354 364
Sise, 187 200
Skates, 289
Slade, 90 329
Sloper, 51 73 80
Small, 221
Smith, 11 to 15 47 87 114 145 to 147 329
Snell, 65 335
Spalding, 287
Sparhawk, 147 261 342 362
Spencer, 18 221
Spence, 329
Spinney, 48 70 162
St. Clair, 277
Stanley, 119 to 122 125
Stanyan, 50
Stark, 116 154 365
Stavers, 103 108 189 to 195 246 262 266 274 312
Staples, 330
Stephens, 338
Stevens, 92 211
Stewart, 339
Stiles, 329 332 344
Stilson, 165
Stileman, 28 86
Stocker, 334
Stoodley, 165 239 315 to 317
Storer, 137 146 234 243 269 270 363 364
Story, 42 to 45 56 86
Strong, 95 96
Sullivan, 116 147 to 150 197 220 to 222 225 255 256 262 266 364 365
Swaden, 50
Symonds, 18

Taft, 306
Taler, 41
Talleyrand, 207
Tappan, 279 329 330
Tarlton, 50 144
Tetherly, 330
Thacher, 144
Thomas, 335 338
Thompson, 17 188 215 221 222 228 321 328 338 352
Tompson, 233 241 242
Thorn, 181
Tibbetts, 329
Tilton, 188 342
Titcomb, 255 308
Toppan, 121 124
Toscan, 147
Towle, 356
Trail, 152 276
Traip, 373
Treadwell, 45 46 121 133 to 139 153 154 165 185 287 329
Trefethen, 87
Tuckerman, 35
Tufton, 132
Turrell, 88
Twamlin, 35

Underwood, 52 170
Upham, 180 181
Usher, 55

Vaudreuil, 246 370
Vaughan, 18 31 to 33 42 43 65 100 101 126 128 159 329 330 354 357 358

Walden, 159 258
Waldron, 34 40 56 65 102 167 230 232 328 339
Walford, 18
Walker, 68 80 159 166 232 249 329 330
Wall, 18 41
Wallaston, 132

Wallis, 162
Ward, 125
Wardrobe, 147
Warner, 133 140 141 165 211 217 234 to 236 258 343
Warnerton, 18 20
Washington, 105 117 123 197 254 to 272 278 279 286 298 306 308 319 320 328 331 352 358 362 363 368
Waterhouse, 134 135 159 162 345 374
Watts, 126
Weare, 214 225
Webster, 171 180 181 311 to 315 328 356
Weeks, 42 80
Wedgewood, 32
Wendell, 145 234 258 307
Wentworth, 39 79 84 96 to 106 108 110 to 118 123 124 141 145 152 165 170 177 200 205 217 220 222 258 259 266 286 307 315 316 342 343 355 357 361
West, 58
Westbrook, 159
Wheelwright, 60
Whidden, 177 178 181 329 330 363 364
Whipple, 151 to 158 177 211 230 262 287 321 328
White, 76 87 351 363
Whitefield, 360 361
Whiting, 328
Whitney, 130
Wibird, 159 299
Wiggin, 34 132
Wiggins, 23
Wincall, 33
Willard, 350
Willey, 266
Williams, 18 20 34 35 41
Wilson, 34 329
Wingate, 126 255
Winkley, 93 329 363
Winslow, 360
Withers, 18
Wolten, 41
Woodbury, 167

Yeaton, 87 194 284 329

---

*From the North American Review, April*, 1859.

## RAMBLES ABOUT PORTSMOUTH.

Portsmouth, New Hampshire, was the residence, in the last and the preceding century, of many men of mark and families of distinction, and the theatre of not a few events that formed a large part of the history of the times, as well as of numerous incidents and transactions, in themselves of less importance, which yet throw essential light upon that history. It abounds too in ancient sites and dwellings, which have each a story of its own. Mr. Brewster, a native of Portsmouth, and of an old Portsmouth family, has inherited much of this local lore, has made diligent inquiry and research among its still remaining memorials and depositories, and has compiled the results of which he has received, heard and learned, in this singularly rich, entertaining, and instructive volume.

The Penhallow, Cutts, Wentworth, Sherburne, Livermore and Langdon families; the somewhat curious ecclesiastical history of the town; the reminiscences of a peculiarly luxurious and ostentatious series of office-holders under the crown, and of high life in the *quasi* court circle; the characteristic anecdotes attached to well known names; the eccentric personages whose memory yet lingers about their former haunts,—these and other similar themes are given, not by any pre-determined method, but in a series of Chapters or "Rambles," each of which has a unity of its own, representing some single group, or train of events, or series of family portraits. We have thus a volume much more piquant and interesting than a formal history could have been, and at the same time a compend of materials, many of which must else have been irrevocably lost, from which some future author may compile the annals of the town. The work is admirably done, and alike in its literary skill and its mechanical execution, does great credit to the ability, accuracy and taste of its esteemed author.

# APPENDIX.

On the occasion of the Reunion of the 'Sons of Portsmouth,' July 4, 1873, the following list of names of those residing abroad was collected. It is given without pretension to perfect accuracy, but is as near that as those who have the matter in hand have been able to make it.

A

Abbott W. Banfield, Hampstead, Tex.
Abbott Nathaniel Mrs., Prospect House Northampton, Mass.
Aborn James Mrs., Wall St., West Lynn.
Adams Eunice Miss, Chelsea, Mass.
Adams Geo. M. Rev., Wellesley, Mass.
Adams Lousia D. Mrs., " "
Adams John G. Rev., Lowell, Mass,
Adams John Q., 287 Meridian St., East Boston.
Adams John Q. Mrs., 287 Meridian St., East Boston.
Adams John Q., Box 64, Valejo, Cal.
Adams John Q. Mrs., Box 64, Valejo, California.
Adams Rufus G. Mrs., Dudley St., Brookline, Mass.
Adams Charles C. Rev., Manhattanville, N. Y.
Adams Charles C. Mrs., Manhattanville, N. Y.
Adams Thomas A., New Orleans, La.
Adams Benj., Dedham, Mass.
Adams George W., 300 Broadway, N. Y.
Adams Rufus, East Boston
Adams A. A. Miss, Newburyport Mass.
Adams George Mrs., Greenwood, Mass.
Adams George L., " "
Adams George L. Mrs., " "
Adams Clara K., Ellsworth, Peirce Co., Wis.
Adams James N., " "
Adams Lucy M. Mrs., " "
Adams Mary A., " "
Adams W. Henry T. " "
Adams Whitney K., " "
Adams Woodbury, Eliot, Me.
Adamson Edward A. Mrs., 27 Porter St., Boston.
Adwers George, Lawrence, Kansas.
Adwers George M., 89 Mast St., Boston.
Akerman Benj.. San Francisco, Cal.
Akerman Albert E. Mrs., Alvarado, Alameda Co., Cal.
Akerman Amos T., Cartersville, Ga.
Akerman Wm. H., San Jose, Santa Clara Co., Cal.
Aldrich Thomas B. Boston.
Aldrich Mrs., 3 W. 38th St., N. Y.
Allen E. H. Rev. Mrs., Haverhill, Mass.
Ames James, East Boston.
Anderson Horace P., Pt. Townsend, Washington Ter.
Andrews William Mrs., Salem, Mass.
Appleton Sophia H., Mrs. 432 Main St. Hartford, Conn.
Appleton Augusta J., 432 Main Street, Hartford, Conn.
Appleton Sophia Mrs., Cambridge. Mass.
Appleton Mary Briard, Lowell, Mass.
Appolonio N. A. Mrs., City Registrar's office, Boston, Mass.
Arnold Henry A. Mrs., Amesbury, Mass.
Ashby Annie Mrs., Indianapolis, Ind.
Atkinson Sallie A. Mrs., 53 Bridge St. Salem, Mass.
Ayers Chas. L., provisions, 36 Market square, Newburyport, Mass.
Ayers Ira, Malden, Mass.
Ayers Leonard, Newburyport, Mass.

B

Badger Charles, Boston.
Badger Eva Miss, Boston.
Badger James L., Rochester, N. Y.
Badger John S., Boston.
Badger John L. (Melvin & Badger), Boston.
Badger J. L. Mrs., Boston.
Badger Maggie Miss, Boston.
Badger John (Melvin & Badger), Boston.
Badger Lizzie Miss (Melvin & Badger), Boston.
Badger Mary E. Mrs., Reading, Mass.
Badger George A., Boston.
Badger Samuel A., "
Badger Samuel A. Mrs., Boston.
Badger Leonidas V. Mrs., Chicago, Ill.
Badger Caroline C. Mrs., 33 Arnold St., Providence, R. I.
Badger Lavinia E. Mrs., Chicago, Ill.
Badger Mary M. Mrs., Chicago, Ill.
Badger John B. Mrs., Boston.
Bailey Daniel A., Manchester, Mass.
Bailey James E. Boston
Bailey Sarah Mrs., Dorchester, Mass.
Bailey Nath'l Mrs., " "
Bailey Sophia Miss, " "
Baker John M. Mrs., Covington, Ky.
Baker Francis, Brooklyn, N. Y.
Balcom Lydia E. Mrs., San Francisco, Cal.
Ball Abbie A. Miss, Northampton, Mass.
Ball Arthur T., 67 Bennington St., Boston.
Ball H. W., Fitchburg Depot, Boston.
Ball H. W. Mrs., " "
Ball John M., 8 Wood St., Charlestown, Mass.
Ball Geo., 8 Wood St., Charlestown, Ms.
Ball Elizabeth Mrs., Salem, Mass.
Ball Eben W. Boston.
Ball Lizzie Miss, Packer's Institute, Brooklyn, N. Y.
Ball N. Haven, San Francisco, Cal.
Banfield Joseph Rev., Boston.
Banfield Nathaniel, Wolfboro', N. H.
Barber Lucy, Kingston, N. H.
Barnard Benjamin, Portland, Me.
Barnard Silas, Portland, Me.
Barnes Samuel H., 11 King St., Boston Highlands.
Barnes Henry, Chickering's Piano Manufactory, Boston.
Barnes Samuel, Lynn, Mass.
Bartlett John H., Salem, Mass.
Bartlet John Mrs., Salem, Mass.
Barton N. Miss, Amherst, Mass.
Barrett Frances Mrs., New Bedford, Mass.
Barrett Frances Mrs., Boston.
Bartlett John K. Dr., Milwaukie, Wis.
Bassett Christopher Mrs., Amesbury, Mass.
Bates Anna M. Mrs., Canandaigua, N. Y.

Bazin Joseph W., Charlestown, Mass.
Bazin Richard E., " "
Bazin Coson C., Cross St., Charlestown, Mass.
Bazin Joshua, Charlestown, Mass.
Beal Edward J., So. New Market, N. H.
Beal Henry R., Hogg, Brown & Taylor, Boston.
Beck Gideon, 164 Tremont St., Boston.
Beck Lewis, Boston.
Beck Lyman H., Woodstock, Me.
Beck James W., Woodstock, Me.
Bell Theodore, 89 Washington Street, Boston.
Bell Harriet, Boston.
Bell John M., Charlestown, Mass.
Bell Lucy L., 174 Pearl St., Brooklyn N. Y.
Bell Sophia, 174 Pearl St., Brooklyn, N. Y.
Bell James, 89 Washington St., Boston.
Beal Joseph G., 89 Washington Street, Boston
Bell Martin G. Mrs., Hoosac Falls, N. Y.
Benjamin D. M. Mrs. Grand Rapids, Mich.
Bennett Ada L. Mrs., New Britain, Conn.
Bennett John B., Dale, Ross & Co., Phila., Pa.
Bennett John R., 1822 Marine Street, Phila., Pa.
Bernard John W., 109 Chauncy Street, Boston.
Berry Charles O., Hartford Foundry and Machine Co., Hartford, Conn.
Berry Geo. W., New York.
Berry Horace, M. D., cor. Broadway and Elm Sts., Cambridgeport, Mass.
Berry J. N., 242 8th St., So. Boston.
Berry Horace, East Boston.
Berry Marcellus F., American Ex. Co., Chicago, Ill.
Berry Lyman Mrs., Charlestown, Mass.
Betton Frank H., Pomeroy, Kansas.
Bigelow H. H. Mrs., San Francisco, Cal.
Bigelow Kate Miss, 701 Tremont St., Boston.
Bigelow James R., Hyde Park, Mass.
Bigelow Jackson Mrs., Dorchester, Mass.
Bishop Henry B. Mrs., Occidental Hotel, San Francisco, Cal.
Black Charles H., Waltham, Mass.
Black Charles H. Mrs., Waltham, Mass.
Black Homer, Chelsea, Mass.
Black James A., Chelsea, Mass.
Black L. Abby, Waltham, Mass.
Black William, jr., Chelsea, Mass.
Blair Montgomery Mrs., Washington, D. C.
Blaisdell John C., Lexington, Mass.
Blanchard Amos, Mrs, Lowell, Mass.
Bliss Frank Mrs., American Pub. Co., Hartford, Conn.
Blunt Albert M. Mrs., 20 Chester sq., Boston.
Blunt Charles E., Col. U. S. Eng'r Corps., Key West, Florida.
Blunt John, 46 Gates Avenue, Brooklyn, N. Y.
Blunt M. Marsh, Col. U. S. A., Governor's Island, N. Y.
Blunt Stanhope, Lieut. U. S. A., Salt Lake City, Utah Ter.
Boardman G. Adlebert, High Street, Providence, R. I.
Boardman Herbert, High St., Providence, R. I.
Boardman Herbert Mrs., High Street, Providence, R. I.
Boardman Charles, San Jose, Cal.
Boardman Thomas, W. Epping, N. H.
Bodge Edward A., Malden, Mass.
Bonimus Lydia T. Mrs., 10 Anderson St., Boston.
Bonin Benj. F., Jamaica Plain, Mass.
Bowden Thomas A., Mrs., Butterfield St., Chicago, Ill.
Bowen Frances Mrs., Cambridgeport, Mass.
Bowles B. F. Rev., Philadelphia, Pa.
Bowles Hiram A., South Boston
Bowles Sarah R. Mrs., 67 Indiana St., Boston.
Bowles Samuel B. Dr., Greenfield, Mo.
Boyd Elizabeth Miss, Boston.
Boyd Ira A., New Orleans, La.
Boyd Robert Mrs., New Orleans, La.
Boyden Nellie Mrs., Worcester, Mass.
Brackett John L. Mrs., Greenland, N. H.
Bradbury Charles W. Mrs., 51 W. 12th St., New York.
Bradbury Lousia Mrs., Cambridge, Mass.
Bradford Sarah E. Mrs., 2 Bunker Hill Street, Charlestown, Mass.
Bragdon Oren D. New Orleans, La.
Bragdon Mary W. Miss, }
Bragdon Alice G. }
Bragdon Emma. } So. Boston.
Bragdon William A. }
Bragdon A. H. Mrs. }
Branigan Thomas Mrs., Broadway, So. Boston.
Brazier A. M. Mrs., Drytown, Cal.
Brewster Charles G., Natural History Store, 486 Washington St., Boston, house 14 Moreland.
Brewster Sam'l L., Pier 45, New York.
Brewster Sarah Mrs., 154 Saratoga St., East Boston.
Briard Edwin, Philadelphia, Pa.
Briard Capt. " "
Briard William A., retired merchant, Madison, Wis.
Bridge Abby Mrs., Boston.
Bridge Jos. H. Mrs., 790 Washington St., Boston.
Britton Margaret A. Mrs., Boston Highlands
Brooks John G. Rev., Philadelphia, Pa.
Brown Nellie S. Miss, 19 and 22 Dock square, Boston
Brown Joseph S., Lowell, Mass.
Brown Jos. S. Mrs., " "
Brown Mary Mrs., Candia, N. H.
Brown Isaac H., postmaster, Massillon, Ohio
Brown Mary L. Mrs., 57 Melrose St., Boston
Brown Horatio G., jr., 297 3d Street, St. Paul, Minn.
Brown Sophia B. Mrs., Havana, Schuyler Co., N. Y.
Brown Elizabeth B. Mrs., Kensington, N. H.
Brown Olive Miss, Dover, N. H.
Brown Charles W. Mrs., West Lynn, Mass.
Brown Thomas W. Mrs. Rev., Dover, N. H.
Brown William R., Boston
Brown Josie Mrs., Mystic, Mass.
Brown J. A., San Francisco, Cal.
Brown Washington, Philadelphia, Pa.
Brown Moses Mrs., Brooklyn, N. Y.
Brown S. Mrs., Hyde Park, Mass.
Brown Addison, Lynn, Mass.

Brown Alonzo F. Mrs., San Francisco, Cal.
Brown Helen M., New York City
Brown Ira A., 48 Bartlett St., Charlestown, Mass.
Brown John, Boston
Brown Joel T., Manchester, N. H.
Brown Mary F. R., San Francisco, Cal.
Brown Martha E. Mrs., Charlestown, Mass.
Brown S. Boardman, Lynn, Mass.
Brown William, Dover, N. H.
Bruce Lewis P., 158 Tremont St., Boston
Bruce Joseph L., " " "
Bruce William, " " "
Bruce Lewis A., Winchester, Mass.
Bruce L. A. Mrs., " "
Bruce Wallace Mrs., " "
Bruce Fred., " "
Bruce Fred. A., 126 Cambridge St., E. Cambridge
Bruce Chas. W., So. Boston, Mass.
Bruce Paschal A., Chelsea, Mass.
Bryam Wm. H. Mrs., Pittsburg, Pa.
Buchman Seward Mrs., Calais, Me.
Buffum Clementine M. Mrs., Charlestown, Mass.
Burke Joseph J., Boston
Burnham Ira F., 24 Winter St., Boston
Burnham Joseph B., Chelsea, Mass.
Butler Benjamin F., 23 Princeton, E. Boston
Butler Benj. F. Mrs., 23 Princeton, E. Boston
Butler Horace B., 23 Princeton, East Boston
Butland Charles C., upholsterer, 281 Essex, h. 29 Brown St., Salem, Mass.
Butler Augustus, 233 Water S., N. York
Butler Philip Mrs., So. Framingham, Mass.
Butler J. Edward, So. Berwick, Me.
Butler Mary Mrs., Augusta, Ga.
Butler N. H,, Augusta, Ga.
Butterfield Benj. F. Mrs., Jamestown, Tuolumne Co., Cal.

## C

Caban Samuel, Kittery Foreside, Me.
Caban Samuel Mrs., Kittery Foreside, Me.
Caneday Annie S. Mrs., St. Joseph, Mo.
Canovan Sarah B. Mrs., Richmond, Va.
Carlton George A., Stockton, Cal.
Carlton Fred., " "
Carroll John W., Waverley, Ill.
Carroll Chas. E., New London, Wis.
Carruthers Pamelia, Franklin, Tenn.
Carruthers Renie Mrs., 52 Maverick St., E. Boston
Carter Ezra Mrs., Concord, N. H.
Carter Wm. H., Salem, Mass.
Carter John M., Newburyport, Mass.
Casco Almira Mrs., Eutaw St., East Boston
Casey Mary Q. S. Mrs., Careyville, Ky.
Casey Sarah L. Mrs., " "
Cassidy P. T., Key, cor. Shawmut av., Jamaica Plain, Mass.
Caswell Lemuel E., crockery and glass ware, 153 Milk, Boston (see advt. front colored page
Caswell Frances Mrs., Weare, N. H.
Caswell John R., Cambridgeport, Ms.
Caswell Mark, Cambridgeport, Mass.
Cate John S., 104 Water St., Boston
Cate Chas. F., Boston
Cate Chas. F. Mrs., Boston
Cate Wm., Boston
Cate Samuel, 7½ Central wharf, Boston, Mass.
Cate Wm. H., Jamaica Plain, Mass.
Cate Alphonso, Jamaica Plain, Mass.
Cate Wm. H., blockmaker, Navy Yard, Charlestown, h. Everett, Mass.
Cate Elizabeth Mrs., Everett, Mass.
Chambers Mary Mrs., Kittery Point, Me.
Chamberlain Mary A. Miss, Dover, N. H.
Chase Margaret A. Mrs., Haverhill, Mass.
Chase Nathaniel, Pittsfield, N. H.
Chaffee Edward D. Mrs., East Providence, R. I.
Chamberlain Mehitable C. Mrs., Chelsea, Mass.
Chapin Anna M. Mrs., Melrose, Mass.
Chapin Samuel H., E. Salisbury, Mass.
Chapin Sam'l H. Mrs., " "
Chapin Frank, " "
Chapman John H. Mrs., New Bedford, Mass.
Chapman A. H. Mrs., 92 Washington St., Boston
Chapman Wm. W. Mrs., Jacksonville, Fla.
Chapman E. A. Mrs., Jamaica Plain, Mass.
Chapman Albert, Jamaica Plain, Mass.
Chapman David, Newmarket, N. H.
Chapman John, Newmarket, N. H.
Cheever William, Boston
Cheever Wm. Mrs., "
Cheever Joseph Dr., "
Cheever David Dr., "
Cheever John, physician, Charlestown, Mass.
Cheever N. P. Mrs., 88 Zeigler St., Boston
Chesley Lydia Mrs., Alton, N. H.
Chesley Annie M. Y. Miss, Northampton, Mass.
Clapham C. Thomas, Coso House, San Francisco, Cal.
Clapham Mahala, Northampton, Mass.
Clark Geo. H., 6 Trenton St., Charlestown, Mass.
Clark Geo. H. Mrs., 6 Trenton Street, Charlestown, Mass.
Clark Charles H., 70 Linden Street, Springfield, Mass.
Clark Frederic S., Biddeford, Me.
Clark Matthew Mrs., Randolph, Mass.
Clark Charles W., San Jose, Cal.
Clark Chas. W. Mrs., " "
Clark Brackett Mrs., Dover, N. H.
Clark Andrew, South Orange, N. J.
Clark Anderson, " "
Clark Elizabeth W., St. Louis, Mo.
Clark Annie M. Miss, Hartford, Ct.
Clark Arthur, 34 Willet, N. Y. City
Clark Charles H., Hartford, Ct.
Clark Clara Miss, 11 Davis St., Boston
Clark Daniel, Manchester, N. H.
Clark Daniel Mrs., Manchester, N. H.
Clark Daniel P., 153 Harrison avenue, Boston
Clark D. P., Charlestown, Mass.
Clark Edmund, Randolph, Mass.
Clark Emma Miss, 34 Willet St., New York
Clark H. G. Dr. Mrs., Beacon St., Boston
Clark John C., New York City
Clark John N., Barre, Mass.
Clark Matthew, Randolph, Mass.
Clark Horace P., ship Anna Decatur, Valencia, Spain

Clark Richard E., 341 Cherry St., N. Y.
Clark Richmond, New York City
Clark Rev. Rufus W., jr., Columbus, Ohio
Clark Samuel, Randolph, Mass.
Clark Samuel Mrs., Randolph, Mass.
Clarinbole John, Lynn, Mass.
Clarinbole Geo., " "
Clarinbole Joseph, " "
Clash Richard J., A. D. Hillyer, Pier 6, North River, New York
Clash Arthur, R. J. Clash, Pier 6, No. River, New York
Clements Hiram L., Hampton, N. H.
Clements Lucy M. Mrs., Newburyport, Mass.
Close Hannah Mrs., Melrose, Mass.
Clough Clarence A. E., 12 Pemberton Sq., Boston
Cobb H. E. Mrs., 633 Brookline Street, Boston
Cobb Sophronia Miss, Boston
Cobbett Geo. A., Waldo, Me.
Cobbett H. E. Mrs., " "
Coburn Lydia H. Mrs., 18 Pickman st., Salem, Mass.
Coffin Nathaniel J., ship Polaris, Arctic Expedition
Coffin Nathaniel, Manchester, N. H.
Coffin Charles E., " "
Coffin Lou Miss, " "
Coffin Florence I., South Boston
Coffin John N., 31 and 33 Haverhill St., Boston
Coffin Enoch, South Boston
Coffin Enoch Mrs., "
Coffin James, 9 Stamford St., Boston
Coffin James Mrs., Boston
Coffin Charles, Manchester, N. H.
Coffin Chas. E. Mrs., " "
Coffin Elizabeth, South Boston
Coffin George, Chelsea, Mass.
Coffin Henry, Charlestown, Mass.
Coffin Wm. G., Damariscotta, Me.
Cogswell Sarah D. Mrs., 301 Tremont St., San Francisco
Cogswell Warren, 364 Tremont Street, San Francisco, Cal.
Collins Jacob, Big Lorraine, Gt. Britain
Collins Jacob Mrs., Big Lorraine, Gt. Britain
Collins Wm., Boston
Colcord Samuel M. (T. Metcalf & Co.), Boston
Coleman Elizabeth Mrs., Ipswich, Ms.
Coleman Jas. Dr., San Francisco, Cal.
Coleman John E. W., San Francisco, Cal.
Coleman Lewis B., Boston
Coleman Corinne, Newington, N. H.
Conant J. H. Mrs., Banner of Light, Boston
Copeland Ann Mrs., Boston
Corliss Emily A. Mrs., Meredith Village, N. H.
Cook Emily C., Atchison, Kansas
Cotton Wm., Boston
Cowden Eliot C. Mrs., Champs Elysees, Paris
Crane Rufus R., paper-box manufacturer, Blackstone, Millbury, Mass.
Crane Anna W., " "
Crane Hosea, " "
Critchley Thomas H., Philadelphia
Culbert A. M. Mrs., Drytown, Cal.
Cummings Charles Mrs., 46 Montgomery St., Boston
Cunningham John J., St. John's College, Fordham, N. Y.
Currier Lavinia Miss, Titusville, Pa.
Currier Eva C. Miss, Trenton St., E. Boston
Currier Albert G., Division City, Grayson Co., Texas
Currier Howard F., Amesbury, Mass.
Curtis Geo. B., grocer, Enfield, N. C.
Curtis Geo. B. Mrs., " "
Curtis T. Henry, E. Jaffrey, N. H.
Curtis P. H., E. Jaffrey, N. H.
Curtis Elvira, Amesbury, Mass.
Curtis Woodbury, Topsham, Me.
Curtis Elijah, New York City
Curtis Benjamin, Salem, Mass.
Curtis Wm., East Boston, Mass.
Curtis Moses, Amesbury, Mass.
Cushing Wm. Mrs., Cambridge, Mass.
Cushman Chas. C., Ottumwa, Iowa
Cutter Sarah Mrs., Cambridge, Mass.
Cutter Charles A. Mrs., 51 Oxford St., Cambridge, Mass.
Cutter F. L., 182 Warren St., Brooklyn, N. Y.
Cutter Frank, Chittenden & Co., N. Y.
Cutts Hon. Hampden, No. Hartland, Vt.
Cutts John M. Mrs., Newburyport, Ms.
Cutts Elizabeth T., Chicago, Ill.
Cutts Julia Miss, Cambridge, Mass.

## D

Dame M. N., Allston, Mass.
Dame Calvin, Prescott, Ontario
Dame C. C., Newburyport, Mass.
Dame W. N., Greenland, N. H.
Dame W. N. Mrs., " "
Dame Mary E., 10 Beckler av., S. Boston
Dame Nathaniel B., Kittery, Me.
Dana Alfred S., College physician and surgeon, cor. 23d St. and 4th avenue, New York
Darling Thomas H., 19 North Green St., Chicago, Ill.
Darton John W., East Boston
Darton John W. Mrs., East Boston
Davies T. F. Rev., 717 Pine St., Philadelphia, Pa.
Davis Annie E. (Rugg), Mrs., Salem, Ms.
Davis Willie, " "
Davis J. Frank, machinist, Haverhill St., h. 1 Pacific St., Lawrence, Mass.
Davis Chas. H., lumber dealer, Water, cor. Clinton, Saginaw City, Mich.
Davis Clement, Durham, N. H.
Davis Joseph, Eliot, Me.
Damrell Charles L., bookseller, 135 Washington st., Boston
Damrell Elizabeth, Mrs., Boston
Davis Wm., 296 Washington st., Boston
Dawson William jr. Mrs., 21 Courtland st., Baltimore, Md.
Dearborn Daniel G., Wholesale Druggist, 141 & 143 St. Clair st., h. cor Adams & Franklin Av., Toledo, O.
Dearborn John, Salem, Mass.
Dearing Thomas E., 91 1-2 Chelsea st., Boston,
Decatur Emma V., Chelsea, Mass.
Dennett Benj. T., Newmarket, N. H.
Dennett Julia A. Mrs., Bunker Hill st., Charlestown.
Dennett J. Jas., Bunker Hill st., Charlestown.
Dennett G. Walker, South Framingham, Mass.
Dennett Ephraim, 38 Palmer St., Boston.
Dennett Ephraim Mrs., 38 Palmer St., Boston.
Dennett Charles, 38 Palmer St., Boston

Dennett Charles E., Malden Centre, Mass.
Dennett Erastus Mrs., Cambridge, Mass.
Dennett George, Georgetown, Mass.
Dennett James T., Charlestown, Mass.
Dennett Charles H., piano forte top maker, 720 Wash. St., Boston, h. 101 Russell St., Charlestown, Mass.
Dennett Mary E. Mrs., South Framingham, Mass.
Dennett James G., 322 Bunker Hill, Charlestown, Mass.
Dennett James G. Mrs., 322 Bunker Hill, Charlestown, Mass.
Dennett George B., Lexington, Mass.
Dennett Geo. B. Mrs., " "
Dennett John W., grocer, 162 Main, h 66 Green St., Charlestown, Mass.
Dennett John W. Mrs., " "
Dennett Langley B., 66 Pearl St., Charlestown, Mass.
Dennett Langley B. Mrs., 66 Pearl St., Charlestown, Mass.
Dennett Geo. W., Framingham, Mass.
Dennett Benjamin T., Newmarket, N. H.
Dennett A. M. Mrs., Cambridgeport, Mass.
Dennett H. N., Newburyport, Mass.
Dennett Thomas P. Mrs., Salem, Mass.
Dennett George, " "
Dennett Edward, " "
Dennett Theodore D., Somerville, Mass.
Dennett John D., Taunton, Mass.
Dennett Elizabeth B. Miss, Taunton, Mass.
Dennett Almira Mrs., Beverly, Mass.
Dennett George S., Charlestown, Mass.
Dennett Burnham C., Boston Highlands, Mass.
Dennett B. C. Mrs., " " Mass.
Dennett Charles B., rear of 383 W. Madison St., Chicago, Ill.
Dennett Mark Mrs., Beverly, Mass.
Dennett Boardman L., grocer, Everett, Mass.
Dennett Albert, E. R. R. Car Shop, Salem, Mass.
DeRochemont Chas., Kingston, N. H.
DeRochemont S. F. Mrs., Newington, N. H.
Deverson William, East Boston, Mass.
Deshon Carrie Miss, Waverly,
Dickinson Fannie Mrs., Boston,
Dimick Otis S., Palestine, Texas.
Dixon Alexander A., Stewart, Adair Co., Iowa.
Dixon Sylvester, Tilton, N. H.
Dolloff Anna E. Mrs., St. Albans, Vt.
Doe Mrs., South Berwick, Me.
Dole W. Mrs., Bangor, Me.
Donnell Samuel, Peabody, Mass.
Donnell Samuel jr., " "
Donnell William, grocer, 15 & 17 Lowell, h. Foster St., Peabody, Mass.
Donnell Octavius, Charlestown, Mass.
Donovan Mary E. Mrs., 5 Centre St., Lowell, Mass.
Dow Elizabeth A. Mrs., Boston.
Dow W. W. Rev., Winchendon, Mass.
Dow Mrs., " "
Dow Lizzie, Kensington, N. H.
Dow George S. Mrs., Providence, R. I.
Dow Frank Mrs., " "
Dow Lorenzo Mrs., Kendalls Mills, Me.
Dow S. A. Mrs., North Hampton, N. H.
Downing John E., Newington, N. H.
Downing Ephraim, " "
Downing Fred O., Medford, Mass.
Downing B., Charlestown, Mass.
Downing B. Mrs., " "
Drake Charles A., Rye, N. H.
Dresser Emery A., 560 8th St., South Boston.
Dresser Mary F. Mrs., " "
Dresser L. F., 151 Hanover St., Boston.
Drown Samuel Mrs., Charlestown, Mass.
Drown Wm. A., umbrella manuf., 246 Market, Phila., Pa., & 498 & 500 Broadway, N. Y., h. 121 North 20th St., Phila.
Drown Anna P. Mrs., " Phila.
Drown C. M. Mrs., Charlestown, Mass.
Drown Albion H., " "
Drown Edwin A., " "
Drown Comfort Mrs., " "
Drown T. Appleton, " "
Dunning George Mrs., 6 Grosvenor Place, Boston.
Durgin Charles T., wool sorter, Manchester print works, h. 560 Chestnut, Manchester, N. H.
Durgin Charles T. Mrs., Manchester, N. H.
Durgin Charles, Baton Rouge, La.
Durgin Eliza Ann Tripe Mrs., h. 560 Chestnut St., Manchester, N. H.
Durgin Anna Miss, Raymond, N. H.
Durgin John, Raymond, N. H.
Durgin John E., Boston.
Durgin Josie Miss, Boston.
Durgin Lizzie Miss, Boston.
Durkee Silas Dr., Howard st., Boston.
Dustin Alvarus, Springfield, Mass.

## E

Earing Daniel, Salem, Mass.
Earl William C., Toledo, O.
Earle Wm. C. Mrs., 183 Summit St., Toledo, O.
Eastman Frank, Box 708, Saco, Me.
Eastman Frank Mrs., " " "
Edgecomb Sarah A. Miss, Washington, D. C.
Ela George, Concord, N. H.
Ellis William Mrs., Worcester, Mass.
Edgerly Sylvanus, Haverhill, Mass.
Edgerly Sylvanus Mrs., " "
Edgerly Flora Miss, " "
Edgerly Myra, Lowell, Mass.
Ellis Wm. C., Worcester, "
Elwyn A. Langdon Dr., Phila., Pa.
Ely Charles Mrs., Gramercy Park Hotel, New York City.
Emery Elizabeth Mrs., East Boston, Mass.
Emery Lizzie M. Miss, East Boston.
Emery Woodward 41 State St., Boston.
Emery George P., Boston.
Emery Horace, Boston.
Emery James H. Mrs., East Boston.
Emery Charles T., Newington, N. H.
Emery Woodbury, Boston.
Evans Lavina Miss, Lawrence, Mass.
Evans Charlotte, " "
Evans Anna J., " "
Evans Mary Ilsley Miss, Rock Island, Ill.

## F

Fairbanks Charles A., Dover, N. H.
Fall Otis, Charlestown, Mass.
Farnham George C. Mrs., Kennebunk, Me.
Fayban Joseph, Haverhill, Mass.
Feitel Albert J., vinegar manuf., 71 Pearl St., Charlestown, Mass.
Feitel Albert J. Mrs., " "
Felton N. B. Mrs., Haverhill, N. H.

Ferguson Thomas A., Brookfield, Mass.
Fernald G. W., Kellogg, Iowa.
Fernald L. P., " "
Fernald Amiron E., East Boston.
Fernald Daniel, Lexington St., E. Bos.
Fernald Benjamin F., Police Office, Malden, Mass.
Fernald F. Clinton, care of F. L. Fernald, Navy Yard, Boston.
Fernald F. W. Mrs., 112 Beach St., Boston.
Fernald Woodbury M. Rev., Boston.
Fernald Alice H. Mrs., 90 Tremont St., Boston.
Fields Mary H. J. Mrs., Baltimore, Md.
Fields George A., Boston.
Fields James T., Boston, Mass.
Finney Dorothy Mrs. Wakefield, Mass.
Fisher Andrew P., East Boston.
Fisher Marion B., Marion St., East Boston.
Fisher John, Beverly Farms, Mass.
Fisher Alexander, East Boston.
Fisher John Mrs., Lewiston, Me.
Fisher Howell Mrs., Pottsville, Penn.
Fiske Caroline A. Mrs., Lowell, Mass.
Fitch Albert J., Charlestown, Mass.
Fitch Albert J. Mrs., " "
Fitzgerald Abbie Mrs., Chelsea, Mass.
Fitzgerald George H., Port Townsend, Washington Ter.
Fitzgerald Edward, Andover, Mass.
Fitzgerald Richard, jr., Lawrence, Mass.
Flagg George W., Exeter, N. H.
Flagg W. C., Boston.
Flanders E. A. Mrs., Charlestown, Mass.
Flanders Lewis Mrs., 400 Columbus Av., Boston.
Fletcher L. Augustus, Am. House, Boston.
Folsom John H. Mrs., 50 Bridge St., Salem, Mass.
Folsom Eugene R., Hilo, Hawaiian Islands.
Folsom Eugene R. Mrs. " Islds.
Folsom Mary E. Mrs., Brooklyn, New York.
Folsom Paris H., 4th Aud. Office, Washington, D. C.
Folsom Albert G., Laconia, N. H.
Foss Moses R., Newport, R. I.
Foss Joseph, Elliott, Me.
Foss Charles, Boston, Mass.
Foster Robert F., printer, Suffolk pl., Dennison Tag Factory, Boston.
Foster Fannie E. Miss, 1 Beacon St., Boston.
Foster Joseph, Paymaster, U. S. S. Shawmut, Key West, Fla.
Foster Lyman S., 39 Nassau Street, New York.
Foster William, Sullivan Street, Charlestown, Mass.
Fox Dr., Kingsrising Av., W. Philadelphia, Pa.
Fredson George, 364 Tremont St., Boston, Mass.
Fredson George, Coluso, Coluso Co., Cal.
Freeman Carrie A. Miss, 96 Appleton St, Boston.
Freeman Albert C., 132 Court St., Boston.
Freeman Wallace G., Portland, Me.
French Charlotte E. Mrs., Deerfield Centre, N. H.
French Samuel F. Newburyport, Mass.
French John W. Mrs., Prospect House, Northampton, Mass.
French John M. Northampton, Mass.
French Charles H., Brattle St., Portland, Me.
French Chas. H. Mrs., " "
Frisbee Florence E., Wolfborough, N. H.
Frost R. M., W. Newton, Mass.
Frost Mary E., Malden. "
Frost Ellen, " "
Frost Leander, New York.
Frost John N., 325 Broadway, N. Y.
Frost William, Malden Mass.
Frost William Mrs., " "
Frost Maria Miss, Newton, Mass.
Frost J. L. Mrs., Newburyport, Mass.
Frost John N., 16 & 18 Merchants Row, Boston.
Frost William S., London, Eng.
Frost George E., Malden, Mass.
Frost Albert H., " "
Fuller Frank, Utah.
Fuller Frank Mrs., Utah
Fuller E. N., Chicago, Ill.
Fuller E. N. Mrs., Northwood, N. H.
Furber Thos. G. Mrs., Newington, N. H
Furber Elizabeth L., Somersworth, N. H.
Furber John L. Dr., Valley Brook, Osage Co., Kansas.
Frye Joseph P., Manchester, N. H.
Frye Charlotte, " "
Frye James K., East Cambridge, Mass.
Frye Samuel B. " " "
Frye Isaac, Boston.
Frye Rachel Miss, Boston.
Frye William C. Mrs., Eliot Depot, Me.
Furniss William, 11 Bond St., N. Y.

## G

Gadd Margaret S. Mrs., 303 Columbus Av., Boston.
Gage Fred., Woburn, Mass.
Gage W. L. Rev., Hartford, Conn.
Gaines John, New Orleans, La.
Gale John, Haverhill, Mass.
Gardner George H., Boston.
Gardner George W. Mrs., 42 Adams St., Boston.
Garland Annie W. Kittery, Me.
Garland Joseph C., Dover, N. H.
Garland Mary E., Lowell, Mass.
Garland Daniel, Portland Me.
Garland Daniel, Greenland, N. H.
Garrett George H., South Newmarket, N. H.
Garrett Sarah L., Boston.
Gerrish Frank, 50 Broad St., Boston.
Gerrish Wallace, Boston.
Gerrish Robert Mrs., Kittery Point, Me.
Gerrish Benjamin, Boston.
Gerrish Benj. Mrs., "
Gerrish Fred H. Dr., 297 1-2 Congress St., Portland, Me.
Gerrish Charles C., Saco, Me.
Gerrish Smith, Boston.
Gerrish Joseph R., Deerfield, N. H.
Gerrish Joseph R. Mrs., " "
Gerrish Andrew D., East Boston.
Gerrish Andrew Mrs., " "
Gerrish Elizabeth Mrs., " " "
Gerrish Nellie M., " " "
Gerrish W. Wallace, " " "
Gerrish William R., Boston.
Gerrish George H., Port Townsend, Washington Ter.
Gerrish Benjamin F., Fulton, Ill.
Gerrish Benj. F., Mrs., " "
George William Mrs., 6 Park St., W. Lynn, Mass.
Gerry Lucy Mrs., Boston.
Gilman Stephen, Box 805, Bangor, Me.

Gilman Alfred, Lowell, Mass.
Glines Joseph H., Charlestown, Mass.
Gillespie Marianna, Alfred, Me.
Gillespie Frances, Canterbury, N. H.
Gilpatrick Susan Mrs., Kennebunk Me.
Gilpatrick Elizabeth, " "
Gleason Anna Mrs., Woodside, L. I.
Glover William Mrs., Box 4045 New York.
Gooch William S., Exeter, N. H.
Goodall John N., Cor. Sudbury and Friend St., Boston.
Goodrich Parker H., Haverhill, Mass.
Goodrich Mrs. Parker H., " "
Goodrich Massena Rev. Mrs., Pawtucket, R. I.
Goodrich Emily L., Miss, Pawtucket, R. I.
Goodrich Wm. A., Redwood City, Cal.
Goodwin Wm. H., Jamaica Plain, Mass.
Goodwin Daniel Mrs. 76 Brewster St., Boston.
Goss Daniel J., Hyde Park, Mass. Mass.
Goodrich Taylor, Boston.
Goodrich William A., Woodside, San Mateo Co., Cal.
Goodrich Chas. B., Cambridge, Mass.
Goodrich Chas. B. Mrs., " "
Goodwin Frank, Boston.
Gordon James, Auburndale, Mass.
Gordon Ellen, Exeter, N. H.
Gordon George, Exeter, N. H.
Gove Louis Edwin, farmer, Natick, R. I.
Gove Louis E. Mrs., Natick, R. I.
Gove Clinton, " "
Graham William Mrs., San Francisco.
Grant Stephen Mrs., registrar's office, Boston.
Grant Charles A., Manchester, N. H.
Grant Annie Mrs., Boston.
Grant Henry M., Rollinsford, N. H.
Grant Henry M. Mrs., " "
Grant Stephen M. Mrs., 38 Sharon St., Boston.
Gray George, Dover, N. H.
Gray John S., 33 Polk Street, Charlestown, Mass.
Gray Clarence S., Amesbury, Mass.
Gray Clarence S., Exeter, N. H.
Graves Elizabeth M. Mrs., Lynn, Mass.
Green T. Goodrich, Windsor Mills, Orangeburg District, S. C.
Green Abel B., Sutters Creek, Amador Co., Cal.
Green Robt. H., Clarke's Court, Lynn,
Green Daniel, Pittsfield, Mass.
Green Thomas, 194 State st., Boston, house Warren ave., Chelsea, Mass.
Green Thomas Mrs., 194 State st., Boston, h. Warren ave., Chelsea, Mass.
Green Daniel, 33 Border st., E. Boston.
Green Elizabeth Mrs., Boston.
Green Margaret, 33 Border street, E. Boston.
Green Addie, 33 Border st., E. Boston.
Green Lottie " " "
Green Annie Mrs., Chelsea, Mass.
Greenleaf Albert, Baltimore, Md.
Greenleaf James F., 9 Turner street, Salem, Mass.
Greenleaf James F., Mrs., 9 Turner street, Salem, Mass.
Greenleaf Frank M., 9 Turner street, Salem, Mass.
Greenleaf Myra B., 9 Turner street, Salem, Mass.
Greenough William A., 3 Mason ct., Charlestown.
Greenough William A. Mrs., 3 Mason court, Charlestown.
Greenough William A., jr., publisher, 96 Washington street, Boston, house 13 Baldwin, Charlestown.
Greenough William A., jr., Mrs., 13 Baldwin, Charlestown.
Greenough John, depot master, Lynn, Mass.
Greenough John, jr., Lynn, Mass.
Greenough Frank H., tinplate worker, Charlestown, Mass.
Greenough J. A. Mrs., Charlestown, Mass.
Gregory John B., 261 Westminster st., Providence, R. I.
Gregory George, 58 H street, Washington, D. C.
Gregory Albert Mrs., Providence, R.I.
Griffin John, carriage trimmer, Dover, N. H.
Grogan J. Mortimer, Lowell, Mass.
Grover William, agent Hadley Co., h. Race street, Holyoke, Mass.
Grover Benjamin, Holyoke, Mass.
Grover Thomas, " "
Gunnison Josephine Mrs., box 708, Saco, Maine.
Gurney Charles W., Sacramento, Cal.

## H

Hackett Frank W., 323 4½ st., Washington, D. C.
Hall Frank S., 217 Fulton st., N. York.
Hall Robert M., " "
Hall Timothy, Harrison square, Mass.
Hall Charles C., " " "
Hall J. Parker Mrs., Brookline, Mass.
Hall A. J., 91 to 95 W. Dedham street, Boston.
Ham S. F. Dr., Boylston st., Boston.
Ham S. F. Mrs. Dr. " "
Ham Charles E., Chicago, Ill.
Ham Tobias, Lake Village, N. H.
Ham Joseph, Salem, Mass.
Ham Nathaniel, Rollinsford, N. H.
Ham Joseph L., Plymouth, Mass.
Ham Leander, Virginia City, Nevada.
Hamet William, Boston.
Hall William, 27 Lambert st., Boston.
Hall Wm. Mrs., " "
Hall Charles S., " "
Hall Barnabas T., " "
Hall John, Lynn.
Hall Frances W., South Berwick.
Hall Martha, 100 Mt. Vernon street, Boston.
Hall Ann M., 100 Mt. Vernon street, Boston.
Haven Henry, Petaluma, Sonoma Co., Cal.
Haven Chas., 365 W. Lake st., Chicago
Haven Clara, Lynn.
Haven Caroline S., Lynn.
Haven Lucy M., Lynn.
Hammond Joseph G., 141 Everett av., Chelsea.
Hammond Joseph G. Mrs., 141 Everett avenue, Chelsea.
Hammond George H., 141 Everett av., Chelsea.
Haven Washington, 391 Western ave., Lynn.
Hammond Daniel M., Third police station, Boston.
Hammond Frank G., 355 Clairborne street, N. O.
Hahn Nilson W., Eutaw st., E. Boston.

Hahn Emily Mrs., East Boston.
Haley Josiah S., steam engineer, 215 Center st., h. 856 8 ave., New York.
Haley Josiah S. Mrs., " "
Haley Lizzie H. Miss, public library, Boston.
Hall William H., Worcester, Mass.
Hall William A., jr., Mrs., 682 Tremont street, Boston.
Hall George A., 52 Washington street, Boston.
Hall Martha Mrs., Detroit, Mich.
Hall Gorham Mrs., Charlestown, Mass
Hall D. Elden Mrs., Cleveland, Ohio.
Hall Eliza B., 9 Harvard row, Charlestown, Mass.
Ham Joseph L., Somerset, Mass.
Ham Lucy Miss, Dover, N. H.
Ham Elizabeth Miss, Dover, N. H.
Ham Joseph, Bridgewater, Mass.
Ham Henry Mrs., Boston.
Ham T. Leander, Eureka, Nevada.
Ham Alphonzo, Portland, Mich.
Ham Ferna d Mrs., East Lexington, Mass.
Hamm Charles H., 23 Hanson street, Boston.
Hamm Mary S. A. Mrs., 23 Hanson street, Boston.
Hammond Mary E., Everett street, Chelsea, Mass.
Hammond Daniel, Everett st,, Chelsea, Mass.
Hammond Daniel, South Boston.
Hammond Eugene, Concord.
Handy John N., jr., Merrill & Co., E. Saginaw, Mich.
Ha dy Ann M. Miss, Hanover, Mass.
Handy Ira M., " "
Hanscom J. M., cor. 7th and Dorchester streets, South Boston.
Hanscom Delia S. Miss, Salem, Mass.
Hanscom George H., " "
Hanscom Nellie, Alfred, Me.
Hanscom Howard H., New Haven, Conn.
Hanscom Alfred H., Denver, Col.
Hanscom Leander, " "
Hanscom Oliver A., Lawrence, Kan.
Hanscom John O., San Francisco, Cal.
Hanscom Wallace, " "
Hanscom Waldron, " "
Hans om Mortimer, Salem, Mass.
Hanscom Ralph H., Lawrence, Kan.
Hanscom Eliza Mrs., 3 Rutger place, New York.
Hanscom Albert, 3 Rutger place, N. Y.
Hanscomb Jacob Mrs., Alfred, Me.
Hanson Elizabeth, 76 Prince st., Boston
Harding Eva Mrs., 6 Trenton street, Charlestown, Mass.
Harding William, Martine.
Harmon John W., 65 Haverhill street, Boston.
Harmon Charles, Epping, N. H.
Harmon Frank, Charlestown, Mass.
Harmon Frank Mrs., " "
Harratt Charles, New York.
Harratt Albert, "
Harrington Frank, Chicago, Ill.
Harrington Frank Mrs. " "
Harrington Henry, " "
Harris Eunice Mrs., Lexington, Mass.
Harris Theodore S., cor. Tremont and Winter, Boston.
Harris Robert L. Mrs., Adrian, Mich.
Harris Hamilton Mrs., Albany, N. Y.
Harris Frank Mrs., Greenwood, Mass.
Harris Frank Mrs., Greenwood, Mass.
Harris Franklin Mrs., Greenwood, Ms.
Harrold C. W. Lieut., Fort Hamilton, New York.
Harrold Joseph, Franklin, Mass.
Harrold George J., Exeter, N. H.
Hart Jane H., Mrs., 74 Pearl street, Charlestown, Mass.
Hart William W. Mrs., Amherst, Mass.
Hart Wm. P., McMinnisville, Tenn.
Hart Henry, Greenland, N. H.
Hart William, Washington, D. C.
Hart Hanson, Portland, Me.
Hartshorne James F., 240 Washington street, Boston.
Hartwell Sarah L. W. Mrs., Waltham, Mass.
Harvey Marcia S. Miss, Dover, N. H.
Haseltine B. B., Pittsburgh, Pa.
Haselton Ira, Haverhill, Mass.
Haselton J. C., Whiteside, Tenn.
Haselton John B., Suncook, N. H.
Haseltine James E., 125 and 127 Commercial street, Portland, Me.
Hatch Samuel S., box 511, Salt Lake City.
Haven Chas. E., office, 21 No. Seventh street, house 2031 Walnut, Philadelphia, Pa.
Haven John H., Sandwich Center, N. H.
Hayes William, Alvarado, Alameda Co., Cal.
Hayes William Mrs., Alvarado, Alameda Co., Cal.
Hayes John P., 1128 Division, Philadelphia, Pa.
Hayes Isaac, 1128 Division, Phil., Pa.
Hayes Lydia, box 18, Dover, N. H.
Hayes Ivory, Dover, N. H.
Hayes Clinton D., 1141 Wash., Boston.
Hayes Joseph, Alvarado, Alameda Co., Cal.
Hayes Edward, Medford, Mass.
Haynes Victoria E. Mrs., 157 Hanover, Manchester, N. H.
Hayward Cyrus, Salem, Mass.
Heap L. E. Mrs., 19 No. Green, Chicago, Ill.
Hebb Mina G. Mrs., Annapolis, Md.
Hedge Silas L. Mrs., 53 Mill street, Charlestown.
Henderson Charles, St. Clair, Penn.
Henderson Robert, New York.
Henderson Robert, Mrs., New York.
Henderson Jacob, Chelsea.
Henderson Charles, coal dealer, Pottsville, Pa.
Henderson Alex., coal dealer, Pottsville, Pa.
Henderson Robert B., Boston.
Henderson Robert B. Mrs., Boston.
Hersey Charles Mrs., South Boston.
Hervey Elisha H., Exeter, N. H.
Hickey Thomas H. Mrs., Dorchester, Mass.
Hickle William, Boston.
Hicks Mrs., care of Thos. Walden, Russell street, Charlestown.
Hill Aaron M., Needham, Mass.
Hill James F., Marseilles, France.
Hill Matilda S. Mrs, Wolfboro, N.H.
Hill Andrew, Chelsea, Mass.
Hill George E., East Somerville, Mass.
Hill George E., Mrs. " "
Hill James Mrs., Madison, Wis.
Hill Henry Mrs., East Boston.
Hill Edgar, Providence, R. I.
Hill Granville, Boston.
Hill William H., 49 Cornhill, Boston.
Hills Mary E. Mrs., Franklin, Mass.
Hilton John H., Springfield, Ohio.

Hobart Miles Mrs., care G. S. Dow, Providence, R. I.
Hobbs Martha J., E. Cambridge, Mass.
Hodgdon John W., 37 Central street, Boston.
Hodgdon Willis B., E. R. R. car shop, East Boston.
Hodgdon Morrill, cotton planter, Edwards Depot, Hines Co., Miss.
Hodgdon Calvin S., Exeter, N. H.
Hodgdon Calvin S. Mrs., Exeter, N.H.
Hodge G. B., 44 and 46 Winter street, Boston.
Hodge John M., Needham, Mass.
Hodge Martha B., 65 Trenton street, East Boston.
Holbrook William B., South Boston.
Holbrook Eva L. Mrs., Portland, Me.
Holbrook Emeline Mrs., New York.
Holman John, feathers and bedding, 60 Union street, Boston, house, 140 North avenue, Cambridge, Mass.
Holman Geo. W., feathers and bedding, 47 Friend st., Boston, house 140 North av., Cambridge, Mass.
Holman Chas W., Manchester, N. H.
Holman O. P. Mrs., Worcester, Mass.
Holmes Rev. Thomas, Merriam, Ind.
Holmes Edward, Greenland, N. H.
Holmes Edward Mrs., " "
Horn James F. Mrs., Lynn, Mass.
Horton Henry Mrs., 384 Washington ave., Brooklyn
Horton Susan S. Mrs., Dover, N. H.
How Moses Rev., New Bedford, Mass.
How Moses Rev. Mrs., " "
How Dr. Lyman B., Manchester, N.H.
Howe Moses G., 35 Court, Boston
Howe Martin S., Haverhill, Mass.
Howe John S., Boston
Hoyt Richard H., Newington, N. H.
Hoyt Israel S., " "
Hubbard Dr. Mrs., Louisville, Ky.
Hubbard J. W., Wells, Me.
Hubbard J. W. Mrs., Wells, Me.
Hudson Jacob E., Box 341, Boston
Hugerley H. H. Mrs., 154 Prospect, Cambridgeport, Mass.
Hunter Thomas L., Cambridgeport, Mass.
Hunter Thos. L. Mrs., Cambridgeport, Mass.
Hunter Wm., Bangor, Me.
Huntress Rev. E. S., Maynard, Mass.
Huntress James E., 160 Prospect st., Cambridgeport, Mass.
Huntress James E. Mrs., 160 Prospect st., Cambridgeport, Mass.
Hurd Charles, Lynn, Mass.
Hurd Webster Mrs., 10 Ashland street, Boston.
Hurd James R., 14 Stewart st., Lynn, Mass.
Hurd Geo. E., St. Paul, Minn.
Hurley Wm. P., Rockland, Me.
Hutchings Theodore, Boston
Hutchings Ann, Boston
Hutton Aaron S., 500 W. Broad st., Philadelphia, Pa.

## I

Ingalls Samuel, Lowell, Mass.
Ingalls Oscar F. Mrs., Lynn, Mass.
Irving James Mrs., Ipswich, Mass.

## J

Jackson Wm. J. Mrs., Chelsea, Mass.
Jackson Charles M., " "
Jackson Richard P., Charlestown, "
Jackson Nathan B., " "
Jackson Ada Miss, Charlestown, Mass.
Jackson Carrie Miss, " "
Jackson Isabel Miss., " "
Jackson Fred A., " "
Jackson Geo. E., Boston
Jackson Susan Mrs., 65 Trenton st., East Boston
Jackson Gilman D., Boston
Jackson Gilman D. Mrs., Boston
Jackson Edward, "
Jackson Edward Mrs., "
Jackson Daniel B., "
Jackson Daniel B. Mrs., "
Jackson Wm., Worcester, Mass.
Jackson Alex., Newburyport, Mass.
Jackson Charles, Boston
Jackson Joseph, "
Jackson William, "
Jackson Wm., Chelsea, Mass.
Jackson Leonard, " "
Jackson Howard A., 32 Court sq., Boston
Jackson Thomas M., Treasury Dept., Washington, D. C.
Jackson John H., Custom House, Boston
Jewett George Mrs., Bangor, Me.
Jewett John, New York
Jackson Charles E., Jamaica Plain, Mass.
Jackson Wm., Charlestown, Mass.
Janvrin Geo., San Francisco, Cal.
Janvrin James, " "
Jarvis Russell Mrs., Claremont, N. H.
Jarvis Wm. H., N. & C. R. R. Shop, Nashville, Tenn.
Jenkins Wallace H. Mrs., Lynn, Mass.
Jenkins Edward L., Boston
Jenkins Charles W., Peabody, Mass.
Jenkins Wm. D. Mrs., Brooklyn, N.Y.
Johnson Jeremiah Mrs., Johnson & Dauchy, N. Y. City
Jones Thomas Mrs., Broad st., Lynn, Mass.
Jones Edwin F. Mrs., Broad st., Lynn, Mass.
Junkins George P., Boston
Junkins Wallace, Charlestown, Mass.
Jenkins Thos., 36 Webster st., E. Boston
Jenkins Margaret Mrs., 36 Webster st., East Boston
Jenkins L. Edward, Chelsea, Mass.
Jenkins Loyal, Merchants Bank, Boston
Jewett Dr. Theodore, S. Berwick, Me.
Johnson Lucy M. Mrs., Baltimore, Md.
Johnson Charles F. Mrs., Mt. Vernon st., Charlestown, Mass.
Johnson Dorothy Mrs., Charlestown, Mass.
Johnson Mrs., Jamaica Plain, Mass.
Johnson Dolly Mrs., Charlestown, Ms.
Jones Joseph D., Jordan, Marsh & Co., Boston
Jones Joseph J., Bangor, Me.
Joy Alfred L., Boston
Julian Luke, Exeter, N. H.
Junkins Orren C., Valejo, Cal.
Junkins Emma F. Miss, 1131 Fulton, Brooklyn, N. Y.

## K

Keith Harriet G. Mrs., Matthews Court House. Va.
Kennedy Carrie I. Mrs., Peoria, Ill.
Kennedy C. H., Lynn, Mass.
Kidney James W. Mrs., Sullivan st., Charlestown, Mass.
Kimball Reuben, lumber dealer' Water, cor. Clinton, Saginaw, Mich.

Kingsley Wm. L., New Haven, Ct.
Kingsbury Charles Mrs., N. Y. City
Knight Annie A. Mrs., Randolph, Ms.
Knight S. Newhall, agt. American Express Co., Third st., h. N. W. corner Sanborn and Huff, Winona, Minn.
Knight Eben Mrs., New York City
Knight Abby Miss, " "
Knight Maria Miss, Salem, Mass.
Knight Lizzie Miss, " "
Knowlton L. U. C. Miss, 293 Fulton st., Chicago
Knowlton W. H. H., 293 Fulton st., Chicago
Knowlton Willis T., 881 So. Halstead st., Chicago
Knowlton Mary Miss, Hartford, Ct.
Knowlton John Mrs., Orphan Asylum, Hartford, Ct.
Knowlton Howard C., 16 Monument st., Portland, Me.
Knowlton James J., San Francisco, Cal.
Knowlton Wm., 42 and 44 Duane st., New York
Knowlton Epes Mrs., East Boston
Knowlton J. S. Mrs., " "
Kennard Martin P., 331 Washington, Boston
Kennard Manning, Florence, Italy
Kennard Wm. M., Newport, Pa.
Kennard Wm. H., Boston
Kennard Charles W., Tremont street, Boston
Kennard M. P. Mrs., Boston
Kennedy Thomas, Box 51, Ipswich, Mass.
Kennedy Thos. H., Box 51, Ipswich, Mass.
Kennedy Anna Mrs., St. Joseph, Mo.
Keyes Benj. F., E. R. R., Lynn, Mass.
Keyes Benj. F. Mrs., " " "
Knowlton J. Edward, 137 Washington st., Boston
Knowlton J. Edward Mrs., 137 Washington st., Boston
Knowlton Willis T., Chicago, Ill.
Krans Edward H. Mrs., La Grange House, Boston

## L

Labree J. G., Schenectady, N. Y.
Ladd Eliphalet, Auburndale, Mass.
Laighton N. Parker, Tremont Brewery, Boston
Laighton N. Parker Mrs., Tremont Brewery, Boston
Laighton Samuel, 128 Manderville st., New Orleans, La.
Laighton Sam'l Mrs., 128 Manderville st., New Orleans, La.
Laighton W. Fernald, Navy Yard, Charlestown, Mass.
Laighton James A., Palmer, Batchelders & Co., Boston
Laighton Ivan, Charlestown, Mass.
Laighton Thos. B. Mrs., Isle of Shoals, N. H.
Laighton Oscar, Isle of Shoals, N. H.
Laighton Cedric, " "
Laighton Mary P., Treas. Dept., Washington, D. C.
Laighton Edgar Mrs., G. Falls, N. H.
Lamos James C., Dover, "
Lang Thomas W., Boston
Langdon Frank E., S. Berwick, N. H.
Larkin George, Lynn, Mass.
Larkin Thomas, Natick, Mass.
Larkin Thos., jr., " "
Larrabee James, Alfred, Me.
Lary Charles, New York City
Lacoste John H., Beal, Hooper & Co., Boston
Ladd Wm. F., New York City
Ladd James S., Zanesville, Ohio
Ladd F. M., Salisbury, Mass.
Ladd C. E., West Newton, Mass.
Ladd Eliphalet, East Windsor, Ct.
Laighton W. Fernald, New London, Ct.
Laighton Parker Mrs., Indiana Place, Boston
Lambert Fred N., 174 Commercial st., Boston
Lambert Addie F. Miss, Box 268, New Orleans, La.
Lambert Wm. Mrs., Boston
Lambert Mary Miss, "
Lancaster Hattie A. Mrs., Boston
Lancaster W. D. Mrs., 76 Webster st., East Boston
Lane Mary J., Natick, Mass.
Lang Thomas W., Sible,y Osecola Co., Iowa
Lang Lottie A. Mrs., Wampanoag, Mills, Fall River, Mass.
Lang Charles T., Wampanoag Mills Fall River, Mass.
Lang J. Whidden, Meridith Village, N. H.
Lang T. Elwyn, Meredith Village, N. H.
Langfo rd Joseph C., farmer, Candia, N. H.
Langdon John, Buenos Ayres, South America
Lathrop Caroline Mrs., Melrose, Mass.
Lawrence Parker Mrs., Chelsea, Mass.
Laws John W., Boston
Laws Wm. H., Jamaica Plain, Mass.
Leach Alex., Newburyport, Mass.
Lear Wm. H., East Boston.
Lear John, Pacific Mills, Lawrence, Mass.
Leavitt Charles W., Oshkosh, Minn.
Leet Fred Dr. Mrs., Greenville, Mercer Co., Pa.
Lefavour Mary A. Miss, Dover, N. H.
Leonard Francis D., Barnes & Co., Boston
LeRoy Wm. A. Mrs., Lynn, Mass.
Leslie G. Fred., Haverhill, Mass.
Lester Wm. Mrs., Stratham, N. H.
Libbey I. Putnam, Washington, D. C.
Libbey Henry Mrs., Mt. Washington Glass Co., New Bedford, Mass.
Little Martha A. Mrs., Epping, N. H.
Little Susan Mrs., 29 Green street, Portland, Me.
Littlefield John L., Eliot Depot, Me.
Long Nathan'l R., hardware, 19 and 21 Main, Penn Yan, Yates Co., N. Y.
Long Wm., Jordan, Marsh & Co., Boston
Lord Theresa Mrs., Boston
Loring Dolly Mrs., Gloucester, Mass.
Lovering John D. Mrs., Chelsea, Mass.
Lowd Daniel Y. Mrs., Mendota, Ill.
Lowd Mark, Salem, Mass.
Lunt Charles, Boston Highlands
Lunt Ellen Miss, "
Lunt Sarah Miss, "
Lyman John, Boston
Lynn Albert, 186 Hanover st., Boston
Lyons Mary A. Mrs., Elliot, Me.
Lyons Robert Mrs., Staten Island, N.Y.
Leach Wm. H., Boston
Leach Samuel, Melrose, Mass.
Leach John S., Rye, N. H.
Lester Wm., Stratham, N.H.

Libbey Israel P., Waltham, Mass.
Libbey Wm., L., agt. Mt. Wash. Glass Works, Boston.
Lindsay Geo. Mrs., 1084 Washington st., Boston
Little Wm. D., Newburyport, Mass.
Little J. Gardner, Newburyport, Mass.
Locke Martha Miss, 10 Ashland street, Boston
Locke Emily M. Miss, 10 Ashland st., Boston
Locke J. J., Box 945, Haverhill, Mass.
Locke John S. Charlestown, "
Locke Martha R. Mrs., Charlestown, Mass.
Locke James W. Mrs., Key West, Fla.
Locke J. J., Mrs., Haverhill, Mass.
Long Samuel P., Exeter, N. H.
Lowd J. C., Temple Place, Boston
Lyford G. C. Mrs., Exeter, N. H.
Lyman P., 40 State st., Boston
Lyman Charles A., Philadelphia, Pa.

## M

Main Chas. Mrs., San Francisco, Cal.
Main Jane Ann, Boston
Manent Eliza Miss, 3 Rutger st., New York City
Mann Herbert, Haverhill, Mass,
Mann N. P., Boston
Mann N. P. Mrs., Boston.
Mann N. P., jr., Boston
March John S., Boston
Manson Alvah C., painter, Warsaw, N. Y.
Marden James, N. Hampton, N. H.
Marden S. B. Mrs., Providence, R. I.
Marden Francis, Georgetown, Mass.
Marden Geo. N., Stoughton, Mass.
Marden Almira Mrs., No. Hampton, N. H.
Marden David, Boston
Marden Wm., "
Marden Daniel, Hartford, Ct.
Marden C. W., Hartford, Ct.
Marks Lucy H. S., 43 Forrester st., Salem, Mass.
Marks Mary H., 43 Forrester st., Salam, Mass.
Marr Henry N. Boston
Marsh Frank P., Rochester, N. Y.
Marsh M. Sheafe, W. Washington st., Chicago, Ill.
Marshall Andrew, Barnstead, N. H.
Marston Simon L., Haverhill, Mass.}
Marston John J., Gardiner, Me.
Marston John J. Mrs., " "
Marston Alice C.. " "
Mack John S., Cambridgeport
Manent Charles, 3 Rutger st., N. York
Manent Chas. Mrs., " "
Manent Henry, " "
Manent Augustus, " "
Manent James, " "
Manent Wm., 9th st., Brooklyn
Manent Harry, 258 Monroe st., New York
Manson John Mrs., Cambridge
Marden Edwin, 8 Mulberry st., Providence
Marden Edwin Mrs., 8 Mulberry st., Providence
Marden Andrew, 8 Mulberry st., Providence
Marden W. H. Boston
Marsh Charles, Salem
Marshall Wm. G., N. Y. C. & H. R. R., Rochester, N. Y.
Marston J. Edward, 32 Cabot st., Beverly
Marston Jacob, Rye, N. H.
Marston Benning, Newburyport, Mass.
Marston William A. Mrs., 28 Oxford St.. Boston,
Marston James, North Hampton, N. H.
Marston Lucy A. Mrs., " "
Marston Sherburn, " "
Marston James, " "
Marston James Mrs., " "
Marston John G., Bangor, Maine.
Marston Sarah E. Mrs., " "
artin Richard, Boston.
Martin George W., San Francisco, Cal.
Martin John, Great Falls, N. H.
Martin Chas. W., merchant tailor, Post Office block, h. 65 Emerson, Haverhill, Mass.
Marvel James T., Ipswich, Mass.
Marvel James T. Mrs., Ipswich, Mass.
Mason Charlotte A. H. Mrs., Berlin, Wis.
Mason Robert M. Boston.
Mason Charles Mrs. Medford, Mass;
Mason Gustavus W., Chelsea, Mass.
Mathes Frances A. Miss, Dedham, Mass.
Mathes T. H. Mrs., Dover, N. H.
Maynard Charles E., Arizona.
Maxwell Mr. and Mrs., Oliver F., Central Iron Foundry, E. Boston.
Maxwell Oliver E., Boston.
McDonald Joseph H., Charlestown, Mass.
McGaw Thomas, 19 No. Green, Chicago, Ill.
McGaw Robert, 108 Bartlett, Charlestown, Mass.
McLane Allan, Nice, France.
McIntosh Adelaide M. Mrs., Bath, Me.
Mead Mrs. Elizabeth, 123 Chestnut, Chelsea, Mass.
Medbury Andrew N., Seekonk, Mass.
Medbury Mrs. Andrew N., " "
Melcher George, Custom House, Boston.
Melcher Chas. C., B. & A. R. R.,office, 40 State, Boston.
Melcher Nellie Miss, 32 Doane, Boston,
Melcher William N., Lynn, Mass.
Melcher John L., New York.
Melcher William, Mittineague, Mass.
Melcher Mary Miss, Dover, N. H.
Melcher Almira Miss, " "
Melcher Charles F., 40 State St., Boston.
March Benjamin D., Genl Post Office, New York.
Marshall J. Otis Mrs., Lynn, Mass.
Meinerth Charles A., Newburyport, Mass.
Meinerth John Haven, Newburyport, Mass.
Meinerth Josephine L., Newburyport, Mass.
Meinerth George G., Newburyport, Mass.
Melvin R. S. Miss, 14 Concord square, Boston.
Melvin James S., Boston
Mendum Caroline A., Newfield, N. J.
M endum J. Albert, Boston.
Mendum James D. Newfield, N. J.
Mendum Jas. D. Mrs., Newfield, N, J.
Mendum Willis B., grocer, 162 Dorchester avenue, So. Boston.
Mendum George E., Boston,
Mendum George, Charlestown, Mass.
Merriam J. Warren Mrs., 1228 Wabash avenue, Chicago, Ill.
Merrill George E., station agent and telegraphic operator, E. R. R., W. Ossipee, New York.

Merrill Sylvester P., Amesbury, Mass.
Merrill E. G. Mrs., Newburyport, Mass.
Merrill L. E. N. Mrs., " "
Merrill Albion K., Waukegan, Ill.
Merrill Albion K. Mrs., Waukegan, Ill.
Miles Gilbert Mrs., Box 4045 N. Y. city
Milles George, Lynn.
Milton Sarah M. Mrs., 40 Union Street. Boston.
Milton Miss Viola, 40 Union St., Boston.
Milton George B., dry goods, 427 Washington st., Boston.
Milton Horace P., 427 Washington St., Boston.
Milton Andrew T., 427 Washington St., Boston.
Milton A. T. Mrs., 427 Washington, Street, Boston,
Milton Wallace, New Orleans, La.
Mitchell Mrs. Mattie, Norwich, Conn.
Mitchell Eliza A. Mrs. Manchester. N. H.
Mitchell Robert Mrs., Kennebunkport, Me.
Moody Elias Mrs., Dover, N. H.
Moore Edward Mrs., 360 No. Eutaw St., Baltimore, Md.
Moore Eveline Mrs., Boston.
Monroe George E., 116 London Street, East Boston.
Monroe Mary E. Mrs., 19 North Green St., Chicago, Ill.
Monroe Nathan Mrs., So. Seekonk, Mass.
Monroe Joel Mrs., Pembroke Mass.
Moran Harrison, Box 23, St. Helena, Napa Co., Cal.
Moran W. W., Brownsville, Texas.
Moran Andrew, Somerset, Mass.
Moran Henry W., Box 203, East Somerville, Mass.
Moran Andrew D., Durham, N. H.
Moran John Mrs., Cambridge, Mass.
Morgan James Mrs., Manchester, Mass.
Morrison Eliza D. Miss., Dorchester, Mass.
Morrow Helen .M, Baugor, Me.
Morrow Mary P., " "
Morton Sarah A. Mrs., E. Somerville, Mass.
Morton William H., Salmon Falls, N. H.
Moses John W., Mill Center, Wis.
Moses John H., Everett, Mass.
Mosher Josie W. Mrs., 104 Decatur St., East Boston.
Moulton E. A., Simpson, Nowell & Co., Chicago.
Moulton Wallace S., Biddeford, Me.
Moulton Charles, Portland, Me.
Moulton N. Thayer, Colorado Ter.
Moulton W. S., merchant tailor, Biddeford, Maine.
Moulton N. Thayer Mrs., Biddeford, Maine.
Moulton William, Boston.
Moulton John Mrs., Amesbury, Mass.
Mudge Andrew A., Boston.
Mudge Alfred, "
Mudge George A., "
Mudge Edward, "
Mudge Margaret Mrs., Plaistow, N. H.
Mullin W. Frank, leather dealer, No. 1 Rowe's Wharf, Boston.
Mullin Mrs. W. F., No. 1 Rowe's whf., Boston.
Mullin Frederic B., Boston.
Mullin Frederic H., "
Mugridge Daniel S., 904½ Michigan av., Chicago.
Murray William Mrs., Salem, Mass.
Murray Lizzie A. Miss, Lynn.
Manson Alvah C., Warsaw, Wyoming MCo., N. Y.
Merrill Albion K., Waukegan, Ill.
Merrill Albion K. Mrs., " "
Merrill William, E. R. R. Car shop, Salem, Mass.
Merrill William P., Wollaston Heights, Salem, Mass.
Merrill Elbridge G., Newburyport, Mass.
Merrill Sylvester P., Newburyport, Mass.
Merrill George E., Newburyport, Mass.,
Meserve John S., Huntingdon, W. Va.
Messer Reed, 195 Sumner St., East Boston.
Miller Harriet A. Mrs., Drytown, Amador Co., Cal.
Minot George Mrs., Concord, N. H.
Mitchell Margaret G. Mrs., Salem, Mass.
Mitchell Charles Mrs., Kittery.
Mitchell James, Hovey's, 33 Summer street, Boston.
Mix Wm. N. Mrs., Independent, Van Buren Co., Io.
McKinnon John G., Boston.
Moore Martha F., Boston.
Moore William P., Boston.
Moore Elisha, Boston.
Moran Walter, Somerville, Mass.
Moreland E. G. Mrs., nurse, Chicago, Ill.
Moses J. Wesley, Mrs., Manchester N. H.
Moses Clarence, Manchester, N. H.
Moses Erank, " "
Moses Irving S., " "
Moulton Jos. H., San Francisco, Cal.
Moulton C. Buchanan, Cambridge, Mass.
Moulton C. Buchanan Mrs., Cambridge, Mass.
Moulton Edwin, Chicago, Ill.
Moulton Benjamin, Stratham, N. H.
Mudge Charles, Boston.
Mudge S. W., Rice, Kendall & Co., Boston.
Mudge S. W. Mrs., Rice, Kendall & Co., Boston.
Mudge George W., Rice, Kendall & Co., Boston.
Mudie R. A. Mrs., Chicago.
Mullen Henry T., Whitney St., W. Lynn, Mass.
Mullen Charles H., Lynn, Mass.
Mullen James D., 37 Washington St., Lynn, Mass.
Mullen Asa E., Lynn, Mass.
Murray William, Salem, Mass.

## N

Nason John, Woonsocket, R. I.
Navy Ann O Mrs., 76 Prince, Boston.
Neal George W., Boston
Neal Ida Miss, Salem, Mass.
Neal Charles, Kittery, Me.
Neal John, Kittery.
Neal Samuel B., Box 1479, Boston
Nelson Isaac F. Mrs., 4 Dana place, Boston
Nelson Clara Miss, do.
Nelson Ella Miss, do.
Newhall O. D., Harrison av., Boston.
Newhall Frank H., 35 Bromfield, Boston
Newton Mary Mrs., Key st., cor. Shawmut ave., Jamaica Plain
Nickerson Frances A. Mrs., New Orleans, La.

Nickerson Frederic Mrs., So. Boston.
Nichols Ralph, Lower Lake, Cal.
Nichols Chas. Mrs., San Francisco, Cal.
Nichols John H., 269 Lowell, Lawrence, Mass.
Nichols Phineas Mrs., San Francisco.
Noble Robert V., roofing slate and roofing materials, Hudson, N. Y., h. Greenport, Columbia Co., N. Y.
Norris Joseph Mr. & Mrs., 205 West Newton, Boston
Norris Moses, morocco manufacturer, 156 Market, house 86 Summer, Lynn, Mass.
Norris Edward, Charlestown, Mass.
Norris Lucy Mrs., Newburyport, Mass.
Norton Thomas Mrs. Salem, Mass.
Norton Andrew J. Mrs., Greenland, N. H.
Norton Thomas H., 509 Hayes, San Francisco, Cal.
Norton Robert G., E. Somerville, Mass.
Norton Sarah Miss, East Somerville, Mass.
Noble Robert, New York.
Norris George W. Mrs., Chelsea.
Norris Isaiah B., Malden
Norris Isaiah B. Miss, Malden
Norton Abby Miss, Salem, Mass.
Norton Thomas Mrs., "
Norris Joseph, Boston.
Norris Joseph Mrs., Boston.
Norwood George Mrs., Russell street, Charlestown, Mass.
Nowell William G., Malden, Mass.
Nowell Wm. G. Mrs., " "
Nowell S. M. Miss, Camb'gep't, Mass.
Nowell A. C. Miss, " "
Nowell James A., " "
Nowell Joseph S., " "
Nowell Ellen Mrs., Lycoming Co., Penn.
Nowell Mina Miss, Lycoming Co., Penn.
Nutter William, Kittery Point, Me.
Nutter William A., Haverhill, Mass.
Nutter Sarah O. Mrs., Lake Village, N. H.
Nutter Philander E., Boston.
Nutter Sarah H. Mrs., E. Somerville, Mass.
Nutter B. F., 39 Adams, Boston
Nowell Sarah J. Mrs., Inman st., Cambridgeport, Mass.
Nowell Fred D., 37 Park Row, New York City
Noyes Clementine P. Mrs., Lafayette, Ind.
Nutter Johnson, East Boston
Nutter Johnson Mrs., East Boston
Nutter Charles, "
Nutter Frank, "
Nutter Emma, "
Nutter Charles W., Newington, N. H.
Nutter William, "
Nutter Joshua M., Bath, Me.
Nutter Nathaniel, Greenland, N. H.

## O

O'Brien Michael, Lawrence, Mass.
Odiorne Daniel, Holbrook, Mass.
Odiorne Eliza B. Mrs., "
Odiorne Charles B., "
Odiorne Leonard H., Boston Highlands
Odiorne Charles E., Gorham, N. H.
Odiorne Joseph, 80 Washington st., Boston
Odiorne George W., So. Newmarket, N. H.
Oliver Louise Mrs., 214 7th st., South Boston
O'Neal Charles, Rock Island, Ill.
Ordway C. D., Natick, Mass.
Ormsby L. M. Mrs., Hermitage, Mercer Co., Penn.
Otis James M., Concord, N. H.
Otis O. B., Haverhill, Mass.
Otis William M., Kittery, Me.
Odiorne Simeon S.,
Odiorne Mattie A. Miss.
Odiorne Charles, East Boston.
Odion Henry W., Chicago.
Otis Harrison G., Concord, N. H.
Otis William H., Kittery

## P

Packer William C. Mrs., Greenland, N. H.
Page Josiah, Freeborn, Freeborn Co., Minn.
Paine Lucy M. Miss, Lawrence, Mass.
Paine Mary E. R. Mrs., "
Palmer R. H. Mrs., Pittsburgh, Penn.
Palmer Robert M., Haverhill, Mass.
Parker Charles C. P., San Francisco, Cal.
Parker Hannah R., Somerville, Mass.
Parker John D., Boston.
Parker Francis E., "
Parker George W., No. Andover, Mass
Parker Benjamin, " "
Parker William H., " "
Parker Anna J., " "
Parker Ida F., " "
Parker John H. Mrs., Lewiston, Me.
Parker Amasa Mrs., Albany, N. Y.
Parker C, E. R. Mrs., Delhi, N. Y.
Parker Adelaide E. M. Mrs., Bristol, Bucks Co., Penn.
Parker Ada A. Miss., Bristol, Bucks Co., Penn.
Parker Virginia A. Miss, Bristol, Bucks Co., Penn.
Parker Abby, Wolfeboro', N. H.
Parker Wm. A. Capt,, U. S. N., Maverick House, E. Boston.
Parker Belia M. Miss, 321 Dudley st., Boston.
Parker John H., Raymond, N. H.
Parks Albert, Police dept., Cincinnati, O.
Parks Joseph, Newburyport
Parmenter Annie M. Mrs., Randolph, Mass.
Parrott Commodore E. G,, Charlestown. Mass.
Parrott Robert P., Cold Spring, Putnam Co., N. Y.
Parrott Peter P., Greenwood Iron Works, Orange Co., N. Y.
Parry Edward Randolph, Brevet Major U. S. A., Fortress Munroe
Parry Mrs., " "
Parsons Samuel, No. Beverly.
Parsons John H., Salem, Mass.
Parsons J. M., " "
Parsons Warren, Newburyport.
Parsons Nathaniel P., Drytown, Amado Co., Cal.
Parsons Nathaniel P. Mrs., do.
Parsons Daniel, Charlestown.
Parsons D. B., Boston.
Parsons Louis P., Boston.
Parsons William, "
Partridge Charles C., 13 Boylston st., Boston.
Partridge James, Boston.

Patten N. S., Butler, Ky.
Patten Lucy Miss, Kellogg, Iowa.
Patterson A. J. Rev., Boston
Patterson A. J. Rev. Mrs., Boston.
Paul George N. Mrs., 37 Laurel, Worcester, Mass.
Paul Arthur H., East Somerville, Mass.
Paul Herbert, cor. Chauncy and Summer, Boston.
Paul J. Fletcher, "lifting cure," 149 A. Tremont, cor. West, Boston, h. Jamaica Plain.
Paul Stephen Mrs., Newington.
Paul William, 47th st., Harlem, N. Y.
Paul William Mrs., " "
Paul Carrie M. Miss, Jamaica Plain.
Paul Lucy A. Mrs., "
Paul George E., St. Jose, Mo.
Paul Charles W., " "
Paul Henry K., Bristol, Conn.
Payson Clark, Kensington, N. H.
Payson Robert, Lynn, Mass.
Peabody Mary Rantoul, Cambridge, Mass.
Peabody M. Ladd, Cambridge, Mass.
Peabody Caroline E., " "
Peabody Helen T., " "
Peabody A. P. Rev., Cambridge.
Peabody A. P. Rev. Mrs., "
Pearson Nathaniel, Portland, Me.
Pearson Oliver G., 17 Province, Boston
Pearson Edmund, 17 Province, Boston
Pearson G. W., 109 Saratoga, East Boston.
Pearson Robert, 40 Shepherd street, Lynn.
Peirce Chas. W., 611 Vine, Philadelphia, Pa.
Peirce Clarence, 242 Washington, Boston.
Peirce John, Xenia, Ill.
Peirce Ruth O., Bristol, Penn.
Peirce Charles Mrs., Amesbury, Mass.
Peirce Andrew Mrs., Dover, N. H.
Peirce Mrs., care J. L. Smith, Dover, N. H.
Peirce Jas. L., cor. 11th and Wallace, Philadelphia.
Peirce Ruth S. Mrs., Bristol, Conn.
Penhallow Benj., Lowell, Mass.
Penhallow L. E., " "
Penhallow S. P., " "
Penhallow Thomas W., 7 St. James ave., Boston.
Penhallow Thos. W. Mrs., 7 St. James ave., Boston.
Penhallow Charles I., 7 St. James av., Boston.
Penhallow Peirce, 7 St. James ave., Boston.
Penhallow Susan, Philadelphia, Pa.
Penhallow B. H., "
Pennington John Mrs., E. Boston.
Pennington Adeline E. Mrs., 20 White st., E. Boston
Pennington Henry, do.
Pennington George A., do.
Perkins Joseph O., Sudbury st., Boston
Perkins John Mrs., Salem, Mass.
Perkins Alfred, E. R. R. Car Shop, Salem, Mass.
Perkins Mary Mrs., Gloucester, Mass.
Perkins George, Nahant.
Perkins James, Lynn.
Perkins John A., "
Perry Henry E., So. Newmarket, N. H.
Peterson Edwin A., Greenland.
Peterson Edwin A. Mrs., Greenland, N. H.
Peterson William E. Mrs., Greenland, N. H.
Peyser William, Boston.
Peyser Wm. Mrs., "
Peyser Elizabeth, "
Peverley William, Chelsea.
Philbrook Henry Mrs., Charlestown, Mass.
Phillips Quincy Mrs., Cambridge.
Pickering J. Howard, Boston.
Pickering Charles E. "
Pickering John I. Mrs., Newington.
Pickering Ephraim J., "
Pickering Lydia Mrs., Greenland.
Pickering Daniel N., Boston.
Pickering Isaac, "
Pickering Isaac Mrs., "
Pickering William L. New York.
Pickering James F., 108 Tremont St., Boston.
Pierce Abby S. Mrs., Lawrence Mass.
Pierce Martin Luther, Pres. 1st National Bank, Lafayette, Ind.
Pike Edward L., Cambridge.
Pike George "
Pike Annie R. C., Antrim, N. H.
Pike J. F. G. Dr., Pavilion, Tremont St., Boston.
Pike J. Thornton, 2d Comp. Office, Washington.
Pinkham Isaac, Lynn.
Pinkham Margaret Mrs., Newmarket, N. H.
Piper J. H., Salem St., Maplewood, Mass.
Piper J. H. Mrs., " "
Piper William H., 131 & 133 Washington St., Boston.
Piper Moses H., " " "
Piper James M., 101 W. Springfield St., Boston.
Piper Benj. C., State House, Boston.
Piper Chas., 131 Washington st., Boston
Piper Harriet Miss, South Boston.
Pitman Thomas, Charlestown.
Pitman George, "
Pitman Ezekiel, "
Place George H., East Walpole, Mass.
Place Geo. H. Mrs., " "
Place Jas. E., Cohoes, N. Y.
Platt Abbie M. Mrs., Boston.
Plumer Henry, 95 Commercial Street, Boston.
Plumer Mary, Charlestown.
Plumer Abbie Miss, Somerville, Mass.
Plumer Sarah O., Mrs., Richmond, Ind.
Plumer J. P., 339 Washington St., Boston.
Pollard Mrs., 323 W 32d St., New York.
Pollard Andrew Mrs., South Boston.
Poor Charles V. Mrs., 29 & 30 India St., Boston.
Pope M. Mrs., cor. Wash. and Bowdoin Sts., Boston.
Porter George, E. R. R. Car Shop, Salem, Mass.
Porter Frank, Salem, Mass.
Porter Fannie Mrs., Salem, Mass.
Porter Isaac Mrs., Wenham, Mass.
Porter George N. Mrs., 3 Lothrop St., Salem, Mass.
Porter Hattie W. Miss, " "
Porter Howard, " "
Pote Fronie Mrs., 476 Sumner St., East Boston.
Potter Treat, Manchester, N. H.
Potter Drown "

Powers Wm. Mrs., Malden.
Powers Clara A. Mrs., Malden.
Pray Wm. P., 116 N. 11th St., Phila.
Pray James, Fort Madison, Iowa.
Pray E. P. S. Mrs., Washington, D. C.
Pray William, East Boston.
Pray Elma Mrs., Charlestown.
Prescott Henry W., 40th W. 9th St. New York.
Prescott Henry W. Mrs., " "
Prescott James, " " "
Prescott Frank, " " "
Prescott Oliver " " "
Prescott Walter " " "
Prescott John, Grafton.
Prescott Charles W., 242 Washington St., Boston.
Preston Sarah Mrs., Nebraska City, Neb.
Preston Wm. H., Smith Doolittle & Smith, Boston.
Preston Margaret Mrs., East Canaan.
Priest M. L., physician, New Bedford.
Priest M. L. Mrs., " "
Priest Franklin, So. Scituate, Mass.
Priest John, Newington, N. H.
Priest Mary Mrs., North Cohasset, Mass
Prouty Sarah A. Mrs., East Boston.
Pryor Charles, Salem, Mass.
Pryor Joseph, East Boston.
Pryor Roscoe, "
Putnam F. C. Rev., Bergen, N. Y.
Putnam Hannah Miss, Newburyport.
Putnam James R., painter, Boston.

## R

Raitt John W., Fitchburg, Mass.
Ramsdell N. Rogers, 51 Hanover, Boston.
Rand Samuel S., Claremont.
Rand Warren L., 361 Meridian St., Boston.
Rand Edwin R., 5 Hersey Place, Boston
Rand Wallace, C. W. Kennards, "
Rand David, S. B. & A. R. R. Shop, Boston.
Rand William, " " " "
Rand George S., Hyannis, Mass.
Rand Edward S., Lebanon Centre.
Rand David H., Oakland, Cal.
Rand Edward A., S. Boston.
Rand W. Wallace, "
Rand Manning K, 148 Tremont, Boston
Rand Charles F., 53 Tufts, Charlestown.
Rand Annie L., 114 Decatur, E. Boston
Rand Frank P., North Hampton, N. H.
Rand John W., hatter and furrier, 71 Main, Charlestown, Mass.
Rand Gilman, 59 E. Brookline, Boston.
Rand Moses jr., hats, &c., 175 Washington, Boston.
Rand Streeter, Claremont, N. H.
Randall Edward, Seabrook, N. H.
Randall Frank B., State st., Boston.
Randall Reuben S., police officer, 172 Chelsea street, Charlestown, Mass.
Rea Samuel, Crescent place, Boston.
Rea Adelaide, " " "
Rea Pierpont, " " "
Rea Samuel, jr., " " "
Reding Chas. W. Rev., Milford, Mass.
Reding H. Warren, Centralia, Kansas.
Reding J. Warren, Haverhill, N. H.
Reding M. A. Miss, Millford, Mass.
Reding Sylvester, " "
Reed John S., Pawtucket, R. I.
Reed John S. Mrs. " "
Remick Albert, Tiffany & Co., N. York.
Remick Albert Mrs., " "
Remick Herman, Boston.
Remick John, Kittery, Me.
Remick Joseph jr., East Boston.
Remick Mary A. Mrs., New York City.
Remick William, Melrose.
Remick Frances Miss, Brooklyn, N. Y.
Rhodes Edward B. Mrs., Suncook, N. H
Rice Stephen Mrs., San Francisco.
Rice Chas. B., 316 Madison ave., N. Y.
Rice Oliver P., " " "
Rice Wm. A. Mrs. " " "
Rice Edwin T. Mrs., " " "
Rice Richard H., homœopathic physician, 48 Farwell, Newport, R. I.
Rice George F., Lynn, Mass.
Rice William F., Salem, Mass.
Rice George, Boston.
Richards Louisa S. Mrs., St. Louis, Mo.
Richardson Joseph P. Mrs., Newburyport, Mass.
Richardson Nellie Mrs., So. Boston.
Richardson Mary Mrs., Knoxville, Tenn.
Richter Emile Mrs. Dr., Baltimore, Md.
Ricker Marian A. Miss, Boston.
Ricker Elijah, Exeter.
Ricker Samuel, Exeter.
Ricker James W., city treasurer's office, Boston.
Ricker Thomas, South Berwick, Me.
Riley Charles W., carpenter, Causeway, cor. Friend, Boston, house Salem st., Maplewood, Mass.
Riley Sarah E. Mrs., Salem st., Maplewood, Mass.
Riley Frank E., organ builder, Mason & Hamlin, Boston, house Salem st., Maplewood, Mass.
Riley Villa B. Miss, Salem street, Maplewood, Mass.
Rindge John Mrs., Elsworth Ave., Cambridgeport, Mass.
Roberts James Mrs. Gen'l, Fortress Monroe.
Roberts Maria Miss, New York City.
Roberts Mary, Brooklyn, N. Y.
Roberts John K., Salem, Mass.
Robertson James Mrs., 298 Sackett street, Brooklyn, N. Y.
Robinson Horace F. Mrs., Chicago, Ill.
Robinson Horace E., Mrs., Detroit, Mich.
Robinson Eva E. Mrs., 214 7th street, South Boston.
Robinson John F. Mrs., Jamaica Plain.
Robinson Horace C. Mrs , 293 Fulton street, Chicago, Ill.
Robinson Abby Mrs., Brooklyn, N. Y.
Robinson Abby Miss, Boston Highlands
Robinson Frank W., 10 Woodland terrace, Philadelphia.
Rob nson Catherine S. Mrs., 32 Canal street, Boston,
Robinson Helen Miss, 32 Canal street, Boston.
Robinson A., Stratham, N. H.
Robinson Walter, Boston.
Rollins John P. Mrs., Cedar Rapids, Linn Co., Ia.
Rollins W. Manning, 97 Commercial street, Boston.
Rollins T. E. Mrs., Corning, N. Y.
Rollins Daniel G., Great Falls, N. H.
Rose Edwin F., 35 Devonshire street, Boston.
Rose Horace C., Boston.
Rose Horace C. Mrs., Boston.
Rothwell Josephine E. Mrs., Dover, N. H.
Rowe Frank, Salisbury, Mass.
Rowe Lucy " "

Rowe Albert, Alexander, Gennessee Co., N. Y.
Rowe Charles F., Crystal Spring, San Mateo Co., Cal.
Rowe Edwin, Crystal Spring, San Mateo Co., Cal.
Rowe Enoch P., Crystal Spring, San Mateo Co., Cal.
Rowe Fred A., Crystal Spring, San Mateo Co., Cal.
Rowe Frederic Mrs., Crystal Spring, San Mateo Co., Cal.
Rowe Jennie Miss, Crystal Spring, San Mateo Co., Cal.
Rowe Wil iam F., Crystal Spring, San Mateo Co., Cal.
Rugg Arthur H., grain & commission merchant, next to Board of Trade, Peoria, Ill.
Rugg H. I., Mrs., Peoria, Ill.
Rundlett J. Dwight, Choate's Drug store, Boston.
Rundlett E. C. Miss, 217 Broadway, Cambridgeport, Mass.
Rundlett Frank P., Emporium, Pa.
Rundlett N. A. Miss, 217 Broadway, Cambridgeport, Mass.
Rundlett T. M. Mrs., 217 Broadway, Cambridgeport, Mass.
Russell Benjamin F., Charles street, Lowell, Mass.
Russell Charles, Charles street, Lowell, Mass.
Russell Granville Mrs., 6 Hollis place, Boston.
Russell Edward Mrs., Newburyport, Mass.
Russell Thomas, Newburyport, Mass.
Rutledge John, Bangor, Me.
Rymes Washington, Newington, N. H.
Rymes Christopher E., machinery, Charlestown, h. Somerville, Mass.
Rymes Christopher E. Mrs., Somerville, Mass.

## S

Safford Sarah, 2 Lilly, So. Boston.
Safford Samuel, " " "
Salter Charles H. Mrs., Greenland, N. H.
Salter Charles H., China, Me.
Salter James H. Mr. & Mrs., 10 Pineapple, Brooklyn, N. Y.
Salter George, Newington.
Salter Wm. F., New York.
Sanborn Daniel,
Sanborn John D., Lynn Mass.
Sanborn John D. Mrs., Lynn, Mass.
Sanborn Lewis D., Dover, N. H.
Sanborn Nelson, Box 765, Saco, Me.
Sanborn Nelson Mrs., Box 795, Saco, Me.
Sanborn George E. Mrs., Orphan Asylum, Hartford, Conn.
Sanders Susan Mrs., Box 18, Dover, N. H.
Sanford Samuel, Boston.
Sanger George P. Mrs., 472 Broadway, Cambridge, Mass.
Sanger John W., 472 Broadway, Cambridge, Mass.
Sanger William, 472 Broadway, Cambridge, Mass.
Sanger George, 472 Broadway, Cambridge, Mass.
Sargent Joseph C., Barre, Mass.
Satterthwaite Anna Sheafe Mrs., New York city.
Saul John W., Concord, N. H.
Saul Jerry, Merrysville, Cal.
Saul Kate Mrs., Exeter.
Saunders Abraham Mrs., Dover, N. H.
Sawtelle David Mrs., 421 Pine Street, San Francisco, Cal.
Sawyer Mary E. Mrs., Lake Village, N. H.
Scott Frank, 4 So. Commerce street, Mobile, Ala.
Scott Winfield, Deerfield Parade, N. H.
Scott W. Elsworth, " " N. H.
Scott Daniel, P. Stratham, N. H.
Scott Daniel W., Deerfield Parade, N. H.
Scott Frances A. Miss, Deerfield Parade.
Scott Ida M. Miss, Deerfield Parade, N. H.
Scriggins John, Kittery, Me.
Scriggins Charles H., Covington, Ky.
Scotton Addie A. Miss, Highlandville Mass.
Scribner Anna Mrs., Raymond, N. H.
Sewards Henry H., Chelsea, Mass.
Sewards Henry H., jr., " "
Sewards Charles W., " "
Sewards Horace E., " "
Sewards George W., " "
Seed John T., 227 Central st., Lowell, Mass.
Seed John T. Mrs., 227 Central street, Lowell, Mass.
Seavey James Mrs., Bangor, Me.
Seavey Izette Mrs., Bangor, Me.
Seavey Anna Miss, Exeter, N. H.
Seavey Augusta Miss, " "
Seavey Kate Miss, " "
Seavey Andrew J., Dover, N. H.
Senter James, Tuft's College, Medford, Mass.
Senter William, Portland, Me.
Senter Emma Mrs. Portland, Me.
Senter J. H. Cambridge, Mass.
Shackford Nathaniel, Lake Village, N. H.
Shaw Jennie E. B. Miss, 29 Rue De Provence, Paris.
Shaw William F., 24 Kneeland, Boston
Shackford Nathaniel Mrs., Lake Village, N. H.
Shackford Charles Rev., Lynn, Mass.
Shackford William G., 29 Carrondelet, New Orleans, La.
Shackford Charles C. Rev., Ithaca, N. Y.
Shackley Fred A., Alleghanyville. R. R. Co., West Penn. Junc., Pa.
Shannon Robert, Boston.
Shannon Charles H., 50 Bridge, Salem, Mass.
Shannon George D., Kittery.
Shannon Mrs. Geo. D. "
Shannon Frank P., "
Shannon Geo. H., "
Shannon Nellie, "
Shannon Nettie, "
Shapley Fred A., 51 5th av., Pittsburg, Pa.
Shapleigh Augustus W., St. Louis, Mo.
Shapleigh Marshall S., importer, 625 Chestnut st., Philadelphia, Pa.
Sheafe Albert A., 560 8th Street, So. Boston
Sheafe Clara Mrs., 560 8th st., S. Boston
Sheafe John H., Baring Bros., Rome, Italy.
Sheafe Marsh W., Janesville, Wiss.
Sheafe M. L. Mrs., Boston.
Sheafe William, Boston.
Shehan James, Biddeford, Me.
Sheldon Geo. M. M. Mrs., Salem, Mass.

Shepherd Riol, Medford, Mass.
Sherburne B. Frank, Taunton, Mass.
Sherburne Sarah E., Taunton, Mass.
Sherburne Wm. A., painter, Taunton, Mass.
Sherburn John, Davis & Furber, No. Andover.
Sheridan James F., Shawmut Iron Works, Cambridgeport, Mass.
Shillaber Benjamin P. author, Chelsea, Mass.
Shillaber Charles E., San Francisco, Cal.
Shores Sally Miss, Boston.
Shores Foster, 164 22d st., Chicago, Ill.
Shorey Julia Mrs., Hoosic Falls, N. Y.
Shute Michael, East Boston.
Shute James, Charlestown, Mass.
Sides Thomas A., South Groveland, Mass.
Sides George, Juan Fernandez.
Simes William, jr., 10 Cent'l st Boston.
Simes James, " " "
Simes M. F. Miss, Charleston, S. C.
Simes M. E. Miss, Stratham, N. H.
Simes John P., " "
Simes Joseph, South Plymouth, Mass.
Simes Joseph S., Boston.
Simmons John O., Jamaica Plains.
Simmons John O. Mrs., " "
Simpson Lizzie Mrs., Boston.
Sise Albert F., Boston.
Sise Chas. F., "
Sise George, New Zealand.
Slack Sarah A. Mrs., Decatur street, East Boston.
Slater Hayden H., Amesbury, Mass.
Smart Fred, Chelsea, "
Smart Annie Miss, Highlandville. Ms.
Smart Theodore, San Francisco, Cal.
Smith Jas. O. Mrs., Mill Centre, Wis.
Smith Sarah, Dover, N. H.
Smith Wm. B. Mrs., Dover, N. H.
Smith Geo. W., " "
Smith James O., Mill Centre, Wis.
Smith Leonard Mrs., Dover, N. H.
Smith Dana Z. Mrs., Salem, Mass.
Smith George Mrs., " "
Smith Emma Miss, Lynn, "
Smith G. W. F., Newington, N. H.
Smith G. W. F. Mrs., Newington, N.H.
Smith Thomas L. Dr., Dover, N. H.
Smith Geo. W., E. R. R. Car Shop, Salem, Mass.
Somerby J. C., 782 Shawmut avenue, Boston.
Somerby J. C. Mrs., 782 Shawmut avenue, Boston.
Somerby George K., 782 Shawmut avenue, Boston.
Somerby Frank, 74 Ship st., Providence, R. I.
Somerby John, 2d. Salem, Mass.
Somerby John 2d Mrs., " "
Sparhawk David H., Boston.
Spinney F. Thornton, Charlestown, Mass.
Spinney Joseph F. Mrs., 1472 Tremont st., Boston.
Spear Henry F. Mrs., Boston.
Spinney Eliza A. Mrs., Raymond, N.H.
Spinney Charles L., 5 Hamilton st., Boston.
Spinney R. Morrison, South Boston.
Spinney G. Chesley, " "
Springer Lyman, Pico, Peru.
Stacy Lucy P. Miss, Greenland, N. H.
Stacy Augusta Mrs., Philadelphia, Pa.
Stacy M. P. Mrs., 10 Woodland terrace, W. Philadelphia, Pa.
Stacy M. P., 10 Woodland terrace, Philadelphia, Pa.
Stacy E. P., do.
Stanwood Isaac H., Philadelphia, Pa.
Stanwood J. H., Tigerville, Terribonne Co., Parish La.
Staples Alfred, Portland, Me.
Staples Joshua Mrs., 368 No. New Jersey st., Indianapolis, Ind.
Staples Rebecca Miss, 368 No. New Jersey st., Indianapolis, Ind.
Staples Joshua, 368 No. New Jersey st., Indianapolis, Ind.
Stevens Charles Mrs., Concord, N. H.
Stevens C. Belle, Malden, Mass.
Stevens Louisa E. Mrs. Malden, Mass.
Stickney Margaret Mrs., Phila., Pa.
Stickney Joseph H., 225 Cambridge street, Boston.
Stickney Lewis H., 114 Cambridge st., Boston.
Stocker Wm., Newburg, N. Y.
Stocker Alfred A., Newton, Mass.
Stocking John W. Mrs., Sullivan st., Charlestown, Mass.
Stocking Mark E., New York City.
Stokell Geo. L., 710 Harrison avenue, Boston.
Stokell Geo. L., jr., do.
Stokell Wallace S., do.
Stoodley Benjamin, Worcester, Mass.
Story Lucy A., New York City.
Story Albert, Manchester, N. H.
Stowell Sarah A. Mrs., Leroy, N. Y.
Sturtevant Lizzie Mrs., East Boston.
Sullivan Annie M. Mrs., 122 Oxford st., Portland, Me.
Stanwood Jas. R., 13 Doane st., Boston.
Stavers John W., Bushwick & Stavers, Chicago, Ill.
Stavers John W. Mrs., do.
Stewart Lewis Mrs., Vallejo, Cal.
Stevens Ezra A. jr., agt. Barstow Stove Co., Malden, Mass. (see advt. inside back cover).
Stevens Fred B., " "
Stevenson Jas. Mrs., Wolfeboro', N.H.
Stickney Horace W., South Boston.
Stiles Frank J., c. Maude & Clement streets, Malden, Mass.
Stiles Storer E., South Berwick, Me.
Stoddard E. M. Mrs., box 73, Portsmouth, Va.
Stone Henry L. Mrs., Edinboro' st., Boston.
Strong Mary E. Mrs., 32 Canal street, Boston.
Sughrue Julia Miss, Boston.
Swasey Sarah A. Mrs., Charlestown, Mass.
Sweetlove Eliza Mrs., 52 Webster st., East Boston.

## T

Tabb Eliza Mrs., Dover, N. H.
Talbot Benjamin Mrs., Tremont St., Boston.
Tapley Clara A. Mrs., Dover, N. H.
Taggard Robert A. Mrs., Ashland, Mass.
Tarlton William B., 81 Bremen St., East Boston.
Tarlton Frank D., clerk Boston & Albany Milk Depot, West Orange St., Boston, h. 2 Poplar Place.
Tarlton Hermon A., Middletown, Conn
Tarlton Hermon A. Mrs., " "
Tarlton Stephen, Leicester, Mass.
Tarlton Stephen Mrs., "
Tarlton Albert F., "

Taylor Margaret H. Mrs., St. Louis, Mo
Taylor Mary J. Mrs., North Hampton, N. H.
Taylor Admiral, Aiken, Ga.
Taylor Mrs., " " "
Taylor Daniel Mrs,, 16 Louisburg Sq., Boston.
Teague Jer., Greenland, N. H.
Teague Freeman B., Somerville Mass.
Tebbetts Allan C. Mrs., 20 Lexington St., E. Boston.
Tetherly William, E. Chatham, N. Y.
Thayer Mary E. Mrs., Boston.
Thayer Nathan Mrs., Orange, N. J.
Thomas Mary B. Miss, LeRoy, N. Y.
Thomas H. G., 158 State, Chicago, Ill.
Thomas Henry M., Manchester, N. H.
Thomas Charles, Eliot, Me.
Thomas George Rev., Stratham, N. H.
Thompson Henry M., agt., Manchester Print Works, h. Franklin cor. Pleasant, Manchester, N. H.
Thompson Luther, Newfield, Me.
Thompson Luther Mrs., " "
Thompson Henry G., photographic stock, 158 State, h. 775 W. Adams, Chicago, Ill.
Thompson George W., Mt. Wash. Glass Co., New Bedford, Mass.
Thompson Frank K. P., Mt. Wash. Glass Co., New Bedford, Mass.
Thorn Saml. G., New Haven, Conn.
Thorn Saml. G. Mrs. " "
Thurston James Rev., Dover, N. H.
Tibbetts Frederick B. Mrs., Dover, N. H.
Tobey Stephen, 36 Everett, Charlestown, Mass.
Tobey William, Salem, Mass.
Todd Augustus, "
Todd Joseph G., Kittery Point, Me.
Todd Jos. G. Mrs., " "
Todd Eva G. Miss., " "
Todd Benjamin, West Lynn Mass.
Towle Jennie A. Mrs., So Newmarket, N. H.
Tracy Chas. W., U. S. N., Annapolis, Md.
Tracy Charles W. Mrs., Annapolis, Md.
Treadwell William H., Gotha, Germany
Treadwell Robert O. Dr., " "
Tredick Henry, California.
Trefethren John Y. Mr. and Mrs., Cambridge, Mass.
Trefethen Clifton, Kittery, Me.
Trefethen Lewis B., Chelsea, Mass.
Trefethen Andrew, South Boston.
Trefethen Charles, Boston Highlands.
Trickey J. Frank, Stoneham, Mass.
Trickey J. Frank, Mrs., " "
Trickey John, " "
Trickey William, Charlestown, Mass.
Trickey William, Boston.
Trott Amos, Jamaica Plain.
Tucker Hosea, Salem, Mass.
Tucker Thomas, "
Tucker Henry, Charlestown, Mass.
Tucker William, Randolph, Mass.
Tucker Appleton, " "
Tuckerman Elizabeth, Lancaster, N.H.
Tuckerman Wm. H., Brooklyn, N. Y.
Tuckerman Henry, North Ashburnham, Mass.
Tuckerman John H., Lancaster, N. H.
Tuckerman Geo. W., real estate, constable and locksmith, 205 South, and 5 Telegraph, Boston.
Turrell Garland, New York City.
Turner Sarah Mrs., Philadelphia, Pa.
Turner Isabella Mrs., 1 Chester Park, Boston.
Turner Henry A. Mrs., 56 West Cedar St., Boston.
Tuttle Hugh H. Mrs., Boston.
Twombly Mary A. Mrs., 97 Sudbury St. Boston.
Twombly Samuel, Lake Village, N. H.
Twombly Orison, " " "
Twombly Thomas O. Mrs., Great Falls, N. H.
Tucker E. G., Mrs., 11 Ashburton Pl. Boston.
Tucker James M. Rye, Winchester Co., New York.
Tucker Levi B. Mrs., Plaistow, N. H.,
Tucker Henry, Boston.
Tucker Woodward H., Chelsea, Mass.
Tucker Alfred W., " "
Tucker Horace A., Port Townsend Wash. Terr.
Tucker J. Appleton, " "
Tyler William, Charlestown, Mass.

## U

Upham Charlotte M. Miss, New Haven, Ct.
Upham Joseph B., U. S. S. Hartford, Yokohama, Japan

## V

Varney Frank, Springfield, Mass.
Varney Eliphalet, Manchester, N. H.
Varney Martha, " "
Varrell Charles W., 194 State, Boston, h. Franklin ave, Chelsea, Mass.
Varrell Frank M., U. S. S. Wyoming, East India Squadron
Varrell John H., Ipswich, Mass.
Varrell John H., Harrisburg, Pa.
Vaughan James Mrs., Boston
Vennard Freeman C., E. R. R. Car Shop, Salem, Mass.
Vennard Matthew B., jr., De Valls Bluff, Ark.
Vennard Malcolm H., De Valls Bluff, Ark.
Vennard Marcellus A., 93 Fulton st., New York
Vennard Jonathan T., Seabrook, N.H.
Vennard Edward S., Manchester, N.H.
Vennard Freeman E., Elizabethport, N. J.
Vennard Henry T., New Orleans, La.
Vennard John C., Lynn, Mass.
Vennard Malcolm H., New Orleans, La.
Vennard Marcellus, Sidney, Australia
Vinton A. M. Mrs., 28 Oxford, Boston

## W

Wadleigh Edwin A., Boston
Wadsworth S. A. Mrs., Maplewood, Mass.
Waite Percy, Chelsea, Mass.
Walden Andrew D., Camden, Me.
Walden James, " "
Walden Alfred, Chelsea, Mass.
Walden Alfred Mrs., " "
Walden Thos., Russell st., Charlesto'n.
Walden Thos. Mrs., " "
Walden Charles, " "
Waldron Henry, Brooklyn, N. Y.
Waldron S. W. Mrs., 2 East 37th st., New York
Waldron Asa D., coal dealer, Kirzie, cor. Kingsbury, h. at Kirwood, Chicago, Ill.
Waldron Asa D. Mrs., Kirwood, Ill.
Waldron Daniel, merchant, Augusta, Me.
Waldron E. G. S. Rev., Pikesville, Md.
Waldron Isaac, 2 E. 37th St., N. Y.

Walker Nath'l, 295 Merrimack street, Manchester
Walker Nath'l Mrs., Merrimack street, Manchester
Walker Stacy G., Merrimuck st., Manchester
Walker Arthur W., Box 2421, Boston.
Walker George, Charlestown.
Walker Geo. S., Boston.
Walker Geo. S. Mrs., Boston.
Walker Wm. B., Custom House, Boston
Walker Elizabeth P., Box 4045, New York
Walker Maggie Miss, Jamaica Plain, Mass.
Walker Stacy G., Manchester, N. H.
Walker Mary Mrs., Reading, Mass.
Walker Joseph C. Mrs., 53 Bridge, Salem, Mass.
Walker Dwight C., E. R. R. Car Shop, Salem, Mass.
Wallace Lizzie A. Miss, Lynn, Mass.
Walsh Richard E., 227 Fulton street, Brooklyn, N. Y.
Walton M. E. Mrs., Seabrook, N. H.
Warburton Henry A., Worcester, Mass
Warburton Henry A., Mrs., " "
Warburton John, 729 Wyoming, Phila.
Warburton John Mrs., " "
Warren Wm. H., U. S. S., Nansemond, Savannah
Warren G. N. Mrs., Jamaica Plain, Mass.
Warren Jno. W. Mrs., Jamaica Plain, Mass.
Washburn J. H. Mrs., Michigan St., Erie, Pa.
Watkins Geo. W., New York Times Office, N. Y.
Webb John, Gold st., New York
Webber Ed. G., salesman, 339 Broadway, h. 71 Second ave., N. Y. City.
Webber James B., 76 Sudbury, Boston
Webster John, Gas Works, Adrian, Mich.
Webster Merritt, 34 School st., Boston
Webster Sophia L. Mrs., Dover, N. H.
Webster David L., 75 Blackstone, Boston
Weed Geo. F. Mrs., Dixmont, Me.
Weeks J. Calvin Mrs., Greenland, N. H.
Wendell A. Q., jr., hardware, Boston
Wentworth Jane S.Mrs.,Salmon Falls, N. H.
Wentworth J. Langdon, Salmon Falls, N. H.
Wendell Daniel, Rock Island, Ill.
Wendell Daniel Mrs., " "
Wendell Charles, Chicago, Ill.
Webster John G., 75 Blackstone St., Boston.
Wendell Annie Thompson, Quincy Farm, Wollaston, Mass.
Wendell Jacob, Philadelphia, Pa.
Wendell Geo. W., Great Falls, N. H.
Wendell Geo, Mrs., " " "
Wendell Geo. B., Quincy granite, 37 Central street, Boston, h. Quincy Farm, Wollaston, Mass.
Wendell Geo., Jamaica Plain, Mass.
Wendell Jacob L., Jamaica Pl., Mass.
Wendell Kate Thaxter, Quincy Farm, Wollaston, Mass.
Wendell Mary E. Mrs., Quincy Farm, Wollaston, Mass.
Wendell Mark R., Jamaica Pl., Mass.
Wendell C. B., 783 Wabash avenue, Chicago., Ill.
Wendell Helen Miss, Somerville, Mass
Wentworth Emma Mrs., 89 Pembroke street, Boston.
Wentworth Wm. B., Exeter, N. H.
Wentworth Samuel Mrs., Rollinsford, N. H.
Wentworth Charles E., 2 Wentworth street, St. Louis, Mo.
Wentworth Charles E. Mrs., 2 Wentworth street, St. Louis, Mo.
Wentz Hannah Mrs., 1502 Warnock, Philadelphia.
Weymouth Carrie Miss, 1 Adams, Charlestown.
Whalley James, 18 and 20 Essex, Boston.
Wheeler John H., Nebraska City, Neb.
Wheelright Abbie, Wells, Me.
Whidden H. Frank, tack manufacturer, South Abington, Mass.
Whidden John H., Gloucester, Mass.
Whidden Alfred S., Dover, N. H.
Whidden A. S. Mrs., "
Whidden Henry M., house and sign painter, Main st., Peabody, Mass.
Whidden Andrew J., E. R. R. Car Shop, Salem, Mass.
Whidden Andrew, East Boston.
Whidden Stephen, "
Whidden Charlotte Mrs.,Howard st. Boston.
Whidden Joseph, oil dealer, Boston. h. 150 Prospect, Cambridgeport, Mass
Whidden Frances G. Miss, Dover, N.H
Whidden Wm., Alvarado, Alameda Co., Cal.
Whidden Wm. Mrs., Alvarado, Alameda Co., Cal.
Whidden Thos. J., Jamaica Pl., Mass.
Whidden Joseph Mrs., 150 Prospect, Cambridgeport, Mass.
Whidden Joseph W., Newington, N.H.
Whidden Thomas J., 37 Upton, Boston
Whipple Edward Mrs., 15 Greenville st., Boston.
Whitcomb George H., Charlestown, Mass.
Whitcomb J. D., 115 Worcester street, Boston.
White Lydia A., 1599 Washington st., Boston.
White William B., Greencove, Fla.
White Wm. B. Mrs., " "
White James H., Amesbury, Mass.
White Benj. T., postmaster, College Hill, Mass.
White Benj. T. Mrs., College Hill, Mass.
White William B., Greenboro', Fla.
White Fannie A. Mrs., "
White J. W., jr., Boston.
Whitehouse Elizabeth H. Mrs., Dover, N. H.
Whitehouse George Mrs., Rollinsford, N. H.
Whitney Julia A., Mrs., Bunkerhill st., Charlestown, Mass.
Whitney Lincoln Mrs., Millbury, Mass.
Whitney Kate M. Mrs., Honolulu, Sandwich Islands.
Whitney L. Rev., Janesville, Wis.
Whiton Louis Mrs., South Boston.
Whittem Joseph, Mobile, Ala.
Whittemore William H., So. Boston.
Whittemore James H. Mrs. Salem, Mass.
Whittemore Charles C., Custom House Boston.
Whittemore Charles S., 36 Essex st., Rochester, N. Y.
Whittemore Samuel N., U. S. S. Constellation, Annapolis.

Walker Elizabeth L. Miss, Matthews Court House, Va.
Walker Lucy M. Miss, Matthews Court House, Va.
Walker Wm. L., So. Newmarket, N. H.
Wiley Sarah J. Mrs., Kennebunkport, Me.
Wise William G., Auburn, N. Y.
Wise Annie P. Mrs., " "
Whittle Sarah Mrs., York, Me.
Wiggin Sarah Mrs., Boston Highlands.
Wiggin Caleb Mrs., Stratham, N. H.
Wiggin Mary A. Mrs., Dover, N. H.
Wiggin Jacob B., Salem, Mass.
Wiggin Jacob B. Mrs., do.
Wiggin Geo. H. Mrs., 11 Wyman, Boston.
Wiggin Sadie M Miss, Salem, Mass.
Wiggin Carrie L. Miss, " "
Wiggin Ida M. Miss, " "
Wiggin Charles, Dover, N. H.
Wiggin Sam'l A., treas. Dept., Washington.
Wiggin Samuel A. Mrs., do.
Wiggin Thomas B., 130 Tremont st., Boston.
Wilcox Chas. E. Mrs., 710 Harrison avenue, Boston.
Willey Chas. E., May Port, E. Florida
Willey Benning, 131 Chelsea st., East Boston
Willey Phineas J., Portland, Me.
Willey James L., " "
Williams Frank, 199 Bridge st., Salem, Mass.
Williams F. E. Mrs., Northboro, Mass.
Williams W. H., Burlington, Vt.
Williams Addie Mrs., Boston.
Wilson Albion, Buffalo, N. Y.
Wilson John W. Mrs., Chicago, Ill.
Wilson Charles E., New Scandinavia, Republic Co., Kansas.
Wilson Thomas, 74 E. 128th st., New York Ci y.
Wilson Josiah P., box 83, Poughkeepsie, N. Y.
Wilson Chas. A., 25 Winter st., Boston
Wilson Leonard, Buffalo, N. Y.
Wilson Leonard Mrs., do.
Winder William, Annapolis, Md.
Wingate E. B., Friendship, Alleghany Co., N. Y.
Wingate Geo. E., U. S. S. Richmond, Va.
Winkley Samuel Rev., Boston.
Winslow Edward Mrs., Lowell, Mass.
Wise Wm. G., Auburn, N. Y.
Wise Wm. Mrs., " "
Wise Geo. E., Washington, D. C.
Wise Geo. D., Boston.
Wise Geo. D. Mrs., do.
Wise George, Natick, Mass.
Wood Edgar D., E. R. R. Depot, Boston
Wood Chas. H. Mrs., 115 Leverett st., Boston.
Wood Maria Mrs., 1 Worcester place, Boston.
Woodbury Chas. Levi, Boston.
Woodman Briard, 259 Broadway, So. Boston.
Woodman Sarah Mrs., 10 Crosby, Lynn, Mass.
Woodman Emma Miss, do.
Woodman William, Old Colony R. R., 214 7th st., South Boston.
Woodman John W., 124 Crawford st., Portsmouth, Va.
Woodman Wm. B., dry goods, 259 Broadway, h. 214 Seventh, South Boston.
Woodman James A., Deerfield, N. H.
Woodman James A. Mrs., " "
Woodman Carrie A. Miss, " "
Woods John, Boston.
Woodsum Charles E., Hyde Park, Mass.
Woodsum Benjamin, Mobile, Ala.
Worthen Lizzie W. Mrs., Lowell.
Worthern Lucy E. Miss, "
Wortman Mary, Boston.

## Y

Yeaton Boardman, Boston, Mass.
Yeaton James R., Brentwood, N. H.
Yeaton Jas. R. Mrs., " "
Yeaton John, Brooklyn, N. Y.
Yeaton John, Stratham, N. H.
Yeaton John H., builder, h. 842 8th avenue, New York City.
Yeaton Moses, jr., Independent, Van Buren Co., Ia.
Yeaton John Mrs., 29 Green St., Portland, Me.
Yeaton Geo. H., Hautsport, Hauts Co. Nova Scotia.
Yeaton Charles B., pressman, 3 Cornhill, Boston.
Yeaton Chas. B., Mrs., "
Yeaton James, 34 Union St., Boston.
Yeaton Edward T., Rochester, N. H.
Yeaton George M., 33 Summer St., Boston.
Young Acanthus, Barnstead, N. H.
Young Acanthus, Mrs., " "
Young Elijah B., 91 W. Dedham St., Boston, Mass.
Young Henry, Bridgeport, Conn.
Young Henry C., New Haven, Conn.
Young Mary Mrs., Manchester, N. H.
Young Mary P., 91 W. Dedham St., Boston.
Young Monroe, Lynn, Mass.

## Z

Zevelly A. N., Washington, N. H.
Zevelly A. N. Mrs., Washington, N. H.

www.ingramcontent.com/pod-product-compliance
Lightning Source LLC
LaVergne TN
LVHW020114110826
845151LV00001B/151

* 9 7 8 1 4 2 5 5 4 3 5 0 1 *